For a Voice and the Vote

FOR A
VOICE
AND THE
VOTE

MY JOURNEY WITH THE MISSISSIPPI
FREEDOM DEMOCRATIC PARTY

LISA ANDERSON TODD

UNIVERSITY PRESS OF KENTUCKY

Published by the University Press of Kentucky

Scholarly publisher for the Commonwealth,
serving Bellarmine University, Berea College, Centre College of Kentucky, Eastern
Kentucky University, The Filson Historical Society, Georgetown College, Kentucky
Historical Society, Kentucky State University, Morehead State University, Murray
State University, Northern Kentucky University, Transylvania University, University
of Kentucky, University of Louisville, and Western Kentucky University.
All rights reserved.

Editorial and Sales Offices: The University Press of Kentucky
663 South Limestone Street, Lexington, Kentucky 40508-4008
www.kentuckypress.com

Cataloging-in-Publication data is available from the Library of Congress.

ISBN 978-0-8131-4715-4 (hardcover : alk. paper)
ISBN 978-0-8131-4716-1 (epub)
ISBN 978-0-8131-4717-8 (pdf)

This book is printed on acid-free paper meeting
the requirements of the American National Standard
for Permanence in Paper for Printed Library Materials.

Manufactured in the United States of America.

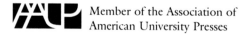

Member of the Association of
American University Presses

To my parents,
Carl M. Anderson (1905–1972)
and Ida Johnson Anderson (1903–1996)

It was not a great victory, but it was symbolic, and it involved the pledge of high party officials to work with the Freedom Party for the next four years to gain registered voters and political strength in Mississippi.

But there was no compromise for these persons who had risked their lives to get this far.

—Martin Luther King Jr.,
The Autobiography of Martin Luther King, Jr.

Contents

Abbreviations

AFSC	American Friends Service Committee
COFO	Council of Federated Organizations
CORE	Congress of Racial Equality
CURW	Cornell United Religious Work
EVS	Ecumenical Voluntary Service, World Council of Churches
FBI	Federal Bureau of Investigation
LBJ	Lyndon Baines Johnson
MFDP	Mississippi Freedom Democratic Party
MSU	Mississippi Student Union
NAACP	National Association for the Advancement of Colored People
NCC	National Council of Churches
SCLC	Southern Christian Leadership Conference
SNCC	Student Nonviolent Coordinating Committee
UAW	United Automobile Workers
UPO	United Planning Organization
VEP	Voter Education Project, Southern Regional Council

Introduction

My summer as a voter registration volunteer in the civil rights movement was a life-changing experience for me, and this book permits me to share with readers what the volunteers confronted while living and working in circumstances that were so different from their own worlds. The Mississippi Summer Project—also known as Freedom Summer—involved more than five hundred mostly white college student volunteers who spent two months in Mississippi in the struggle for freedom, justice, and voting rights for the black citizens of the state. In the summer of 1964, three civil rights workers—James Chaney, Andrew Goodman, and Michael Schwerner—were murdered by the Ku Klux Klan in Neshoba County, Mississippi. Blacks were denied the right to vote and were subject to arrest, violence, and economic retaliation if they attended a mass meeting, applied to register to vote, or participated in a nonviolent demonstration. The political parties and the schools ignored the needs of blacks in Mississippi, which resulted in the creative development of nonviolent alternative institutions—the Mississippi Freedom Democratic Party (MFDP) and the Freedom Schools—in which they could participate.

I have written about my family, childhood, and previous summer experiences to reveal my motivation in joining the project. I describe the politically moderate community of Greenville where I was assigned for voter registration, including the families I lived with, my fellow volunteers, the young black staff, canvassing in black neighborhoods, precinct work for the new MFDP, the local MFDP county convention, my fear, and my sense of the Beloved Community—the state of living in harmony where distinctions of race or class do not matter.

My principal motivation in writing this book is to explain the MFDP Challenge to the seating of the discriminatory all-white Mississippi Democratic Party at the Democratic National Convention that nominated

1

Lyndon B. Johnson for the presidency in Atlantic City, New Jersey, at the end of August 1964. Sixty-eight delegates, mostly poor, rural, black residents were elected in MFDP precinct and county meetings and at a state convention to represent Mississippi at the national convention. Their purpose was to challenge the racism in Mississippi that prevented their participation in politics and the racism in the national Democratic Party that allowed segregated delegations from the southern states. This history has not been told. Only parts of the story are scattered in other books, as I have noted in my bibliography. I have discovered revelations and details unnoticed, unreported, or underreported. My account is based not only on secondary sources, but on Ph.D. dissertations, oral interviews, contemporaneous documents, newspaper and magazine articles, and Lyndon Johnson's taped telephone conversations. In addition, I conducted interviews with several principals who implemented the MFDP strategy at the convention, as referenced in my endnotes. I also include my perspective as a participant-observer who went to Atlantic City as a supporting summer volunteer.

The most compelling part of my summer involved the people I lived and worked with in Mississippi. They led me to focus on the grassroots delegates who went to Atlantic City. I include information about some of these individuals—how they risked their lives, their optimism, and their reactions to the politics that swirled around them. Bob Moses, the Summer Project program director, insisted, to the extent he could, that the MFDP delegates be kept informed and participate in the discussions regarding delegate seating in order to be prepared to make their own decisions at the Democratic National Convention. The delegates were courageous and deserve credit for confronting the official authorities and vigilantes arrayed against them and for carrying out the MFDP's nonviolent program.

In addition to the MFDP delegates, I discuss political leaders remembered for their liberal views and contributions to freedom, justice, and social welfare. Not only Johnson but civil rights warrior Senator Hubert Humphrey, young Minnesota state attorney general Walter Mondale, high-profile leader of the civil rights movement Martin Luther King Jr., organizer of the March on Washington Bayard Rustin, union leader Walter Reuther, Democratic insider and liberal Washington attorney Joseph

L. Rauh Jr., and Bob Moses, respected for his sincerity and integrity, had significant and controversial roles at the convention.

The book includes a chronology of five days in Atlantic City that begins with Fannie Lou Hamer's testimony to the Democratic Party Credentials Committee on Saturday, August 22, 1964, continues to the opening of the convention on Monday, when the Mississippi seats were empty, the conclusion of the Challenge on Tuesday, and, finally, the all-day discussions of the convention's decision on Wednesday. I compare what we knew during the convention, or what I thought we knew, with what history has taught us since. During my research, I often thought, "I never knew that." The book is not a comprehensive history of the MFDP, which has yet to be written, but it offers background of why and how the party was created in April 1964. I end the book with the end to the Challenge. The MFDP's subsequent activities are beyond the scope of this writing.

The politics of 1964 reverberate today. Both the Democratic and Republican Parties began losing their historic coalitions. Ultraconservatives had taken control of the Republican delegation-selection process and excluded all but fourteen blacks out of the thousands of delegates to the San Francisco convention in 1964. While the Democrats began the reform process of opening the party, the Republicans engaged in a simultaneous process of closing their ranks to blacks, Hispanics, immigrants, and other minorities. After ultraconservatives took control and nominated Barry Goldwater, moderate Rockefeller Republicans—William Scranton, Charles Percy, and George Romney—proved unable to regain influence over the party, and ultraconservatives—today those who make up the Tea Party, remained in control.

About the terminology in my writing: I consider race a useful identifying feature and so identify individuals as white or black or "Negro," the term of respect in use before *black* or *African American*. I chose to use the term *black* throughout my writing to be consistent. I distinguish who was black and who was white for information and in line with my thinking that a concern for social justice warrants considerations of race.

My story is only one of many. I have tried to present an accurate account of a historic moment in time on behalf of the courageous black residents of Mississippi who risked their lives for freedom and to share my own stories so that others can learn from the past and become inspired to join the struggle for freedom, justice, and an improved democracy that continues today.

I hope my story will make you understand why I care.

1

In Atlantic City for the Democratic Convention

Go tell it on the mountain, over the hills and everywhere;
go tell it on the mountain, to let my people go.
                                                    —traditional spiritual

On Sunday that last week of August 1964, I was excited to be going to my first political convention. The Mississippi Freedom Democratic Party (MFDP), a new, integrated, parallel political party, was challenging the seating of the all-white, segregationist Mississippi Democratic Party delegation because that party barred blacks from participation in party affairs and supported the state in denying blacks the right to vote through literacy tests, poll taxes, intimidation, and violence. The MFDP delegates went to the convention seeking recognition as Democrats from the state of Mississippi with the right to choose their own representatives and wanting to purge the national Democratic Party of its racism. I had helped organize the MFDP as a summer voter registration volunteer, and now I wanted to see the elected MFDP delegates recognized, seated, and voting for Mississippi at the national convention.

I was with my new friend Pat Vail, a fellow volunteer in Mississippi. Pat was short and had short, dark hair; a strong voice; and a hearty laugh. She was, as she said, a "functionary for freedom."[1] She was assigned to clerical work in the voter registration office but not given secretarial responsibility. We had driven from Summit, New Jersey, my birthplace and hometown. Summit is a couple of hours north from Atlantic City on the Garden State Parkway. Pat and I were eager to continue the fight to seat the MFDP delegates and optimistic that the MFDP would succeed.

5

I was twenty-two, just out of college, and the Mississippi Summer Project, as it had been named, had ended the previous Friday. I had gone to Mississippi that dangerous summer as a volunteer in the pursuit of freedom, justice, and equality for *all* Americans. I wanted to do my part. I differed from my high school and college friends, none of whom decided to join the civil rights movement. They were content with the status quo or otherwise occupied. Families could and did prevent students from going to Mississippi under threat of withdrawal of financial or emotional support.

I didn't want poor black families to continue to have to live without the basic rights of citizenship that I had. Something had to be done to bring them freedom and justice. The violence, oppression, and hostility had to end. I knew that Mississippi was the worst state for racial discrimination in the country and that attention needed to be paid to what was happening there. The beatings and jailings reported in the newspapers and on television meant that many students were too scared to volunteer. Perhaps I should have been concerned about my safety, but what I remember feeling was an overwhelming sense of the need to fight injustice. When I asked a black Mississippi civil rights veteran years later if *she* was scared, she replied, "I think we were just too young to be scared. We didn't know any better."

I had survived Mississippi, but instead of resting at home, I went straight on to Atlantic City, concentrating on the Democratic National Convention with almost the same intensity that I gave to the Summer Project. The MFDP delegates were local people who had risked their lives in the struggle for freedom. Now they were challenging the racism in Mississippi and in the Democratic Party. They, as well as supporting staff members and volunteers, lobbied state delegates day and night for their support of the Challenge. All the MFDP delegates had stories to tell of life in faraway Mississippi, how they had tried to register to vote, and what had happened to them as a result: threatening phone calls, nightriders shooting or throwing firebombs into their homes, loss of jobs or credit, or other actions taken to intimidate them and their neighbors. Young civil rights workers advised and assisted them but were not MFDP decision makers.

Arriving in Atlantic City midday Sunday, Pat and I soon saw for the first time Convention Hall, located on the six-mile-long boardwalk, an immense building covering seven acres, dating from 1929, which had hosted annual Miss America pageants, horse shows, and auto races. Convention Hall had also served as an army training center for 500,000 men during World War II.

We saw a new bust of President John F. Kennedy in an arcade, looking out at the vast, mysterious Atlantic Ocean, reminding us of his assassination not long before on November 22, 1963. The nation was beginning to come out of its overwhelming grief at the loss of the young, handsome president who had inspired us in so many ways.

Now Kennedy was gone, and the country was left in the hands of Lyndon Johnson, the Texan who had become politically powerful as a conservative southern leader in the Senate, unsure of how he would follow the policies of his predecessor. Despite a great deal of controversy, Kennedy had named him as his running mate at the 1960 convention, and after a close election in which Kennedy defeated Richard Nixon, Johnson became the vice president. I didn't know what to expect of Johnson but sentimentally wished we could see more of John Kennedy's younger brothers, Bobby and Teddy, his elegant widow, Jackie, and his little children, Caroline and John-John. Actually, the Kennedys were there in Atlantic City, protecting their privacy, but they would pay tribute to the fallen president one evening of the convention. Since Johnson considered Bobby Kennedy a threat to his commanding political presence, and this convention would be Johnson's to control, the Kennedy tribute was not scheduled until the last night of the convention after all decisions had been made. Pat and I had not come to commemorate Kennedy and would leave town before then.

The convention was typical of the time. Drew Pearson, a popular newspaper columnist of the day, described political conventions as "America's greatest political circus, featuring star-spangled-banner blondes waving flags in hotel lobbies, not knowing what it is all about; a record amount of mustard, hot dogs, and soda pop disappearing down delegates' gullets; and Miss Tiparillo of 1964 or her equivalent passing out record numbers of free cigars."[2]

The most famous resort in America at the time but in decline since the end of World War II, Atlantic City gave the delegates plenty to do. With

Demonstrating on Monday to seat the MFDP at the Democratic National Convention. Courtesy of Nancy Schieffelin.

free tickets for the Atlantic City racetrack, they had the option of watching the horse races. Major corporations offered free cars with chauffeurs; a lounge with sandwiches, coffee, and snacks served by waiters from the Pennsylvania Railroad dining cars; and hideaways serving distilled spirits. The pharmaceutical industry made free aspirin tablets available for those with "political headaches." Many of the delegates were there wanting to party, but the MFDP, with its moral claim to justice tried to slow them down. Pat and I were part of this effort to keep their attention on the issue presented.

MFDP supporters began an around-the-clock demonstration on the boardwalk to call attention to their demand for MFDP seating. At times, it was a solemn, dignified silent vigil of about three hundred people, many of whom were from the Congress of Racial Equality (CORE); at other times the demonstrators walked in a picket line with signs calling for seating the MFDP.

Near the entrance to the Convention Hall, everyone could see a display of oversize charcoal drawings of the martyred James Chaney, a black man, and Andrew Goodman and Michael Schwerner, two white men. From widespread press coverage, delegates knew about the three civil rights workers who were arrested in Neshoba County at the beginning of the summer and then released to waiting Ku Klux Klan members, who murdered them and buried them in an earthen dam. After a forty-four-day search, federal authorities found their bodies in early August. Pat and I gravitated to this spot, where delegates passed by regularly, to ask them to support seating the MFDP. The display was on a raised platform that held a gutted, burned-out car believed to be the station wagon used on the fatal trip.[3] The bell taken from the burned Neshoba County church, which the three civil rights workers had traveled to inspect, added to the stark reality the convention goers faced.

This location near Convention Hall also served as center stage for rallies and groups singing freedom songs, which gave us encouragement just as they had strengthened protestors in jail, on demonstrations or marches, and in mass meetings in small, spare Mississippi churches.[4] Pat and I joined in the enthusiastic, dedicated singing, following the lead and picking up on all the words.

When Fannie Lou Hamer—the strongest, most musical, and most inspirational of freedom singer leaders—joined in, a larger crowd would gather to listen or sing along. Mrs. Hamer became known for her leadership and courage in the Mississippi civil rights movement after her nationally televised testimony at the convention. She is associated with "This Little Light of Mine," one of the few if not the only freedom song that uses "I" rather than "we," but she had a different favorite in Atlantic City. There she used her hearty voice on the boardwalk to lead us in "Go Tell It on the Mountain," substituting "let my people go" for the phrase "Jesus Christ is born" in the traditional spiritual. I found the singing heartwarming, and as I joined in, white passers-by, sympathetic or not, seemingly could only look on, remaining outside our circle. Some of the protesters invited strangers to be part of the singing group. We frequently sang the theme song of the civil rights movement, "We Shall Overcome," the words of which we deeply believed.

No one had given the volunteers an assignment in Atlantic City before we left Mississippi, and Pat and I did not take the initiative to find the

Joe Rauh, Fannie Lou Hamer, and supporters singing "We Shall Overcome" at the 1964 Democratic National Convention. Courtesy of George Ballis/Take Stock.

coordinators and sign up to lobby specific state delegates. We nevertheless knew what all of us were supposed to do—target the delegates from our home states to persuade them to vote to seat the MFDP. We proceeded on a freelance basis, spending the days walking and looking around.

Andrew Young, a principal aide to Dr. Martin Luther King Jr., wrote in his book *An Easy Burden* that young people like me had "unrealistic expectations" and were too "ideological."[5] He was in Atlantic City for the convention and told me later that he tried to get us to tone down our "rhetoric."[6] He considered that he and Dr. King were more mature and more politically sophisticated than the militant student activists working in Mississippi. He knew that they had risked danger to provide encouragement and moral support to blacks seeking to vote, but he still did not accept their position.

I had taken sides in the controversy that swirled around me in Atlantic City. I was militant and convinced of the righteousness of the MFDP cause as I tried to convey to delegates and others *why* the black residents of Mississippi were entitled to equal treatment. I could not conceive of a basis for defeat of the MFDP. Pat also believed that the Challenge would succeed: we had worked so hard that summer, and "the story was so compelling."[7] Or both the Mississippi Democratic Party delegates *and* the MFDP delegates would be seated; surely the MFDP delegates would not be excluded.

It was great to be there on the boardwalk and near Convention Hall, involved and excited. I had been "flung with no transition into the world of deals and decisions," into the unreal "pop-art, circus quality of Atlantic City" after my "confrontation with Southern reality." That's the way journalist Sally Belfrage, a summer volunteer, put it in her memoir, *Freedom Summer.*[8]

On Tuesday, August 25, the end came. I loved being a part of what we now know was history in the making, just as I had been the previous two months in Mississippi. I did not realize the meaning of the five days in August 1964 in Atlantic City then, but I wanted to understand what had happened and why. Atlantic City has been on my mind in one way or another ever since. It was the crowning event of the most important summer in civil rights history. It was also the culmination of a personal journey that had started, for me, long before.

2

My Life before Mississippi

> It is within the fragile yet formidable walls of your own family that you learn, or do not learn, what the phrase *human family* means.
> —Frederick Buechner, *Beyond Words*[1]

I lived in a harmonious family in a four-bedroom, wood-frame, colonial-style home in Summit, New Jersey, until I was eighteen. Summit was an attractive Republican community of about 30,000 that appealed to Wall Street commuters.

My father, Carl M. Anderson, was a corporate lawyer who commanded respect in his work with a major New Jersey corporation, its affiliated trade associations, and its international relations. A lifelong Republican, he was disciplined, kind, loyal, honest, and prudent. He was also cautious: he would not sign petitions for fear of finding his name on a list that he had thought was innocent but was actually tainted. That caution was bred in the McCarthy era of Red baiting.

My mother, Ida Johnson Anderson—who gave up her career as a psychiatric social worker to stay home and take care of the three children—was modest, frank, friendly, intellectual, and wise. She was probably a Democrat, but she honored my father and said that she voted Republican. She participated in numerous activities in the community, volunteering to serve disabled children at a specialized hospital, interviewing girls applying for American Association of University Women scholarships, and sorting books for that organization's annual book sale. When I turned thirteen, she took a job as a junior high school guidance counselor in a neighboring community but worked for only one year, realizing that she couldn't do it all.

My father was active in the Lutheran Church. In 1966, the Lutheran

With my parents and my brothers, John *(left)* and Eric, at my graduation from Cornell on June 15, 1964. Lisa Anderson Todd Collection.

Church of America elected him as treasurer of the national church. I was baptized at First Lutheran Church in Summit. Every week my father drove my brothers and me to Sunday school. I didn't like going because I was a tomboy and didn't like getting dressed up and wearing fussy patent-leather Mary Jane shoes. I remember singing "Jesus Loves Me This I Know" and "This Little Light of Mine" better than any Bible stories.

Unlike my father, my mother had nothing to do with the church, though she went to church with the rest of the family on the special days of the church year. She would not sing "A Mighty Fortress Is Our God," one of Martin Luther's best-known hymns, presumably because it was too militaristic.

My parents raised me and my two older brothers, Eric and John, to be honest, considerate, fair, disciplined, patient, kind, modest, and unassuming. To respect the dignity of others. My father handed down to me, his "favorite daughter," his determination and conscientiousness, which came along with an unfortunate inclination to perfectionism. From my mother I gained a sense of looking out for others, no matter their station in life.

I resolved early on that because I could not beat up my brothers and had no younger brother or sister to pick on, I would be a good girl and compete with them at school. However, I never wanted to show off, raise my hand in class, or participate in a formal discussion, though when the teacher called on me, I generally knew the answer. I preferred working alone and even today know that I have never liked anything about what I would call a "group."

When I was very young and begged, "Mommy, what can I do?" she would simply tell me to go and read a book. I did a lot of reading as a child, in particular the childhood stories of presidents, founding fathers, and heroes that some of us remember as "the orange biographies." They made me aspire to be famous myself some day.

I spent seven formative summers at Camp Hagan on the Delaware River in Pennsylvania. I liked the idea of starting over there, a place where no one knew anything about me. Near the end of the summer of 1955, during the torrential rains of Hurricane Diane, the governor ordered our evacuation. Buses took my group to an orphanage in New York City, where our parents could pick us up. It was there that I saw deprivation for the first time. The homeless children stared at us parading through in our silly-looking brown uniforms—cotton short shorts and pullover short-sleeved shirts. I knew then how fortunate I was. My mother once told me that I was too emotional to become a social worker because I would be unable to separate myself as a professional from clients.

My parents, children of Swedish and Swede-Finn immigrants, placed a high value on education. They wanted my brothers and me to achieve but did not make me feel any pressure to do or be more than I was. They gave me opportunities to learn, enjoy life, and grow in my own way. Under my father's influence, I took music-appreciation classes, played the piano, and in fourth grade learned to play the trumpet, which was not an instrument girls chose in the 1950s. I played in the junior high school orchestra and took private lessons, aiming to be in the All State Band and Orchestra, but I soon said to Nelson Keller, my teacher, "I hate the trumpet." I have never forgotten his advice, "Don't ever get hate in your heart." Nevertheless, I became embarrassed at age fourteen and stopped playing the trumpet.

I chose to go to Kent Place School, a private all girls' day school in Summit, for my four years of high school. I liked the environment and was unconcerned about my status with boys, both inside and outside the classroom. We wore comfortable uniforms that removed further competition in what to wear every day. I studied hard and got good grades—even though I still never raised my hand in class—graduating third in my class of fifty-two girls. I didn't feel that smart but considered myself an overachiever. I participated after school in glee club, dramatics, and varsity team sports, including field hockey, basketball, and softball. My class elected me president both my junior and senior years.

I saw a mix of personalities in the school at a time when there was barely any economic, political, racial, or religious diversity at such schools. I can't think of any black fellow students then, and only two Jewish girls were in my class. I wanted to know and find value in everyone in the class. At the same time, I enjoyed popularity in a clique of many lifelong friends. Neither my mother nor I was interested in getting me into the debutante group; I was more likely to identify with the underdog.

I was a seventh grader in 1955, caught up in the suburban routine of home and school and unaware of the progress of the civil rights movement.[2] The National Association for the Advancement of Colored People (NAACP), dating from 1909, established chapters of at least fifty members each in Mississippi, beginning in Vicksburg in 1918. Members faced threats and intimidation, and chapters would go out of existence but could regroup under another name to protest injustice and advance black voter registration. In the mid-1940s, black veterans, after experiencing a freer and more democratic way of life in other parts of the country and overseas, came home from World War II with added determination to end segregation and discrimination.

In August 1955, Emmett Till's mother let the world know, through photographs from an open-casket funeral in Chicago, that her fourteen-year-old son who was visiting family in Money, Tallahatchie County,

Mississippi, had been brutally murdered and disfigured, reportedly for whistling at a white woman in a store. The state failed to bring his murderers to justice. That news gave Joyce Ladner and Dorie Ladner—two of the early student organizers in Mississippi—the conviction that something had to be done to stop the lynching of more children such as Emmett Till. Blacks in Mississippi "reacted defiantly," and according to local black NAACP leader Amzie Moore, it was a turning point that is a better mark to begin the civil rights movement in Mississippi than the 1954 *Brown v. Board of Education* Supreme Court decision.[3]

Also in 1955, Rosa Parks engaged in her protest against segregation, as she had learned in the NAACP and at Highlander Folk School in Tennessee. She faced arrest for not moving to the back of the bus and became famous, along with the best-known civil rights leader, Dr. Martin Luther King Jr., as they led the successful 366-day bus boycott in Montgomery, Alabama.

My parents did not impart liberal political views to me when I was young; in fact, after my brother Eric returned from college with new ideas, my father's conservatism on the issues of the day became more apparent to me. As a lifelong Republican, he was a traditionalist. However, both my parents were involved in public service. As a result of his corporate work as president of the company's foundation, my father also served on the board of directors of the United Negro College Fund and was the national campaign chairman in 1964 and 1965. Because of this connection, he learned more about black society and culture than a typical Republican lawyer would have at the time. I was proud of his commitment but mortified when he told me he sat next to Lorraine Hansberry at a dinner and asked her what she did. Apparently he didn't know that she was the noted black playwright and author of *A Raisin in the Sun*. Neither he nor I had any exposure to blacks in our suburban community. I only knew our cleaning woman, who came once a week and sometimes baby-sat us. I did see black kids in my classes in junior high school, but I wasn't aware of those in need, never volunteered, and made no effort to help the poor.

I knew where I wanted to go to college: a top academic school that was co-ed and located anywhere in the Northeast. My first choice was Radcliffe, and Radcliffe's thin letter of rejection sent me into total despair. My mother thought—correctly—that a serious blow early would make me better able to cope with life's disappointments in the future. I attended Cornell instead. College was not always what I expected, but I maintained my self-confidence, and the rigorous life at Cornell University prepared me for the future, including my 1969 summer in Mississippi.

The diversity of the big university unsettled the prep school kid I was. I was lost at Cornell my first semester, feeling lonely and unloved. My fantasy about college had included participating in fascinating and stimulating intellectual discussions with classmates, when I would stay up until all hours talking about the Cold War, Cuba, the nuclear threat, and other weighty subjects. But in real life I did not find anyone nearby who met my narrow-minded standards for such a discussion.

With my limited experience, I probably came across as a prejudiced snob. I stereotyped the many Jewish students, in particular those from New York City and Long Island, as brainy and brilliant, and the upstate New York residents, who went to Cornell's state-supported Colleges of Agriculture and Home Economics, as little better than country hicks.[4] No wonder I had difficulty making friends. We had a number of foreign students on campus, in particular Asians and Africans, but few American blacks. I remember only two black women in a freshman class totaling 2,200.

That fall of 1960 I stayed up into the early morning hours sitting in the big, plaid-upholstered, comfortable chairs with wide wooden arms in the basement to watch the presidential election results on the one TV in Risley Dorm. I felt like a groupie for political news and major events, waiting for the Chicago poll returns to make sure that John F. Kennedy was elected. He was my clear favorite—however my parents may have been voting. As for local politics, I ran in a campus-wide election that year, but my lack of support, inability to campaign, and abysmal showing turned me off other student organizations and extracurricular activities.

During this time, student civil rights protests got national attention after the Greensboro, North Carolina, sit-in on February 1, 1960, but I paid little attention. In 1959, Nashville students, including John Lewis and Diane Nash, studied the theories and methods of nonviolent resistance with Reverend James M. Lawson Jr. and engaged in several sit-ins before Greensboro. In April 1960, they founded the Student Nonviolent Coordinating Committee (SNCC) along with other students objecting to segregated facilities in the South. On March 27, 1961, nine black Tougaloo College students went to the main branch of the Jackson Public Library for the first Mississippi sit-in, a "read-in" that protested the exclusion of blacks from all library services.[5] The students sat quietly reading books that were unavailable at the black library and were asked to leave; when they refused, the police arrested them for disturbing the peace. I missed the debate on my campus between Malcolm X and James Farmer, the national director of CORE, that same month. And later that year Freedom Riders traveling on interstate buses ended up in penitentiary confinement in Mississippi before the federal government issued new orders for enforcement of desegregation in interstate bus travel. Other civil rights activity then involved voter registration, political action, and community organizing. It was that year that Bob Moses began a SNCC project in Mississippi.

But I was not yet a civil rights activist. I just needed to adjust to Cornell. I was a little happier my second semester when I met other students who made me feel comfortable, and we became friends. Soon rushing to join a sorority absorbed my interest, and, scornful of the superficial, I joined the smart, independent, politically liberal Kappa Alpha Thetas, who had a wide range of personalities and interests, some truly bizarre, that were more to my liking. I lived in the sorority house my sophomore year, and that October we followed the news of the Cuban Missile Crisis.

Theta at Cornell resisted the membership rules of its national organization that operated to exclude Jews. About one-fourth of my pledge class was Jewish, and the year after I graduated the national officers went to Ithaca to supervise rushing and to enforce the national sorority's discriminatory system. In response, the Cornell girls stopped rushing, got evicted from the sorority house, and lost their charter. National Theta claimed it was ending "inappropriate social behavior" at the chapter. Some of us *were* a little wild, but the real reason lay with the local Theta commitment to diversity, which the university administration supported.

I thus learned from personal experience about prejudice and began to become aware of racial injustice in the South from news events. I elected to take a sociology course in race relations my junior year and eventually chose a major in American studies with a minor in government.

My parents supported me financially and encouraged me to have fun in college, without any need to work to meet expenses. My father didn't understand my telling him I *wanted* to get a job. He resisted the idea, thinking I should not take a university job from a student with financial need, and he did not want to provide financial information to the university. After he finally consented, I worked part-time one semester my junior year for a dollar an hour in the new high-rise Olin Library.

After my sophomore year, when I was twenty, I chose to participate in the Experiment in International Living and went to live for a month with a family in northern Sweden. We had a cross-section of girls in our group, including a black girl from Greensboro, North Carolina, whom I judged quickly as someone overly anxious to please, while I was sticking to a clique of three girls with sharp personalities. Recognizing that I was not being very nice, I became more aware of how hurtful it can be to the loner who is left out of the group.

I lived on a farm with the Lydén family. At first I felt isolated and frustrated, but by the end of the home stay I really liked the family and would not have wanted to be in the village or with rich people. We had a group farewell party that included an American meal, dancing, and singing of American and Swedish songs. I noted the emotional closing in my diary as "a friendship circle (right over left)" when we sang "Auld Lang Syne." This was the same style of singing "We Shall Overcome"—emotionally, with hands held and arms crossed while gently swaying from side to side—that I would later do so many times during the summer of 1964 in Mississippi.

My Experiment in International Living trip to Sweden was a real adventure, an experience that prepared me for Mississippi. Strangers welcomed me and made me comfortable in a foreign culture, and I adapted to new and different ways. I was connecting with new people, different from me, and communicating with effort to make myself understood and, I hoped, appreciated. Before I got back home, I thought about the free time I would have after another year of college. I wanted to go back to Europe, travel, and do different things—study, bicycle, or join a work camp. But I soon realized that I wanted to do something more socially useful than foster international cross-cultural understanding on what might amount only to a vacation.

I had the idea of a work camp—where a group living in community provides some service—from my brother Eric, who joined an American Friends Service Committee (AFSC) international work camp to build a school in a village in southern Italy. But the United States had its own problems. I inquired at the AFSC and researched domestic work camps in the library back at Cornell. During my junior year, I mailed in applications to two groups.

3

Mississippi, 1963

Keeping the Waters Troubled

> Wade in the water, wade in the water, children,
> wade in the water, God's gonna trouble the water.
> —traditional spiritual

"I was full of apprehensions this morning." That's how scared I was when I started my summer diary on Saturday, July 6, 1963, the summer after my junior year in college and the year before I went on the Mississippi Summer Project. I flew from Newark, New Jersey, to Jackson, Mississippi, for a one-month work camp at Tougaloo College, the small, historically black college just north of Jackson. The Ecumenical Voluntary Service (EVS) of the World Council of Churches was sponsoring a group of college students of different racial, national, and denominational backgrounds to live in the dorms, help the campus maintenance staff, and attend social science seminars to learn about racial problems in Mississippi.[1] We were only to "keep the waters troubled" as we devoted our efforts toward racial reconciliation.

Considering how fearful I was and knowing about the recent Jackson civil rights demonstrations, my parents too must have been worried but didn't show it in their good-byes. Airplane travel was new for me when I was twenty-one—I had taken very few flights—and I was traveling alone. When we took off, the jet engine outside my window caught fire. I saw the flare, but I didn't know it was unusual *and* a serious problem until the plane turned around and landed safely at Newark. The sight of my parents at the end of the Jetway when we got off the plane overwhelmed me. Wouldn't it be wiser to stay home with them for the summer? Thinking of the recent civil rights arrests in Jackson, I wondered—would I be getting into that?

I knew little of what was coming. An EVS memo told me about the leader and local hosts of our group and included a short reading list: *Killers of the Dream* by Lillian Smith, "Letter from Birmingham City Jail" by Martin Luther King Jr., and *Black Like Me* by John Griffin. We needed "adequate" work clothes for "very HOT" weather. The memo reminded us, "Bring your Bible." The EVS director also reassured us: "I suppose I should go into more detail about your concern for the situation in Jackson . . . [but suffice it to say that] life goes on as usual outside the limited areas of action and activity, which means that one can keep a safe distance from the activity."

Without additional information, I was left with my determination and my parents' understanding support. They expected that I would follow through on what I had decided to do, and I got on the next plane going to Mississippi. The time to think on a slow Eastern Airlines plane had me imagining the project and reviewing what I knew about the Mississippi civil rights movement. I could not realize then how significant and life changing my summer would be.

Tougaloo held a unique status in Mississippi as an "oasis" for civil rights activists. The college had an integrated faculty, a handful of white students in the student body of fewer than five hundred, and no state funding, which would have dictated strict policies of segregation. Tougaloo took an unequivocal stand on integration, whatever the consequences. I had been reading news about Tougaloo students: they were in that first library read-in in 1961, and on May 28 of this year several of them, including Memphis Norman, a black sociology student, and Joan Trumpauer, a white transfer student from Duke, held a sit-in at a lunch counter reserved for whites in the Woolworth's store in downtown Jackson. They stayed for two hours without being served. White racist hecklers brutally beat them while police and the store management looked on, doing nothing until the mob grew and then finally turning off the lights and closing the store. Bloody, pelted with ketchup and mustard, struck with broken glass, their cuts salted and burned with lit cigarettes, the students then left safely with a police escort.

This event energized the Jackson movement.[2] In late 1962, blacks had organized a selective-buying campaign that boycotted the downtown white shopping area on Capitol Street. They demanded integration of facilities, equal employment opportunities, and elimination of discriminatory business practices, but they received no concessions from the mayor. They turned out in large numbers for mass meetings, demonstrations, and marches to downtown Capitol Street. Then a court injunction against the protests led to mass arrests and brutal treatment in jail. These events reached a climax on June 12, 1963, when Medgar Evers, the NAACP state field secretary who was the revered local leader of the Jackson protests, was shot in the back in his driveway. This was the kind of front-page news I had been reading at home.

The assassination of the thirty-eight-year-old, respected, popular Evers drew 2,800 to the funeral in the Masonic Temple and an estimated 5,000 for a mass march behind the hearse to the Collins Funeral Home. What was silent and solemn changed as people spontaneously turned toward Capitol Street with singing and cries of "We want freedom! Freedom! Freedom!" The phalanx of city police and highway patrolmen with rifles and shotguns, dogs, and billy clubs that met them did not make arrests but blocked Capitol Street and pushed the demonstrators back. After the police shot over the heads of people into windows and did some bloody clubbing, tension increased as some young blacks, angry that the leadership of the Jackson movement was not more militant, and some street kids lacking the discipline of the nonviolent movement, began throwing bricks and bottles at the advancing police. John Doar, the assistant attorney general for civil rights in the U.S. Justice Department, his white shirt sleeves rolled up in the extreme heat, dramatically held up his hands to speak to the protestors, pleading with them to go home. The area slowly cleared, with both demonstrators and police dispersing.

President Kennedy intervened with Jackson's mayor to obtain an agreement for the hiring of a few black city workers so that the conservative local black NAACP leadership could persuade everyone to end the demonstrations. Roy Wilkins, the executive director of the national NAACP, arrived to announce a stop to NAACP money for bail to get people out of jail. Many had not wanted the demonstrations to end because the token concessions fell far short of the blacks' demands for desegregation and an end to hiring discrimination. John Salter, a white sociology professor at

Tougaloo, and Ed King, a white southerner who was the chaplain at the college—the strong, forceful, militant leaders of the young protestors— wanted the people to continue moving forward. Offered an opportunity to leave Mississippi to avoid threats to their personal safety, both men declined. On June 18, 1963, serious injuries from a car wreck hospitalized them and kept them from the mass meeting that evening where the NAACP leadership presented the city's agreement and called for ending the protests. The demonstrations stopped, but the struggle for freedom would continue.

By early July, when I was arriving in Mississippi, Charles Evers, Medgar's brother, had taken over the state NAACP and changed its focus to urging blacks to register to vote, an effort that the federal government wanted to be conducted without major publicity. Hinds County officials, still adamantly opposed to civil rights progress in Mississippi, responded by closing the Jackson registration office for a month.

After my arrival in Jackson, Pharis Harvey, our group leader, a tall, thin, young Methodist minister, drove me and a truckload of other students from the airport to the Tougaloo campus. I met John and Margrit Garner, our hosts for the program, and the other nine members of the group. John, a white professor of physics, and Margrit, from Switzerland, had met at an EVS work camp abroad. The other students were from Oregon, Iowa, Kentucky, Oklahoma, and Texas, and one young man, Diethelm Steinberg, was from Germany. We represented diverse Protestant religions: United Church of Christ, Methodist, Lutheran, and others. There were two blacks in our group: Thelma Sadberry, a Tougaloo student, and Ivory Phillips, who had just graduated from Jackson State. At the time, students at Jackson State could not participate in the civil rights movement on their campus because they knew they would be expelled if they did.

The Tougaloo campus, on five hundred acres of land, impressed me with its traditional and new buildings in a spacious, open environment. The president's home, a modern ranch-style house, bordered the entry drive, and the student union had been built recently, but I stayed in an old dorm that was hot and humid.

After supper in the campus dining hall, we saw the movie *A Raisin in the Sun*, which had been released in 1961. Then we met at the Garners' to learn about the maintenance work we would be doing and our schedule. They lived in a small house on the campus, where they were sleeping with their baby in the living room because shots had been fired through the windows just three nights before. After the murder of Medgar Evers, racial tensions had increased, a group of twenty students prepared to provide protection with guns for self-defense, and the college added a night watchman to guard the campus border adjacent to a main road. Our church group would not be going where the action was, though. Despite what I heard that night about Tougaloo, I told myself I would be safe. And I prayed. I was not involved. I was not a civil rights worker.

Our day would start at 6:15 a.m. for "office," a religious service that was totally unfamiliar to me. After breakfast, we would work from 7:00 to 12:00, and after lunch we had free afternoons. Another religious discussion was scheduled from 5:00 to 6:00, and after supper we would attend evening seminars. We would be joining the summer-school students, who were mostly high school age, in the student union for all our meals. The Garners advised us to try to call the students by their last names because they had always been called only by their first names, and using the courtesy titles *Miss* or *Mr.* would bestow respect. Also, we were to avoid asking about the students' families because some didn't know where or who their fathers were.

By the end of that first long day, I wrote enthusiastically, "Now I'm quite eager and excited. The people are good people and the place is vital as can be."

The Tougaloo project gave me my first direct significant exposure to black people and the civil rights movement. I met people who had been deprived of the rights and privileges that I enjoyed and took for granted, and I saw the life of fear and humiliation that they endured. I also gained an understanding of how important nonviolence was in adding a moral dimension to the movement. Blacks did not fight back against the threats, violence, and brutality. This was not a war, and demonstrators did not react with force, but with disciplined restraint. I received an exceptional educational opportunity and saw firsthand what the organizers were doing in Mississippi.

We led fairly sheltered lives in the dorms, where we did not feel threatened and were not risking arrest. We courted some danger when we were in Jackson, particularly on Sundays when trying to integrate churches, but we intentionally avoided confrontation that could lead to arrest.

The project gave me a daily rhythm, with a work obligation only in the mornings, when we hoped to dodge the heat of the sun. Some of the work was difficult, and I was physically tired after five hours. The job I remember most vividly was tedious and had been left undone for a year: putting together tall, gray, metal lockers with lots of those tiny screws, washers, and nuts, which I have noticed in gym locker rooms ever since. We procrastinated and took more than three weeks assembling the lockers, a few at a time.

Other work was more fun as we learned in conversation with one another to be cooperative and sensitive to each other's needs for help or relief. We tore down an old, useless three-carriage garage, carting the debris to a cistern and throwing the concrete chunks into the water; washed windows in the library; cut down trees; and cleared brush. I liked taking down a forty-three-foot-tall tree better than washing windows. We got used to the very hot weather and enjoyed an iced-tea break midmorning at the Garners' house. I had never liked iced tea, but it was just fine at Tougaloo.

I can picture our group members—Tom, Paul, Tremon, Dickie, Sharon, Pam, and Bobbie—although I lost track of everyone shortly after the summer, with one exception. Karen Pate, from the University of Oregon, and I corresponded for years. We both were volunteers on the Summer Project in 1964, and she visited me once at Stanford. Karen was an open, friendly Westerner, concerned and conscientious. She had short brown hair and was a little taller and heavier than I. She, Pam—an attractive strawberry blonde also from Oregon—and I spent most of our time together, but all of the participants in the program were a group together. No one in the group was strange, weird, or too pious for me. I took note in my diary of things that Thelma and Ivory, the two black students in the group, had to say and learned from them: "Thelma said, 'I take people at face value. I like to give them a hundred and then subtract rather than givin' 'em zero and then adding.' . . . Ivory says he thinks you should give them 50 and then go up or down from there."

Ivory had a legal mind and a good sense of humor, and he often engaged in banter when we were working. He knew the precautions we needed to take. Thelma was a gentle person, reserved, confident in her religious faith, and composed. I found it curious that my parents were as old as her grandparents. Everyone in the group treated each other in a friendly, respectful manner.

We called Diethelm, the twenty-five-year-old from Berlin, "Dickie." He impressed all of us with his strength and hard work; he had an entertaining personality, and I credit him for much of our fun while we were working. On one occasion, Dickie initiated a discussion of race relations and gave us examples of problems around the world. He could simplify things and also made serious, thoughtful comments.

The work camp was not only work, but an introduction to the Mississippi civil rights movement. On my first full day, SNCC field secretaries Jesse Harris, John O'Neal, and Carol Johnson spoke to us in the Social Science Lab. Dr. Ernst Borinski, a German refugee scholar who had come to the United States in 1948 and was a professor in the Sociology Department at Tougaloo, had created this unique forum to sponsor talk across racial lines. He invited students at Millsaps, a small Methodist-sponsored, all-white private college in Jackson, to the lab for discussions. This summer Memphis Norman, the student who had been beaten unconscious at Woolworth's, chaired the lab while Professor Borinski was away.

I was learning about SNCC for the first time. The staff explained their voter registration work in Greenwood, about one hundred miles north of Jackson in the Mississippi Delta. I understood that SNCC's approach was to go to a black community after some injustice had occurred in order to encourage that community to come out and register. I saw right away that SNCC was not at all bureaucratic. SNCC workers were not outside agitators but went into a community when local people requested their help and "let the people decide." There were sixty-six SNCC field secretaries in the South then; each received only subsistence wages. Intrigued, I knew I wanted to hear from SNCC again.

None of the members of my group participated in the discussion with SNCC because everything about it was so new and different to us. Although I had never wanted to raise my hand in school, now I told myself that I must speak up more. Near the end of the month I recognized what a difference participation can make as I found myself much more interested one day than I had been the day before. This notion is fundamental, but it seemed a major revelation for me when I was twenty-one.

That same Sunday afternoon we met with a couple of white folks. The Garners invited friends from their church, Galloway Methodist, to come out to Tougaloo to meet us. Our group took credit for getting them on the predominantly black Tougaloo campus for the first time. But after the husband spoke to us, I was pessimistic that anyone could bring about social change in Mississippi. I wrote that it was "so impossible to talk and reason with Southern whites because they get so emotional." They probably felt the same way about us, even though we didn't consider ourselves radical. On our second day in Mississippi, we were just a bunch of pretty ignorant, do-gooder kids.

The next evening, Monday, Dave Dennis and Jerome Smith from CORE came to Tougaloo to conduct a nonviolence workshop and recruit students for demonstrations. They were skilled at involving people in learning the techniques for anyone to use at demonstrations but were ambivalent about nonviolence for local residents who believed in self-defense. I also heard about the other issue raised by nonviolence: Was it a way of life or only a tactic? Dave Dennis gave me his answer, which I wrote down: "Dave said for 99% it is merely a tactic. He can no longer tell a Negro to put down his gun although he wouldn't carry one himself. Things have been happening so fast around here. 10 people have been shot down in the last few months and one is dead, Medgar Evers."

We were sheltered, yet we were hearing directly about civil rights violence in Mississippi. Young civil rights activists experienced in the field, rather than professors, were teaching our lessons. I asked about the participation of young children in demonstrations, as shown on TV in the Birmingham, Alabama, protests. CORE wanted children removed from the protectiveness of their parents to learn to fight for their civil rights before they know and learn and live anything else—a new thought for me.

The CORE representatives set up role playing with the scene of a white boy and a black girl holding hands, and the white boy is attacked for this transgression of southern white mores: "We learned what to do—hands folded on top of the spinal column (back of the neck), elbows in stomach, and the one [on] the ground curled up because it takes a specially placed kick to hurt the back. The idea of CORE and the nonviolent movement is to try and reach that man's mind—to say 'Why are you doing that, Brother?' in a calm tone to break his thrust of excitement."

I thought it must be very difficult to face such a situation: "It must take a superhuman strength. And such a knowledge of oneself—or an acknowledgment of the confusion in a man's mind—for an individual. In this kind of a situation truly man is acting and thinking for himself and not as part of a well-defined group that can hand out answers. In hypothetical situations that are mentioned they cannot say what they would do. They are conflicted—my dignity as a man and my responsibility to the movement."

For the first time I had to think about nonviolence in practical terms.

My interest in the political issues led me to talk to the Tougaloo students to learn more about the Jackson movement and what had happened in the spring. I compared notes about college experiences with girls I met in the dorm where we lived. Students working at the college earned an amazingly low forty-five cents an hour, whereas I had received a dollar an hour at Cornell. At first, I was awkward with the black students who grew up in Mississippi because my family's economic status was so different from theirs, but I was seeing real dorm living—something I missed when I first went to Cornell—a lot of noise and yelling and laughing. All of the girls in our group became more comfortable as the days went by, and we could join in the fun.

I had a long talk one day with Freddie Kirk, a girl who lived next door to me in the dorm. She had participated in the Jackson demonstrations and was on the march when John Salter, the white Tougaloo professor, was hauled off the front porch of a house by the police and beaten. The police arrested her and held her and other demonstrators in a paddy wagon for half an hour after closing its windows and turning on the heat. She spent thirty hours in jail under terrible conditions: the "guards gave them hot water, called them the worst possible names, food 'not fit for a dog,' a bed she wouldn't call a cot . . . [but] the night cops were nice and slipped them food." The boys who had been jailed talked back to the cops, and the cops were afraid, she said, to go to the boys' section. Freddie Kirk disagreed about ending the demonstrations after Medgar Evers was killed. She said, "When the tension grew high—just keep going and exert pressure."

Joan Trumpauer told me about the 1961 Freedom Rides. She had spent three months on the Parchman prison farm after she was arrested in Jackson. My admiration increased for the Freedom Riders, who refused bail and stayed in jail. I thought about my friends in the North who got their information only from newspapers, magazines, and television, while I began feeling an emotional alliance with participants in the Mississippi civil rights movement as a result of these contacts.

It was not all serious all the time. We had plenty of fun, including bonfires and singing. We went to a Saturday night dance in the student union, where I felt flattered that a Tougaloo student asked me to dance. I saw Bob Moses there that evening, but he had declined to speak to our group, which disappointed me. I had first heard about him from Jane Stembridge, who was living at Tougaloo during the summer of 1963, writing a training manual for an adult literacy pilot project. A white southerner, she was a student at Union Theological Seminary in New York before becoming the first executive secretary of SNCC in Atlanta in 1960. She knew Bob Moses well from sharing an office with him before Moses ended his New York teaching contract and went to Mississippi in the summer of 1961. Although he was in charge, he never sought publicity. He was not at all pretentious, but sensitive and charismatic. My first reaction to him was maddening. I didn't see an excuse for his not talking to our group. He said he had to leave but then showed up at the dance. But the more I saw of Bob Moses and his style of leadership, the more I understood his reputation and respected him.

Jane called him a saint. Frederick Buechner, a Presbyterian minister and one of my favorite writers, makes the term fit Bob Moses: "[T]he feet of saints are as much of clay as everybody else's, and their sainthood consists less of what they have done than of what God has for some reason chosen to do through them. . . . [S]aints are essentially life-givers. To be with them is to become more alive."[3]

I would learn how Bob Moses was working to give life—the critical courage it took for blacks in Mississippi to apply to register to vote.

I enjoyed the personalities and humor of both the Tougaloo students and the kids in my group. "These kids are a lot of fun," I wrote. "True, I can't understand [the dialect of the local students] at times when they're talking to each other. . . . I can respect everyone for their goodness and humor and forget about brainpower."

Obviously I still sounded like a snob, judging "brainpower" by the academic standards I knew, but I was trying to be sensitive to others. I wanted to maintain good relations within the group and was very interested in relating to black students at Tougaloo.

One day three of us had a wonderful work assignment that gave us a chance to make a minor contribution to the civil rights movement and to see Jackson. We had been assigned to work in the office of the *Mississippi Free Press,* a four-page alternative newspaper that had outside financial support. The office was located on Farish Street in the main black neighborhood in Jackson. Most of the nine *Free Press* staff members were on leave from liberal Oberlin College in Ohio, and we had been put to work alphabetizing a new list of 8,000 Mississippi teachers received from the Mississippi Teachers' Alliance. Later we copied the teachers' names and addresses on a subscription form to protect the newspaper and the Teachers' Alliance from reprisals if there were an inspection of the *Free Press's* records. The file would show that each teacher wanted to subscribe to the paper and thus insulate the Teacher's Alliance from the negative association of supporting the civil rights movement.

At the corner grocery where we bought popsicles, it seemed to me that the owners in a black neighborhood should be black, but here they were white. That day I saw blacks living in neighborhoods less segregated from whites than in the neighborhoods I knew in the North. These residential patterns allowed black and white children to play together while they were growing up despite the prohibition on going to school together. The all-black neighborhoods in Jackson gave me a new view: "The neighborhoods are by blocks—Negro then white the next block. It isn't necessarily divided into very large areas. And you can tell right away which are the Negro blocks. The houses are barely painted and so often have chairs out on the porch for sitting. I noticed also the way the houses are perched on cement blocks at the corners—no basement."

In suburban New Jersey, I never saw small, unpainted houses with people sitting out front to enjoy the cooler air.

Dickie served as our guide for a tour of the capitol building, pointing out the segregationist signs: "White Men," "Colored Men," and upstairs a room marked for "Gentlemen." Another sign, "For White Only," was by a vending counter on the bottom floor where a blind man was working. I saw the phrase "Dieu et les Dames" on the ceiling of the Senate chamber and wondered about the translation—"God and women," receiving the same reverence from Mississippi white men. I knew the racists placed their white women on a pedestal and sought to protect them from black men by any means available, but this pairing seemed to go too far.

We also saw the life-size statue of the notorious demagogue Senator Theodore G. Bilbo, who was a very short five foot two; his statue was the centerpiece in the rotunda of the capitol, greeting visitors for thirty years until 1979, when the governor ordered it moved to a side corridor in the basement. In the summer of 1963, a guide told us, "We feature our schools and churches," without mentioning that both were all white.

Travel to nearby Madison County opened my eyes to the way blacks lived in a rural area. Tom Johnson, a Baptist minister and social worker, showed us slides and then guided us on an afternoon trip. Ed King told us how he and his wife "nearly got sentenced to ten years in prison on a perjury charge. They sought police protection for their home after trouble because of his missionary work with Negroes."[4] Large families relaxing on a Sunday afternoon gave us friendly greetings. We saw their fields of cotton, corn, okra, and watermelon; we visited, ate some watermelon, met an eighty-five-year-old man, the son of a slave who had bought eighty acres of his own property; he interestingly had a habit of carrying around $1,500 in his pocket—a habit he had recently given up at Johnson's urging. Johnson told us, as I heard later in orientation in Oxford, "how important it is for Negroes to meet friendly whites in giving them dignity and self respect."

Madison County had consolidated its high schools in new buildings to bolster its claim that the schools were "separate but equal" in defiance of the school desegregation mandate. Johnson told us how unequal the schools in fact were. Students in the black schools read ragged, out-of-date textbooks discarded by the white schools, and their typewriters for typing class were not fully functional. While we were standing around an old closed black high school, some local people recognized Johnson and came over to talk, but others held back because they were too afraid to be seen talking to whites.

We gathered in the Social Science Lab at Tougaloo many times for presentations by outside speakers and discussions. Allan Knight Chalmers, a United Church of Christ minister from New York City and the chairman of the NAACP Legal Defense and Educational Fund, known just as the NAACP Legal Defense Fund or the Inc. Fund, spoke to our group for an hour. He explained to us why he considered Jackson the worst area attempting civil rights progress: forceful resistance to integration and an absence of responsible leadership in the white community resulted from Jackson's provincial orientation, its citizens having moved in from rural areas, and from its being dependent on locally owned light industry. He contrasted Birmingham, Alabama, which had northern corporate headquarters that required accountability in response to local opposition to integration. Political power and social prestige in Jackson, he said, attached to membership in the Citizens' Council, and local newspapers engaged in inflammatory rhetoric, invective, and biased reporting. There was no one in the power structure who could be trusted. No one wanted the right solution.

Chalmers anticipated that boycotting the white shopping area and holding mass demonstrations without a group of local whites supporting the blacks would be a long two- or three-year struggle. The grassroots organizing that had brought out more than two hundred people for the spring demonstrations had been good for educating young people. He called himself a strategist—dealing with communities to solve their problems. He didn't like moderates, saying that they salve rather than solve the problem. Regarding what was happening on the national front, he told us that the March on Washington for Jobs and Freedom that was planned for the end of August was expected to draw 100,000 young people. He feared it would go off as a dud.

Tim Jenkins, a black law student from Yale and a Howard University graduate, spoke to us a couple of times in the Social Science Lab. In one session, he described the bill pending in Congress to desegregate public accommodations. We also heard about a more liberal bill sponsored by Congressman Robert W. Kastenmeier, a Democrat from Wisconsin, which would add a guarantee of voting rights and penalties for police brutality. Tim expressed pessimism about that bill because he thought congressmen were "ivory tower legislators who didn't really know what was going on."

Dr. A. Daniel Beittel, the white president of Tougaloo college since 1960, told us about the civil rights groups in response to our questions, most of which I asked. The NAACP was a well-established organization that thought it should do the job but was criticized for sending outsiders into a local area. SNCC and CORE used local people, and Dr. Beittel agreed that the leadership should be local. He said he had no knowledge of the Tougaloo students' library sit-in in 1961, emphasizing that the purpose of the college was education. But later he showed up as a supporter at the Woolworth's sit-ins.

I was also learning a great deal from attending mass meetings. When I went with some of our group to my first, held at the vast Masonic Temple in Jackson, only five whites were in the packed audience. Bishop Spottswood Robinson, chairman of the board of directors of the NAACP, and Charles Evers led the rally to renew the spring demonstrations. The local NAACP supported the protests, provided the students demonstrated only in small groups and did not risk arrest. SNCC field secretary Bobby Talbert and a girl with him, a wild young high school senior whose name I didn't get, greeted our group and invited us to sit with them on the stage. They told us about arrests and beatings and gave us SNCC and CORE buttons, which I was happy to have. It didn't make sense to me that our predominantly white group was singled out for attention, but I couldn't object.

These mass meetings were not only organizational tools but also religious events, and more than one minister participated in this one. There was an opening prayer, a message based in scripture, and the meeting closed with a benediction. A choir of about fifteen students on the stage led the singing of freedom songs.

This was the first time that I heard the magnificent music so important to the civil rights movement. Freedom songs inspired courage in those trying to register to vote, gave voice to the picket lines, and raised the spirits of imprisoned students, letting their jailers know they were not afraid. Freedom songs could be sung by everybody. The music was easy to learn, the tunes from black hymns and spirituals were familiar, and following the leader for each verse and joining in the repetitive chorus allowed everyone to participate. I don't know which songs I heard and sang that evening, but some that I have always loved are "We Are Soldiers in the

Army," "Which Side Are You On?" "We'll Never Turn Back," "Oh Freedom," "Woke Up This Morning," and "Keep Your Eyes on the Prize."

I loved the singing, but the clapping that frequently began during the
first verse was problematic for me. I couldn't seem to get the beat right
and would stand not clapping, feeling like an altogether stiff jerk. After
more than a year, I figured out that I could watch someone else, put my
hands together tentatively, keep watching, and then, once I got the beat,
relax and clap merrily along with the others. This procedure distracted me
from just singing, which was what I wanted to do, but succeeded in making me feel more comfortable.

I talked to my parents on the phone occasionally and was pleased
when my mother "encouraged my individuality," as I wrote in my diary.
That individuality posed something of a problem for me, however, in the
other major focus of the work camp—religion. I had not gone to church
much since I was confirmed at age fifteen and was not feeling particularly
religious in July 1963. The first evening, Pharis, our Methodist minister
leader, had us pledge "a covenant" to "a life of mutual accountability"
with the "risk of exposing ourselves."

Each of us took turns with responsibility for the morning worship.
I made mine short, read it all, and was pleased to receive a compliment
from Pharis. After supper, we got into long unguided discussions that I
considered too theological and uninteresting. I was unable to concen-
trate, but knowing we would end no later than 6:00 p.m. to watch the
Huntley–Brinkley news show on TV helped me get through many a boring session. But I began to participate more and later admitted to myself
that evening devotions were interesting—we were talking about "real
things." I started questioning the role of the church. Was it service? Was
it worship? Or was it both?

I reached my limit of tolerance, however, when Pharis proposed that
the group take communion—though not the Eucharist—"in remembrance of Christ." He announced that everyone in the group would participate, or no one would take communion. I believed that Christ is truly
present in the sacrament and thought that communion should be given
in a church. If I could not receive it according to my Lutheran faith,
I chose not to participate. As the only one who refused, I created an
issue that required group discussion on more than one occasion. Insensi-

tive and unyielding, I deprived the other group members of something they clearly wanted. Communion was as important to them as it was to me, and our doctrinal differences should not have harmed anyone in the group, but I was unwilling to suspend my beliefs. I felt the responsibility: "But I don't feel I should partake for the sake of the group," I wrote. "It seems so very informal and I can't adjust to the idea that it is not the Eucharist (Holy Communion). If it is not what is its purpose?"

Unlike the others, perhaps I was more interested in civil rights, the political issues, and the Tougaloo students than in religion and our little group.

Part of our mission was racial reconciliation, which I had to learn about for the first time. "Reconciliation between people [involves] a mutual journey, requiring reciprocal participation . . . includ[ing] a willingness to acknowledge wrongs done . . . and make restorative changes that help build trust."[5] If only people could be "set right"—healed, restored, and brought closer together—changes could occur for the better. Reconciliation, also known as confession, is even a sacrament in some churches as an individual makes changes to become closer to God. In the time and place where I found myself, reconciliation offered the possibility of transformation of race relations where change had not taken place before.

In one session with the white Millsaps students, we reached a black–white consensus that the church would be the last institution to integrate. Too many people would prefer that the waters not be troubled; they wanted to be comfortable in church, with their own kind, receiving solace and avoiding any confrontation with difficult issues. Our discussion heated up after a Millsaps student said that blacks were not participating and working to help themselves gain what their leaders were demanding. My position was that "you shouldn't have to do anything because you're a citizen and a person." In my mind, the struggle for freedom was a matter of rights, not privileges, a matter of entitlement, not benefits to be earned.

John Wilkerson, a Millsaps student who was formerly a neighbor of the Tougaloo chaplain Ed King in Vicksburg, expressed his disagreement with the aggressive approach under way to open Millsaps public events to Tougaloo students. He said, "Every time [Ed King] . . . does something (try to get in concerts, etc.) the relationship between the two schools goes down. It's just hurting things by making such a big push. Rev. King can't understand them, but they're not ready to make the complete commitment."

I was inclined to agree with Ed King, yet I also thought that moving too fast on integration might be less likely to obtain desired results. I held conflicting views. I was in a position then to want to hear the other side. I also thought maybe I could persuade a fellow college student to my point of view, tentative as it was.

The more I learned about the civil rights movement and began to understand the oppression of blacks, however, the less I was interested in reconciliation and a patient, slow approach to integration. On Saturday, July 27, Carl Zeitlow, the director of all the ecumenical work camps, visited our project and talked about the work of the National Council of Churches (NCC). In early June 1963, the NCC established the Commission on Race and Religion to advocate passage of the pending civil rights bill and influence public opinion in support of the civil rights movement. He talked about reconciliation, and so, troubled as I was about my commitment to the movement, I asked Mr. Zeitlow what he thought about us demonstrating. He was encouraging, but he also saw a problem: "In general he is for participation in order to really get involved," I wrote later. "And this is true, I think. It's frustrating to sing about freedom and yet not go out and march for it. You wonder how much you really mean it and how willing you are to work for it. More specifically he talked about our function of reconciliation giving the example of our talking with Millsaps students. If we demonstrated, we wouldn't be as effective doing that."

I did my polite talking with the white students but began to realize that getting involved was not waiting for others to engage in discussion but rather "standing up." One could talk, talk, talk or make a real commitment and be willing to take a risk. The opportunity soon came for me to take a first minimal risk.

We spent a lot of time with Ed King after meeting him at the CORE nonviolence workshop. He was young, tall, and lanky, and I appreciated how well informed he was. The large bandage on one side of his face made me feel badly for him, remembering that he had been in a car wreck just weeks earlier. He suggested that we participate in the downtown Jackson church visits. During the spring, he had tried repeatedly to integrate all-white churches by going with black Tougaloo students to attend worship services in these churches. Only St. Andrews Episcopal Church had opened its doors to an integrated group. He continued to be the inspiration and coordinator for these integration efforts until all the churches adopted open policies years later.

During devotions on our third evening, our group leader, Pharis, asked us to consider risking arrest to integrate a major white church in Jackson. After what we had learned about nonviolence that day, I was feeling solemn. No one in our group had been in jail after a civil rights demonstration. The issue was whether we were going to be *part* of the Mississippi civil rights movement—demonstrating and risking arrest. Was this part of the deal? I know I was apprehensive and, being cautious and reserved, not ready to stand up.

Pharis told us that the Garners wanted us to join them on Sunday, July 21, in worshipping at the all-white Galloway Methodist Church, where they were members. Pharis insisted that this be a group decision. But he also told us that a black church had invited us to help survey a black neighborhood in Jackson to which the church was planning to move. We would walk house to house with kids from the church in biracial teams of three. We would also face possible arrest if we chose to participate in the survey.

Thelma was opposed to going to Galloway because she did not think we would accomplish anything. Ivory expressed concern about his family and could not consider his own willingness to participate without think-ing of others who would be involved. We worried about what an arrest would mean for either Thelma or Ivory and deferred to them in making our decision. We felt that the brunt of any violence would fall on Ivory, and if we did go, we should not press the refusal of admission but leave willingly and not risk arrest. The group decided not to go to Galloway because the possible negatives outweighed the positives. The possibility of getting thrown in jail and needing bail and a lawyer seemed a far cry from the work camp proposal and my summer expectations.

Instead of going to Galloway, our group decided to attend the open St. Andrews Episcopal Church on Sunday, July 14. Pharis courteously called the church to tell them we were coming. With a policeman watching our arrival, Ivory advised Pharis to feed *two* parking meters to make sure we didn't get a ticket. Going into the church, I overheard a man saying with a nasty tone in his voice, "I see we have visitors." Ushers seated us near the back of the church for the formal liturgical service. During the service, we got funny looks that I called "continued blank firm stares." I wondered what was "running through their poor sick minds." Only one white boy shook hands with Ivory, and one Millsaps girl spoke to us after the service ended. When we were driving away, a policeman on a motorcycle recorded our license plate number and swerved in front of our car.

Ed King planned that all the churches would be visited the following Sunday, July 21. To avoid risking arrest, we would leave peacefully if turned away. Our group went first to a 9:30 a.m. service at Tougaloo, and then I went with Pharis and a few others to the First Presbyterian Church. Three men met us in front of a closed door. Pharis asked if it was a Christian church, and we heard in response that it was the First Presbyterian Church. The men did not think they had to answer other questions and suggested that "our colored friends worship at the chapel they set up for their employees." Asking to speak to the pastor was ineffective. The men guarding the church doors said that he did not have anything to do with the way things were run around there. They had "such hardened looks on their faces." Dickie later wrote to the pastor, contrasting the lack of welcome he had received with the West Berliners' "screaming, cheering, flag-moving, confetti-tossing welcome" given President Kennedy at about the same time. Someone from a foreign country would be astonished that the church was open only to white people.

That same Sunday Pharis also went with Joan Trumpauer and a black Tougaloo student to Galloway Methodist. The church turned them away. None of the other churches were integrated that Sunday either: Trinity Lutheran, First Baptist, United Church of Christ, Disciples of Christ. Pharis contacted United Press, thinking it would be newsworthy that an integrated group sponsored by the World Council of Churches was not allowed to attend a church service in Mississippi. I never read about our efforts in any newspapers, but we believed they were useful in beginning to challenge segregated worship in Jackson.

The next Sunday we went to Trinity Lutheran for an early service of matins. The previous Sunday, a Lutheran minister, his wife, and four Tougaloo students had been turned away. Ivory was leading Thelma and me in while Pharis held the door. The usher said to us in a friendly manner, "Come in, come in." "I never knew I could feel such a thrill at entering a church," I wrote later. The warm welcome was a pleasant surprise. Several people in the congregation engaged us in conversation after the service. The preacher, who was a visiting minister from Millsaps, let us know later that our presence "had quite an emotional impact on the people—the most meaningful worship service they had had in a long time."

When we were standing outside, however, a layman refused to shake hands with Pharis, saying that he could not extend the hand of welcome to him and that the people in the church were not sincere. He asked Pharis where he was from and, hearing Oklahoma, said something like, "You've got a lot to do there." This opinion was a common objection to the presence of volunteers in the South: Why don't you go home and clean up your own backyard? Pharis had a great comeback: "We've got a lot to do all over the world."

The Trinity Lutherans invited us to stay for Sunday School, which was for all ages, unlike at my home church in New Jersey, where it was just for children. In my class, I heard about responsibility for spilling blood—Planned Parenthood, capital punishment, and war—but nothing about race relations. I was emotional that Sunday about going to church: "It's a very exciting thing to integrate a church. Actually, it's very sad that this action came as such a surprise to us. Why should it get so magnified out of all proportion? Merely going to church, something that's taken so far for granted[,] can be a very real experience."

On our last Sunday, August 4, wanting to go back to Trinity Lutheran, six of us went to the same early service, but this time the ushers turned us away. "I felt so forlorn faced by their spokesman's 'You're not welcome here.' . . . Their action was explained as being the result of there being 'two groups' in the church. They were different ushers for this month. Isn't it pathetic that these men have to worry and be so afraid? Fear such as that must be a horrible thing to live with."

A police car followed us as we walked over to St. Andrews, where we entered without a problem: "No one spoke to us except a nod from one woman still seated in her pew and a man who said to me, 'We wear hats in the Episcopal Church.'"

That same day we went to the New Hope Baptist Church, the black church where Thelma was a member. There we were welcomed by all without question, suspicion, or stares. I noticed a deacon sitting next to me singing parts of the prayers and could feel the spirit of freedom and emotion that the congregation was enjoying. The rhythm affected people when they heard not only the word, but also the music in the background. The congregation was singing "Throw Out the Lifeline," the minister was preaching energetically and emotionally, and people were walking down to the front of the church. I learned that the women wearing white, including white gloves, at the front pews worked as nurses in case of anyone "falling out" from the high stimulation of the service. For the first time, I saw "the call," when members of the congregation are so profoundly moved that they go to the altar to accept Jesus Christ as their savior.

At one of the Jackson mass meetings, Ed King spoke about the church integration efforts and asked students for testimonials about their experiences "visiting" the white Jackson churches. One girl spoke about having been turned away from a Methodist church by a policeman who used profane language. Ed told about a minister who had said to him that if a group got inside his church, he was confident the congregation would beat up the integrationists. When Ed asked, "What would you do then?" "the same girl said self-protection and prayer if she could. She said she would ask that they be forgiven for not acting like the Christians they were supposed to be."

I felt better about church in Jackson when I met Mrs. Jane Schutt. She was a handsome, distinguished, well-dressed, fifty-year-old white southerner. Not a native, she had moved to Jackson when she was twenty-one years old. She was the chairman of the Mississippi Advisory Committee to the U.S. Commission on Civil Rights, on which she served with Dr. Beittel, the president of Tougaloo. We learned that after too few people attended the commission's biracial workshops, the Advisory Committee reestablished the Mississippi Human Relations Council, which was more successful in holding interracial meetings. Since May 1962, they had had as many as sixty people participating. Since few whites would serve as officers, Dr. Beittel was the chairman, and Mrs. Schutt was the secretary of that organization.

White residents in Mississippi were unwilling to speak up for civil rights and risk ostracism from their families and friends. Mrs. Schutt's answer to that was, "I may have felt some ostracism but I haven't noticed it. I've been so busy. They say you'll be out of 'polite society,' but what is that?" I hoped that she had some immunity from racist pressures because of her official position with the Advisory Committee, but I found out later that in December 1963 the Ku Klux Klan burned a cross on her lawn; in response, she placed Christmas lights on the charred remains.

Mrs. Schutt considered the independent Interracial Prayer Fellowship that met at the Pearl Street Church in Jackson more effective in bringing the races together. Attendance might be as low as twelve or as high as forty, and the ratio of blacks and whites also varied widely. Close relationships developed over two years through study and prayer in these small groups. Mrs. Schutt impressed me with her sincerity: "She believes certain things and she acts on them because to believe is to live your belief, as she said," I wrote. "She spoke very sincerely and meaningfully. . . . I'm sure she must be doing great work in the white community. She said she couldn't see what would happen in the long run, but she just looks to see what she can do that day."

In the end, the religious aspects of this work camp had a positive impact on me. Pharis challenged us in our thinking as he dealt with his own reactions. One day I noted: "[Pharis] . . . questioned his fear this morning, and he admitted that it was the man he was wrongfully trying to fight instead of the system. Always we are to practice Christian love and brotherhood. The white Southerners who hate as much as they do cannot be hated, but only pitied really. They are fearful men. And of what?"

His influence, my experiences in the Jackson churches, and what I learned from Mrs. Schutt about reaching black and white women together in prayer groups led me to a new view of the civil rights movement as a religious endeavor. "Unlike in my sociology course," I noted, "race relations is now in a Christian framework."

Despite the new NAACP policy to avoid arrest, on July 19 the police charged twelve students present in two city parks with *threatening* to disturb the peace. That evening Johnny Frazier, the NAACP Jackson field secretary for youth, spoke to us at Tougaloo about the targeted city parks and Mississippi Coliseum, the arrests, and the NAACP's hopes to increase attendance at the evening mass meetings. The following day, which was a Saturday, 150 people went to the mass meeting at the Masonic Temple and started a march down Capitol Street, where they were forbidden to demonstrate and had always been stopped by the police. The marchers sang freedom songs face to face with police holding rifles, shotguns, and billy clubs and then turned back before any arrests were made.

Ed King told us how we could contribute to the movement without engaging in a sit-in. At the trial of the arrested twelve students set for the following Friday, Ed King gave us the job of spotters—being on the scene unobtrusively, neutral in attitude. We were to be "observers responsible to call if any violence broke out." Once a spotter became known, the individual would no longer be useful. Ed pointed out the difficulties of finding and accepting where to be useful in the movement, even though one might not necessarily be in the thick of the action. "You want to join, but your job is better done by not joining," he said. I was excited about this opportunity because it would be a way of getting involved without actually demonstrating and facing arrest. I was in awe that the twelve who had been arrested, students like myself, planned to stay in jail, a very real situation that I couldn't imagine for myself. But I missed my chance because the court postponed the trial. However, Ed King's thoughts about finding a useful place in the movement were provocative and stayed with me.

On July 22, we went into Jackson for another workshop in nonviolence, but only fifty kids showed up, a discouragingly small number. Why the lack of interest? Probably because the kids had gotten very roughed up in the spring and were not confident they could remain nonviolent. They also expected to be arrested, and jail would be even more of a risk to their personal safety when they could not be bailed out. Jackson had increased the cost of bail to $1,500 for a first arrest and $3,000 for a second, and the NAACP had ended its contribution of bail money after the killing of Medgar Evers.

We went to another mass meeting held at Pratt Memorial Church in Jackson. Johnny Frazier told a story of getting into the governor's office with a Nigerian reporter. The governor was shocked when Johnny said his name was Frazier, indicating he was not from Nigeria. Johnny had applied three times to go to the segregated Mississippi Southern University in pursuit of the quest that Clyde Kennard had begun. In response to

Kennard's audacity, officials had framed him for a crime, convicted him, and sentenced him to serve time in Parchman. He later died after prison officials refused to treat his cancer. Johnny was waiting for a court decision about his admission. When Ed King talked at the end of the meeting about integrating the all-white churches in Jackson, I was pleased that he got the same standing ovation as Johnny. I liked and respected Ed and did not want the black crowd to treat him differently because he was white or was talking about churches.

On our last Sunday, five of our group went to the city jail to visit Thelma's first cousin, Jesse Harris, one of the SNCC field secretaries who had inspired me at the very beginning of the work camp. I didn't know then what he had experienced: spending forty-five days in Parchman after he joined the 1961 Freedom Rides and then being beaten in the county jail after an arrest for refusing to sit in a segregated courtroom. I hadn't heard the cause for this new arrest. Thelma could not visit him, and we just saw him through the screen on his fourth floor cell, waving his handkerchief, but couldn't hear what he said. She told us he was "so stubborn he won't come out unless he's sick!"

I had my run-in with the police that Sunday when they stopped our integrated car near the city line on our way back to Tougaloo. They asked us to get out of the car, confronting me first for my name, address, and where I worked. It was hard to do, but I answered as calmly as I could. I found Thelma's composure unbelievable as she waited for direct questions before she gave her name. She had not had bad experiences with the police before. She knew the police could do nothing to her mother because she did not work. The other Tougaloo student was scared, worried that the police would go to her home.

On August 1, 1963, the most important day of my summer, we had accepted a SNCC invitation to visit the Delta. Leaving at 5:30 a.m. to avoid notice as an interracial group, we drove through the deserted, desolate, flat Mississippi countryside two and a half hours north on the two-lane highway from Jackson to Greenwood, not stopping for anything. Through the rolling hills of Yazoo City, I saw the kudzu covering everything in its path, forming grotesque shapes as it engulfed tree limbs and stumps. Then in the Delta we saw the surroundings change to large green fields of cotton in a wide-open and endless landscape.

We arrived in Greenwood without incident and in time for breakfast in the SNCC office, two good-size basement rooms. The office impressed me as being in quite good order, whereas the upstairs NAACP office, a room with two empty desks, looked bureaucratic and inactive. A dozen young people and several adults were working and milling around in the SNCC office, making me feel shy about any conversation.

Sam Block from Cleveland, Mississippi, had begun the SNCC work in Greenwood in 1962, and after Bob Moses moved there from McComb in January 1963, the SNCC Mississippi staff were headquartered in this office. Willie Peacock, also a Mississippi native, spoke to us about changing people's attitudes through voter registration. We sat in the front room, which was called "the chapel" and was set up with five long benches and a lectern for any type of meeting. The state requirement that the names of those who applied to register to vote be printed in the newspaper for two weeks, theoretically to allow time for complaints about disqualifying moral character, in reality provided the information that white employers, landlords, and bankers could use against blacks who applied to register. SNCC believed that the state's responsibility for illiteracy imposed an obligation to make provision for blacks who could not read or write and that this obligation also applied to voter registration. I read some letters from black residents complaining of intimidation and the loss of homes, jobs, or welfare. The sanctions as well as physical harm and property damage were often severe. SNCC did not have resources for a welfare program for families without income, but they did solicit and receive donations of food and clothing from sympathetic supporters in the North and distributed them as fairly as they could.

SNCC stayed in Greenwood supporting the local people despite extreme opposition to its voter registration activity. Frequent arrests and firebombing of the SNCC offices did not stop the fearless SNCC organizers. On February 28, 1963, three white men in an unlicensed car had followed Bob Moses, Jimmie Travis, and a third black man, Randolph Blackwell, who was visiting from the Voter Education Project (VEP) in Atlanta, as they left Greenwood. Overtaking them on the highway, the whites shot the car full of seventeen slugs, hitting the driver, Travis, in the neck and arm but missing the other two, who were able to duck. Miraculously, Jimmie Travis survived his wounds, although the closest hospital that would treat him was more than a two-hour drive away in Jackson. Wiley Branton, director of the VEP, called on all the SNCC workers in Mississippi to converge on Greenwood to show that no degree of violence would cause the workers to back down and leave town.

I tried to imagine the courage it took for blacks to take these risks to claim their right to first-class citizenship. I gave the SNCC workers credit for their bravery in living among the local citizens and encouraging them to apply to register to vote, and I attributed much of the success, limited as it was in terms of the number of new registered voters, to Bob Moses.

We toured Greenwood, taking precautions to seat Ivory in the back of the car with the boys, and we saw the big old homes that reflected white wealth from the Delta agrarian economy. After our day of listening and learning, we organized smaller groups to go to an evening mass meeting. Pharis assigned me to go to Clarksdale, where I wanted to go because of Aaron Henry, the pharmacist who was state president of the NAACP. He had just been arrested a few days earlier for parading without a permit and was one of more than a hundred currently in jail. Put on a demeaning garbage truck detail, he had only two pieces of dried bread and a spoonful of grits to eat per *day*. To go to Clarksdale as the white girl in the integrated group, I would have to ride on the floor in the backseat out of sight, which was okay with me, but the SNCC workers found that too dangerous and wouldn't go, which meant I couldn't go either. That evening the police did stop others in our group while they were returning from Clarksdale and would have arrested them but for Dickie. His foreign status confused the cops, and so they did nothing.

Instead I went to Ruleville, a small rural town in nearby Sunflower County, with SNCC staff going in a separate car. Ruleville was known for Senator James O. Eastland, the powerful segregationist chairman of the Senate Judiciary Committee who had served in Congress for thirty-six years. His plantation was near Ruleville, and he had an office in town.

We went to a home where we would have dinner, not knowing what to expect. I recorded that we were "greeted by a big man in overalls and a fat woman with her hair sticking straight out" and received a warm welcome. Fannie Lou Hamer, forty-five, a former sharecropper who had been evicted from the plantation where she had worked for eighteen years just for attempting to register to vote, was our hostess. We had not heard of her then, but her spirit and personality soon impressed me in conversation. Because she was registered, I asked her if she was going to vote. She said she did not think she would be allowed to because you had to pay a poll tax for *two* years before you could vote, and the county had refused to accept her first payment of the tax. The inflection in her voice made that answer poetically plaintive, but at the same time she was undaunted.

Mrs. Hamer told us what she'd suffered because of her registration. Her house did not have running water, just two faucets outside, but her water bill had jumped to $15 from $2.60 a month. Nightriders shot into her house six times one night; luckily, she was staying elsewhere with her niece because her husband had thought something might happen.

Then, while traveling from a citizenship-training session in South Carolina, she and her companions had gotten off the Trailways bus in Winona, Mississippi—some to get served in the bus station. Federal law requiring interstate bus facilities to desegregate had established the right for blacks to use these public accommodations. State highway patrolmen, county sheriffs, and city police were supposed to enforce the law. Euvester Simpson, who had joined the movement when she was just out of the all-black Itta Bena high school in June 1963, was on the same trip. She states that they intentionally used "the white side of the bus terminal . . . every time there was a rest stop." She speculated that after Columbus, Mississippi, the patrolmen at the next stop, Winona, had been warned because they "were there waiting for us . . . [and] would not let us into the white side of the bus station."[6] Annelle Ponder, a Southern Christian Leadership Conference (SCLC) worker who recruited local black Mississippians for citizenship training, wrote down the license number of the patrol car, and the police took all seven of them to jail.

On the order of the jailer, fellow black prisoners beat Mrs. Hamer badly. "She said she didn't know human flesh could get so hard from beating," I wrote in my diary on August 1, 1963. Annelle Ponder and June Johnson, a sixteen-year-old girl from a movement family in Greenwood, also were badly beaten. No one beat Euvester Simpson because, as she guessed, "phone calls were coming in from all over . . . [and] they were afraid to do any more." She shared a cell with Mrs. Hamer and described how Mrs. Hamer had suffered from the beating: "I remember sitting up the rest of the night with Mrs. Hamer. She had put her hands back to try to keep some of the straps from hitting her head. And so her hands were all black-and-blue and swollen. She got really sick during the night and developed a fever. I put cold towels on her forehead, trying to get the fever down. She was really sick, and we were all so upset. Nobody got any sleep. So you know what we did? We sang freedom songs all through the night."[7]

When SNCC heard about the arrest, Lawrence Guyot went to the jail to post bond for their release. Instead, he too was brutally beaten and jailed in an unbelievably harrowing experience. They all remained in jail for four days.

I described Mrs. Hamer earlier as "fat," but that description does not do justice to this short, strong, energetic woman. She gave us, as I exclaimed in my diary, "a warm welcome." She looked tired to me. She said many times, "All my life I've been sick and tired. Now I'm sick and tired of being sick and tired."[8] She showed a toughness that did not make her sound like a victim, and as she told her stories with a sense of humor in a rhythmic voice, I was hanging on every word from this remarkable woman.

She truly was another saint. I have read that if you want to meet a saint, look to the poor—those who have little getting in the way of their experience of God. She didn't tell us all that happened that time in Winona, but I have read of how her Christian faith "transformed . . . [her] perception of her torturers" and led her to a conversation with the jailer's wife about the life of faith.[9] In her book *Freedom Song*, after describing Mrs. Hamer as "a woman of wisdom, grit, and discernment," Mary King quotes the following poem by Jane Stembridge:

Mrs. Hamer is more educated than I am. That is, she knows more.

. . .

. . . What? She knows *she is good.*

If she didn't, she couldn't sing the way that she sings. She couldn't stand, head back, and sing. She couldn't speak the way that she speaks—she *announces.*

It is not the story she tells—dramatic, true, terrible, real. It isn't the facts, but the way that she stands to announce.[10]

Known in the movement for her wonderful voice and fervor in leading freedom songs, Fannie Lou Hamer once said, "Singing brings out the soul."[11]

We ate dinner while the SNCC workers were out soliciting affidavits regarding a denial of the right to vote from anyone willing to sign them. If the individual's name was not on the rolls when he or she went to vote, an affidavit of qualification could be presented. If the manager of elections also signed the affidavit, the individual's ballot in the upcoming state elections would be counted. I thought there was little chance that the affidavits would be accepted, but knowing they should be as provided by Mississippi state law, I believed presenting the affidavits would be a legitimate protest. I don't remember what our meal was, but I can guess that it was chicken, greens, corn bread, and iced tea. Mrs. Hamer stood in the doorway of her hot kitchen until *we* invited *her* to eat with us. Then she told us how nervous she had been the first time she ate with whites—at Tougaloo in the faculty dining room.

Fannie Lou Hamer told us how she felt about white people. We had heard earlier in the month that it was important for blacks to meet friendly whites who treated them with courtesy and respect. She praised us for what we were doing and said how glad she was to see that some white people cared. She assured us that the knowledge that we cared gave them the courage to go on. Suddenly we seemed more important than I had thought possible. She continued, telling us that she didn't hate whites because she could understand. They've been keeping blacks down for so long, and "You know, if you had a shade tree, you wouldn't want to give it up. Now, would you?" And she was emphatic in her generosity. Whatever she had, we were welcome to it.

The mass meeting started at 7:30 p.m., just around the corner from the Hamers' house, in Williams Chapel, the only church in the area that could be used for such meetings. Mrs. Hamer said ministers, speaking generally, were the worst—unwilling to help the movement for fear of losing what they had as leaders in the community. We had been to mass meetings in Jackson, but this one was different for me. The place was smaller, and the atmosphere less formal, more intense, and more emotional. The church was full. We sat together as a group on the hard wooden pews in the one-room wooden church. We were in the rural

Delta, where there was more white hatred, oppression, and violence than in Jackson. The older adults attending this meeting, more women than men, were in more danger than the mostly young students who gathered for the meetings in Jackson.

Mass meetings were important not for assembling a large crowd of people, but for summoning the courage of the black community to challenge its oppressors. Gathering together socially in the evening for religious inspiration and political rallying lessened the fear as neighbors gained strength from one another. SNCC staff would typically explain the process of registering to vote and urge participation, discussing what they knew from local people was significant for their community. Then participants at the meeting, new potential leaders, might rise to "testify" as to their life stories, beliefs, and recent experiences in order to encourage their neighbors. Joining in intermittent freedom songs inspired action, lessened individual doubts, and connected people to each other. Before the conclusion of a mass meeting, SNCC would announce the next date it planned to take a group to register and ask for volunteers. Sometimes only a few hands would go up: they were, after all, being asked to be ready to risk their personal safety, their jobs, and their homes.

At the meeting we attended in Ruleville, a Reverend Morris began with a sermon about brotherhood. He didn't believe a man could preach the Bible without preaching freedom. For me, hearing the audience respond, usually just "oh yes" or "amen" after every sentence spoken by the minister, was different and notable for a political gathering. Some of the women were even singing their responses. Charles McLaurin, the SNCC field secretary who had worked in Ruleville since the previous summer, spoke words of encouragement. All but three of the people there had tried to register. He talked about how the women had gone down to the courthouse in August the previous year and "got the ball rolling," and it hadn't stopped. The minister's constant refrain was "keep on keeping on."

I didn't expect the meeting to be so religious, but I was learning how important Christian beliefs were in sustaining these older black men and women in the rural South. Everyone put a great deal of energy into the spirited singing of freedom songs even though it was a very hot evening.

The contributions at the meeting totaled $4.51, a pretty small amount but still important for SNCC's work.

Mass meetings always ended with the singing of the anthem of the civil rights movement, "We Shall Overcome," as we did that evening, standing arm over arm, with hands held, including the verse, "Black and white together, / Black and white together, / Black and white together now!" and the chorus, "Oh deep in my heart, I do believe. / We shall overcome some day." After the meeting, I shook hands with six women who enthusiastically told me how glad they were that we came. I felt very welcome. To have attended this mass meeting in a plain, small church was a special privilege and a memorable occasion.

On that August day in 1963, I made my commitment to civil rights. Just a few months earlier, I had decided to go on a service project but had no political ideals motivating me to go to Mississippi. Now I felt involved with black Mississippians who had entrusted me with their gratitude. They may have assumed I would forget and abandon them, go home without doing anything more to help. But meeting Fannie Lou Hamer and the honest, straightforward, courageous people in Ruleville had a powerful influence on me. I started thinking about what I could do to give something back and feel less guilty about all that I had. I wrote the following: "Today had a real meaning for me. The contrast between what a person like Mrs. Hamer is doing and what I am about in this world is indescribable. We felt guilty being there. So how can we return home and do nothing? If we can't do nothing, how much can we do? And how much will we do?"

A few days later I sent a thank-you note to Mrs. Hamer for her generous hospitality and the delicious meal. But I thanked her for much more that she had given us. My letter said: "You gave us something more important than food that evening. Your strength and courage was [sic] an inspiration that cannot be forgotten. I only hope that we can do half as much as you are doing in this fight for freedom. Somehow all Americans must understand the meaning of such giving and suffering."

And I went on, uncharacteristically, to invoke God in the closing lines: "May God be with you all in your striving toward freedom. This fight will be won!"

I was optimistic.

We spent one day during the last week evaluating the work camp. We basically wanted to be more directly involved in the civil rights movement and thought the work on campus should be more purposeful. My notes stated: "Expressions of both satisfaction and enjoyment of being physically tired, and also discontent that the work was not more closely related to the movement. In this way it could have been more significant but not necessarily as satisfactory. Work was part of the daily rhythm of life."

The work camp aimed at racial reconciliation, however, and did not make me feel that I was participating in the civil rights movement. As Pharis put it, we were there to "keep the waters troubled." At that time, a real commitment meant joining a demonstration, knowing the techniques of nonviolence, risking arrest and physical harm from the police or hostile bystanders, and deciding whether to accept bail or stay in jail. But I didn't yet know the meaning of my commitment. That first summer in Mississippi I was just stirring things up a little bit without taking any risk. But sometimes risk could be as little as taking a different position within your family or before your friends. I knew I could make that commitment.

Back at Tougaloo for a few more days of routine, work, and religion, I began looking forward to a voter registration project at the next work camp—in North Carolina. I expected less racial segregation and discrimination there than in Mississippi and hoped for more freedom than we had in our sheltered existence at Tougaloo. I had learned a great deal about the civil rights movement, and with my commitment I now wanted to call myself a civil rights worker.

What I did not anticipate was how different the atmosphere would be in my next interracial group of students.

4

On to Greensboro, North Carolina, and Back to Cornell

They came from almost every state in the union; they came in every
form of transportation. . . . It was a fighting army, but no one could
mistake that its most powerful weapon was love.

—Martin Luther King Jr.,
The Autobiography of Martin Luther King, Jr.[1]

I arrived in Greensboro, North Carolina, in early August 1963, the month
of the March on Washington for Jobs and Freedom, for a three-week
voter registration project sponsored by the AFSC, the national Quaker
organization headquartered in Philadelphia.[2] This time I was not alone as
my new friend Karen Pate had also signed up for the project, and we took
the bus together to Greensboro. Eighteen of us, all college students, ate
and slept in the basement of St. Stephen Church, a member church of the
United Church of Christ. The twelve girls slept in bunk beds on one side
of a divider wall, and the six boys on the other side. One bathroom served
all of us; showers were four blocks away at the Y.

On our first Sunday, the group split up to go to several churches in
the black neighborhoods to introduce ourselves and urge voter registration. We asked to say a few words. I went to a Lutheran church. What a
contrast to my first black church experience in Jackson. The pastor was
a young white man who welcomed us with a favorable introduction as
young people "doing the Lord's work." The service was "sober and drab
as compared with the usual Negro service," I wrote in my diary. No one
seemed to notice our white presence in the all-black congregation.

I was immediately struck by the difference between the black kids

In the vacant lot across from the church in Greensboro, North Carolina, August 1963. Courtesy of Randolyn Johnson Story.

from Greensboro in our group and the students I had gotten to know in Mississippi. These kids were asserting their independence, and I thought their *self*-concern came first. They were not very friendly the first night, when they went out to a party without us. But this first impression lasted only a day. I realized that these local black girls were really sharp. They joked together because they were friends and easy-going. Robert Tyrone "Pat" Patterson, a student at A&T (now North Carolina Agricultural and Technical State University) and the one black guy on the project, was very good-looking, well dressed, cool, and kind. The black girls taught me a new word that defined Pat—*pressed*. He wore a friendly smile most of the time, and I found him attractive. He was a sensitive, thoughtful guy who asked me if I had always felt the same way about people. I guess I had, but I had not known many people different from myself before Cornell and my summer experiences during college.

Soon we were all partying together with local black kids. The parties started late, about 11:00 p.m., with music, dancing, maybe some beer, and card playing. I wondered what to do, how to conduct myself when the black guys paid attention to me. I acted pleasant, talked to them, but I had to struggle to understand a different manner of speaking that was more than just a southern accent. I met Charles Wells, an A&T graduate who was going to American University in Washington for a master's degree, and we paired off one evening, just talking, nothing romantic. I liked him, but there was a problem. It would have been a really interesting evening had I been able to understand most of what he said. He mumbled and spoke too fast. But I thought he was nice. When he drove me to get some food, I saw the looks from the blacks at the drive-in, but it didn't seem too strange to be there. Of course, I knew about the taboo against interracial dating but didn't want social pressure to influence me in what I did or did not want to do. The black boys' interest in us—the white girls—continued through the project, and we were friendly in return. I learned another local word, *program,* as in these guys were out to condition the girls in picking up any of us. With all the guys around, I concluded that I wasn't prepared to accept dates, which I felt would make things too complicated. I saw my volunteer experience in Greensboro as a great opportunity to know a whole different group of young people.

Despite my resolve not to complicate things by dating, I did spend some time with another guy named Greenwood Allen. He was twenty-five, had been born in Harlem, had attended private schools in North Carolina, and had graduated from A&T a couple of years earlier. He was working in Tillery, North Carolina, teaching social studies in a school and in a prison. I wrote about him: "He really is such a fine respectable interesting person. Drives an Impala convertible and is 'pressed.' We agreed that our interest in each other was initiated by curiosity, but certainly there was more to knowing him the past three days than knowing a Negro boy. . . . Such a good looking guy!"

This relationship made me wonder about others' irrational fears. I wrote my questioning: "It makes you wonder what the fear of mixed marriages really is. What difference does skin color make? All the fears come back to this as the ultimate evil, but why? It is so ungrounded. I can understand this, knowing this guy as an individual. He's just like anyone else."

When I heard that Allen and his girlfriend had broken up three days later, I was surprised, felt guilty, and hoped I was not hated. He left town to go back to work, and I didn't write. This dating stuff would get complicated.

Dr. George Simkins Jr., the president of the Greensboro NAACP chapter, spoke to us about race relations in the city, which were good only in relation to other places in the South. After a CORE-led selective-buying campaign from May 11 to June 7, 1963, against Greensboro merchants who discriminated, black college and high school students faced arrest for demonstrating for desegregated public accommodations and merit hiring by the city.[3] They blocked entrances to restaurants and theaters to get arrested. Filling the jails became a primary strategy for putting pressure on the city. After more than a thousand students were arrested, officials responded to this strategy by releasing them from the overcrowded prison farm, an old polio hospital, and the National Guard Armory. They then threatened expulsion from A&T for further participation in the protests. The black community, more than 2,000 strong, supported the students in a somber, silent march of black ministers, doctors, teachers, and average citizens that forced the beginning of a negotiated settlement. Tension mounted with new demonstrations when progress toward an agreement failed. The arrest of student leader Jesse Jackson provoked the final confrontation between demonstrators sitting in the central business area of downtown and the police, who arrested them for obstructing traffic. Finally, the city had no choice but to support desegregation of public accommodations. The demonstrations had interfered with routine police operations and cost the city $1,300 a day to feed and house the arrested demonstrators. They succeeded in getting an agreement from four hundred merchants to open their facilities on a fair and equal basis.

Dr. Simkins told us about the requirements for voter registration, and Mrs. Margaret Schechter, the executive secretary of the Board of Elections, gave us more details about registration and voting in the county. Her statistics showed that registration qualifications were minimal: one-year residence in the state, thirty days residence at a local address, and the ability to read an oath. But whereas two-thirds of eligible whites were registered, only one-third of eligible blacks were. Mrs. Schechter emphasized to us how important the vote was, telling us to always vote, and so I have.

Demonstrating the hand-held voting machine model to a prospective voter, August 1963. Photograph by Richard Ramsay, courtesy of Lewis A. Brandon III.

The spring demonstrations had made residents receptive to our voter registration campaign. We went out as integrated pairs during the hours people were likely to be home, asking them to register. We assumed residents were not registered to avoid hearing them claim that they were. I found the canvassing challenging: "It's a challenge to make the people feel easy and start on the lowest level," I wrote. "You register first, just get your name on the books after reading a short paragraph and signing your name. Then you can vote in any of the coming elections—city, county, state and President Kennedy."

We encountered little apathy, and I was glad to find that most of the people we talked to were receptive. When young children were in the front yard, talking to them in a playful way and getting them giggling helped me bridge any gap in communication with their parents. One or two registrars volunteered to wait at the nearby Y or a community center while we were canvassing, ready with on-the-spot registration for those who came in and filled out the application form. If residents needed a ride, we provided transportation. The first evening twenty-five people were standing in line at the registration site when we finished canvassing at 9:00 p.m.

We wrote a card for every house to identify individuals eligible to register to vote and kept an exact tally of the numbers registered each day by neighborhoods in the five black precincts in the city. The registrar gave us small, hand-held models of the voting machine used to show citizenship classes what new voters were supposed to do. No one in the group liked being stuck in one place with the job of demonstrating the models to applicants at our registration site, but I found it a good opportunity to talk and be constructive.

My challenge was to make the most of my three weeks, when each of us was on his or her own without the cohesiveness that we had at Tougaloo working as a group. Teams of two canvassed, with several local kids helping us out. I felt that we didn't make the best use of our time during the day. Exhausted after the parties and late-night talking, I slept more than usual, and I often found our long, boring meetings a waste of time. We spent hours sitting along the steps to the basement of the church talking with the Greensboro kids, relaxed and happy. The more moderate racial climate here made North Carolina seem far away from Mississippi.

One Sunday we decided to integrate some white churches. Elfreda Ardis, one of the local black members of the group, and a few white members of the group went to the West Market Methodist Church, a surprisingly large, plush church with cushioned pews set nearly in the round, and three balconies. Unlike in Jackson, we were admitted, and we felt welcome: there were looks, but the congregation did not stare at us. I thought the sermon was good: "The message was love thy neighbor and I thought the minister said an awful lot without speaking on the racial situation directly. Never would so much be said in Mississippi certainly. He said we should go out on the streets of Greensboro and look people in the eye and see their 'fears, anxieties and frustrations.'"

Segregation, with its underlying suspicion and hatred, was depriving people of the ability to reach out to others and feel the power of love.

The project gave us education and touring opportunities during the day. At a textile-manufacturing factory, we got a direct look at discrimination and decided to protest to the management. Cone Mills, Greens-

Randy in the front, with the other girls paying attention to Dick, August 1963.
Courtesy of Randolyn Johnson Story.

boro's largest employer, had 2,000 people, men and women, both whites and blacks, working in the factory we visited. We saw "Colored" signs on drinking fountains and learned that no blacks held the higher-paying jobs as supervisors. Pat signed our group letter to the Cone brothers urging that they "end discriminatory practices and adopt fair employment policies."

Our action, however, offended our sponsor, the local AFSC, which had an established program of seeking merit employment without regard to race. One of the Cones called Mrs. Sarah Herbin at the AFSC to complain, telling her that most of the signs had come down and that we didn't know what we were talking about. Mrs. Herbin showed up at the church disturbed because she was connected with us, and we did look like troublemakers. We didn't excuse Mr. Cone and stuck to our guns, defending our letter.

My new friends Elfreda Ardis and Bunky Dansby, who had been arrested in the spring demonstrations, were going to trial on August 26, and I went with them to a protesters' strategy meeting. CORE asked the group to decide: If the demonstrators received a guilty verdict and were sentenced, should they appeal the sentence or go to jail? I thought about what I would do and could not imagine being arrested and going to jail. Most planned on jail as a further protest against segregation, but the sentence, thirty days in jail or a $25 fine, turned out to be a decision the group appealed.

The highlight for me on this project was the time spent with the local black girls from Greensboro. We gossiped, analyzed others in the group, and talked honestly about race. Karen and I could learn about black people's feelings from them because they were open to expressing their anger to us. They were committed to the civil rights movement and resented blacks who did not support working for freedom and justice. And they did not accept any black person "passing" as a white person. The parties and the dating gave us common ground for conversation. We reviewed all the boys, particularly the ones in our group. I noted in my diary that "they [the local black girls] raved about Tod for ten minutes" because he was so good looking—tall, blond, and preppy. We talked—and laughed—at our bunks before going to sleep some nights as late as three or four in the morning. Their words, phrases, and humor entertained me. Although we gossiped, we also talked seriously, learning from each other.

I was angry and disappointed when I learned that the project director had decided that we could not go to the March on Washington on August 28 because of our job in Greensboro. "First things first," he said. We talked about why we all *should* go to the march. I felt differently from the girl who wanted to go to have fun: "I want to participate which means demonstrate. Right now I feel very committed but I know I can't claim to be until I have been in a demonstration. Being in one demands a decision and thus in some way changes the individual. It's a step—you have to act. You can talk forever. So we were fairly upset to hear negative feelings because we've got to go—for more important reasons than being in on history to tell our grandchildren."

The director eventually changed his mind, and three buses from

Greensboro left our church at 1:00 a.m. I was disappointed with the bus assignments because I didn't get on the CORE bus with all the swinging kids. The March on Washington for Jobs and Freedom was being held to demand civil rights legislation, a public-works program that would provide jobs, an increase in the minimum wage, federal protection for demonstrators against police brutality, the implementation of school desegregation, and self-government for the District of Columbia. President Kennedy supported the civil rights bill pending in Congress but opposed the march. Apprehensive about violent attacks on the demonstrators and afraid of losing support for passage of the legislation, he tried to cancel the event. He called A. Philip Randolph, the tall, distinguished, elderly leader of the Brotherhood of Sleeping Car Porters, the principal organizer of the march, and other national civil rights leaders to meet at the White House. The organizers assured the president that the marchers would be peaceful and refused to call off the march.

When I woke up about 9:00 a.m. as the bus moved freely into the city, I noticed the array of military police, which made me wonder how peaceful the march would actually be. Our group was unable to stay together, but some of us held hands to get through the crowd gathering at the Washington Monument. I became afraid that I would lose everyone, but ten of us, part of the group and some local kids, managed to stick together all morning.

Folk singers provided entertainment as the marchers slowly arrived. Joan Baez was singing when we found a place on the monument grounds. Most of the people there were blacks, young and old, well dressed, but there were also many whites in the crowd. The huge size of the crowd impressed me the most, and I remember noticing that many of the printed signs displayed an identical message and used a uniform format. Some just said, "JOBS AND FREEDOM," as seen in the photographs of the march. I knew that labor unions were supporting the march and thought that they had financed the signs. I have read that the march organizers discussed possible slogans and approved only those that would avoid offensive declarations against the president and the Congress.[4]

I loved it all for the spirit of harmony the crowd gave me. I could feel that we all were in agreement about civil rights that morning. Peter, Paul, and Mary; Bob Dylan, who was called "Bobby" then; and Odetta sang.

Young black kids from Clarksdale, Mississippi, and Louisiana—many just out of jail, including SNCC's Bobby Talbert in his overalls (the student who had greeted us at the Jackson mass meeting)—sang "This Little Light of Mine" and other freedom songs.

By 10:30 that morning, 90,000 people had arrived. Dr. King wrote about the march in his autobiography:

> [T]here were many dignitaries and many celebrities, but the stir-ring emotion came from the mass of ordinary people who stood in majestic dignity as witnesses to their single-minded determina-tion to achieve democracy in their time.
>
> They came from almost every state in the union; they came in every form of transportation; they gave up from one to three days' pay plus the cost of transportation, which for many was a heavy financial sacrifice. They were good-humored and relaxed, yet disciplined and thoughtful. They applauded their leaders gen-erously. . . . The enormous multitude was the living, beating heart of an indefinitely noble movement. It was an army without guns, but not without strength. It was an army into which no one had to be drafted. It was white, and Negro, and of all ages. It had adherents of every faith, members of every class, every profession, every political party, united by a single ideal. It was a fighting army, but no one could mistake that its most powerful weapon was love.[5]

A call for a minute of silence in memory of W. E. B. DuBois, the black historian who had died the night before at the age of ninety-six in Ghana, silenced the polite, orderly, disciplined crowd. I wrote: "This was what was so wonderful about the day—[the announcer] got silence. The indi-viduals in these crowds were very polite and orderly—it was difficult to get through but it was possible. Everyone wanted to listen to what was going on, too. Fears [of violence] were ungrounded, for it was a disci-plined group."

The time eventually came for the march to begin on two parallel streets, east from the Fifteenth Street area of the Washington Monument to the Twenty-Third Street area of the Lincoln Memorial for the after-

noon program. We held hands to stay together three in a line in the mul-
tiracial crowd that Avon Rollins Sr., a member of the SNCC Executive
Committee, described as united by "their dedication, their sincerity, their
somberness, and their unspoken resolve to make a difference."[6] We sang
only one freedom song, "We Shall Overcome." One verse says, "We'll
walk hand in hand," and another, "Black and white together." I felt I was
doing more marching than nearly every other white person I saw that day
because I was with black friends. Randy Johnson, who had become my
good friend, told me the wonderful feeling she had when no one stared
at her as a black in an integrated group.

Near the Lincoln Memorial, pushing for a spot in the shade began.
Not everyone could be in the shade, but my group, now down to six,
managed to stop near a tree, where we ate our bag lunches. After eating,
we eased our way closer up to the front, but it was even more difficult to
see the far-away speakers at the Lincoln Memorial than at the Washington Monument in the morning. We were standing up in the sun most of
the afternoon, but at times we sat down on the street, and we also took
a break to take our shoes off and put our feet in the shallow water of the
Reflecting Pool.

There was more singing, notably from Mahalia Jackson, before the
speeches. I thought of Marian Anderson, who had sung on the steps
of the Lincoln Memorial in 1939 when the Daughters of the American
Revolution refused permission for her to sing to an integrated audience
in their Constitution Hall.

Although many women participated in the movement, providing leadership, getting arrested, and going to jail, the official leaders of the six
national civil rights organizations—all male—did not include Dorothy
Height, president of the National Council of Negro Women. Recognition of women leaders and the presence of Ms. Height on the platform
was the extent of the gender diversity in the speeches that day. Myrlie
Evers, the widow of Medgar Evers who had been murdered on June 12
that year, was on the program to speak, but she was unable to attend.
John Lewis, the twenty-four-year-old chairman of SNCC and future congressman from Georgia, created controversy with prepared remarks that
were circulated to others, who deemed his words "inflammatory" and
improperly critical of President Kennedy's civil rights bill.[7] Washington's

archbishop Patrick O'Boyle, scheduled to deliver the invocation, contacted the White House and threatened to withdraw his participation because of Lewis's prepared remarks. SNCC was opposing the administration's civil rights bill because it did not go far enough to guarantee voting rights and protect blacks from police brutality. Lewis planned to ask, "Which side is the federal government on?" but that question was taken out of his speech. Other changes had to be made, but the speech was still strong, and the message was not compromised. This controversy made front-page news in the *Washington Post* the next day as the press at first overlooked what Martin Luther King Jr. said. Lewis did say, "'ONE MAN, ONE VOTE' is the African cry. It is ours, too. It must be ours." He had seen a demonstrator's sign, "One Man, One Vote," in a televised documentary from Africa not long before the march.[8] Those words became a SNCC motto, along with "Freedom Now!"

The announcer thrilled the crowd with word that the estimates of participants had been off: 200,000 had come to the march, and buses were still arriving. In the end, the estimated total attendance was more than 250,000.

It was a long afternoon, but I didn't get impatient until I felt as if I had been waiting forever to hear Martin Luther King Jr., who was the last speaker on the program. He had a three-page planned text that concerned not only racial inequality but also economic inequality faced by blacks. He spoke of the life of the black "badly crippled by the manacles of segregation and the chains of discrimination." He said that the black "lives on a lonely island of poverty in the midst of a vast ocean of material prosperity." America had promised inalienable rights of life, liberty, and the pursuit of happiness for all but had defaulted on its promise to its citizens of color. Blacks had received a "bad check that had come back marked 'insufficient funds.'" Now they had "come to cash that check" and refused to believe that the "bank of justice" was "bankrupt."[9]

Only then did he disregard his text and begin what is remembered as the essence of the "I Have a Dream" speech, including, "We will not be satisfied until justice rolls down like waters, and righteousness like a mighty stream. . . . [L]et freedom ring. . . . [A]ll men are created equal . . . [all] will be able to sit down together at the table of brotherhood. . . . [C]hildren will not be judged by the color of their skin but by the content of their character."[10] King's speech was the highlight of the day for me—and probably for thousands of others. That was my chance to see him.

King had previously included the rhetoric of the dream in his speeches, with more emphasis on the call for economic justice than in the speech he gave at the Lincoln Memorial. On December 11, 1961, he said in the closing address at the AFL-CIO's national convention in Miami, Florida, that "the dream of American democracy" was "a dream unfulfilled." Appealing to the labor leaders to join the struggle for racial equality, he described a "dream of equality of opportunity, of privilege and property widely distributed; a dream of a land where men will not take necessities from the many to give luxuries to the few . . . the dream of a country where every man will respect the dignity and worth of human personality—that is the dream."[11] And two months before the march, at a protest in Detroit, King saw the problem of racial injustice as a national problem and again stated his vision in economic terms: "I have a dream this afternoon that one day, right here in Detroit, Negroes will be able to buy a house or rent a house anywhere that their money will carry them and that they will be able to get a job."[12]

There was so much more to Martin Luther King Jr.'s leadership than the mythology that surrounds a single speech. He had a crucially important role in the MFDP Convention Challenge in Atlantic City that usually goes unnoticed, and, while retaining his confidence in nonviolence, King became far more radical, taking positions to end poverty and unemployment in black communities and against Johnson's war in Vietnam before he was gunned down on April 4, 1968. Legal segregation in the form of Jim Crow laws would eventually end, but racism continues to this day, and we can still see vast differences in the economic position of blacks and whites today.

Those of us in Washington that day took a pledge of personal commitment to achieve the march's goals:

Standing before the Lincoln memorial on the 28th of August, in the Centennial Year of Emancipation, I affirm my complete personal commitment to the struggle for Jobs and Freedom for all Americans.

Singing freedom songs after the March on Washington, August 1963. Courtesy of Randolyn Johnson Story.

To fulfill that commitment, I pledge that I will not relax until victory is won. I pledge that I will join and support all actions undertaken in good faith and accord with the time-honored democratic tradition of nonviolent protest, of peaceful assembly and petition, and of redress through the courts and the legislative process.

I pledge to carry the message of the march to my friends and neighbors back home and to arouse them to an equal commitment and an equal effort. I will march, and I will write letters. I will demonstrate, and I will vote. I will work to make sure that my voice and those of my brothers ring clear and determined from every corner of our land.

I pledge my heart and my mind and my body, unequivocally and without regard to personal sacrifice, to the achievement of social peace through social justice.

The march was over by 5:00 p.m. as the demonstrators scattered to their cars and buses. To kill time until our scheduled departure hour, we sat on the curb, stood, and walked from one end of the blocked-off street to the other, feeling inspired and singing freedom songs. I felt proud to be showing in public a commitment to civil rights.

Back in Greensboro, we had only one more day before the project would come to an end. After an evening evaluation of the project by local residents, Mr. Butler, a black man active in the church where we stayed, hosted some of us for barbecue sandwiches at a local restaurant. He gave us some perspective about racism from his fifty years that I, as a white, was still trying to understand. His best line was: "You know the only two people who have their freedom? The white man and the Negro woman. If you look around at me and Elfreda and Randy, you can see that that freedom has been exercised." We all laughed without getting serious about the historical origins of blacks' fair complexions in the conditions of slavery.

At 1:00 a.m., we went on to Dr. Elizabeth Laisner's apartment, where the rest of the group, Paula Jewell, and Jim Upchurch were having a good time toasting the project with a couple bottles of sherry. Dr. Laisner was an Austrian professor of French and German at Bennett College who was supportive of the movement and had befriended our group. I described her in my diary as "an old maid," with "straight hair, glasses, a chain smoker, foreign, and *dedicated*." She was also a talker. Paula was the black girl who had been in my Experiment in International Living group in Sweden the previous summer, and Jim was a white southerner, a Guilford College student, who had been participating in the movement since June. I sympathized with him because his parents had stopped speaking to him, something I couldn't imagine my family doing to me.

About 3:00 a.m., back at the church, Dick Miles, a graduate Russian student from Indiana University, showed pictures he had taken of our project, and I felt that I didn't want the project to end. Karen, Randy, and I ate watermelon in the kitchen and continued talking until six, when the sun was rising. Karen spent the rest of the weekend with Elfreda at her family home in Greensboro. Randy invited me to stay with her, but I had to get home for my mother's birthday.

The next day, Friday, August 30, at different times members of the group left with a lot of hugging and kissing at the bus station. A local white woman who noticed our interracial group told us, "That's what I like to see." We knew we had touched at least one person. I contrasted in my mind the hatred at the Jackson bus station. I finally left with Pell Fender, a Stanford student in our group, on a 10:30 p.m. bus to Washington, D.C., where he boarded a bus home to San Francisco, and I took the bus to Newark.

I finished a typed, ten-page report for the AFSC at home, describing the project, the voter registration requirements, the areas we covered in canvassing, our techniques, the importance of publicity and organization, and the need for voter education. We had missed our goal of registering a thousand, but we did register 803 blacks in the three weeks: 606 Democrats, 83 Republicans, and 33 Independents. I concluded: "We hope that more work can be done in both registration and voter education in all of North Carolina as well as the rest of the South. Only through such concentrated efforts can the Negro vote become soon the power it should be in our American democracy."[13]

I valued my experience in Greensboro more for my relations with black students than for the work I did. In Mississippi, we were more likely to have been singled out by the black population for respect, as we were at the Jackson mass meeting. In North Carolina, we did not receive special treatment or notice from the group members, either positive or negative. Learning to live together and to cooperate and coming together despite our different perspectives, races, and personalities gave me confidence for the future, when I would be meeting and working with other people with different racial, economic, and social backgrounds.

Randy agreed with this perspective:

It gave me friends. The friendship was just wonderful. Those relationships were for a lifetime. We still write and stay in touch with each other. But it was a learning experience. Finding out that you guys were no different from us. We were one and the same. Just kids. Same philosophies, same likes, same dislikes. There was no difference at all. And I thought I sensed that because I lived in such close proximity to white people [growing up] in Smithfield [North Carolina]. But because of other experiences you thought there might have been some differences. But in the final analysis, there are not a lot of differences.[14]

Back home for a few weeks, I found it difficult to describe how much the summer had meant to me, but I did proudly announce that we had registered eight hundred new black voters in North Carolina. I also wrote a letter to the local *Summit Herald* that was published on September 5, 1963. Reporting what I had done in the summer, I wanted the citizens of Summit to "understand what is going on in America today." I wanted everyone "freed from the fear of integration." I said it was momentous for me to be at the March on Washington and made the point that "as long as I could not go where I wished with my friends this summer, whether it was the movies on Saturday night or church on Sunday morning, I know that I am not free," and I speculated at the end: "I wonder what I in a Northern suburban community like Summit am doing for freedom and America."[15] I questioned the commitment I had proclaimed in response to Fannie Lou Hamer and in the pledge to work for social peace through justice at the March on Washington. But I decided to try to become a civil rights worker in Mississippi after graduation.

During my last year at Cornell, the racial oppression in Mississippi and elsewhere continued as SNCC tried for more media exposure and the forces of hate drew interest from northern newspapers and television broadcasters. Soon after the March on Washington, the bombing of the Sixteenth Street Baptist Church in Birmingham, Alabama, on September 15, 1963, killed four young black girls. I participated in a sad March of Mourning in Ithaca, a silent march from the student union to a park downtown, where local clergyman conducted a memorial service. Later in the fall, Ithaca staged a lively Songfest for Freedom in the high school auditorium. A local black doctor who had met a high school student from Durham, North Carolina, at the March on Washington encouraged local students to raise money to bring a dozen high school students from Durham north for a concert. Joyce McKissick, the daughter of the prominent civil rights lawyer and CORE leader Floyd McKissick, led the group, introducing and explaining the freedom songs on the program. Parents and friends who came to see the local student sponsors sitting on the stage filled the auditorium. I joined in the singing of songs I had learned at Tougaloo—"We Are Soldiers of the Cross" and "If You Can't See Me at the Back of the Bus." The crowd linked arms and sang "We

Shall Overcome" to end the program, which served as a reminder for me to renew my civil rights commitment.

Jane Stembridge, the SNCC worker I had known on the Tougaloo campus, contacted headquarters in Atlanta to make sure the work campers received information and knew about SNCC's need for funding. Sandra "Casey" Hayden, the white northern coordinator in the Atlanta office, sent me a letter, and I immediately subscribed to SNCC's weekly newsletter, *Student Voice*. I also ordered the *Mississippi Free Press* and the *Southern Patriot* to keep up with news of the civil rights struggles as they continued in the South.

My junior-year roommate at Cornell, Suzanne Peckham, told me later, "You were a different person" when I came back for senior year. Now I had a passion. Although I did not take the initiative to organize a Friends of SNCC chapter for fund-raising, I did volunteer for civil rights activities at Cornell United Religious Work (CURW) and became the editor of the *Civil Rights Newsletter,* providing local and national up-to-date civil rights information. Paul Gibbons, a white minister in the United Church of Christ, and Polly Allen, a white lay deacon in the Episcopal Church, worked on civil rights at CURW. We focused on passage of the civil rights bill, then in hearings before committees in the Congress. Writing letters, asking for signatures on petitions, attending lectures and conferences, and making a trip to Washington to lobby filled my spare time.

During spring vacation, Jeanne Laux, Joan Karliner, and I traveled south to observe firsthand current civil rights activities. In Atlanta, I attended the all-day open meeting of SNCC field secretaries and hangers-on like me, listening to the unending discussions in which anyone could participate. There seemed to be no fixed agenda, and there was little attempt to cut off debate in the interests of reaching understanding, acceptance, and maintaining program support from everyone. The group was composed largely of young black men, with a few whites and some women. Knowing about the violence and danger for civil rights workers in the South, I appreciated the fact that they greeted one another as close friends. I knew only a few people by sight—Bob Moses, Willie Peacock, Charles McLaurin, Bobby Talbert. From that first meeting on, I did not seek to be close with any SNCC group because I did not have the qualifications. I did not expect to be accepted. I would work and be conscious of avoiding offense.

At Cornell as a senior, I started thinking about what I wanted to do after graduation with a major in American studies that did not equip me for any specific employment. I did not want to teach. I considered graduate school in government or history, but not for any special reason. And, of course, there were my memories of Mississippi and the commitment I had made to civil rights.

I soon decided that I would fare better in law school than in graduate school. The NAACP was advancing civil rights progress through litigation at a time when the Supreme Court was enforcing constitutional provisions for equal justice. I could foresee making my contribution with a law degree. So I submitted applications for law schools for the fall of 1964. I chose Stanford for its smaller size and location in California, where I had never traveled.

In that year, when Betty Friedan, who had just published *The Feminine Mystique,* came to campus to speak, I sat at a card table by the entry asking for signatures on a CURW petition supporting passage of the civil rights bill. I met her when she arrived, and someone told her that I planned to go to law school, which was unusual for a woman in 1964. In her opening remarks, calling attention to the civil rights bill petition, Betty Friedan spoke about me: "The student at that table asking for your name on the civil rights petition is going to law school. She'll become a lawyer, and she can also marry and have children. There are no limits today on what a woman can do." If *she* said so, I *could* do it all.

My stand for civil rights was not difficult or controversial for me in the supportive environment at Cornell, where other progressive students were also becoming activists for civil rights. Cornell students adopted Fayette County, Tennessee, as a project to support. After going to register to vote, black sharecroppers in the county were evicted from their homes and were living in a tent city, needing food, clothing, and shelter while they figured out new ways to support themselves and their families independent of white landowners. Undergraduates volunteered for the Fayette County project during school vacations and raised funds through student government.

Because I had been so impressed with SNCC the previous summer,

I wrote to SNCC asking for work, learned about the Mississippi Summer Project for volunteers, and applied. My family had given me both the independence and the confidence to make this choice. I recognized injustice and was not afraid of social condemnation for taking a position on what I thought was right. When I saw how Mississippi treated its black citizens, I knew it was wrong. With free time and financial resources, I asked for the chance to do something about this injustice. My timing coincided with the Mississippi Summer Project.

5

Planning for the Summer Project

The Mississippi Summer Project was the most exciting, creative, issue-oriented, self-propelling political activity in the history of America.
                                                                    —Lawrence Guyot[1]

The 1964 Mississippi Summer Project is unique in civil rights milestones for recruiting large numbers of northern college students to live and work in cooperation with local leaders of the Mississippi civil rights movement. Its primary focus was voter registration using volunteers like me to encourage black residents to apply to register to vote and participate in the Mississippi Freedom Democratic Party.

The Fifteenth Amendment to the U.S. Constitution, ratified in 1870, prohibited states from denying voting rights on the basis of color. However, almost a century later, some jurisdictions still had entrenched mechanisms of evading this ban. In Mississippi, with rare exceptions, blacks could not register to vote due to restrictive state laws, discrimination by county registrars, violence, harassment, and intimidation by white racists, who were determined, with the blessing and participation of public officials, to maintain white supremacy and deny access to blacks.

The statistics about Mississippi voter registration in 1964 were that only 28,500, or 6.7 percent of more than 422,000 blacks of voting age, were registered voters, whereas 525,000 whites were registered.[2] The literacy test, the publicity, and the poll tax were effective in keeping blacks off the voter rolls—all official measures that operated along with the unofficial violence, intimidation, harassment, and economic reprisals that kept many immobilized with fear. After the Civil War and the end to slavery, 190,000 blacks in Mississippi had been registered to vote, but when federal troops were withdrawn in 1877 and white southerners returned to power after Reconstruction, they systematically institutionalized separation of the races through Jim Crow laws and removed blacks from the voter rolls. By arbitrarily using violence against blacks—lynchings, kidnappings, shootings, and beatings—white Mississippians kept blacks in their assigned place with no recourse to the police or the courts for self-protection. The blacks could hardly retaliate with organized threats or violence, which had no chance of succeeding, but they could refuse to cooperate covertly by employing work slowdowns and other creative measures.

The Mississippi NAACP and the Negro Voting Leagues made limited progress with black registration in the first half of the twentieth century, particularly after World War II, with new leaders among returning veterans. But their accomplishments were later erased. In 1954, the backlash to the Supreme Court's school desegregation decision in *Brown v. Board of Education* was the creation of Citizens' Councils in Indianola, Mississippi. The councils would enable businessmen and community leaders to adopt so-called legal, peaceful means to maintain segregation as a substitute for what they saw as the lawless violence of the vigilantes, which they deemed undignified and bad for the state's reputation. The Ku Klux Klan, renowned for cross-burnings and the white robes and hoods they wore to remain anonymous, had not been active as an institution since the 1930s, but a feeling that the battle for white supremacy was being lost led to its revival in Mississippi in late 1963. On a single day in the spring of 1964, they coordinated cross burnings in sixty-four of the state's eighty-two counties, causing particular worry to responsible whites. The State Sovereignty Commission, a spy agency with investigative powers, took the names of anyone who wavered from the state's policies of segregation and funded the Citizens' Councils. At the same time, the white political powers erected new barriers, making voting by blacks even more difficult than it had been.

The right to vote is the most essential and fundamental right of citizenship, but in Mississippi an individual did not register to vote. An individual *applied* to register to vote. Registration could take place in only one location, at the courthouse in the county, and the four-page application form—to be filled out without assistance, one at a time, in the registrar's office—included twenty-one questions plus a requirement to define citizenship. It included straightforward identifying questions (name, address, age, etc.) and asked about criminal convictions as well as the applicant's employer. It ended with items that could be difficult and challenging for blacks and whites alike: they had to copy a selected section from among the 285 sections of the Mississippi Constitution, state "a reasonable interpretation (the meaning) of the section" just copied, and set forth their "understanding of the duties and obligations of citizenship under a constitutional form of government."

The white registrar in each county exercised broad discretion to select the provision for examination, making it easy for whites and difficult for blacks. The registrar also had full authority in an exercise of discretion to decide whether the applicant's response was sufficient to qualify the applicant for registration. And because registrars could easily see the race of the applicant, in practice they freely accepted applications from whites and denied the ones from blacks.

Few blacks could overcome such obstacles. Moreover, the mere process of applying to register to vote intimidated them: noticeably passing through town to the courthouse, formally going by oneself before a hostile registrar of voters, and leaving through a crowd of menacing whites who frequently gathered to stare, call out names, and even threaten to attack—all while the police stood by. Blacks could anticipate threats, violence, and loss of a job, bank loan, or credit as soon as they were recognized as having applied to register to vote.

The likelihood of economic retaliation against an applicant increased with publicity. Local newspapers listed for two weeks the names of individuals applying to register, purportedly to allow residents to comment on the individual's moral character. The system was "totally corrupt." Only a person defined as "white, twenty-one, and breathing" could vote.[3]

To diminish voting by blacks, Mississippi also used poll taxes, the per person tax required for voting and designed to disenfranchise poor people. If an applicant were successfully registered, two payments of the two-dollar state poll tax, proven by receipts, qualified the applicant to vote. Having the money to pay, getting the payment accepted, and keeping track of the receipt were final hurdles to voting.

The local black residents who courageously led the grassroots organizing made the difference for future generations. Amzie Moore, fifty-three, a World War II veteran, postal worker, independent businessman, and president of the NAACP in Cleveland, Mississippi, was an early Mississippi freedom fighter who paved the way for the student movement in Mississippi. He was fearless. He said, "I'm not leaving," when whites tried to force him to leave town, and he slept with two guns in a bedroom with a window high above the level of his bed.[4] Moore, Aaron Henry in Clarksdale, C. C. Bryant in McComb, and E. W. Steptoe in Amite County, among others, took tremendous risks throughout the 1950s and 1960s, and they somehow survived without being run out of the state. Others were less fortunate: in 1955, George W. Lee was murdered in Belzoni and Lamar Smith in Brookhaven, and Gus Courts left the state after he was shot in the arm in Belzoni. I have high regard for these men, who still remain largely unsung. Among the local courageous women, not only Fannie Lou Hamer but Victoria Gray, Annie Devine, Unita Blackwell, Winson Hudson, and Alyene Quinn, among others, deserve recognition for taking risks and making their contributions. These local leaders welcomed the first SNCC and CORE workers into their communities. They befriended, advised, and protected many young students in their homes.

The student civil rights movement of the 1960s began with direct action. On February 1, 1960—when I was an unknowing senior in high school—four black college students began the student sit-ins by demanding service at a segregated lunch counter in Greensboro, North Carolina. Student sit-ins soon swept to more than one hundred other southern cities and towns, including Nashville, where a group of students had become knowledgeable about Gandhi's philosophy of nonviolence. That spring at a conference at Shaw University in Raleigh, North Carolina, the students formed SNCC to continue their initiative. They decided to work independently of adults, whom they considered to be gradualists in matters of civil rights. As Diane Nash, a student leader from Nashville, told David J. Garrow, Martin Luther King Jr.'s biographer: "If people think that it was Martin Luther King's movement, then today they—young people—are more likely to say, 'gosh, I wish we had a Martin Luther King here today to lead us.' . . . If people knew how that movement started, then the question they would ask themselves is, 'What can I do?'"[5]

By naming the new organization the "Student *Nonviolent* Coordinating Committee," the students, some religiously oriented and others viewing nonviolence as only a tactic, highlighted the importance of non-violence as the new group's framework. They wanted the group "coordinated," not hierarchically organized. As a group of equals, they wanted shared understandings that were acceptable to everyone. SNCC's purpose was to encourage self-initiative as the young workers set out to inform, to inspire, and to motivate the oppressed people in Mississippi and elsewhere in the segregated South to claim their civil rights. They worked with people where they were. SNCC's idea of leadership was based on listening to and valuing the opinions of all members of a group, including the domestic worker, the farm laborer, and the illiterate. I understood what this philosophy meant as a practical matter within SNCC during the spring 1964 SNCC meeting that I observed in Atlanta. Everyone had the opportunity to voice concerns before the organization reached a decision. Open discussion that sometimes appeared unduly long and aimless was characteristic of SNCC operations.

When Bob Moses first went to Mississippi, Amzie Moore influenced him to work in voter registration to gain *political* power. Direct action in Mississippi was far too dangerous. In the 1960–1964 period, SNCC was emphatically not the radical, revolutionary organization associated with militant black nationalism that it came to be known as in the late 1960s. It was merely seeking to have the U.S. Constitution and judicial system apply to all citizens without regard to skin color in a fully integrated society, although it also nurtured what historian Howard Zinn calls a "vision beyond race." He describes the vision as one "of a revolution beyond race, against other forms of injustice, challenging the entire value-system of the nation and of smug middle-class society everywhere."[6] Under the Kennedy and Johnson administrations, the federal government generally refused to take the initiative required to guarantee blacks constitutional rights; to do so would have alienated powerful white southern Democratic allies. After the use of federal troops in Little Rock in 1957 and at Ole Miss in 1962, government inaction against lawlessness allowed the established patterns of segregation and discrimination to continue. Federal Bureau of Investigation (FBI) agents witnessed violence without taking any action to stop it. The few exceptions were Justice Department suits filed against county registrars to enjoin discrimination in voter registration under authority of the Civil Rights Act of 1957 and the work of John Doar, deputy director of the Civil Rights Division of the Justice Department, who acted within his authority on behalf of the movement. Through *Brown v. Board of Education* and the Civil Rights Act of 1964, the government did lift legal restrictions—in public schools, interstate transportation, public accommodations, and public facilities—but federal laws went unenforced, and integration was not a reality in Mississippi.

Nevertheless, black students in the South continued to believe in change *within* the political system; they thought that if white liberals learned what was going on, political pressure would be brought to bear on the federal government. SNCC, according to the Christian concept of redemption, assumed that nonviolence would successfully appeal to the nation's moral conscience and looked forward to reconciliation of the races in a truly integrated society.

Several events led to reconsideration of SNCC's straightforward approach to voter registration and community organizing.[7] Severe reprisals against the aggressive major voter registration campaign in Greenwood, including the shooting of Jimmie Travis, made people even more vulnerable to physical harm. The Justice Department decision to withdraw its injunction action in federal court against further interference in the Greenwood registration campaign for fear of a federal–state showdown over violence led to a deal that would end further federal support to make Greenwood a showcase of effective voter registration. The VEP of the Southern Regional Council provided foundation funding for nonpartisan voter registration programs in Mississippi, but low registration numbers led the VEP to cut off its funding. Minimal results of the voter registration campaigns showed by the end of the summer of 1963 that it was not possible to register blacks in Mississippi in more than token numbers. At the current rate of progress, it would require 135 years to register half of the eligible blacks.[8] The unified local forces who were determined to maintain white supremacy opposed any civil rights progress. They caused fear and inertia among blacks, and the Kennedy administration refused all pleas for federal protection against retaliation, presumably to avoid alienating its white southern political allies. The situation called for new tactics, which involved running candidates for office.

The Freedom Vote, a mock election meant to demonstrate that blacks would vote if given the opportunity, in the fall of 1963 ran Aaron Henry, the state president of the NAACP, and Ed King, the white chaplain at Tougaloo, for governor and lieutenant governor. Sixty-four volunteers from Stanford and Yale went to Mississippi for one or two weeks to travel throughout the state to get out the vote. The Justice Department became concerned about potential violence after the white students arrived in the state and assigned more FBI agents to witness incidents of harassment or violence. And journalists took more interest in the Stanford and Yale students in Mississippi than they had in local black civil rights workers, with press coverage temporarily increasing. More than 80,000 local blacks participated in the election, casting their ballots throughout the state in grocery stores, barber shops, and churches in the black community or by mail, thus demonstrating blacks' interest in voting and political participation.

Before the summer, Freedom Days, first tried in Canton and then Hattiesburg and Greenwood, Mississippi, involved a large number of applicants lining up to register, accompanied by picketers protesting the denial of rights to blacks. In this way, nonviolent direct action was combined with a voter registration drive. The presence of white supporters, largely ministers recruited by the NCC, added to the helpful publicity and thus lessened the potential for brutal treatment of the applicants. These protests served to mobilize the black communities, but arrests frequently followed, and not many residents were added to the voting rolls. More activity was needed.

Wanting to build on the momentum of the Freedom Vote, Bob Moses discussed with SNCC a plan to recruit as many as 2,000 volunteers for a summer project. He believed that the presence of a large number of northern white students would bring awareness of the unending, intolerable conditions, offer blacks protection against violence, and provide resources for community organizing and political participation that SNCC did not have. Students would relay their observations and experiences to influential people in the rest of the country, their families, friends, readers of newspapers in their scattered communities, and their congressmen.

Moses knew that bringing a large number of young white students into the state could be extremely dangerous. Civil rights activity had provoked arrests and violence for years, and the project could ignite even more extreme action by Mississippi authorities and vigilantes. No one was more sensitive to the risk of the potential death of a white volunteer than Bob Moses. Medgar Evers, the NAACP state field secretary; Herbert Lee, a local ally of SNCC when Moses worked in Amite County in 1961; and Louis Allen, a witness to the killing of Herbert Lee, murdered on January 31, 1964, the night before he was planning to leave the state, had all been close to Moses. If a white student were killed, Moses knew the death would be sensational news. A free Mississippi required the eyes of the nation to see it as not just another of the fifty states, but as a state that was defying the Constitution and federal laws. Outweighing the risk of more lost lives was the increased possibility of obtaining federal action to end the terrorism and oppression and to bring freedom, justice, and hope for democracy to Mississippi.

Other SNCC activists also worried about the dangers and objected to the plan Moses presented for more than one reason. In November 1963, heated debate of the issues continued over three days at a meeting in Greenville. Throughout my summer in Mississippi, I was totally unaware of the strongly held staff objections to the Summer Project and was very surprised to learn later that Charlie Cobb, who was to be my director in Washington County in the summer of 1964, led the opposition and continued to believe the Summer Project was a mistake when he was interviewed years afterward.[9] Some SNCC staff held the opinion that the white volunteers would overwhelm their organization. What some local organizers worked hard to do, they reasoned, would come more easily to formally educated, socially sophisticated, articulate white student volunteers. And they feared that incipient organizing by new local leaders at the grassroots level could be undone by white volunteers taking over tasks that residents should decide and handle by themselves. The volunteers would be interested in doing as much as possible as fast as possible, and, according to Mississippi native Hollis Watkins, who opposed the project, "speed was the wrong approach." Local black residents, accustomed to obeying white authority, would likely follow the leadership of the white students. If the volunteers exhibited their self-confidence and began giving directions, Watkins said, they "would take over and change the course of the movement,"[10] with the result that local blacks would cease to rely on their own experience and instincts as to what was needed.

Some SNCC activists were also resentful. They could not accomplish what Bob Moses knew was required, but they considered themselves more deserving of publicity than the white volunteers, and they knew they would still be around at the end of the summer, when the white volunteers would leave for home. All of the SNCC field secretaries' concerns reflected North–South issues more than black–white issues.

But Moses had support. Lawrence Guyot, known just as "Guyot," a twenty-four-year-old native Mississippi field secretary recently graduated from Tougaloo; Fannie Lou Hamer; and Victoria Gray, a thirty-seven-year-old independent businesswoman from Hattiesburg who was also a SNCC field secretary, endorsed the project from the beginning. Local resident activists wanted the help and had no theoretical problem with bringing in white volunteers. In December 1963, the SNCC Executive Committee in Atlanta accepted Moses's recommendations for the Summer Project, but the discussion in Greenville had been so heated that the decision included a limit of only one hundred volunteers. In January 1964 at another long, open meeting in Greenville, SNCC explored the issues, heard the objections, and arrived at a consensus to expand voter registration without addressing the issue of white volunteers. The murder of Louis Allen on January 31, 1964, changed minds, however, as SNCC field workers realized they themselves could not expect to continue to be immune from being killed. Bob Moses appealed to his "foot soldiers," who had deserted him in voting against the project: "you got to help me on this."[11] Field secretary Frank Smith responded to this appeal and changed his vote. In February, Moses ultimately prevailed in getting SNCC's commitment to invite up to a thousand volunteers to enable a statewide project that SNCC lacked the manpower and financial resources to conduct. Charlie Cobb recognized that pragmatic local black residents wanted change, and if it required bringing in white student volunteers, SNCC staff more inclined to consider ideological issues should not thwart their wishes. Charlie accepted the decision and was thoroughly hospitable to us in Greenville.

Once the decision was made for the Summer Project, SNCC and CORE staff traveled to local communities to inform residents of the plan at mass meetings. They went to the communities in Mississippi where SNCC and CORE had been working since 1961—McComb, Hattiesburg, Greenwood, Ruleville, and Clarksdale, to name a few—to line up activity facilities and arrange housing for the volunteers. They planned project sites in these towns and cities and considered how they could expand to neighboring counties. Although fearful of white reaction, black residents looked forward to receiving the outside assistance and would welcome the volunteers. They omitted counties where severe risk of violence to civil rights workers made any integrated activities unwise.

The Council of Federated Organizations (COFO), a coalition formed in 1961 from all the national, state, and local civil rights and citizenship education groups operating in the state, sponsored the Summer Project. SNCC would be the principal organization in charge. COFO would coordinate all protest groups in the state to build a strong unified front on behalf of the local people. The organizers hoped that competition in obtaining limited funding available for civil rights activity would decrease. Local resident activists in COFO had participated in voter registration drives, held monthly meetings in Jackson before the summer of 1964, and recognized the need for massive numbers of volunteers to come into the state for the summer. COFO assumed responsibility for accepting volunteers for the project, while SNCC raised funds, hired staff, and managed the project in most of Mississippi. Bob Moses served as program director. I had seen Bob only one day at Tougaloo, once in Greenwood the previous summer, and at the SNCC meeting in Atlanta but knew how important he was. He would inspire the students, manage the overall project from Jackson, effectively strategize the MFDP's political plans, and thus become one of my heroes in the movement.

COFO created a five-person committee with contacts on northern college campuses to recruit white volunteers older than eighteen to spend the summer in the Mississippi movement, using personnel in SNCC offices and campus Friends of SNCC groups in New York, Washington, Boston, the Bay Area of California, Ann Arbor, and elsewhere as well as CORE chapters, called Freedom Centers, to recruit, interview, and evaluate applicants. In personal interviews, recruiters assessed the potential volunteers' stability, intelligence, self-control, and self-discipline. They expected volunteers to be able to treat the black community with respect, to be willing to go to church, and to be appropriate in their dress and appearance. They were not interested in "those who are looking for a new kind of 'kick,' sexual or otherwise; and those evangelical souls who would arrive in Mississippi with no more understanding of the situation than to turn their eyes skyward and say, 'Lord, here I am.'"[12] They recruited at elite colleges and universities, where students could bear the costs of a summer in Mississippi.[13] But as Dottie Zellner, the white SNCC activist who recruited in the Boston area, told me, they did not seek or favor applicants from famous families.[14]

COFO also planned to use professionals—teachers, lawyers, librarians, ministers, doctors, nurses, architects—as volunteers. But unlike the students and except for teachers, these professionals had full-time employment in the summer and would go to Mississippi for only a few weeks. In my view, they would be going down to Mississippi ignorant, having not gone to the week of orientation held for student volunteers.

In response to my request to work for SNCC in Mississippi, Walter Tillow, a white SNCC staff member, sent me a letter about the SNCC plans for the project, which had just been announced in February: "SNCC will have a project this summer in Mississippi part of which will be a law students project, another part will deal with Freedom Schools, Community Centers, and voter registration. This project is being handled by our Mississippi Office and I suggest you write to Miss Penny Patch, SNCC . . . for an application and further details."[15]

Tillow signed the letter "Freedom," echoing the frequent cry from civil rights demonstrations in the 1960s, when people of color demanded "FREEDOM NOW!" I did not participate in the Freedom Schools, Community Centers, research project, white community project, or law student project, all of which were important parts of the Summer Project, so I do not discuss them here.

I applied promptly, emphasizing that I had experience from the previous summer. In addition to the educational exposure to Mississippi at the Tougaloo work camp, my qualifications included three weeks of voter registration in Greensboro, North Carolina.

The COFO letter acknowledging my application cautioned that it would be several weeks before the large number of applications could be processed and information given on an assignment and acceptance. According to white SNCC staff member Penny Patch, the Jackson office was sorting through hundreds of applications with "much discussion and difference of opinion as to how many and whom to accept."[16] She perceived the reservations about bringing in massive numbers of volunteers, between 1,000 and 2,000, which could both overwhelm the emerging young local leaders and endanger black staff and residents by provoking violence as they worked beside blacks as equals. Because of the potential dangers, SNCC white staff had worked largely in office jobs up to this point rather than in the field in voter registration and community organizing. I didn't realize it then, but I was asking to be among the first whites to be at risk of arrest and injury by working directly with young black SNCC field secretaries such as the ones I had met during the previous summer. Optimistic, I felt confident that SNCC would accept me based on my experience.

I learned of my acceptance by form letter in early April 1964, which urged me to become involved in the work of northern support groups and start general fund-raising for administrative expenses. I had applied to law school but wasn't sure I wanted to go and was delighted to hear about Mississippi so soon. I felt relieved at gaining *some* certainty of what I would be doing right after I graduated from Cornell.

The acceptance letter requested three photographs of myself and told me that I would "need funds for . . . transportation, living expenses, and personal needs (estimate: $15–$20 per week or $150 for the entire summer)." I could begin raising funds as needed and should ensure the availability of bond "in the event of arrest." I did not get any information about the dates, location, or nature of my specific assignment or of the required orientation. But there was an assurance of further notice "as soon as possible." At least I knew I would find out more before I left school. Apparently someone was considering taking me on as paid staff because a postscript included COFO's offer to try and work something out for me on the finances. But I had my savings to use for my expenses and knew that my father would post bond if I were arrested. I believed I could function just as well as a volunteer and didn't push to be hired as staff.

I was reading everything I could about the southern civil rights movement during my last restless year in college but still didn't know a lot about the plans for the summer. I was interested only in voter registration. The early brochure *Mississippi Summer Project,* used for recruiting and fund-raising, explained the need for the involvement of massive numbers of Americans in the struggle for freedom in Mississippi. Two objectives were (1) the mobilization of the black community in Mississippi through the development of local leadership and organization and (2) "a heightened awareness throughout the country of the need for massive federal intervention to ensure voting rights."[17] The laws as well as state and local officials had doomed black voter registration in the numbers necessary for political power to change the white supremacist culture of Mississippi. Since 1961, few blacks had successfully registered, and too high a price had been paid in the loss of lives, beatings, firebombing of homes, burning of black churches, economic reprisals, and harassment. The country as a whole, with the power and authority of the federal government, would have to be enlisted to change the closed society of Mississippi.[18]

The brochure included ambitious plans for voter registration in rural counties and two or three cities such as Jackson, Meridian, and Greenville, which would be saturated with about one hundred students. I knew that only men would work on the plantations and in the backwoods areas of the state because the mere sight of white women canvassing with black men would risk violence in these rough areas. COFO also planned Freedom Registration. Residents would be asked to fill out a simple unofficial form that would parallel the registration requirements in northern states but without the accompanying fear of reprisals involved in applying to register officially at the county courthouse. The number of residents willing to sign Freedom Registration forms would demonstrate the interest of disenfranchised blacks in voting and political participation, as the Freedom Vote had in the fall of 1963. These forms would also form a basis to challenge the legality of the Mississippi delegation to the Democratic National Convention and the validity of the fall federal elections.

I received notice of my assignment to work in voter registration by a letter in May, which included literature about what I would be doing in Mississippi. The new tactics of the Mississippi Summer Project, bringing in massive numbers of volunteers to focus on voter registration, involved the more significant Freedom Registration, which was part of the initiative of organizing the MFDP. This new, open, parallel political party, an alternative nonviolent institution, would challenge the Democratic Party at the

Democratic National Convention to end its acceptance of segregated, racist delegations from Mississippi. The MFDP would demonstrate that disenfranchised blacks wanted to participate in politics. The party would provide an opportunity for them to learn the workings of the political process at the local level. Sponsoring candidates in national elections would give choices in voting despite the unlikelihood of victory. Because it was so difficult for blacks to elect representatives to Congress and to register to vote, alternative candidates, Freedom Elections, and Freedom Registration would not only provide opportunities for local political participation but also convey the news outside Mississippi that the system was broken. Mississippi was a "closed society" without leadership or moral resources to reform itself. Political, economic, and social justice would not come to Mississippi without the interest and support of the country as a whole, backed by the authority of the federal government.

The state Democratic Party in Mississippi excluded blacks from most meetings, even if they were registered voters. The Jackson Municipal Auditorium and the Heidelburg Hotel, both segregated facilities, hosted the state convention. Controlled by Democratic officials, the legislature set the exclusive and restrictive voter registration requirements; the executive was elected on the basis of a campaign to keep blacks from registering to vote; the judicial system did not give blacks relief in voting cases; and county registrars were elected in this discriminatory system. Exclusion from the right to vote meant exclusion from the Democratic Party. The Mississippi Democratic Party adopted a platform in 1960 in direct opposition to that of the national party, rejecting the latter's stand in support of civil rights, and it was not expected to support Lyndon Johnson. Because the Mississippi Democratic Party discriminated against the black citizens of the state, did not adopt the party's policies, and did not support the candidates, COFO believed the MFDP could challenge the seating of Mississippi's party at the national convention on legal grounds and would have both political and moral support for its position.

COFO staff planned the necessary steps to implement the MFDP Convention Challenge with advice and counsel from northern liberal-labor supporters. Bayard Rustin, the independent national civil rights leader who organized the March on Washington, acted as adviser to Bob Moses on the upcoming Convention Challenge for a reform of the Democratic

Party that he had long wanted. In late November 1963, he sent his protégé and deputy Rachelle Horowitz to Jackson to help. She researched
the Democratic primaries in Mississippi and the method of selecting delegates to the national convention so that COFO could duplicate that
machinery in contesting the regularly designated delegates to the convention. Horowitz stayed two and a half months in Jackson and found
the situation "terribly complicated."[19] Once back in New York, she realized that without a single authority in the North, the local young people
should organize on their own.

Rustin saw the MFDP effort as "one issue that was of the utmost
importance."[20] Moses wanted him to spend time in Mississippi so that he
could "interpret his findings" to potential supporters in the North.[21] Rustin worried, however, as his biographer John D'Emilio wrote, whether
SNCC "could pull off a campaign of this magnitude without accepting
the resources—and hence the constraints—that working cooperatively
with the larger movement and with national Democratic Party allies
demanded."[22]

During the summer, the volunteers would assist in Freedom Registration and in the campaigns of freedom candidates for Congress. Local registrars in every precinct would maintain registration books that could be
used to challenge the validity of the fall elections. A document, "Freedom
Candidates," described four MFDP campaigns for three of the five U.S.
House seats and one Senate seat in the Democratic primary scheduled for
June 2, 1964, before the Summer Project began. COFO wanted to register disenfranchised blacks as an organizing mechanism for participation in
Freedom Elections to be held not only in the primary elections, but also
in the fall elections. This participation would demonstrate that thousands
of blacks denied the right to vote would vote if they were able to. The
further plan was to challenge the seating of the officially elected candidates to Congress after the fall election on the grounds of discrimination
against a significant portion of the voting-age population.

I became more interested in the part of the COFO political program
to send an alternative delegation to the national convention in Atlantic
City. Registered MFDP members would choose delegates in open meetings, and they would attempt to unseat the regular Mississippi Democratic Party delegates on the grounds that the latter were chosen by

undemocratic means and had opposed the nominees and platform of the national Democratic Party in 1960.

The letter instructed us to begin our summer political work by discussing the Convention Challenge with anyone we knew with influence in the Democratic Party—I couldn't think of anyone—to solicit support and to send any contact information to Casey Hayden at the COFO office. COFO knew it would need northern support to unseat the all-white, segregationist Mississippi Democratic Party delegation, and it would rely in part on volunteers' contacts to find that support.

COFO wanted participants to have a common basis of knowledge and suggested that we read at least the first three of the following books, ranked in order of importance, before coming to Mississippi:

W. E. B. DuBois, *Souls of Black Folk* (1903)
W. J. Cash, *The Mind of the South* (1941)
Michael Harrington, *The Other America* (1962)
Martin Luther King Jr., *Stride Toward Freedom* (1958)
Lillian Smith, *Killers of the Dream* (1949)

Because I had been doing independent reading during my senior year, I had made a head start on this list.

The letter's enclosed memos included an appeal from COFO that everyone who possibly could should bring a car. I had a VW bug my senior year at Cornell, but my father was against my taking it south for the summer, and I actually had no interest in running the risk of driving it in Mississippi. Either selfishly or wisely, I did not want to be responsible for driving myself or others. The memos also described orientation periods lasting about four days that would be held in mid-June at Berea College, a location later changed to Western College for Women (now Miami University). COFO noted the right of "the Mississippi leadership" to "deselect" any volunteer during orientation or in Mississippi during the summer. In addition, COFO urged volunteers to raise some money through a northern support center or independently, describing its "very critical financial condition"—it was "absolutely broke."

The next memo to Summer Project voter registration workers concerned materials to bring for the summer. It included a list of what we must bring and another list of what was not required but "desperately needed." For example, it enclosed the application for registration to vote in Mississippi and sample sections of the Mississippi Constitution for us to mimeograph five hundred copies in the same layout and take them to Mississippi with us. In 1964, there were no Xerox machines, so one had to type the document first on a stencil and then run the stencil on an inked mimeograph machine. I knew how onerous the application process was, but I was seeing the twenty-one-question form for the first time. The memo we received for duplication included only nine examples of the 285 sections of the state constitution that a registrar might ask an applicant to copy and interpret. COFO also requested that we bring a typewriter, stencils, a clipboard, pencils and pens, and office supplies. I brought my Smith-Corona portable typewriter and some office supplies, but I was unable to donate larger items that COFO needed, such as duplicating machines, tape recorders, or film projectors.

COFO expected that the young, predominantly white volunteers, new to conditions in Mississippi, would be unaware of how we should act. It feared for the safety of the volunteers as well as for its own staff and local residents if we behaved arrogantly or carelessly or showed a lack of understanding of the rules by which blacks had to live. COFO knew that in the interests of everyone's safety a training program was necessary and wanted that training to take place *before* we entered the state.

I don't think I realized at the outset how much the volunteers would be asked to focus on federal protection. SNCC workers needed protection from the violence that they encountered and had made repeated requests for action by the FBI and the Justice Department on their own behalf and on behalf of residents whom they persuaded to apply to register and to get involved in the movement. With large numbers of volunteers arriving in the state for the Summer Project, there was an even greater need for federal protection. In early April, Bob Moses sent a memorandum to supporters—including celebrities such as Harry Belafonte, James Baldwin, and Marlon Brando—asking that they seek a meeting with President Johnson to secure that protection. Many appeals were made, but the Johnson administration did not respond.

Unable to get a congressional committee hearing, COFO held its own all-day hearing on June 8, 1964, at the National Theater in Washington, D.C., to inform the country about the situation in Mississippi and to arouse public interest in the need for government protection.[23] COFO invited a panel of distinguished attorneys, educators, and authors to hear testimony from Mississippi. Dr. Harold Taylor, former president of Sarah Lawrence College and later with the Eleanor Roosevelt Foundation, presided, and the panelists included the novelist Joseph Heller, author of *Catch-22;* Murray Kempton of the *New Republic;* Dr. Robert Coles, research psychiatrist with the Harvard University Health Service; and Monroe Freedman from the George Washington School of Law. Sixteen witnesses testified about the violence, suffering, and apparent federal indifference. Lawyers cited the federal laws that for years had prohibited states from denying the vote and the physical brutality described by the witnesses at the hearing. COFO issued a press release, and the transcript of the hearing was included in the *Congressional Record* on June 16, 1964. Unfortunately, the effort proved unsuccessful. The Johnson administration paid no official public attention to the pleas, and the press gave little, if any, coverage of the event.

A COFO memorandum dated June 11, 1964, asked that the applicants accepted for the Mississippi Summer Project appeal to their senators, representatives, local officials, relatives, friends, and all interested parties in every way possible to add to the pressure it was putting on the administration to provide some sort of protection for the hundreds of volunteers coming to Mississippi. I felt I was too busy with my course work and plans for graduation to call or write my congressmen. But COFO knew and was making sure we volunteers knew that we would be at risk of serious harm or even death unless we could convince the government to intervene.

Bob Moses, Aaron Henry from the NAACP, and Dave Dennis from CORE sent a letter to President Johnson requesting a meeting on June 18 or 19 to discuss preparations for the summer, but again the administration ignored the request. COFO clearly feared dire consequences if hundreds of volunteers arrived in Mississippi without assurances of federal protection. But the absence of assurances did not deter me.

I soon learned that I was to arrive at Western College for Women in Oxford, Ohio, on Sunday, June 14, for my orientation and training, which would end at noon on Saturday, June 20, when we would leave for our field assignments. Although COFO emphasized that it was "crucial that you attend the orientation to which you have been assigned," I had a major conflict. Graduation was Monday, June 15, and I would not miss that. COFO anticipated problems and requested immediate notice if someone was unable to attend orientation, so I notified the Jackson office that I would be late. I had never heard of Western College for Women or Oxford, Ohio, but I learned that they were thirty-five miles northwest of Cincinnati. We were also advised that women should not wear short shorts or tight Bermudas or slacks, and we would need a sleeping bag or one set of bed linens.

I thought that by this time I knew a lot about the history and culture of Mississippi race relations and the Mississippi movement, but all of us had to realize how dangerous the project conditions would be. If during training COFO impressed that on all the volunteers, who were newcomers and outsiders, we would be more careful to protect ourselves—*and* others.

6

Orientation

How the Student Volunteers Were Prepared

> If we can go and come back alive, then that is something. If you can go
> into Negro homes and just sit and talk, that will be a huge job.
> —Bob Moses to the Mississippi Summer Project volunteers[1]

After my last college exams, I drove the VW home with all my belong-
ings and then returned to Cornell for the weekend, graduation, and two
friends' wedding. I was able to rationalize making myself late for the orientation: friends were inviting me to a wedding for the first time, and I
already had a head start in orientation from my weeks in Mississippi the
previous summer.

I got a ride with classmates going to the voter registration project in
Fayette County, Tennessee. On Wednesday morning, June 17, I arrived
to register at Peabody Hall, one of the old buildings on the sprawling,
traditional, two-hundred-acre Western College campus in quiet, conservative, rural western Ohio, joining the two hundred other volunteers
already there.[2] I knew no one. Gwen Gillon, a SNCC field secretary, was
my roommate in the college dormitory.

Orientation consisted of all-day programs of lectures, workshops, and
informal gatherings with staff that had come up from Mississippi. With
new information and new people in a new place, I was looking forward
to time away from what was familiar—hearing what to expect and receiving instructions on to how to behave living in the black community. My
letters home jog my memory of the summer, and some events made an
indelible impression. Failures of volunteers' memories of events nearly
fifty years ago can be understood. Doug McAdam, who wrote a socio-

logical study of the volunteers, *Freedom Summer,* has noted that we were "feeling, seeing, experiencing too much." He observed that "[t]hings happened too quickly to allow time for the reflection required to commit specific events to long term memory."[3]

The NCC, in its new initiative to become involved in the civil rights movement, had agreed to sponsor the training through its Commission on Race and Religion. It had planned to use Berea College, founded in 1855 in Berea, Kentucky, as one memo had told the volunteers. However, influential Berea alumni, thinking the project not well conceived, expected it to cause more racial turmoil than improvement in race relations and threatened to cut off their donations to the college. Berea cancelled, and Western College for Women, despite similar objections from its alumnae, agreed to host the orientation, but only for 2 one-week sessions. From what I know now, I wish the orientation had been conducted in the more politically conducive atmosphere at Berea, which was closer to Mississippi, but I cannot regret the comfortable and pleasant, although hot, surroundings in Oxford, Ohio.

The NCC relied on the project leadership, outside experts, and seventy-five experienced Mississippi SNCC and CORE civil rights staff for presentations to the volunteers. Although some SNCC organizers had initially opposed the project, they taught the volunteers freedom songs, gave us warnings, scared us with their war stories, and showed us their support. They needed to ensure that we knew how to behave when we arrived in Mississippi.

Looking around, I saw volunteers who were predominantly white, nice-looking, middle-class college kids. Now I no longer had to come up with reasons why I wanted to join the struggle for civil rights in Mississippi when my friends, knowing it would be so dangerous, asked me. I was with like-minded souls who had the same aspirations. I was not very friendly with them, being something of a loner and preoccupied in my own world, probably exhausted from my last days at Cornell and the trip. I was not making new friends in Oxford. I guessed that the blacks I saw were staff, but a few were volunteers like me. The project wanted more black volunteers, but the economic circumstances of most interested black students made it difficult for them to pay their own way, post bond in the event of arrest, and forgo spending the summer earning the following year's college expenses. Other black students did not have the interest in leaving the relative safety of the North and facing racism their families had left behind in the South.

In the morning of the orientation week, we sat close in the crowded, un-air-conditioned Peabody auditorium, filling every seat. I listened carefully, eager to learn and be prepared for arrival in Mississippi, not knowing where I would be working. The map of the congressional districts of Mississippi, showing five districts and the location of the thirty-two Mississippi projects by cities and towns and rural areas in the state's eighty-two counties, soon became familiar to me. COFO headquarters were in Jackson, and SNCC headquarters moved from Atlanta, Georgia, to Greenwood, Mississippi, for the summer. There were SNCC project directors in four of the five congressional districts: (1) Clarksdale, Batesville, and Holly Springs in the north; (2) the Delta area, including Greenwood, Ruleville, and Greenville, where I would finally be assigned; (3) Jackson and McComb; and (5) Hattiesburg and the Gulf Coast cities to the south. CORE operated exclusively in Meridian and Canton in District 4, which was also south of my eventual location.

Bob Moses was principally responsible for preparing us to be the new nonviolent warriors in the fight for freedom in Mississippi. He impressed me with his calm, quiet, thoughtful manner. Bob was twenty-nine years old at the time, not very tall, but broad-shouldered, compact, and strong looking, with a consistent serious demeanor. He wore horn-rimmed glasses, a clean white T-shirt, and blue denim overalls. The SNCC "uniform" of overalls originated in the Mississippi Delta as civil rights workers, dressed like field hands to avoid notice, trespassed on private property to contact blacks living and working on the cotton plantations. Bob would stand to the side of the podium as he modestly and thoroughly presented critical information and his personal views. As I listened to him, I did not fully appreciate the personal toll he was subjecting himself to as the primary advocate for bringing volunteers into Mississippi to confront dangers he knew well. He was asking that we use our educated, privileged status to work and appeal for justice and equality at the risk of our lives. At most, he could only tell us how to try to protect ourselves and black residents as much as possible.

In my view, Bob Moses remains the foremost hero of the Mississippi

HOLLY SPRINGS

BATESVILLE

TUPELO

CLARKSDALE

CHARLESTON

2

1

CLEVELAND

SHAW • RULEVILLE

ABERDEEN

INDIANOLA

GREENWOOD

COLUMBUS

ITTA BENA

STARKVILLE

GREENVILLE

TCHULA

BELZONI •

CARTHAGE

PHILADELPHIA

CANTON

FLORA

4

MERIDIAN

VICKSBURG

JACKSON

3

LAUREL

NATCHEZ

HATTIESBURG

McCOMB •

5

• Location of Mississippi projects

MOSS POINT

GULFPORT   BILOXI   PASCAGOULA

Congressional Districts of Mississippi

"Congressional Districts of Mississippi," from Elizabeth Sutherland, ed., *Letters from Mississippi* (New York: McGraw Hill, 1965), 66.

Bob Moses. Courtesy of Steve Schapiro.

civil rights movement, a status he shuns despite many such attributions. In addition to being called a saint, which I had heard during the previous summer, he has been described in countless ways, among them "awesome," "influential," "unparalleled," "the solitary movement mystic," "having virtually a sacred mystique," "possessing goodness as a person," and "a figure of strength." When Nicolaus Mills interviewed me for his book about the Mississippi Summer Project, *Like a Holy Crusade*, I shared my sentiments about Bob Moses: "Bob Moses stood out for everybody. He was an incredibly strong figure. He was calm. He was effective. What he said made sense, and you wanted to do what he said should be done."[4]

The volunteers uniformly respected him for his quiet demeanor, his charisma, his creativity, his intellect, his ability to articulate the issues, his sincerity, and his leadership ability. I know I did.

A volunteer's comments about him from that time provide a picture of this remarkable, courageous man: "When he talked, he was not in the least dynamic, but he forced you by what he said and by his manner of saying it, to want to partake of him, to come to him. He was not in any way outgoing, yet when he spoke you felt close to him. Instead of giving himself to you or forcing himself upon you, he created such a great desire in you to draw on him that you were able to feel you were doing so when he spoke."[5]

Another volunteer wrote about him that summer in a letter published in *Letters from Mississippi*, a compilation of anonymous letters from Summer Project volunteers: "He is a careful thinker, expresses himself with great economy and honesty, and with every word, one is amazed at the amount of caring in the man."[6]

Nancy Schieffelin, my friend from Summit who volunteered as a Freedom School teacher and was assinged to Greenville, attended orientation the following week and reacted the same way. Her parents allowed her to go, but relatives and neighbors were opposed, telling her that the project was too dangerous and Communist inspired and that she shouldn't be messing things up down there. She described Bob Moses as "the most engaging, quiet, calming, wise" person and said that it was he, during the Oxford orientation, who gave her the confidence to go to Mississippi.[7]

Bob did most of the talking in the general sessions I attended and provided the most interesting and inspiring parts of the orientation for me. First, he presented the background of the Mississippi civil rights movement and the history of Mississippi and COFO; then with the district map of Mississippi I have copied here, he described the project, the areas of the state that were project locations, and the attitudes that prevailed among whites and blacks in these areas in Mississippi. He explained economic and cultural differences among the regions in the state and stated that before the people of Mississippi could be better off, many would be hurt, and some would be killed. He wanted to curb any overly optimistic enthusiasm that we might have regarding bringing about any significant change. He said, "If we can go and come back alive, then that is something. If you can go into Negro homes and just sit and talk that will be a huge job."[8] By intentionally lowering our expectations of accomplishment, Bob deterred the idealists with missionary zeal who might want to claim personal virtue for bringing freedom and justice to the downtrodden in Mississippi. He said, "Don't think that you're going to save something for democracy—just that there's a dirty job to be done."[9]

Bob Moses knew that we would find people slow to respond and urged us to be patient with Mississippi. Many had never met friendly whites willing to converse with them on terms of equality. They would be having a new experience: encountering and coming to know white people who considered them equals and treated them with respect. Some would welcome us, but the volunteers would have to be patient in working with apprehensive or apathetic residents, long intimidated and fearful, to activate them in the struggle for voting rights and equality.

Second, Moses made sure that we knew about the possibility of arrest. State law authorized curfews and prohibited picketing on all city streets and sidewalks, and a new criminal syndicalism law made it a felony just to suggest any political or social change. Arrests of civil rights workers, often on the highways, were arbitrary and did not always follow an offense. The Mississippi cops had a reputation for avoiding identification by not wearing badges. Jack Greenberg, chief counsel of the NAACP Legal Defense Fund, and John M. Pratt, an attorney with the NCC, were not memorable in discussing legal problems we might face, but I remember Jess Brown, a wiry, tough, fifty-one-year-old black lawyer from Jackson. As one of three black Mississippi lawyers who would defend civil rights cases, he knew about police practices and how to make his points with his local mannerisms of speech.[10] He said that if "the police stop you, and arrest you, don't get out and argue with the cop and say 'I know my rights.' . . . There ain't any use standing out there trying to teach him some constitutional law at 12 o'clock." He advised that we go on to jail and wait for our lawyer. Once white Mississippians knew our views on racial matters, we would no longer be classified as white but, in his view, could expect rougher treatment. White Mississippi would consider the two groups, in his words, "niggers and nigger-lovers."[11]

We were told that arrests were even more likely if we engaged in mass demonstrations, protests, or sit-ins. Congress had just passed the civil rights bill, which would be enacted July 2, 1964, and some volunteers might be tempted to use sit-ins to test Mississippi compliance with the law. Bob Moses made clear that COFO forbade demonstrating. Direct action was not a part of the Summer Project; COFO wanted us at work, not in jail using up limited legal and financial resources. The question of legal representation and the subject of communism in the civil rights movement came before the volunteers in this context. The NCC said that none of its ministers would be represented by lawyers from the National Lawyers Guild, the oldest human rights bar association, founded in 1937 as a racially integrated alternative to the American Bar Association. The Guild had long been labeled subversive for its unrestricted membership policies and its defense work during the McCarthy era. But Bob Moses firmly told us that Red baiting of the Guild was politics of the past that was irrelevant to the freedom struggle in the 1960s. SNCC had needed lawyers to defend its field secretaries and local blacks arrested for exercising basic rights in Mississippi and consistently received effective legal counsel from Guild volunteer lawyers. Because SNCC welcomed outside help, Moses did not want to hear talk of communism; it was too divisive. In Mississippi, when I heard the attacks on COFO as a Communist or Communist-infiltrated organization and on radical-sounding volunteers as Communist, I knew they had no merit but were used by opponents only to discredit our work.

Third, Moses gave us basic instructions that were soon second nature for me: no guns. The movement was nonviolent. No one in SNCC carried a gun, and there were no guns in SNCC offices. The position on what local people did regarding guns was less clear, but I feel fortunate that I never got close to mention of a gun when I was in Greenville. SNCC was aware that local residents owned rifles to defend their homes and families, and the general belief was that the organization could not tell a homeowner what to do.

COFO was particularly concerned with how the white volunteers would behave. We were advised to treat the local residents with respect, according them a dignity not granted by white Mississippians. We were to talk to blacks as we would address our parents' friends, by using the courtesy titles *Mr., Mrs.,* or *Miss.* Aware of the danger we presented for local residents, we would not give out the name or address of the person with whom we were living or the names of any local person associated with us. Mississippi was a dry state, but the general availability of liquor required a prohibition on liquor in the Freedom Houses, the places for housing that also served as offices for the movement.

A three-page COFO security handbook contained the rules: don't go anywhere alone, avoid travel at night, be conscious of cars that circle offices or Freedom Houses, take notice of cars without tags, record tag numbers of suspicious cars, carry identification at all times, follow the dress code—avoid "bizarre or provocative clothing." I understood that we should dress to avoid the beatnik or weirdo stereotype: girls in dresses, not shorts, jeans, or slacks; boys in shirts and pants, always clean shaven and with short hair; and in both cases nothing too colorful that would draw attention to us. Girls generally didn't wear pants then as they do now, and I didn't have any blue jeans or slacks with me. We were to be neat and clean and polite. Poor people who could not afford to dress up did not expect anyone to dress down, and I saw no reason to try to look poor. I wanted to dress as well as I could in clean clothes, sandals, skirts, and sleeveless cotton blouses for the hot weather. I realized I would have to spend my free time washing and ironing.

COFO wanted us to know how dangerous the work would be. James Forman, thirty-six, a formidable, forceful, big man, very different in appearance from Bob Moses, was the intellectual SNCC executive director. He had spoken on Monday, before I arrived, preparing volunteers to witness poverty in the private homes in the black community where they would be staying. The *New York Times* reported that when volunteers laughed at the thought of using outhouses in the absence of indoor plumbing in some rural areas, he sobered them up: "I may be killed and you may be killed."[12] That was a very clear message in the orientation, conveyed in many different ways, but it did not alter my determination.

Another major topic of the general sessions was nonviolence, presented by James Lawson, thirty-six, a former divinity student from Nashville and now a minister who was a founding member of SNCC; Bayard Rustin, fifty-two, the activist organizer and Quaker pacifist who had been imprisoned for refusing to serve in the military in World War II; and Vincent Harding, thirty-three, a scholarly, activist Mennonite minister from Atlanta. They explained the history and philosophy of nonviolence, which was a way of life for the more spiritual participants in the civil rights movement, and told the volunteers how critically important it was as a tactic.

Among these three speakers, Vincent Harding impressed me the most as he talked to us in his frank and honest manner, which he successfully blended with humor. There had been apprehension about what "kooks" would be volunteering, and he said he was very much impressed with "the kind of seriousness, and yet avoiding a somberness" with which we were taking our assignment. He reiterated what Bob Moses had said: that "the most important thing that you will do will simply be being present." In addition to giving us the historical background of race relations, he projected what the volunteers would encounter—deferential local blacks, hostile whites living in fear, and tempting interracial sex. He spoke about racial prejudice and its effect on blacks in outlining different situations we would find. He said to "recognize that no matter how many times you come to Mississippi, you are probably bringing some [white racism] along with you. And you have to admit this."[13] Prejudice was also part of who we were, and he exposed our own prejudice, making the white volunteers confront our attitudes toward blacks. I could no longer assume that I did not have any prejudices but had to consider that I had preconceived opinions about blacks and about any racial, religious, or ethnic group different from my own. I welcomed this new idea, attempting to relate it to myself and my attitudes while growing up. Despite any doubts I may have had, I knew I had the desire to *live* in the black community and be a part of the Mississippi movement. I hoped I would feel a willing, open tolerance toward all when I met the local residents.

Many national journalists were covering the story of the white summer volunteers. Their presence told me that we were involved in a big deal—history in the making. Bob Moses was right—the press coverage would be huge. They reported on the atmosphere of orientation, perceiving racial tension between the black Mississippi staff members, considered professionals by the press, and the white student volunteers, called novices. The press highlighted the differences in the two groups, eager white volunteers and worn black activists, but the difference apparent to me was the color of our skin. Others talked about the gulf between us in terms of race and class and wrote of the fundamental facts of the country's history of slavery, prejudice, and discrimination: blacks feeling resentful of the privileged, well-educated volunteers who knew more about how to get things done with their writing and public-speaking skills; whites feeling guilt regarding our role in and responsibility for the historic treatment of blacks. What was difficult for blacks with less formal education, whites might do with ease. But here we were setting out together to do something to right the wrongs, and I did not see tension and friction. The singing of freedom songs, which other volunteers may have been hearing for the first time and had to learn, brought us together, and as events unfolded, observers noticed the groups coming closer together.

The press picked up two incidents during orientation as evidence of what reporters decided to label as racial tension or friction between the experienced workers and the new recruits. Claude Sitton, the veteran southern civil rights reporter for the *New York Times,* told of a specific incident on Tuesday night, before I arrived. Watching a television documentary film that showed a slovenly, fat, white southern man blocking the door so blacks could not register to vote, whites in the audience laughed at the ridiculous scene they thought couldn't possibly be real. Six black staff walked out, dismayed at how much education the volunteers needed. They and the country had no idea how racist Mississippi was. The black staff members knew that the white southern man was a real man: Theron Lynd, the notorious registrar of voters in Hattiesburg, where many had gone together on Freedom Days to attempt to register to vote. When the film ended, they spoke about their criticism of the volunteers, and the volunteers, who had been insensitive to the meaning of the registrar's conduct for black residents, gained understanding that would bring the group closer together. The telling comment was, "I can only hope that by the time the summer is over, you will not be able to laugh anymore."[14] That was a time for white volunteers to remain quiet, as I remember I once did watching a movie with blacks the previous summer. Different groups will find humor in different things.

The other incident frequently related, from the second week of orientation, concerned Charles Morgan's interrupting his presentation to recognize a black staff member who had raised his hand and how a torrent of emotion poured forth. Morgan, thirty-four, was a white southern lawyer who was driven out of Birmingham for a letter he wrote blaming all opponents of the civil rights movement for the church bombing that killed four young black girls in September 1963. He was making the point to the volunteers that white southerners were held back from supporting civil rights by peer pressure to maintain the status quo of segregation. The young black man who interrupted made a long emotional statement repeating many of the same phrases: "It's hell in Mississippi" and "We've got to change the system." He warned, "You're going to be treated worse than black[s]."[15] Drained from speaking, he slumped and then left. Silence filled the room. The white students found his statement particularly moving and expressed their appreciation with applause. Dorie Ladner, a kind and generous but outspoken black SNCC field secretary from Hattiesburg, Mississippi, criticized the applause. She identified the man as Jimmie Travis, a Mississippi native and a SNCC veteran of the movement who had been shot in the neck in 1963. What he said was something that had to be said, that he needed to say, but was not presented for recognition by an audience—"You just don't applaud. It's hard. It's hard." As Dorie told me later, "I told the people to be serious."[16] The white students still felt the need to express their support for Jimmie, and after Dorie reprimanded them, they applauded again. The white volunteers had not yet gotten sensitized to their circumstances.

The reporters, all of them white, appeared less comfortable with the blacks and focused on stories of white volunteers. No reporter approached me, and I never talked to any of them. One of the questions they asked was, "Why did you want to join the Summer Project?"—a question that volunteers, without an intellectual justification, found difficult to answer, giving "only the vaguest of explanations," as Claude Sitton wrote in the

New York Times.[17] I would have given my straightforward, simple, somewhat glib answer, "Because I wanted to do something about the problems I saw last summer in Mississippi," which I know now is not very satisfactory. One volunteer wrote in a letter that *Look* magazine was "searching for the ideal naïve Northern middle-class white girl," a phrase used later by others.[18]

I did not see the tension and friction between white volunteers and black veterans that reporters seemed to find, and I also did not feel that I was in an uncomfortable place. I have been surprised when reading about white volunteers' expectations in Oxford. *Letters from Mississippi* includes letters from volunteers who felt that people were not friendly and welcoming during orientation. They wrote about small groups that formed, with blacks feeling resentful of whites and whites wanting to be accepted and recognized for what they were doing to help blacks in Mississippi. Sally Belfrage reports in her memoir *Freedom Summer* that volunteers felt left out and wanted to receive expressions of gratitude from the black staff but instead felt that they were being used. They were giving up a privileged, pleasurable summer for the harsh conditions in Mississippi, so surely they would be recognized by black staff as friends.

I found the attitudes of the Mississippi staff that were mystifying to Sally Belfrage perfectly understandable. In *Ready for Revolution: The Life and Struggles of Stokely Carmichael (Kwame Ture)*, Stokely Carmichael denies any rejection of the new volunteers by black staff. I saw the SNCC staffers acting as I had seen them at the meeting I went to in Atlanta in the spring of 1964, glad to see their friends again and reuniting emotionally in their unique "circle of trust, band of brothers."[19] They knew each other and wanted to be together, while the rest of us were strangers in the room—to them and to each other. I saw their behavior as natural, particularly because of the dangers they faced daily working in Mississippi, and so was not offended. I did not feel that I was entitled or welcome to join a group that preferred to stay together without the new white volunteers. We were about to be in the minority in our work in Mississippi and needed to get used to our new status. There the Mississippi staff, the same age that we were, if not younger, would give us our instructions.

We saw the talent of these young Mississippi staff members in workshops during orientation. COFO scheduled role playing and small discussions in the afternoons for local project groups or for canvassing for voter registration. I still have a write-up that includes the following questions for role playing:

1. How would you approach a person in a community you had never seen before?
2. How could you make a person understand what voting is by relating things in his everyday life?
3. How would you talk to a real religious person?
4. How would you talk to a community leader?

Of these questions, the second seemed the most relevant and challenging to me. We heard the following simple example of making voting important. On dirt roads in black neighborhoods, there were no street lights, yet the white part of town had paved streets that did not go dark at sunset, so the argument was that you could work for improvements close to home in your neighborhood. If you were able to vote, you and your neighbors could elect a local representative who would look out for your interests in order to get reelected, see that your roads were paved and street lights installed. But for me improvisation was always more effective than using a script in urging fearful or apathetic blacks to get up, stand up, and go register to vote.

A more interesting afternoon involved role playing on the lawn near Peabody Hall. We all got in on a demonstration of nonviolent tactics. The question was: How would you react to tear gas, fire hoses, dogs, verbal intimidation, cattle prods, and other hostile measures while you were on a picket line or in a march to the courthouse? But we learned about non-violence as a practical matter. Getting outside on the warm, summer days was a welcome change from being inside sitting and listening to speakers in the packed auditorium. Some volunteers took the parts of angry Mississippi whites ready to beat up demonstrators with their fists. Others played the role of victim. Not the aggressive type, I played victim. The Mississippi staff showed us the positions for crouching, rolling up, protecting the most sensitive parts of the body, going limp, and preparing to be dragged away. Volunteers may not have had direct exposure to civil rights demonstrations or might have known something of what to expect

only from television scenes of protestors getting arrested. I was familiar
with the techniques from attending nonviolent workshops.

The press loved the role playing and even participated in these sessions. The television cameramen bustled about to get the best shots of
the action. I remember getting punched in the stomach by Karl Fleming,
the distinguished civil rights reporter from *Newsweek,* when he was acting
in the role of white cop. Fleming, from North Carolina, who, as other
reporters have described him, had "the tall, ruggedly handsome looks of
an action-movie star," teamed with Claude Sitton over three years, moving in and out of black and white southern hot spots, turning regional
stories into national headlines.[20]

The nonviolent role playing and discussions during orientation reinforced the importance of getting a commitment from the government to
protect not only SNCC and CORE staff and local residents seeking the
right to vote, but for our own safety. Bob Moses repeatedly urged us to
write to our local newspapers to spread the word about the oppressive
conditions in Mississippi and to contact our representatives and senators to push for federal protection. I was still too preoccupied during
orientation to do anything but remembered my responsibility later in
the summer, when I wrote letters to the *Summit Herald;* my congresswoman, Florence Dwyer; and my two senators, Clifford Case and Harrison Williams.

Now that we were going to Mississippi, we had to consider the effect
of law enforcement policies and practices on us. The FBI was notorious for standing by, observing, and taking notes while blacks were being
beaten and jailed for peacefully attempting to register to vote. The government lawyers would conduct interviews, investigate, and report their
findings to Washington, but no prosecutions followed. COFO intentionally emphasized the probability of arrests and the possibility of violence
and death to make us face our fears. Moreover, if we acted carelessly or
improperly, project staff and local black residents would suffer while we
would probably survive. We needed to realize our responsibility if retali-
ations were taken out on them.

Bob Moses knew the reality of violence from his own beatings, arrests,
and time spent in jail, although he didn't regale us with those stories, and
they are not frequently told. Instead, he gave us accounts of two mur-

ders that had acutely affected him: the murder of Herbert Lee in 1961, a local man who had helped with voter registration in Amite County, and the subsequent killing of Louis Allen, who had witnessed the murder of Lee and suffered years of threats and harassment. On January 31, 1964, Allen had told Bob he was moving to Milwaukee the next day, but that night assailants, never identified, murdered him. These deaths occurred in Liberty, Mississippi, and gave meaning to the sign you could see in the SNCC office in Greenwood:

There's a street in Itta Bena called FREEDOM
There's a town in Mississippi called LIBERTY
There's a department in Washington called JUSTICE

To warn us of the dangers, COFO told us the Mississippi war stories: bombings, arrests, beatings, shootings, and killings. We heard about the incredible hostility and brutality suffered over years of incidents in Mississippi. The grave demeanor of the Mississippi staff made us believe in the accuracy of these accounts. Was this volunteer scared? I must have been, but I don't remember feeling overwhelmingly frightened. My safety during the previous summer gave me illusions that I would be safe. If I came home alive then, surely I would return home at the end of this summer. I wonder now if I should have had other feelings, but I do not believe they would have changed my plans. The next week's orientation of the second group of three hundred Freedom School teachers and Community Center volunteers would be even more sobering, including reports about three civil rights workers who went missing in Mississippi on June 21.

Taking precautions against the coming dangers in the summer, COFO assigned at least one volunteer on each project to communications, responsible for knowing the whereabouts of staff and volunteers and for coordinating inquiries from the press. The Jackson headquarters office had two wide-area telephone service lines. Anyone leaving a project to go to another town had to call Jackson: call in when leaving, call in on arrival, and call in after returning. That was imperative for keeping track of everyone working in the Summer Project.

On the last day of our Oxford orientation, John Doar, the deputy director of the Civil Rights Division of the Justice Department, spoke to us for an hour about federal law enforcement. Federal law provided for arrest for violations of the civil rights of all citizens. Congress had intended that the Civil Rights Acts of 1957 and 1960 should end discrimination against blacks in voting, but there was no federal will to enforce these laws. I respected the institutions of government and believed in their representatives, but now I was struck by the inconsistencies. Although we hoped for assurances about a stronger federal presence in Mississippi during the summer of 1964, Doar was not encouraging. He emphasized that law enforcement was the responsibility of state and local governments. Direct questions forced him to tell the volunteers with no ambiguity that the federal government would not protect us. We would be in the same position that local black residents had been in since 1877, when federal troops withdrew from Mississippi at the end of Reconstruction after the Civil War. He simply said, "We don't have any national police force." I recorded in a postcard home: "John Doar spoke for an hour today at noon and definitely got put on the spot—he said the FBI will not be protecting us. Yet someone read from the U.S. Criminal Code that FBI officers do have the power of arrest if the offense is committed in his presence. No answer."

Another volunteer wrote in a letter that John Doar said that "they would keep very close watch on us and try to watch for trouble brewing,"[21] but I don't recall even that amount of reassurance.

I already knew that the federal government was not living up to expectations in Mississippi, but hearing the blatant statements from a high-ranking Justice Department official upset me. The government had not acted to prevent the loss of black lives, and now *our* lives were also at risk—a realization that worried me and added to my dismay about the government in Washington. Little did I know that there was more disillusionment to come.

Although some volunteers criticized the program's inefficiencies, in my view the organizers and speakers succeeded in our first week of orientation. One of the memos had warned that we might be "deselected," but I paid little attention to that possibility. SNCC carefully screened applicants before acceptance, and few volunteers, if any, got dropped. The sessions also succeeded in testing the volunteers' resolve to join the project. They increased their commitment, and I didn't hear about anyone who went home.

I didn't receive my assignment to Greenville until it was almost time to leave Oxford. COFO gave each of us a postcard to inform our parents where we would be. I wrote about Greenville:

> I'm going to Greenville which is on the Mississippi River to work in the office. About 15 will be working on voter registration. Address is 940 Sidney, Greenville, Mississippi. Phone number is 335-2173.
>
> We're leaving tomorrow by bus chartered to Memphis and then in our separate groups to our destination.
>
> Greenville is known as a liberal city, home of Hodding Carter's Delta-Democrat Times. Can move around there.

I do not know who decided my assignment; no one discussed it with me. However, I surmised that a city with a moderate reputation was a logical destination for me as one of the few white women in voter registration.

I just wanted to get on with the job, but I did hope my parents were following the story and would "cut and save" the articles for me. In my postcard, I showed them my confidence and excitement, squeezing in a lot of information, including a report on the press coverage. I said: "Claude Sitton of the Times is here—quite a guy and Karl Fleming of Newsweek."

I alerted them to features in such popular magazines as the *Saturday Evening Post, Life,* and *Look.* In addition, CBS television had scheduled a program for the following Wednesday. After the three Mississippi civil rights workers disappeared on Sunday, June 21, the newsworthiness of the orientation sessions increased, and press coverage intensified. By the next week, all the parents of volunteers, wondering and worrying, would watch the news for these stories.

What the volunteers learned that week was life changing, as we made a commitment to risk our own lives in the Mississippi freedom struggle. We were anticipating life-threatening experiences. I already knew something of what was presented during orientation, but being there was critically important for me. Bob Moses inspired me, and I absorbed all the precautions I needed to take if I were to be a safe and effective volunteer. NCC and COFO sent us off thus prepared—serious-minded, clean-cut, nice-looking kids with instructions to be polite and mannerly, singing freedom songs, saying good-byes, feeling a bit brave and eager to begin new experiences and accept new challenges.

7

June 21, 1964

> I feel that the only meaningful type of work is the Movement but I don't want myself or anyone I've met to have to die. . . . I'm no different from anyone else and if they're risking their lives, then so must I. But I just can't comprehend why people must die to achieve something so basic and simple as Freedom.
> —letter from a Mississippi Summer Project volunteer[1]

On Saturday, June 20, hundreds of volunteers left Oxford, Ohio, for the Mississippi Summer Project. A volunteer had a car going to Greenville, and someone elected me, or else I volunteered, to go by car rather than by bus. This was obviously a preferable way of taking a long, more than twelve-hour trip.

All four of us in the VW bug with an Oregon license plate were college-age kids. Pam Trotman, a black volunteer from New York and a recent Howard graduate, shared the backseat with me, and two white guys who were also voter registration volunteers sat in the front and did the driving. We did most of the trip on Saturday, going through Ohio, Kentucky, and Tennessee. I'm reserved with people I don't know, and I don't think we were doing much talking. I think I took the time to think and sleep, wondering what lay ahead.

We arrived in Memphis at 12:30 a.m., "obviously the wrong time," I said, writing to my parents. We were in danger: an integrated group, arriving late at night in a city not known for its racial tolerance. Better than Mississippi, but not good. A week later I heard from volunteers traveling by bus how scared they were when the police and a threatening mob of white thugs were waiting for their buses arriving in Memphis in broad daylight.

115

Someone from the Summer Project or in our group knew an artist in Memphis and arranged for us to sleep at his house. After staying up to talk, we slept on the floor from 3:00 to 6:00. This artist's place was the messiest house I'd ever been in, but I didn't care. I was safe enough and excited, knowing I was going back to Mississippi. This summer I would not just be learning about the civil rights movement but had been qualified as a civil rights worker.

Leaving Memphis was the time to worry as we crossed the state line right away and entered Mississippi. We were part of the invasion of summer civil rights workers that had received a great deal of local and national publicity. Anyone who noticed us had to know that the four of us were part of the Summer Project: the timing of our travel, out-of-state plates, young, integrated travelers. The police might stop us anywhere for questioning, harassment, beatings, or fines. They might arrest us and take us to jail for a traffic violation that had not occurred. The police would at least record a description of the car and its license plate for possible future targeting. In March of that year, the governor of the state had referred to the summer volunteers as "organized revolutionaries" out to substitute federal law enforcement authority for state authority. The state police were trained in riot-control techniques and given full power in civil disorders rather than restricted to traffic law enforcement. The state legislature had given the governor power to send the state police into areas with authority over local law enforcement. The local press used derogatory words, calling us a "broken-down, motley bunch of atheists," "malcontents," and "wild-eyed left wing nuts" to encourage readers to oppose us and to deter black support of the voter registration activities Mississippi was so anxious to stop.[2]

Jackson had experienced massive demonstrations in the spring of 1963, and the city, completely opposed to civil rights, prepared to deal with the same thing again. It had increased the state police from 275 to 475 men and added equipment—shotguns, tear gas, troop trucks, vehicles to haul demonstrators to detention compounds, and even a 13,000-pound tank (named "Thompson's Tank" after the mayor)—in anticipation of the incursion of the outside agitators, even though we were a nonviolent army and had no plans for protest activities.

The local media, Mississippi politicians, and a network of the State

Sovereignty Commission, the Citizens' Councils, and the Ku Klux Klan prevented the civil rights movement from making progress in Mississippi. They effectively segregated the way of life for all but a handful of independent white citizens. As long as a threat of violence could intimidate and the federal government remained acquiescent, public officials successfully kept blacks in their traditionally subservient place, a place that blacks knew well and that some would transgress with full knowledge of the risks. I was young but feeling bold for leaving the comforts of my home to urge older people of a different color from mine to take those risks in the struggle for freedom. Now it seems strange that I was so determined and did not consider the complexities of the endeavor.

I thought about the stories we heard at orientation of the police brutality, shootings, and harassment used to preserve the Mississippi way of life that we were setting out to change. I would be among the first to arrive. I was traveling in total uncertainty. Anything could happen.

We drove into Mississippi on Sunday morning, past a big welcome sign along the highway letting us know that we had arrived in the Magnolia State. I have a bad sense of direction and just knew we were headed straight south, downhill on the map, in the southern state where racial segregation was the most entrenched and where the most extreme violence was taken to preserve white supremacy. We saw kudzu in spots, the deep green, large-leafed vine that grows so incredibly fast that it overtakes the landscape, stretching endlessly up and down the hillsides. Where it covers the limbs of dead trees, monstrous outlines provoke images of strange creatures. The sight of kudzu has always given me the chills after I heard that it was a threatened resting place for an "uppity Negro." Such lush landscape was not beautiful, but unfriendly, in what I considered hostile territory. Yet it was a place I had willingly chosen to go.

We were on a straight, two-lane highway, going through flat, dry, treeless country. This was the Mississippi Delta, the rich agricultural region in the northwest sector of the state bordering the Mississippi River. The large plantations supported wealthy cotton planters, including the powerful Senator James O. Eastland, who lived luxuriously on a two-hundred-acre plantation. Farming mechanization and chemical weed killers were beginning to change lives. As black labor would become surplus, millions would be forced off their land, and many would migrate to Chicago and other northern cities to look for jobs and a better life. In the early 1960s, though, blacks still lived and worked on the plantations in Delta counties, stooped over, chopping (weeding) and picking cotton in the hot sun. They lived in small, unpainted, tarpaper shacks without foundations and used nearby outhouses for bathroom facilities. Blacks walked or rode on mules or in wagons or traveled in broken-down cars to go to town to shop or to church, or they relaxed on front porches to talk or sing and catch a possible hot summer breeze amid the harshness of rural poverty. There were few filling stations or grocery stores or old, red Coke signs—no billboards, neon signs for motels, or fast-food places that would mar the view. I recall a countryside overwhelmingly deserted, desolate, and flat as far as the eye could see. We didn't stop for anything anywhere on the highway. That would have been stupid—and dangerous.

We locked our car doors and nervously watched other cars. Were they occupied by blacks or whites? Did the driver or passengers notice us? Did the gun racks in the back windows of pickup trucks carry guns? Was there a license plate? If so, from where? Probably Mississippi, but maybe Louisiana or another neighboring state—Tennessee, Arkansas, or Alabama. In 1964, I don't think the natural wonders or historic sites drew tourists to vacation in Mississippi. Instead, out-of-state cars likely carried natives yearning for home, traveling back from the places that offered more economic opportunity, cities to which they had fled but where life was not necessarily better and they could be lonely without family who had stayed behind. We were driving in Mississippi in daylight, so I was not as frightened as I would have been at night.

Meanwhile, unknown to me, Andy Goodman, who had just finished his sophomore year at Queens College, had also left Oxford by car to join the Summer Project as a white volunteer. He rode with another young white man, Mickey Schwerner, who was a more experienced white staff member of CORE in Meridian, the county seat of Lauderdale County in southern Mississippi, and who had already been working with a black CORE staff member, James Chaney, a Meridian native, in voter registration. When Mickey attended orientation, he noticed Andy and was impressed by his composure and political awareness. COFO assigned Andy to Vicksburg, but Mickey thought that Andy could conduct a Freedom School planned for nearby rural Neshoba County and got him reassigned to the Meridian project site. James Chaney and some summer volunteers were also in the car. They left Oxford, Ohio, on Saturday at 3:00 a.m. so that they would arrive safely in daylight in one day of driving. Andy was among the first white volunteers to arrive in Mississippi.

Only a small nucleus of strong black community leaders lived in this area of Mississippi, which was known for vigilante terrorism. In the early 1960s, Dave Dennis, the courageous civil rights veteran from CORE who became known for his angry passion as a public speaker as well as his sense of humor and strategic thinking, had begun the work in voter registration in Lauderdale County and neighboring counties. Nothing could be accomplished in the adjacent Neshoba County, however, because of the likelihood, if not certainty, of being met with the violence that intimidated most of the local black community.

On Sunday, as my group was approaching Greenville, "the three boys"—Mickey, James, and Andy—as I called them then (without intending any offense, but only recognizing that they *were* young), settled into Mickey's 1963 blue Ford station wagon a little after noon to drive from Meridian into Neshoba County to investigate the burning of the Mount Zion Methodist Church in Longdale, an all-black community in a rural part of the county. Andy Goodman had time on June 21 to write and send the postcard COFO required that we use to inform our parents about our assignments:

> Dear Mom and Dad,
> I have arrived safely in Meridian Mississippi. This is a wonderful town and the weather is fine. I wish you were here. The people in this city are wonderful and our reception was very good.
> All my love,
> Andy[3]

I didn't meet Andy but understand that he was close to his parents, Carolyn and David Goodman, and had been influenced to volunteer for the Mississippi Summer Project by their activism and the progressive schools he had attended in New York City.

Because James Chaney knew the local roads, he drove. Young Ben

Chaney, James's brother who was only ten, had begged to go, but no one considered that wise, and his mother kept him at home. Mickey specified that they would be back in Meridian by 4:00 p.m. After that hour, project staff would call the surrounding jails and, if the workers could not be found, alert the media, the FBI, and the Justice Department.

The Summer Project included Greenville as one of its sites to continue earlier efforts to register black voters at the Washington County Courthouse located downtown. Other summer activities in Greenville involved Freedom Schools, Community Centers, and research. On the Mississippi River in the heart of the Delta, Greenville was a city of 47,000 in 1964, with blacks in the majority and a growing business center for industry and commerce. The city had a reputation of being the most open society in Mississippi in terms of race relations, which made it conducive for holding SNCC meetings like the ones that had debated and finally approved the Summer Project. Some say river towns are typically more moderate and tolerant of new ideas than other areas of the state that are insulated from outside influence. I heard in Oxford that Greenville was "liberal," which is what I told my parents as soon as I learned of my assignment; another volunteer called it "relatively relaxed and civilized."[4] Many of the white people there had an appreciation for the arts, and in a cultured community they were less likely to condone racism. Greenville was notable for producing famous writers—William Alexander Percy, Walker Percy, Shelby Foote, and Ellen Douglas among more than sixty-five published authors. And so it has been called "the Athens of the Delta."[5]

If the whites in Greenville were so reasonable about race relations, what did I expect? In part, I would be disappointed. In Oxford, I had heard so much about the hostility of Mississippi whites that led to beatings and arrests of civil rights workers. I knew about the local black heroes—first the men, such as Amzie Moore in Cleveland, and soon the women who were awakened by the student activists, such as Fannie Lou Hamer, who had learned about her civil rights for the first time in August 1962, and others in the rural counties. Courageous and militant, they were the leaders taking risks to become first-class citizens. In Greenville, perhaps we would not meet any local people famous in the movement. But I no longer expected to be in grave personal danger. Primarily, I found my assignment reassuring. I thought I would stay safe and cause my parents less worry. Other volunteers might be disappointed if they were looking for adventure, but that was far from my mind.

As the third-largest city in Mississippi after Jackson and Meridian, Greenville offered more economic opportunity for both whites and blacks than the rural areas did. It was the site of an innovative barge-construction industry, tow boats were headquartered there, and it hosted a large carpet-manufacturing plant. A number of other industries were located at Greenville because of the proximity to the Delta's hardwoods and other abundant natural resources. In the booming economy of the 1960s, black middle-class professionals, preachers, teachers, and entrepreneurs had more economic security. They were more apt to hold moderate views about civil rights. I joined in a group view that they were "Uncle Toms" who did not want to risk losing the few benefits they enjoyed, even though some were active leaders of the local NAACP. Blacks employed by the federal government, such as post office workers, lived apart from members of the black elite in town, but they also enjoyed financial security. A federal air force base on the outskirts of town had added to equal employment opportunities in Greenville. A vast complex of three hundred buildings, it had provided a training program for foreign pilots from our allied nations. I believe the base had some influence on race relations in Greenville even though it had closed in 1960.

I was aware of one prominent resident of Greenville, but not sure why Hodding Carter received so much acclaim. I later learned that Hodding Carter Jr. ("Big Hodding") had founded a newspaper in Greenville in 1938 that became the *Delta Democrat-Times*. In 1946, he gained national recognition when he received a Pulitzer Prize for his outspoken, independent editorials when the Japanese were being taken to concentration camps. He also wrote courageously against Senator Theodore G. Bilbo, the popular Mississippi demagogue who was a passionate defender of racial segregation and white supremacy; Bilbo had also been called a "vile degenerate," "moral pervert," and "foul-tongued slanderer" as well as a "bribe taker," "liar," and "crook" for his outrageous bombast.[6] Carter continued to oppose racist demagoguery in novels and editorials and was largely credited for Greenville's significant white tolerance for blacks in the 1950s and 1960s. However, he was also a gradualist who advocated obedience to the law and only token desegregation on the grounds that change could not occur in the South overnight. In 1962, when Hodding Carter Jr. was only fifty-five, his son, Hodding Carter III ("Little Hodding"), had taken unofficial editorial control of the paper.[7] So when we talked about Hodding Carter in 1964, we were referring to the son, who was carrying on the reputation and influence of the paper while his parents were living in New Orleans.

Fortunately for us, the city fathers "decreed there would be no violence."[8] The mayor and the city council followed the orders of the leading white professionals and businessmen. These so-called big shots met regularly as the Friday Evening Tea Club to keep tabs on what went on in the city. Neither the Ku Klux Klan nor the Citizens' Council was allowed in. Actually, Greenville was not "liberal," but it "was better than other places." As a result, though, it was "more difficult to get a strong civil rights movement" developed "due to the apathy that existed among the people."[9]

Under the influence of the city fathers in the civilized atmosphere in Greenville, the police chief, William C. Burnley Jr., who later was elected mayor, devoted himself to upholding the law. He was no "Bull" Connor, the infamous police commissioner who had defended racial segregation in Birmingham, Alabama. Back in May 1963, pictures of black demonstrators in Birmingham, including young children, threatened by attack dogs and thrown to the ground by water from powerful fire hoses made a lasting impression on shocked TV audiences throughout the country. Greenville's chief, in contrast, was conscientious about preserving the city's good reputation. He was a big, gentlemanly white man with a bland face, always in police uniform, with his badge on a clean, white shirt. He was generally known for being fair and reasonable.

We approached the city on Highway 82, the wide main street paved with asphalt. It was hot and dry and looked as though the sun had bleached everything else. Nelson Street was the commercial main street for blacks in this segregated city: grocery stores, dry cleaners, drug stores, cafés, offices. The black community was self-sufficient on Nelson Street and had no need to go downtown, where they would confront what everyone knew were whites-only facilities that they were not allowed to use and where no one would serve them food. The signs "White" and

"Colored" generally made it clear what the boundaries were in public places. Where there were no signs, blacks just knew what to do. Not long before, as Dr. Matthew Page, a black native of Greenville, recalled for me, there was "a time that you couldn't walk on sidewalks . . . you couldn't walk past the white schools . . . when you couldn't even go in the courthouse, and there were certain floors you couldn't go on and not even look at . . . times that you had threats—you could have lost your life if more than five or six whites and blacks got together for a meeting, whether it was social, political, or what have you."[10] Blacks in Greenville remembered these fears and remained careful and cautious not to offend the whites who maintained their supremacy.

It was easy for me to know whether we were in the white part of town or the black part; the people on the segregated streets made it clear when we were in the right place. For me that summer, "the right place" was a new safety zone, the black community. I knew, seeing only blacks walking on the sidewalks or streets, that we were headed in the right direction to the Freedom House. On that first day, we didn't see Main Street or Washington Street, the downtown area, or any big houses in wealthy white neighborhoods but followed instructions received in Oxford and went directly to the Freedom House. That would be my headquarters for the first few weeks of the summer.

I felt relieved when we finally arrived at 940 Sidney Street on the south side of town. Every project had a Freedom House, and in some dangerous areas the address was kept as secret as possible. It was a place for students to live, but more importantly it was the place to gather, get information, and discuss civil rights—an open house for anyone wanting to get involved in the movement.

I saw a tiny, rundown frame house, painted white, but not recently, next to the Disney Chapel, a small plain, white wooden church. There were similar houses on both sides of the street, with folks sitting on their front porches and children playing in the yards. They were staring at the unusual arrival of young white adults (or should I call us boys and girls?). They must have heard about the project, white kids from the North coming to town, more "Freedom Riders." Every civil rights worker in Mississippi had that nickname, which had begun in 1961 when integrationists rode the buses south from Washington, D.C., to challenge discrimination

The former Freedom House at 940 Sidney Street in Greenville, Mississippi, 1964.
Photo by Lisa Anderson Todd, March 2010.

in interstate commerce and landed in jail when they got to Jackson. They
were the real Freedom Riders.

This Freedom House had a concrete front stoop and a small yard in
front and back, no bushes or flowers, not even grass. Walking through
the front screen door, we quickly explored all there was to the one-story,
four-room house. Young people milled around without seeming purpose.
No one welcomed or greeted us in any organized way. The looks and
casual hellos put us on our own. This was my introduction to the disor-
ganization of the militant student civil rights movement, which I would
have to adjust to or abandon.

As soon as we came through the door, we were in the living room,
sparsely furnished with old, broken-down couches and chairs. In the next
room, bunk beds hugged the wall, and peeking in the bedroom, I saw
a double bed and a single bed, which would allow at least five people to
sleep comfortably in the house. There was no second floor or basement.
In the back, the bathroom had a tub, but no shower. A small kitchen

contained a cramped table, chair, and counters littered with mismatched dirty dishes and silverware. No rugs softened the wooden floors. I found it old and grubby, even messier than the artist's house in Memphis. But I could overlook all this because I was in Mississippi, finally involved in the movement.

I heard the news from Meridian some time after arriving in Greenville: three people, including a white volunteer and two CORE staff members, one white and one black, were missing. All news would travel fast in Mississippi that summer, and that startling, frightening, awful piece of news went faster than anything else. There was no meeting, no announcement, and no expectation of a response from volunteers already in Mississippi, but just the informal passing of this heart-stopping news in the Freedom House among the not yet organized group. I was particularly disturbed that the unexplained disappearance had happened so soon, on the *first* day that project volunteers were in the state. If this was a portent of things to come, I knew we *all* were in terrible trouble, and my fear increased beyond the low level I had felt when leaving Oxford. Skeptics and the newspapers and broadcasters were careful to use the word *disappearance* in talking about what happened to Chaney, Goodman, and Schwerner, but when I initially heard the news, I believed that they were dead. Anyone who knew the individuals and the Mississippi civil rights movement had no question about their fate.

For most of the summer volunteers, the news was more challenging because it came to them in Oxford. A solemn Bob Moses made the announcement in the auditorium on Monday morning to the volunteer Freedom School teachers, in their week of orientation after the first group of voter registration volunteers had left. He told them what was known about the three young men who had gone missing. My friend Pat Vail happened to be in the office in Oxford when Rita Schwerner, Mickey's wife, took a telephone call. Pat never forgot hearing Rita say then that she knew the three were dead. She was sure that Mickey would have followed procedure and called if they were delayed past the time they were due back. He had not called because he could not.

The new group of volunteers was consumed with worry and doubt in a way that I had not experienced. Bob Moses wanted them to realize the danger and emphasized that they had the option of returning home. Unlike me, these volunteers faced a test of the commitment they had made. Only four decided not to go on to Mississippi. And there was one already in Mississippi who decided to leave. Of two young men arrested shortly before midnight that week, subjected to a night of mental harassment and intimidation in the county jail and released the next day with no formal charges, one went home to New York; his father chartered a plane for him.

That Sunday, June 21, Meridian office workers sent out word that Mickey and his group had not returned or called the office as required. Staff and volunteers began searching, calling the jails in the surrounding area to ask whether they were being held. They continued calling through the long evening, keeping one line open in the Jackson office for communication with the FBI, the Justice Department, and the three families. A Meridian volunteer wrote that his group was sitting in the office "quietly nervous as hell," not saying the things all of them were thinking could have happened to their colleagues.[11] In a different area of the state, feeling I was in a safe community, I was less focused than others on this tragedy but couldn't help but wonder what had happened.

When we later learned that Andy Goodman was the volunteer who had disappeared and saw his picture, I did not recognize him. I began to question whether there would be more arrests and killings. My uncertainty and concern increased for myself, but I was more worried about other volunteers in more dangerous parts of the state. The killings continued to be a shared heavy weight on the volunteers throughout the summer that we could not forget. As Nancy Schieffelin said later, "They could be us. We could be them."[12] The murders intensified the experiences of all the volunteers, varied as they were, in different circumstances in different Mississippi communities.

On Monday night, June 22, I called my parents from the Freedom House phone to tell them I had arrived safely and everything was fine. To my amazement, they did not sound panicked. I also sent them a letter that day. I had no reservations about my assignment to Greenville, wanted to get to work registering voters, and thought everything was wonderful. Now I had some real tasks, and I would be making a difference. My letter began: "You wouldn't believe it if you saw it. We're just trying to get organized; a fantastic job. We will have four offices in Greenville for the summer, but two of them have to be repaired, cleaned, etc. We came to the Freedom House yesterday morning. About ten of us had to stay here last night because some of the housing fell through." I didn't tell my parents that I was on a bare floor, sleeping in my clothes without any covers for the second night in a row. I also didn't mention in the letter the disappearance of the three civil rights workers in Neshoba County but later learned that they already knew about it. I did tell them how broke the project was and that staff were not always getting paid.

They both promptly wrote reassuring, supportive letters reporting their thoughts and activities and telling me news of family members and friends. On June 25, my mother wrote that she had heard that "Marines will be sent in for protection of civil rights workers" and that a Mississippi congressman had said on the floor of the House of Representatives that "it [the disappearance of the three civil rights workers] was probably all a hoax to get publicity." President Johnson did send in assistance from a nearby federal air station, but only personnel to search for bodies, not marshals for protection of civil rights workers. What my mother called "the horrible news from Mississippi" did not change federal policy. She was going to watch a CBS television program that evening to check on the "many rumors floating around." My mother enclosed a contribution for the project, having decided that she would not buy a cotton dress and summer negligee but make do with what she already had, knowing "this would serve a better purpose." She told me she had spoken to the *Newark News* for a story planned on the volunteers from New Jersey.

My father's letter, dated June 26, was more businesslike. He too sent a check. His was "to be put aside for an emergency, *e.g.*, if President Johnson should ask you all to go home." He could visualize an evacuation of the volunteers, but the possibility never crossed my mind, and I would not have wanted to leave. My father served on the board of directors of the United Negro College Fund and at a recent UNCF conference had visited with Dr. Beittel, the president of Tougaloo, who, my father said, would be glad to see me if I could visit Tougaloo. But Daddy cautioned me against taking "any unnecessary chances" and didn't think it would be a good idea for me to go anywhere "by private automobile." He had read in the *New York Times* about the Citizens' Councils taking down license numbers and circulating them throughout the state.

Soon I got busy in voter registration. Our job was to urge people who had not yet registered to go to the courthouse and apply for the right to vote. Even in Greenville, blacks had met and would continue to meet obstacles in seeking this right. I wrote about my activity to my hometown newspaper, the *Summit Herald*. On July 9, 1964, the paper published "Report from Mississippi," which included my seven paragraphs describing my voter registration work canvassing from house to house, the constitutional interpretation test of the state constitution as the major obstacle to registration, the COFO programs of the other thirty-three volunteers in Greenville, and how I was living in the local black community. I also noted the national concern about the three missing civil rights workers and how to send contributions to meet COFO's need for financial support.

The work to increase voter registration was different than Freedom Registration. Before long, I changed my focus completely. The long letter I wrote my brother Eric on July 10, 1964, reflects my youthful enthusiasm for the upcoming MFDP Challenge at the Democratic National Convention:

> About Mississippi, I wonder where I start. It's a very big job that we have to do. As I say to so many people every day, "Have you heard about the Freedom Democratic Party?" and they haven't as I imagine you haven't. On the basis of (1) lack of support of the national platform and candidates, (2) discrimination against Negroes in registering to vote, (3) examples of unheld, unannounced, and closed precinct meetings, the Mississippi Democratic Party will be challenged at the national convention in representing Mississippi. We have our own registration forms that ask the basic questions asked in the North. They fill out their own unless they are illiterate. All of us are registrars and then we are [working at] finding a registrar in every . . . county [that is not too dangerous] and many deputy registrars.
>
> We are going to get at least 100,000 before the convention

and can then say that the delegation is representative because of this number and because all the meetings are open to those registered, unlike the Democratic Party's precinct, etc. meetings. Four states have already voted to vote at the convention to seat this party and because the eyes of the nation are on this state there is a very real possibility of success.

In early July, I was relying on "the eyes of the nation" for the Challenge to succeed. How it would all happen, whether by convention vote or negotiations, was not clear, but I felt that it would end favorably for the MFDP. With broad political support, the federal government would finally enforce protective federal laws and guarantee constitutional rights to all black residents of Mississippi.

8

Living as a Volunteer in Mississippi, 1964

Wherefore take unto you the whole armour of God, that ye may be able to withstand in the evil day, and having done all, to stand. Stand therefore, having your loins girt about with truth, and having on the breastplate of righteousness; And your feet shod with the preparation of the gospel of peace; Above all, taking the shield of faith, wherewith ye shall be able to quench all the fiery darts of the wicked.
—Ephesians 6:13–16 (King James Version)

Greenville is a stately southern city with two wide avenues running its length as you drive in from Highway 82 toward the Mississippi River. In the 1960s, the office of the influential *Delta Democrat-Times* anchored Main Street, which is still lined with many historic public buildings and large imposing houses of worship. The Federal Building containing the post office, city hall, the William Alexander Percy Memorial Library, and the Washington County Courthouse are on Main Street. In addition to the First Baptist Church and St. Joseph's Catholic Church downtown, the influential presence of Jewish merchants and tradespeople in the city is reflected in the large Hebrew Union synagogue that dates from 1906. Washington Street is the busy retail area parallel to Main Street, and farther over, also parallel to Main, Nelson Street at the time I was there offered the black community restaurants, shops, and professional services. The Mississippi River flows wide and largely unseen beyond the levee built up to protect the downtown area after the disastrous flood of 1927. Aside from the listlessness caused by the heat of summer, Greenville was as vibrant a community as any in Mississippi in 1964, unique for its more affluent, less conservative, artistic atmosphere.

I saw and appreciated little of Greenville during the summer. I never went to the library or a downtown church and only once set foot on Washington Street. I paid no attention to its famous writers, artists, and musicians. My place was on Nelson Street and in the black neighborhoods.

As I learned after the summer, SNCC had worked in Greenville in 1963, a year before the Summer Project began. Hunter Morey, a white Princeton graduate and later COFO legal coordinator; Charlie Cobb, our regional project director; Charles McLaurin, transplanted from Jackson to Sunflower County; and Ivanhoe Donaldson, assigned to Batesville during the 1964 summer, had laid the groundwork for us. Charlie had "an advantage" coming in because his grandmother was born in Greenville.[1] An active chapter of the NAACP existed there, with membership led by the black middle-class businessmen and professionals, but they were not as assertive or aggressive in advancing civil rights as SNCC wanted. Although more blacks were registered in Washington County than in other areas of the state, the SNCC organizers urged voter registration and political activity while they also advised high school students who wanted to engage in direct-action protests. A July 1963 sit-in at the local Walgreen's drugstore led to arrests and the subsequent closing of the store. Charlie knew local people who would help find housing for the Summer Project volunteers.

During the first week of the project, before we had an office for voter registration, I enjoyed being in the center of the action at the Freedom House. Earlier that year, eager black high school students, befriended by Charlie Cobb and Charles McLaurin, had formed their own organization that they called the Mississippi Student Union (MSU). Their teachers, however, who were among the middle-class blacks dependent on the existing system for their income and social position, did not want to risk their jobs by participating in the new movement in town and came around to the Freedom House only to listen. But the young people in Greenville had less at risk than their parents and gave more support to COFO and its summer volunteers. Only the threat of suspension or expulsion from school might deter them, a punishment that Johnny Frazier—the NAACP youth director I had met at Tougaloo and heard speak at a Jackson mass meeting—had received.[2] The school readmitted him when his grandmother threatened to send him to the white high school.

In his case, the expulsion reinforced his determination to join the struggle for freedom. He went to work in Jackson and applied more than once to be the first black student to be admitted to the University of Southern Mississippi.

During my first days in the Freedom House, I found people to talk to, listened to lots of interesting group discussions, and looked at books and magazines lying around that had information about the movement. I saw that the project was not well organized, and I was ready to begin the job, but until our office space was ready, we had to wait. I spent the time getting my bearings, learning, and talking to my new coworkers

In other more dangerous communities, a SNCC Freedom House would become a target for firebombs, as in Greenwood and Natchez, if its location was not secret. Nightriders driving around the block threatening violence, shouting "Nigger lovers!" and firing warning shots in the air or through windows were possible. Dorie Ladner, a Hattiesburg native who worked for SNCC in Natchez, has told me the story of the bombing intended for the SNCC Freedom House that blew up the house next door due to the attackers' "ignorance." I felt safe in Greenville, but we were nevertheless nervous and watchful, listening to the cars circling around the block our first nights, something we had been told in orientation we should be aware of, but nothing ever happened. I heard that the cars were the police, who, we were told, were there to protect rather than harass us, but I was not confident of their benevolent treatment. I read later, "[T]here were those big glasses up there [surveillance] and the police department and everybody would be looking out for them, you know, to see that no one bothered them."[3]

We could travel in integrated groups without being afraid when we were in Greenville. We went off for one of our first meals in an integrated group to the remaining operations at the location of the air force base, a place where we knew we would be served without discrimination. When there was a car available, I felt free driving around town, but that was only at the beginning of the summer. When we got to work in earnest, there was no time for just driving around.

About fifteen of us who were the first arrivals would be working in voter registration, except for two of the white girls, who were assigned to research. I described our group in Greenville, both staff and volunteers, all college age, in a letter home: "among the Negro boys, a veteran SNCC worker, two from Harvard, three from Mississippi, and the project director is a graduate of University of Chicago; girls are two from Howard; among the whites, boys from Reed, Philadelphia, Boston, New York, and California, and the two other girls are from New Jersey and California."

Charlie Cobb was the veteran SNCC staffer responsible for our regional area—Washington, Issaquena, and Sharkey Counties. Muriel Tillinghast, a graduate of Howard, initially a volunteer in the group Stokely Carmichael recruited from Washington, D.C., became a SNCC staff member before leaving orientation in Oxford and later our project director in Greenville. Pam Trotman, the other black girl I mention, had also just graduated from Howard. The two black guys from Harvard, volunteers Bob Wright and Louis Grant, impressed me with their reasoned, intelligent views of the civil rights movement. I was trying to fit their perspective in with what I had been studying at Cornell and was disappointed that they soon left Greenville to work full time in Issaquena County. I spent most of my time with the "two other [white] girls," Lyn Hamilton, from New Jersey, and Valerie Hogan, from Sacramento, California. We got along and were friendly but lost track of each other after the summer.

As a white girl, I did not expect to be assigned to live and work outside the city limits because it was more dangerous for women than for men to be working side by side with black residents when mixing the races was so offensive to white Mississippians. COFO sent Les Turner, a handsome black volunteer from Chicago, to nearby Leland as the project co-coordinator.[4] His initial efforts involved making contact with police officials, black ministers, store owners, and the local newspaper, among others. He concentrated on voter registration to bring applicants to Greenville for the Freedom Day scheduled for July 16. Morton Thomas, a tall, broad-shouldered, self-assured white volunteer from Harvard, hoped for a hundred applicants from the area of town where he was working, although he reported that "fear of job reprisals runs high. . . . Such fear is particularly strong among several City employees" to whom he had talked.[5] He had earlier received "a vote of confidence" when COFO sent him to Hollandale.[6] But he didn't stay because, as the incident summary reported on June 24, "Police, mayor tell summer volunteer he can't live in Negro section of town and register voters."[7] Louis Grant wanted Muriel Tillinghast to come to Issaquena County and had housing for four volunteers, but no one living in the county was willing to take in whites.[8]

I saw the definite difference between the staff and the volunteers. I knew I wasn't one of the former—the blacks who were more militant than the NAACP and than most, if not all, of the volunteers. I was just a volunteer, thinking I knew more than most of the other volunteers, but sensitive about listening and not acting as if I knew too much.

After the many SNCC fund-raising appeals I had received the previous year, I was not surprised to learn when we arrived that even though our project was one of the largest in one of the largest cities, it had no money. COFO in Jackson had made an allotment of only $50 for the offices in Greenville, and half of that had been spent within a week after I arrived. I did not hear about a budget on a project or state basis, and I had no idea what a fair allocation of scarce dollars would have been. The local staff answer was to "tax" each of the first volunteers $25. That quickly raised $200, which called for opening a bank account. The consensus of the group was that I would be the treasurer of the project funds.

Four of us—integrated—went to a bank downtown to open the account because there was no black bank on Nelson Street. In most places in Mississippi, I don't think a project would have placed its funds in a local white bank, but we were in Greenville. We were not supposed to aggravate race relations through any type of demonstration and did not expect that we would cause any trouble downtown.

We dealt with a surprisingly cordial man at the bank. I found it curious that he suggested we make payments on bank checks that would not show the name COFO. I understood that COFO in Mississippi that summer was as bad as being labeled Communist. White Mississippians were calling the volunteers "COFOs," a term of derision for all civil rights workers. The banker expressed his confidence in the organization and in us, saying he knew that it was a national organization. Actually, he was wrong; COFO was only a state organization, but it had members from national civil rights organizations and support from many people outside the South. I was careful not to correct him.

When money came in, it would go out for whatever need was then most pressing. I never encountered any problem with stealing or dishonesty. COFO spent the money received for legitimate purposes: primarily food, rent, and gas, but also office supplies. I asked my parents to contribute and to encourage their friends to do so as well via money orders by registered mail. SNCC paid staff members a salary of $9.64 a week ($10 less withholding) when it had funds, and the workers did not seem to have any of their own money. I allocated myself $10 a week so that I would spend no more than the staff. I had had $225 in savings transferred to my checking account for my summer living expenses, and I was confident that I had enough money but told my father I might need money for transportation home at the end of the summer.

I also asked for anything my parents could think of to donate for the Freedom House, which had two few sheets for the double bed and the three single beds. There were never enough forks and only one sharp knife. I suggested sheets, kitchen utensils, an iron, and even an ironing board. My mother responded and told me what she was sending. Pharis Harvey, the leader of our Tougaloo work camp, and his wife, Jane, had met my parents during the school year when Pharis was studying at nearby Drew University, and he offered to bring these things to me when they drove to Mississippi to visit Jane's family. Maybe the delivery was made when I was not around, but I have no memory of my parents' donations arriving at the Freedom House or seeing Pharis and Jane. I am confident, though, that Greenville or some other project received and used them.

On Monday, my first full day in the Freedom House, a white minister showed up to invite one of the white northern volunteers to speak to the all-white Greenville Ministry Alliance. I was surprised to see a local white man in our black part of town, but I realized that his appearance was an indication of what Greenville was like: "They're proud of their image, and if we don't bother them, they won't bother us," I wrote in a letter home. One of the black militants among us, with two others, spoke up to object to the invitation. They cornered the minister to ask him why he was inviting a white to speak. Why not one of the blacks? The minister didn't withdraw the invitation, but I didn't think he could defend himself. I was not about to volunteer to speak to his group, and no one else did either. He offended enough of us, me included, that no one was in a reconciling mood wanting to foster communication between the races. From the experience of my previous summer and knowing about the continuing civil rights struggles during the school year, I was sufficiently radicalized at the beginning of the summer to go along with this militancy by the black guys. Perhaps others were also, or perhaps they were intimidated by the militants among us and would not buck this peer pressure on the very first day of the project.

My isolation from the white community during the summer was nearly complete. After the trip to the bank, on a couple of occasions I talked to the police, all of whom were white but for three pioneers in Greenville who started on the Nelson Street beat on the weekends. Later in the summer a white cop stopped me when I was walking home and asked questions, seemingly curious about our work, wanting to know whether I was staying for the next month and where I was from. I answered him politely, as we had been trained, and felt it strange that my circumstances were so different from what Mississippi blacks endured. It was hard to believe that there was anything courageous about my going to Mississippi if the local police were so friendly.

The pervasive issue in those early days was the three missing civil rights workers in Neshoba County. All of us were eager for news and constantly discussed whatever we had heard. I talked with other volunteers about whether it would be safe traveling back to the office in Meridian late at night and thought that doing so was not wise in such a Klan-infested area of Mississippi. We shared a common concern because the event also brought out fears for our own safety.

I was disturbed that the NAACP leaders in Greenville seemed to be "Uncle Toms," although that is probably too harsh a term for the middle-class business and professional blacks who were active in civil rights. They were not selling out their fellow blacks but seemed to cooperate with rather than oppose the interests of the white establishment. I believed that they should be taking risks and moving more aggressively to organize and increase the political power of the black community in the city. But I was pleased with my assignment. I believed at the beginning that it had terrific potential. I thought surely the registrar in this reasonable, moderate place would register those who applied, and we just needed to encourage more residents to go to the courthouse. I didn't think people in Greenville were too satisfied to not want to register to vote. Besides adding more registered voters, as I had done in Greensboro the previous summer, I had another challenge. Opportunities for blacks in Greenville would be enhanced if we could develop new, energetic, forceful community leadership that could work around the NAACP.

Unexpectedly, all of the first arrivals in Greenville soon got caught up in doing exactly what we were not supposed to be doing. COFO had told us "absolutely no demonstrations." Although we might want to test the new Civil Rights Act of 1964 for compliance, the Summer Project volunteers were not to engage in mass demonstrations, protests, or sit-ins because direct action was likely to involve arrest and provoke violence. All the staff and volunteers' efforts were to be devoted to voter registration and Freedom Registration as well as to organizing for the MFDP Convention Challenge, teaching in Freedom Schools, planning activities in community centers, and other projects.

The MSU—the civil rights organization for high school students that was more militant than the NAACP youth councils—wanted to demonstrate in Greenville. After they heard about the missing civil rights workers in Neshoba County, they planned to protest the lack of federal protection by picketing the Federal Building on Main Street, which housed the federal judiciary, the post office, and several federal agencies. The discussions took place in the Freedom House, and the volunteers quickly got involved in considering what *we* should do. We remembered that John Doar at orientation had not guaranteed the safety of the volunteers, and we knew the importance of the demand for federal protection.

The MSU students did not appreciate COFO's reasons for not demonstrating and were determined to go ahead. Jesse Davis and Fred Anderson, two of the SNCC recruits assigned by COFO Jackson to Greenville for the summer, were outspoken black college students and good friends. They too wanted to demonstrate at the Federal Building. We all discussed plans for the demonstration and the possibility of arrest. Since COFO wanted to develop new local leadership, I felt we should go along with the young students and not frustrate them by opposing their initiative. If we didn't, they would wonder whether we could put our beliefs into action. As Barbara Mutnick, a Greenville volunteer, wrote anonymously in a letter, "If we don't support these kids in their demonstrations, we're not going to get the respect and cooperation we need from them."[9] Charlie Cobb, Muriel Tillinghast, and George Rowell, our first project director in Greenville, were not around for the discussions, and no one told us not to join the students' initiative.

Our opinions divided about the legality of a demonstration. Should we apply for a permit to picket? Should we wait for the permit before we went to the Federal Building? Should we proceed only in accordance with the terms of the permit? Should we demonstrate if we did not receive a permit? Our intellectual debate did not last long. Someone decided to give notice to the police of the plans and go ahead. I explained what happened in a letter home: "Division North and South; volunteers and staff. Fred just called, asked to speak to the police chief, was refused, so gave the message that there would be a demonstration in 15 minutes at the Federal Building, and got the police chief right away. He just said 'Take off' in a sarcastic tone." Discussion ended. The volunteers could not turn back, and, in a supportive mood, I went along to the Federal Building.

So there I was, on Thursday, June 25, in my first demonstration. I had gone to the huge March on Washington, but there I was one of many in the crowd and not facing the risk of being arrested. Now about forty people—the high school students led by Charles Turner, the MSU president; some SNCC staff and white volunteers; and Charles McLaurin, the Sunflower County project director, who brought over a group from Ruleville—walked in a long line around and around on the sidewalk in front of the building, singing freedom songs. We were out in the hot sun for an hour and a half, from 11:30 a.m. to 1:00 p.m. The police were there, and local residents, most of them white, took a good look at this new curiosity as they went about their business in and out of the Federal Building. I wrote: "It was blazing hot, and the whole time we wondered about arrest. Four cops were there watching us besides all the people who came into the post office. We had a plan if they told us to move on, we would leave but two would go to jail. But there's work to be done, and so no one wants to be arrested."

As it turned out, nothing dramatic happened: no shouting, hostility, police brutality, or arrests.[10] My parents, upset when they heard about our demonstration, called me, and I explained why I was out there and reassured them that everything was okay.

Larry Benton, a white volunteer, as spokesman for the project, commented on COFO's reaction to the demonstration for the *Delta Dem-*

MSU and COFO demonstration at the Federal Building, Greenville, June 25, 1964. Illustration by Tracy Sugarman in Tracy Sugarman, *We Had Sneakers, They Had Guns: The Kids Who Fought for Civil Rights in Mississippi* (Syracuse, N.Y.: Syracuse University Press, 2009), illustration 53; courtesy of the Archives and Records Services Division, Mississippi Department of Archives and History.

ocrat-Times: there was no official relationship between COFO and the MSU, and COFO was planning no further demonstrations. He explained: "We do not believe it is our place to come into a town and try to control the Negroes, to tell them exactly how they must act in the civil rights drive."[11]

Bob Moses, who was conducting orientation in Oxford, heard about our activity and told the second wave of volunteers that "the Greenville demonstration was a rumor; it was against COFO policy and couldn't possibly have happened," as I wrote to my parents on June 28. Then he called and checked with somebody from SNCC to find out what was going on and why. Bob advised against the Summer Project volunteers' participation in any further demonstrations.

The more militant Fred and Jesse wanted to continue the protests. They criticized Moses for being too conservative, even saying that he was "on his way out of the movement." I wrote in a July 5 letter to my parents that they wanted to be independent of "Jackson and Bob Moses, who don't know anything about this community." Fred and Jesse's next goal was to test the ban on whites going to the segregated black public swimming pool. I knew that COFO headquarters in Jackson would be opposed, and I didn't think the volunteers should get involved. Alternatively, I thought we could ask COFO for approval, and if it was received, more demonstrating would be okay. In any event, the MSU planned another demonstration for July 4, to be followed by a sit-in, but I didn't get involved that time. The high school students' talk of violent as well as nonviolent demonstrations upset me. Hearing how angry and militant they were, I concluded that in Mississippi you could not talk about reconciliation: "You talk about running and when you're going to be violent," I wrote in a letter home. "Certainly here [nonviolence is] only a tactic—there's no talk about *loving* the white man."

Stokely Carmichael, our twenty-two-year-old district director, also disapproved of our demonstration. Born in Trinidad, a graduate of Bronx High School of Science, and a 1964 Howard graduate who had spent his three summers in college on the Freedom Rides and later working with SNCC in Mississippi, Stokely was tall, handsome, charismatic, funny, and smart. He was living in Greenwood but doing a great deal of traveling because of his responsibility to supervise all the projects in the Second Congressional District. When he came to Greenville, we gathered around, and as Barbara Mutnick said, "It was always such a big deal when Stokely came to town."[12] He was so entertaining and full of talk. He explained his disapproval of demonstrations: "About demonstrations," I wrote in a letter home, "Stokely thinks it's ridiculous to get beaten for a lunch counter or spend 60 days in Parchman [Penitentiary]. He went through all that to get to the point where he is now, but doesn't feel other kids have to because he can tell them about it."

I contrasted Stokely's approach to dealing with the tensions we felt in Mississippi with Bob's approach: "Moses and Stokely are two opposite types of people: Bob takes it all inside and gets very depressed—and Stokely laughs. But he was saying last night it worried him because he laughs at anything—a guy tells him he's been beaten and he says ha, ha, ha. We were discussing which type continues to function better—and had no answer."

Stokely was remarkable in his willingness to sit and talk to us. Of course, he had a captive audience, which he enjoyed, but he was patient and informative and answered many naive questions from volunteers. He respected the whites who had joined SNCC. In his book *Ready for Revolution*, he writes:

> Upon joining us, those comrades stopped being "white" in most conventional American terms, except in the most superficial physical sense of the word. . . .
>
> [T]hey were unusually conscientious and socially aware young people . . . who had no problem working happily in a black organization with black leadership and that worked mostly in rural black communities at considerable risk. That alone would separate them from the general run of their white countrymen—then and now—and entitles them to our respect. . . .
>
> When they experienced the full force of racist hostility from Southern white politicians, police, and public opinion, compounded by the indifference or paralysis of the national political establishment, whatever class and color privileges they might have taken for granted were immediately suspended. At moments of confrontation they were at as great a risk as any of us.[13]

Stokely also respected and understood white summer volunteers. He called us "essentially a group of strangers," many of whom had never really been around black people in any significant way, but we were familiar to *him* because we were like his high school classmates at Bronx Science.

Stokely has been unfairly criticized for what he said about the position of women. Sara Evans claims in her book *Personal Politics,* about the origins of the women's movement, that he was rebutting the pioneering paper on women in the civil rights movement when he said, "The position of women in SNCC is prone!"[14] After a day of intense, charged SNCC meetings in Waveland, Mississippi, in November 1964, Stokely had included this line in an irreverent, politically incorrect, comic monologue to fellow SNCC staff drinking wine out on a dock at the Waveland retreat center.[15] He had roared with laughter, poking fun at his own attitudes, causing hilarity in his audience. The comment can only be understood in this context; Mary King, who was present when he made the comment, attests in her memoir *Freedom Song* that "he was one of the most responsive men" at the time that paper on women in the movement was circulated.[16] As Joyce Ladner has pointed out, the problem was that "the context was missing, the texture of the times was missing."[17] Ekwueme Michael Thelwell, who was also present, attested to the accuracy of Mary's account, thus adding to the historical record when Stokely would merely acknowledge that he said it.[18]

The arrival of the Freedom School teachers after a week brought new excitement. Our numbers in the state increased to about five hundred college-age summer volunteers.[19] I found myself being scornful of the eleven "well dressed white girls" who came to Greenville because they seemed just too naive about the politics of the movement. Three of them went to an NAACP meeting and came back impressed by the old people singing "We Shall Overcome"; they thought the NAACP members were ready to move. I was doubtful, unable to imagine an NAACP group in Mississippi doing anything militant or constructive. I saw the middle-class members of the NAACP in Greenville as the bourgeois leadership we would need to work around as we activated new leadership at the grassroots level among federal workers, laborers, domestics, retirees, and former sharecroppers and farmers who had come to the city for better economic opportunities. Only twenty people attended that local NAACP meeting, an unimpressive turnout in my mind then. I summed up my attitude about the NAACP in a letter: "They're not ready for anything, and most of us realize that's a crying shame. This group is trying to stop the militancy but it can't be done once you understand and *feel* what's going on. Moreover, the NAACP was simply a 'nasty word' to the SNCC activists and me. In Jackson the NAACP had called and 'got all the housing cut out from the COFO people.' They didn't want 'no disturbing.'"

I was not patient with my fellow volunteers, as others had been with me, ignoring the fact that they had not had the benefit of exposure to conditions in Mississippi that I had the previous summer. I felt superior but obviously should have been more accepting and understanding. I considered myself almost as militant as Fred, Jesse, and the high school students, though I did not go along with any possibility of violence. They were looking at racism and discrimination in their local situation without taking into consideration the state or national reaction to demonstrations, and I wanted to understand their point of view. I wished the other white volunteers, in particular the newly arrived Freedom School teachers, could realize why SNCC and the MSU were so militant. I wrote about how different the volunteers were: "Somehow I wish more could realize this. The F.S. teachers can't and they're suffering for it—feeling very left out and hurt. And we're laughing at them—for their naiveté. Of course, it's wrong. One rationale is—in the tension the emotions, the violence comes out among the group rather than outside it."

I was making fun of other volunteers and tried to excuse my disrespect by saying it came from the tension created by our fear in Mississippi. We didn't *know* whether we were in danger and always felt uncertain about how white Mississippians would treat us. If there was nothing else to absorb our feelings, we turned on one another.

When I could turn my attention to work, I was less involved with what was going on for other volunteers. I wrote home on August 7: "I think we've been honest, but when the other side quote unquote has a meeting you only hear about through rumors in which they just luckily lose the vote 8–6 to put an ad in the paper saying that COFO is Communist . . . , there's something you must work against."

White Mississippians and local journalists frequently used the Communist label to discredit our work. Bob Moses had faced this Red baiting and was firm during orientation that we should not be doing any Red baiting ourselves. I learned later about socialist literature lying around the Freedom House, but none of us qualified as dangerous radicals or Communists. I believed in COFO—it was certainly not Communist—and all that we were trying to do.

My parents sent letters to the Freedom House address, and by using only that address or, later in the summer, our office address, we did not disclose information about local black families with whom we stayed. My father wrote after our first phone conversation and after he had received my first letter explaining my set-up in Greenville: "People ask me if we aren't worried about you, and of course I have to admit that we'll be glad when the summer is over. Then they say, 'Why don't you get her to come back?' My answer is to ask just how you go about doing that, even if I wanted to. I know how you would react to such a suggestion and I'm proud of your courage and determination. At the same time I hope you won't take any unnecessary chances."

I appreciated his confidence in me, and I did not want to let him down. But about my "courage," I was thinking, having landed in the moderate and tolerant city of Greenville, that what I was doing did not take much bravery. I was more determined—or stubborn—than courageous. I had made the decision by the end of the previous summer to work in civil rights in Mississippi, and this was just something I had to do. He concluded his letter with "Good luck, and take care of yourself. We're with you!" My mother was also supportive. She told a local reporter that the family had talked over my plans for Mississippi and that I had "never wavered about going"; I had "real convictions about this project."[20]

During the national Lutheran Church of America convention in Pittsburgh, my father got involved with a report on race relations. He wrote to me on July 7 that, if necessary, he planned to take the floor to oppose a statement approving civil disobedience. He said, "Before you flip," he had to explain that he was worried that someone would use it to justify disobedience to the Civil Rights Act, which had just passed on July 2, 1964. In a later letter, he wrote that after he made his "little speech," about a dozen amendments were offered, and the subject was thoroughly confused. He then worked for three late-night hours with a small committee to come up with a revised statement that the convention adopted. He said, "They really listened to me after I told them you were in Mississippi."

I was enormously proud of my father for speaking up on behalf of civil rights at a time when the issue was so controversial. He was a born conservative, but because of the church and his exposure to colleagues in the United Negro College Fund, he thoughtfully was changing his views. I felt my mother was always more inclined, with her background as a social worker, to empathize with and understand the oppression that I saw in Mississippi. My pastor advised me in a letter to appreciate my father, who had a great impact on the Lutheran Church convention. He called my father's "short speech from the floor of the convention one of the real highlights of the whole affair."[21]

My parents continued to support my volunteer work in Mississippi through the summer but told me about the difficulties I caused them. Many in the North opposed the civil rights movement or considered volunteers joining the Summer Project in Mississippi unwise because the place was so dangerous or because we were unduly interfering with local customs. Most of the people my parents knew in their Republican suburban town were appalled that my parents had let me go and did not talk to them about the civil rights news, while my parents "put up a brave front." Apparently, my parents had to live constantly on the defensive. I can imagine how low key and diplomatic they were, not wanting to stir up controversy if they could avoid it. My mother believed the woman who lived next door was a bigot and feared she would ask about me. When she saw her, she was relieved that the subject did not come up because she "just couldn't take it if it had." Mother continued to be a good neighbor but never offered any information about me that would open up an unpleasant discussion. She had an ally in Mrs. Schieffelin, whose daughter Nancy was also a volunteer in Greenville, someone she could talk to without risking a political confrontation. When the Schieffelins left town for a long summer vacation, the Parents' Emergency Committee offered a substitute camaraderie. COFO had organized this network of parents to support the project goals and provide opportunities for meeting parents of other volunteers. I think these activities helped my parents' morale, worried as they were about my safety. On August 2, 1964, the committee solicited contributions in the amount of $150 for the purchase of two-way radios for safe communication when help was needed by someone out in the field. A careful man, my father deliberated about the request and consulted with others before sending in his contribution.

The first weeks of the project were dominated by national news of the tragedy of the three missing civil rights workers. We heard the report that Mickey Schwerner's station wagon was found burned on Tuesday afternoon soon after they had gone missing on Sunday. Amid speculation about what had happened, we thought more people would now be prepared to expect that Chaney, Goodman, and Schwerner were murdered.

Reporters who did not stay in Oxford for the second week of orientation for the Freedom School teachers or go to Meridian, the CORE project site, or to Philadelphia, the county seat of Neshoba County, for stories about the three missing civil rights workers checked on specific projects. Ours was an ideal place to start—relatively safe, with convenient access from Memphis and white-designated motels for lodging—a place to observe a typical project and interview local people, staff, and summer volunteers. And by June 28, our place was crawling with both reporters and photographers.

Two reporters from the *New York Times* impressed me the most. Claude Sitton had been covering civil rights in the South for the *Times* since the Little Rock school desegregation in 1957. An experienced journalist and an enlightened southerner, he was responsible for writing many of the *Times* stories about the Mississippi Summer Project. He had the background to know what was going on and gave fair and objective accounts of what we were trying to do. I met David Halberstam, another *Times* reporter, when he was in Greenville. He started his career in the small town of West Point, Mississippi, and in 1959 lived in Nashville, Tennessee, reporting on the beginnings of the student sit-in movement, which was the basis of his later book *The Children*. He took a serious interest in the volunteers and put a human touch to his stories. Neither he nor any other reporter ever interviewed me, and I might not have been very articulate if I had been. A natural question was why we had volunteered. I knew that I was committed to working to get black Mississippians the freedom that all Americans should be enjoying.

A man named Bern Keating, a local freelance writer and photographer, spent some days with us and impressed me less than the *Times* men had. He also created some problems for the project by attempting to photograph the bedroom at the Freedom House, which I thought was outrageous. That could have brought us bad publicity—I could imagine pictures in the newspaper of unmade beds, gray sheets, and ratty bedspreads as well as suggestions of illicit, interracial sex. Of course, sex in the South—the idea of a relationship or, indeed, any contact between a black man and a white woman—was the big taboo. Segregationists firmly held the belief that miscegenation—"race mixing"—would lead to the demise of the white race and desecrate the southern way of life. Disgusted, we said no to Mr. Keating—he could not take any photos in the bedroom. So the man left and claimed that we were objecting because we didn't trust him. He did not have the credentials of the *Times* reporters, and we were suspicious. I learned not to trust reporters if I didn't know their point of view. Mr. Keating was right; we didn't trust *him*.

Without our knowing how it happened, a reporter managed to find out our names and figure out the colleges we attended and our home states, and we heard that there would be an article about us in the *New York Times Sunday Magazine*. The press was looking "for the ideal naïve Northern middle-class white girl,"[22] and thought they had found me for the *New York Times*. I was surprised to see my picture, with a short article by none other than Bern Keating about the Mississippi Summer Project. Maybe I was doing something important and special. The *Times*, however, made a mistake that annoyed me. The caption under my photo was "Lisa Anderson, California, Cornell," instead of New Jersey.[23] I was not aware that any pictures were being taken and would not have allowed the photograph if I had known. Keating got me in my cute little white sleeveless blouse, sitting on the floor, eyes cast up in rapt attention. Looking naive? Young? Idealistic?

I was not aware then how offensive this publicity about the volunteers was to the Mississippi black staff. I knew that murders of black civil rights workers in Mississippi, with the exception of the Emmett Till killing, had received little attention in the press, but I was unable to relate that omission to the treatment the press gave the white summer volunteers, whom they interviewed and featured without giving recognition and respect to the black staff. It was the black staff that had more significant stories—they had, after all, risked their lives—but the mainstream white media were not interested.

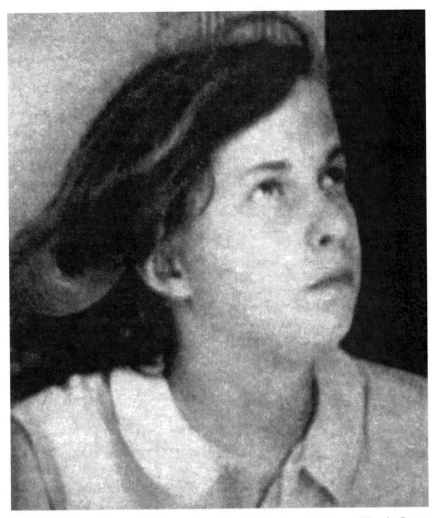

In the Freedom House in Greenville, June 1964. Bern Keating, "Youth Corps in Mississippi," *New York Times Sunday Magazine*, July 5, 1964. Copy in Todd Collection.

Unfortunately, I was oblivious to the feelings of resentment among my black colleagues, who were always polite, if somewhat aloof from us. They spent hours talking to us that first week of the summer and convinced me how vitally important matters of civil rights were and that their opinions were worth hearing. I was not skeptical about what was being said, with the exception of the mention of violent demonstrations, and did not find my own views challenged.

I spent less time in the Freedom House once I got settled in a place to live—which didn't happen automatically. The planned housing for us fell through, and I stayed the first night on the bare floor of the Freedom House, my only option. In a new territory, dependent on others, without transportation, and with little money, I would not just take off for a motel. Remembering the friendly folks we met near Canton the previous summer, I was confident that Charlie would take care of us and didn't worry about where I would be living.

As it turned out, blacks, some very poor, generously invited the volunteers to share their homes despite the risk to themselves and their families for this involvement in the movement. With this arrangement, the volunteers could see at close hand how dignified, strong, spiritual, and hopeful the local people were. But fear was everywhere at the beginning of the summer because no one knew what might happen. After a family decided to help with housing, any reason or no reason could cause a change of mind. More than once a host asked a volunteer to leave because of threats, actual or feared. The blacks who had a guaranteed or more secure source of income from a farm they owned, a small business, federal employment, or federal support payments were more likely to share their houses. Jobs could be lost, but Social Security, disability payments, and veterans' pensions would not be cut off.

By my second day, Valerie, Lyn, and I got a place. It was a typical small, one-story, rundown house, a carbon copy of the Freedom House. Families frequently placed beds in the living room or dining room of these small homes to accommodate a large number of their children or adults who moved back or never left home. More space for sleeping might be available on a back porch. I reassured my parents that I was settled, and the place would be just fine: "Tonight and for as long as she'll have us[,] the three white girls here now . . . will be staying across the street in the dining room and [on the] living room couch of a widow. I don't mind the conditions because she has a bathtub and it's convenient."

The bathtub was the special part. I was anxious to get into a tub of cold water the evening we arrived. By the time I had water covering the bottom of the tub, the elderly, wizened widow yelled through the door, "Don't use too much water." That was the end of my dreams of a luxurious cool bath. But I was able to get clean, and that was satisfactory before a good night's sleep in a bed. In less than a week, however, the worried woman no longer wanted us in her house.

Valerie, Lyn, and I then moved to another widow's house in the South End near the Freedom House. I settled in there for about a month. Mrs. Lola Hardin, sixty-four years old, had a warm personality and welcoming attitude. She had come to Greenville from Crystal Springs, Mississippi, in 1918 after not being able to make a living farming. One daughter, Betty Dean, was living with her, and another daughter was a widow with four children, a new $9,000 house, and a job as a doctor's assistant. We were concerned about the daughter at home and even more concerned about the second daughter with financial responsibilities.

Mrs. Hardin said she would be okay because she had $100 of monthly support in veterans and Social Security payments. But she was worried about her coming light and water bills with more people living in her house. We could have and perhaps we were supposed to pay rent, but after making an offer to supplement her income, I don't think we ever did. She was industrious, picking up and delivering cleaning for which she received half the bill. In a letter home, I admiringly called her "a hustler." I was comparing her to my maternal grandmother in Hibbing, Minnesota, who took in washing to support her six children after she was widowed.

The three of us were comfortable in the front part of this big house while the family slept on the back porch. Mrs. Hardin would give us some meals, which were welcome when she offered, but we did not help ourselves. I felt very much at home with this great woman and liked the fact that she spoke her mind. She told me she was a registered voter but later asked me to teach her at home how to register to vote. When she could be honest with us, I felt we had gained her trust. I enjoyed all the time I could spend with Mrs. Hardin, listening to her and receiving her care. Knowing her was a highlight of my summer as she put me at ease—I was in the black community, not respected and deferred to as a white person in the segregated South, but an equal. When I was in her home, I felt accepted without regard to my race, sex, looks, or status as a privileged, middle-class college graduate. I gained a sense of personal freedom and self-confidence—as in the Beloved Community, the ideal, yet realistically achievable state of living in harmony where racial, class, gender, and age differences are of no significance—that carried me through the rest of the summer.

I also felt accepted in church. Knowing the importance of religion in the lives of the southern blacks we would work with, SNCC project recruiters, interviewing all prospective volunteers—Jewish or Gentile, Protestant or Catholic, faithful, agnostic, or atheistic—asked them if they would be willing to go to church regardless of their individual orientation to religion. The black community would want them to participate in church life. I knew a little about these worship services from the previous summer and a visit to a black church one Sunday at home in Summit. I knew I would enjoy church in Greenville. In Jackson, Mississippi, I had loved the music, the choir, the rousing singing of the congregation, and the hymns that were similar to spirituals, despite the heat and humidity.

In 1964, I had similar experiences. Inside a small wooden church with the windows wide open, we resorted to the standard cardboard fans advertising a funeral home found in every pew to augment only a slight, hot breeze. The rhythm in the preacher's words elicited an "amen" or "tha's right" or "yessuh" from the congregation that would begin quietly, but as the preacher became more involved in his feeling and his words, he would raise his voice while he also quickened the cadence of his speech. Then the replies from the people got louder. The worshipers might stand and raise their arms and nearly taking on dance steps, could get more and more excited in their religious fervor. I found these services awesome, depending on the talent the preacher had for inspiring his people. I treated the black church with reverence as a place where I too could worship, even though my traditions in the staid, liturgical Lutheran Church were very different. I shared in the spirit of freedom and joy.

I was disappointed and saddened when I heard from a boy in the neighborhood that the "Uncle Toms" were ready to run Mrs. Hardin out of the church because she showed up with the three of us—white girls. I couldn't understand why anyone would want to do that and felt badly that our presence had that effect on a woman who just wanted to go to church.

The only problem with living at Mrs. Hardin's was that it was some distance away from the voter registration office on Nelson Street. I usually walked, arriving hot and sweaty in about twenty minutes. I could rarely get a ride because the project had very few cars, and they were supposed to be used for getting outside the city to the surrounding area, the whole of Washington County and the two additional counties, Sharkey and Issaquena. I knew that I could get a free ride in a taxi if the driver were black, but I rarely asked. I eventually moved out of Mrs. Hardin's house for the convenience of living closer to the office; she didn't ask us to leave.

My housing for the rest of the summer was with Mr. and Mrs. Jerry Britton, a black middle-class couple probably in their fifties, whom I respected as dignified professionals. The Brittons lived in a big, brick, air-conditioned house with a large yard: two floors, with a living room, dining room, bedroom, and a sitting room next to a big, open, modern kitchen on the first floor. The three of us—Valerie, Lyn, and I—were still together: I was sharing a bedroom downstairs with Valerie, and Lyn had a room on the second floor. The Brittons owned a drugstore not far from the house where they both worked. Mr. Britton was an authority figure in the household when he appeared, but we saw little of him and only then conversed in superficial pleasantries.

The Brittons were generous about our run of the house. Mrs. Britton cooked for us sometimes and let us poke around the refrigerator at any time of night or day for what we could find that had appeal, which was wonderful when we came in from the heat, tired and hungry. She said in a 1977 interview that she was not afraid for herself or the house in terms of police brutality, but she worried about the volunteers on their way coming home. She thought we were "a very intelligent bunch," that none of us was "riffraff," and that we were interested in the cause, not just in getting away from home.[24] The Brittons offered us everything for free, including washing facilities. That was great because with the heat and the dusty streets and yards I traveled it was a constant chore to keep my clothes clean and to iron the cotton blouses I wore.

Older all-white teachers from New York City who had academic expertise for the Freedom Schools also stayed at the Brittons' for about four weeks. They arrived in Greenville in late July and had not gone through the orientation we had had in Oxford. There were three of them—two women, Norma Becker and another, and one man, Al Schwartz. They rented a 1964 Ford, and I wondered how they could have that kind of money as volunteers. They had rooms on the second floor and seemed to appreciate their air-conditioned accommodations.

The word soon went out about how nice our place was, and other volunteers began coming to eat and sit or stand around talking in the early evenings as the house became a substitute Freedom House. The real one was too far away in the South End to go to after a long day of work. I felt we had run the Brittons out of their sitting room and kitchen, but I didn't want to and couldn't stop anybody from coming over. Seven or eight living in the house seemed a burden on our hosts. I felt I belonged there, doing the political work of a voter registration volunteer out of the nearby office. I wanted Lyn, who left temporarily to go to her grandmother's funeral, to be able to return rather than be reassigned. Peggy Kerr, another white volunteer, had come when the teachers were there. When she arrived crying, upset by the senile woman she was staying with, I was sympathetic with Peggy and wanted her to stay. On behalf of the Brittons, in my own mind, the crowding led me to decide that all the teachers should leave. They could move to a motel.

The New York teachers, who were too new and too sure of themselves for my liking, offended me. I resented their thinking they knew *anything* about the black community in Greenville, where we then felt so comfortable. I perceived that they would *require* air-conditioned housing and be unable to live with a poorer family in a small, hot, airless black home. I didn't like them, and I was not generous to them about sharing mealtimes and discussing the movement. They probably thought I was too young to think I knew so much. Here in the midst of harmonious black and white race relations, where I was so devoted to blacks, it occurred to me that maybe I was prejudiced. I raised the possibility with my parents in a letter home: "We're also having trouble getting along with such different and definite people—is it prejudice? The three are New York Jews. One girl is married. Al's friendly and humorous, but I don't like the humor."

I wrote *we*, but it was my trouble, not anyone else's. I thought my negative reaction was to the fact that they were Jewish rather than to them individually, a reaction that bothered me. I do not attribute prejudice to my fellow white volunteers, and the Brittons treated the teachers the same as they treated all the rest of us. I wrote about my feelings, but I don't think I displayed any outward hostility, and I never actually tried to have them moved out of the house. I had been seeking new ways of living together, but my feelings in this instance represented old prejudices and were nothing like those wished for the Beloved Community.

I will never forget one thing Mrs. Britton said. She would often lie on the couch downstairs in the sitting room with a wet washcloth on her forehead, advising more than once, "Don't ever get these hot flashes." Under the circumstances, she was very patient with all of us invading her cool, air-conditioned home, but one day in August she finally reached her limit. Mr. Britton's foot was giving him a problem, and Mrs. Britton had just had too much. While we were at work, she moved our stuff out of the downstairs bedroom. What a surprise for Valerie and me. Mrs. Britton had decided we would no longer occupy the downstairs bedroom and made the switch without a word to us. One of us was going to be evicting Al from the couch in the second-floor room where he had slept, which probably gave me some pleasure. The teachers were leaving soon, and things would be improving for me and, with fewer folks around, the Brittons. Everything did eventually calm down.

When I left the Brittons' house at the end of my summer, I was not sad to be leaving the state because I was half planning to return for a year instead of going to law school and did not think about missing Mrs. Britton. I did not form the personal, long-lasting ties with the people I knew best in Greenville, as some young volunteers did in other communities. I liked Mrs. Britton very much but had a more distant relationship with her than with Mrs. Hardin. In August, busier at work and more comfortable getting around Greenville, I was looking less to the family that was housing us to meet the needs I had for company. Mrs. Britton seemed more concerned about her own change of life and had less concern about us, knowing we could take care of ourselves. She was generous and kind in giving us what we needed: a comfortable place to sleep and good food to eat.

Meanwhile, as the summer wore on, we hung out where we stayed or where we worked and felt more and more comfortable in the black community. Tracy Sugarman, the Connecticut writer and illustrator who volunteered in Ruleville, described this feeling in his book *Stranger at the Gates:*

> I studied the youngsters. . . . A new intensity, a kind of honed-down quality, was evident in their eyes as they looked about them. . . . [I saw] a growing sense of self and of purpose which was at once respectful and comfortable. The Negroes were beginning to see the students as people they knew and trusted. The students' camaraderie with the Negroes was as easy as it was inevitable. Cut off from the white world they knew, they were finding comfort and warmth within the Negro community. The symbolic identification with the aspirations of the Negro that had brought these youngsters to Mississippi was now being made real by a sharing of fears and disappointments, and the chastening effects of day-by-day life.[25]

We had no rent, no phone costs, and nothing to buy. We worried only about food. As a result, the volunteers depended on local people not only for housing, but also for meals.

When we were not provided for by our hosts, we were on our own and usually ate in two local cafés near the office on Nelson Street. A group would find a booth or a table for a meal, maybe the one full meal of the day—not right at lunchtime or at dinnertime, but sometime in between. At one of the cafés, the daily special, some sort of meat (preferably pork chops for me), a green vegetable, potatoes or rice, and a dinner roll, cost sixty-seven cents. I preferred the full meal but often chose to eat a hamburger, which was only twenty-six cents. When we wanted a beer, we put our coins on the table to see if there was enough for a seventy-five-cent quart of beer that we all could share. I was always there in an integrated group, and locals in the café, strangers to us, knew who we were and sometimes paid for our meals. There was a jukebox, and of course we wanted to hear the music but would not waste our money there. Other customers would, and we would make sure they knew how grateful we were, hoping that they would keep feeding the box. I was an addicted smoker then and spent thirty cents a day for a pack of Salems, ridiculous as that is. I had no other extravagances or even discretionary expenses—no clothes to buy or movies to see. I wouldn't buy a candy bar for ten cents because I couldn't afford it.

I didn't mind being poor, an utterly different experience for a middle-class kid who grew up with an allowance and always had some money to spend. But I did not go hungry, and somehow there was always enough. Our new friends in the community were looking out for us in Greenville, as they did elsewhere. When I appealed for funds from my family, it was not for me, but for supplies for the project.

As for interracial sex on the project, I was generally unaware of whatever went on. Eager to work on the project, I did not intend to date, although I did do some gossiping about the little I knew. I was shocked that one of our volunteers, about my age, left Greenville to return to Illinois with a tall, handsome black volunteer. We knew she was pregnant, although I never heard whether she had the baby, but at that time there was no other legal alternative.

I had no romantic interest in the black guys on the project and did not seek attention from them, contrary to what Dr. Alvin Poussaint, a black Harvard psychiatrist who volunteered in Mississippi in 1965, published in a professional article describing white women's "perverse sexual interest in Negro men."[26] My interest was never that but was only a healthy curiosity as to whether dating blacks would be different. And I had already explored that choice in the freer environment in North Carolina the previous summer. Now I wanted just to get to know people and make whatever contribution I could.

Dr. Poussaint's paper, "The Stresses of the White Female Worker in the Civil Rights Movement in the South," presented to the American Psychiatric Association in 1966, received national attention at the time when it was cited in an article entitled "'African Queen' Complex" and published in *Newsweek*. The article defined the complex as the white worker "see[ing] herself—consciously or unconsciously—as a beautiful, intelligent white woman leading the oppressed black man to freedom."[27] My picture, fortunately without identification, talking to potential voter registrants was included in the *Newsweek* article. Dr. Poussaint claimed that white female civil rights workers suffered anxiety initially as we adjusted to living with poor black families and were treated as special, with obsequious treatment by black residents, publicity in the mass media, and resentment by the black staff because we, not they, were considered brave and courageous. He called us "hung-up chicks," who had to deal with the feelings aroused by attention from black men. Dr. Poussaint continued provocatively, proposing that a "white African Queen complex" resulted from the white female civil rights workers being a target of black anger, to which we reacted with condescension and patronage of black people, guilt, and insufficient strength to survive emotionally. I don't know whether this analysis holds true for any of the other white female volunteers, but the anxiety, special treatment, resentment, guilt, and emotional weakness he described sounded foreign to me and my experience.

Something that happened on the first day of the project confirmed my intention not to date. Most of the new volunteers, myself included, had to sleep in the Freedom House that day, where space was limited. When I woke up, in my clothes, on the floor, one of the black guys was lying on top of me. I didn't wake anyone up with a scream but rolled the guy off me as fast as I could, sat up, and stared him away. I was appalled that he would be so bold.

When another black guy tried to flatter me with his attention, I did not encourage him. I wrote home that although I wasn't accepted at first, I had gotten through to one of the blacks on staff, and another guy had his arm around me that night. My mother, the psychiatric social worker, raised some interesting questions in her reply: "[D]id he understand what that meant to you? (I, of course, assume you accepted it as a gesture of friendship.) Does he understand northern girls? (a Southern girl couldn't do this, could she?) Can you differentiate between Northern and Southern girls? Remember what I told you about [N]egroes meeting mixed-up white girls who *need* attention from [N]egro men because of their personal emotional problems. Remember '*Native Son*'?" My mother knew that I would take the gesture as nothing more than an expression of friendship.

I was never the flighty girl who would get carried away by a black guy expressing interest in what at the time I called "dating" me. I had some self-confidence and would not fall for a guy just because he might be considered intriguing and exotic in a narrow white world. I think both my mother and I felt that some girls could be so desperate for a boy's attention that they might respond positively to anyone. But we weren't totally naive. I'm sure we considered that the young man's putting his arm around me may have been equivalent to a proposition, that he wanted to have sex with me. Since I believed that would be a proposition not to me in particular, not to me selected out among many girls for who I was, but to any young white volunteer on the project, it was better to consider what happened as what she termed "a gesture of friendship."

But with so much ahead for the volunteers to do, I was just not interested. And because of my cool detachment or whatever I projected as such, no one approached me later. I knew that it would be extremely dangerous for a black to be seen with a white woman in any circumstance that could be construed as sexually suggestive. If a black project staff member were found necking with a white girl in a car in a park or a quiet street in the black community, that guy would likely be hauled out of his car, beaten, kidnapped, and in severe danger of being lynched. No rational black civil rights worker would take that risk. But maybe in my imagining, the girl in need of protection had to be a southern white belle and not a female summer volunteer, who was considered the equivalent of white trash. The fury would nevertheless likely descend on the black man, with the white girl left to fend for herself and find her way home, wherever that might be in an unfamiliar town.

I preferred being in the black community, learning from voices new to me and discovering the joy in casual conversation and laughter because we knew that the color of our skin was not something that needed to separate us. I wanted to be with and get to know local black residents. North Carolina had been such a happy experience for me the previous summer as I got to know really sharp, lively local black kids, all in college and my age, who had a sense of humor that brought us closer together. I hoped for at least some of the same feelings on this project.

Volunteers knew the stories of arrests, police brutality, beatings, shootings, firebombs, and even cold-blooded daylight murders and feared that the violence would continue during the summer. COFO used the SNCC system that Julian Bond and Mary King had developed to record and publicize what happened. The volunteer in communications in each project reported arrests and other serious events to COFO in Jackson. In Greenville, white volunteer John Sawyer, from Southern Illinois University, had this responsibility. Mary King explains in her memoir *Freedom Song* how she "asked for information: What? Where? When? Who? How?" and how she and Julian Bond immediately used the details to telephone the news media to place the stories. They used the press this way to let local authorities know they were under scrutiny and to inform the rest of the country. Thus, the problem of racial injustice became a national rather than a regional one. She emphasized how important this function was to the safety of the civil rights workers: "Whatever small protection we had came through news reports that brought our actions to the attention of the nation and broke the cover of secrecy. So little has been written about the civil rights movement from the inside that it is fair to say that, with the exception of those involved at the time, no one knows how important the effective use of the news media was to our safety, and even our lives."[28]

Based on the project reports, COFO prepared the twenty-six-page "Running Summary of Incidents," which provides evidence of the grave risks taken during the summer: 4 project workers killed, 37 black churches bombed or burned, 30 black homes or businesses bombed or burned, 80 workers beaten, and 1,000 people arrested for their civil rights work.[29]

After I was accepted for the project, I must have been afraid about going to Mississippi, but I was able to forget about being in personal danger when I was assigned to Greenville. The COFO report includes only one incident in Greenville and no arrests. But on the night of July 2, 1964, my casual attitude disappeared in a frightening moment. Other white summer volunteers have recorded accounts of surviving physical abuse, threats, and mistreatment by the police and in the jails, but those things were not part of my experience. I feel fortunate that the closest I came to violence was limited to events on one single night.

We were at the VFW. Before this summer, I had thought of the VFW as only a social organization for older veterans who had seen action in the world wars. I didn't know that it was also engaged in community service. The VFW in Greenville invited us to a Friday night dance that would be a benefit for the COFO project. We questioned whether we wanted to go and whether we *should* go.

Typical college students would love to go to a party, but we were not typical in Mississippi. The party was at the black VFW. If there was a white VFW somewhere in town, it excluded blacks and forced them to form their own organization. The VFW hall, where the dance was held, was outside the city limits on a lonely country road. As both blacks and whites on the project, we would go together by car, and the risk to our safety was always high in traveling at night. White men looking for excitement might identify our car, give us chase, and do some shooting with their high-powered rifles, or if they stopped us, they might beat us or kidnap us or worse. Orientation at Oxford included the story of the shooting of Jimmie Travis, and we thought that could happen to us. Because we were committed to nonviolence, we thought of what we had learned.

We debated for a long time whether to go to the dance. The VFW was doing something for us, and my view was that we should be part of the community and show up to indicate our appreciation. Only a handful of other volunteers went with me, all fitting in one car.

We left the city limits in the early evening, not knowing what to expect, but full of anticipation. There was an admission of seventy-five cents that each of us planned to pay. I have no idea how much the VFW contributed to COFO from the proceeds of the dance. Arriving at the large open barn of an old building, we entered the big, darkened room, with just a bar on the far wall, where the men looked young, black, and handsome amid a huge crowd. There were no other whites there. The bar was serving beer, lots of it, and there was probably some moonshine around, too. Each of us got a beer, and we stood around ready to talk about project goals and our activities. My hope was that these men, in particular the young ones, sophisticated after serving in Europe or Korea, were voters. If not, I would try to persuade them to register, but with the loud music it was impossible to have a conversation. I was not there to compete with the local black women—the wives and girlfriends—for attention from the men. The VFW dance for me was a project activity rather than a party.

Before long a VFW man asked me to dance, and as we danced on the hot, crowded dance floor, I felt the cold eyes of the black women directed at me. Although anxious to head back to my friends, I was asked again by another man to dance, and we danced. More than one handsome black man was interested in me, which naturally flattered me. I knew that these guys were interested only because I was available and white. I was aware that I was on display. When my second dance partner asked me to step outside, I left the hot, noisy, airless hall, grateful to get out on the porch for some air, even if it was a hot evening breeze. I hoped that we would be able to talk. Soon my first dance partner arrived to join us. I was shocked when the second guy pulled out a large, shiny, silvery hunting knife on the other guy—an unexpected new experience and a frightful sight. Amazed that they were arguing about which one of them was going to dance with me, I wondered if they were so riled up that the knife was going to be used. All because of me? Dreading what would happen next, I knew I had to get out of there—and fast. Other guys on the porch managed to prevent any violence, and the tension was defused.

That was the end of my dancing. Across the street, a place serving food represented safety. I sat there alone, eating some ribs at an outdoor picnic table, waiting until the others were ready to go back to town to the Freedom House. I did not need to say anything more to any of the VFW men.

We had arrived at the dance at dusk but went back in the pitch black. I always told myself, while in Mississippi, that the car I was in was being followed any time I just felt a car or truck behind me. When I saw a pickup truck, out of habit I would look for a gun rack in the back window and then check to see if there were one or more guns on the rack. From the stories we heard, I knew to be even more frightened if the truck traveled anonymously without tags. That night our headlights did not reveal any shotguns, pointed or not, and nothing happened on the deserted two-lane road, but I remained apprehensive until we were back in the city.

That night's event, brief as it was, made a deep impression on me. I was careful the rest of the summer about my social contacts and avoided all possibility of getting into a relationship. Yet I didn't think you could or should spend too much time worrying about security. I wrote: "All sorts of parents and people are worried this summer but no one can be too worried. That's why Stokely laughs and we live as normal existences as possible. We don't talk about security all the time because it's not worth it. The first few nights I was here I didn't sleep well but you *have to* work hard and forget it."

Although we depended on the local people for our meals, I never gave my hosts any money for food, and I never went to a grocery store to buy food to take home. The volunteers were living on small amounts of money they had brought with them for the summer. Sometimes a generous soul in the black community invited a group of us over for a meal, typically a late weekend afternoon, outdoors, picnic style with lots of southern food. Such get-togethers were joyful occasions. I never developed a taste for mustard greens, collard greens, or okra, but I loved the barbecued ribs, barbecued pork, fried chicken, hot dogs, black-eyed peas, corn bread, potato salad, bean salad, watermelon, and most everything else. Since most of the time I was drinking only water to keep cool and hydrated, ice-cold sodas on these occasions tasted most refreshing. We always looked for a free meal and welcomed the invitations we received.

The Fourth of July was the best of these wonderful occasions. Dr. Noble Frisby, a tall, lean, older man with a medium complexion and sharp features, invited us to his home for that typical southern meal. He was wealthy and generous, and I enjoyed this special and memorable occasion. I considered him the richest black in town—he was an established black doctor, with real estate holdings as well.

Dr. Frisby's friends and neighbors were interested in us, curious to learn about each of us. "What's your name?" "Where are you from?" "Where do you go to college?" were the typical friendly questions they asked. They complimented us for our courage and thanked us for coming, which made me feel good because the thanks were coming from the local black community. The crowd was enjoying the food and mixing well, black and white, celebrating Independence Day. We graciously responded and enjoyed reuniting with our colleagues, who were scattered in various neighborhoods, to compare notes about our experiences.

I had only one social outing in the white community—going downtown for dinner. I forgot my scruples about the white part of town when Polly Allen, my Cornell civil rights friend, invited me to the Downtowner Motel for dinner. The NCC Commission on Race and Religion had recruited her and other white professionals involved in Christian ministry on college and university campuses to find people in Greenville's white Protestant churches who were clear-headed and brave enough to identify and participate as allies in the COFO initiatives.[30] She was in the white community to do the kind of racial reconciliation work the volunteers couldn't do. At first, she had stayed with the family of attorney Doug Wynn, a parishioner in the Episcopal Church in Greenville, but hostile pressure became too much for the Wynn family, and she had moved into the motel. I liked it when she would occasionally show up at our project. If we were in the middle of some deep discussion about the movement, she could listen in and learn more about the issues the student volunteers were confronting. I translated the militancy that seemed to shock her as I was becoming more militant myself.

Polly wanted me to meet her sister and a volunteer minister. My dinner, at what I considered a ritzy motel, was a contrast to my usual evenings and made me feel guilty as I enjoyed such luxury. I justified my indulgence as I tried to convey to Polly and the others in our conversation, as best I could, why I was so committed to the Summer Project goals.

One of them asked me, "How's the voter registration going?"

With this opening, I replied, "Well, actually we are not trying to get people to go down to the courthouse to register to vote officially. Of course, we want them to, if they have not already registered, but we are working hard now to get Freedom Registrations. We are registrars to just take a name, address, and age on forms that anyone over the age of twenty-one can sign to become a voting member of the Mississippi Freedom Democratic Party."

I continued, "We think the MFDP should be seated at the Democratic Convention because blacks are excluded from the regular state Democratic Party, and the regulars do not even support the Democratic platform or candidate. Nothing is going to happen to let blacks vote in Mississippi and open up this closed society until the rest of the country can influence the federal government to enforce federal law. If the MFDP gets seated at the convention at the end of August in Atlantic City, it will be a great victory for civil rights."

The other time I went to the white community was on a shopping excursion. I was alone, which was against the rules, walking, and managed to find Washington Street, where the stores were. No one spoke to me, and I did not speak to anyone, but I could feel animosity and sensed that I was in a more dangerous place. The conversations I heard among neat, properly dressed white women with a heavy southern drawl sounded like a foreign language on those wide, hot, concrete sidewalks.

I was an outsider in a segregated society where I knew I did not belong—an outsider among whites. I could not put on a southern accent to sound like one of them and had no desire to try to conform to be one of them. I wanted to be anonymous and was not interested in disclosing that I was a freedom worker. Unafraid of the hostility I might encounter, I just didn't want to answer any questions and explain myself to people who I was convinced didn't understand anything about how black people felt. I believed they would not have an open mind to hear why I was a part of the Summer Project. After my one expedition, I had seen and heard enough and had no desire to return downtown to the white part of Greenville. Pat Vail told me she also went downtown anonymously—to run into a bank to get in the air conditioning for relief from the oppressive everyday heat.

In the black community, the volunteers were identifying with the hopes and fears of the local blacks, who lived in very different circumstances from their own. I accommodated myself to the new experience as I had been required to do in living with a farm family in northern Sweden two summers earlier. There I was isolated and unable to communicate in a common language. Living in the black community proved to be another challenge for me, but it was something I felt I could handle.

We had arrived young and unsophisticated, but we were armored to withstand the evils of Mississippi segregation. We started with our individual sense of what was right. During orientation in Oxford, we added strict adherence to nonviolence, a principal subject of our training. The incredible, heroic support from the local community sustained us. Our security lay in the black neighborhoods.

As I remember my feelings as a young white girl living within the black community in Mississippi in 1964, I take pleasure thinking of the Beloved Community. The summer in Mississippi has been hailed as the time and place that have come closest to that ideal. All of us—black staff and workers, local residents, and white volunteers—were bound together for mutual protection and support, trusting each other without regard to race or class, in circumstances that gave rise to deep emotional feelings for one another as we sought to build the same beloved community in the society as a whole. Casey Hayden wrote how she felt, expressing our feelings better than I could:

> I think we were the only Americans who will ever experience integration. We were the beloved community, harassed and happy,

and poor. And in those little hot black rural churches, we went into the music, into the sound, and everyone was welcome inside this perfect place. We simply dropped race.

. . . We believed the last should be first, and not only should be first, but in fact *were* first in our value system. . . . We were living in a community so true to itself that all we wanted was to organize everyone into it, make the world beloved with us, make the whole world our beloved.[31]

The notion of the Beloved Community, established before 1964, is part of the nonviolence described in the SNCC founding statement. But no one ever used the term or talked about it in Mississippi. Barney Frank, a Harvard graduate student in political science and future congressman from Massachusetts, helped organize the MFDP as a COFO volunteer in Jackson. He described the same unique interracial environment: "It's so rare to function in an atmosphere of total integration. It's not just that the barriers of race are down. Here, distinctions of class, age, or religion don't matter either. You can see a young Negro girl giving orders to an elderly white man in the office and nobody thinks twice about it. We're all in this together. The person with greater knowledge of the situation is the one in authority."[32]

The history and meaning of this concept, which has been significant for me, is not generally known. The Fellowship of Reconciliation, an interfaith organization dedicated to nonviolence and working for freedom, peace, and justice, first used the term in the early twentieth century. The Fellowship had worked with Martin Luther King Jr. during the bus boycott in Montgomery, Alabama, in 1955 as he adopted Gandhian nonviolent principles for the civil rights movement years before the founding of SNCC.

Nonviolence is also known as passive resistance, but when the Montgomery blacks refused to ride the segregated buses, they were not passive. They were meeting in churches, encouraging each other, and taking direct action in a spirit of love and protest. Nonviolence involves a refusal to retaliate against evil based on the realization that retaliation entails the multiplication of evil. Hating the opposition was immoral as well as bad strategy that would continue a cycle of revenge. Nonviolence had the power to break that cycle and create lasting peace through reconciliation. During orientation, COFO trained the volunteers in the techniques of nonviolence, critical for keeping ourselves and others safe, and we all understood that the ultimate goal of our efforts was integration. But we did not understand then what we would experience that summer.

The aftermath of nonviolence was reconciliation and the creation of the Beloved Community, according to Dr. King. The core value in seeking the Beloved Community was *agape*, love—love that is "understanding, redeeming goodwill for all . . . the love of God operating in the human heart . . . [that is] seeking to preserve and create community."[33] The end was not political power or economic power, but justice—justice not for any one group, but for all people. The Beloved Community would be a place of brotherly love where conflicts arising from differences in class, gender, race, or economic standing do not exist.

In 1959, Martin Luther King Jr. wrote about this larger dimension to nonviolence:

> When Negroes involve themselves in such a struggle, they take a radical step. Their rejection of hatred and oppression in the specific situation cannot be confined to a single issue. For it raises the question of hatred and oppression in the society as a whole, it moves toward an even deeper commitment to a pervasive social change. For out of this one problem, the sense of brotherhood springs as a practical necessity, and once this happens, there is revealed the vision of a society of brotherhood. We seek new ways of human beings living together; free from the spiritual deformation of race hatred—and free also from the deformations of war and economic injustice. And this vision does not belong to Negroes alone. It is the yearning of mankind.[34]

I knew something about the role of reconciliation in nonviolence, but I didn't feel I could do anything to reconcile blacks and whites in Greenville. I found the divide too great and the opportunities too few. The massive numbers of volunteers arriving for the 1964 summer, the local media, and peer pressure put the white community on the defensive and made them generally unreceptive to overtures for reconciliation. Others did make efforts across racial lines—the NCC ministers and the middle-class women, black and white, who visited in white communities in Mississippi on Wednesdays—but the college-age volunteers were not part of these efforts. King's vision of brotherhood has stayed with me based on my summer experiences as we look today to end poverty and prejudice in peaceful times at home and in the world.

Bob Moses understood how the outsider comes into oppressive social situations where the poor and excluded exist but cannot determine whether the people he or she talks to will participate in the movement. He had told us in orientation to be patient with people and just to talk to local blacks, to treat them with dignity and respect. The communication would be an accomplishment as we tried to activate them in the struggle for freedom and equality. Charles Marsh wrote about Moses in his book *The Beloved Community:* "Moses worked patiently to foster an emotional space in which people would feel freely 'called forth by the movement' and in turn feel free to accept, or reject the call. Moses believed that an oppressed people—if affirmed in their created dignity through participation in a supportive community—could find the power to voice their goals and to determine the steps necessary to realize them."[35]

We were less conscious of our differences in the homes of blacks, where we accepted the love that was offered us and returned it as best we could, trying to listen and understand the privation, sufferings, and lack of opportunity experienced at the hands of whites in the community. The local blacks were more receptive to us than the black staff, who made me sensitive to my desire to be accepted. At the beginning of the summer, Muriel Tillinghast, one of the black SNCC staff in Greenville, did not talk to the newcomers as much as I thought she should. When I first met her, we didn't talk at all. She had a very good command of what was going on and what had to be done, was very militant, and had a fantastic sense of humor, which meant a great deal in that environment. My judgment was that she had all the dynamism and smarts you'd ever want. It took time, but I felt I did finally get through to her, and we were able to work together.

There may have been feelings of not being accepted, but conflicts among white volunteers and blacks working in the movement didn't seem to me to exist in the Greenville project. After seeing the Stanford and Yale students working in Mississippi for the Freedom Vote, SNCC was wary about the arrival of smart, young, brash college students in large numbers. Knowing that we would be free to leave at the end of the summer, local blacks might express their resentment in hostility toward individual volunteers, causing hurt, frustration, or even defeat, particularly when the young whites did not have sufficient knowledge or self-awareness to understand the situation. I was sensitive about respecting the black project leaders in Greenville and held back on any ideas I might have had about what we should be doing, particularly when I first arrived. I had always been reserved and did not need to act aggressively to have my way, to influence a situation, or to succeed.

When I first met the other COFO staff and volunteers on the project, I knew they were good people. I noted in my first letter home that there was definitely a difference between the staff and volunteers and that the difference had come to something of a head in Oxford. As the summer progressed, I felt I got along with everyone, although I didn't see much of many of the other volunteers, in particular the Freedom School teachers. After all, we were bound together in the same cause, we were committed to integration, and we really needed to be able to work together, to respect each other, and to appreciate each other's various strengths and weaknesses. I like to think this attitude was simply ingrained in me, and I didn't need to think about it consciously. Although I didn't have to expect major accomplishments, I felt dedicated to doing some work that would make a difference, in contrast to my experiences in the work camp in the summer of 1963, when I was only learning about civil rights problems in Mississippi.

Realizing all this once some days had gone by, I began making distinctions. First, I had some reservations about George Rowell, our project director, who was a graduate student from Chicago. He was a handsome, neat, well-dressed black who was intelligent, capable, and efficient but had never worked in the South. He was very different from the other black staff, who were younger and more militant. They were casual and informal, some with no urgent passion for work but always energized in our discussions. George was stern and businesslike, conscientious about his responsibilities. I thought his style was not going over in Mississippi, a place where going slow helps in making contact with the local people.

When he left the project at the end of July, midway through the project, for reasons I never knew, Muriel Tillinghast, whom I thought highly of, took his place.

We all were working on the same level.[36] I don't remember any meetings or formalities when either George or Muriel acted like my boss. I thought that my project director in Greenville was Charlie Cobb, for whom I developed the greatest respect, but actually his responsibility was all of Washington County, and since Greenville was the county seat, it was the logical place for him to be when he was not elsewhere in the state. His area extended to the neighboring counties to the south, Issaquena and Sharkey, mostly rural areas that had extremely few registered voters.

A Massachusetts native with, as noted earlier, roots in Greenville, twenty-one-year-old Charlie was compact, short, and cheerful; he had a bright smile on his face and a personality that made you want to call him cute. He was the kind of person no one could not like, always smiling and friendly. He was part of the sit-in movement during his freshman year at Howard and planned to attend a civil rights workshop in Houston, Texas, after spring semester. When he reached Jackson, he decided to stop to meet student protestors in Mississippi and was persuaded by Guyot, who was headed up to the Delta, to stay and work with SNCC. Charlie joined Charles McLaurin and others in a new SNCC project in Sunflower County. The fall of 1962 was a tense, violent time of night-rider shootings, arrests, church bombings, and economic harassment following voter registration attempts in the Delta. Charlie's description of the resulting fear is included in the book *My Soul Is Rested* by Howell Raines:

> [W]e couldn't really tell people that we had a way of protecting them, either from economic harassment or from physical violence. . . . So, given that reality, our decision was basically just to be physically present in the county, just to show people. Even more important than bringing people down to the county courthouse, it was important for people to know that despite the physical violence—which increasingly became less directed at us and more directed at the people in the county—that we were prepared to stay and stick it out. And that's basically what we did for

months, just were there talking on porches, holding some meetings, small, in the one church that let us meet.[37]

Charlie went on to organizing in Greenville with other SNCC field secretaries. In my view, he was very much in command of the whole political
situation in 1964. I turned to Charlie with my questions, even though
he seemed to me uninterested in the summer volunteers, and I don't feel
that I got to know him. He was not part of the group lingering in the
cafés drinking beer after a meal but kept his distance from us. I can now
explain his behavior by what I did not know then. He was a *leader* of
the SNCC field secretaries who initially objected to Bob Moses's plan to
bring in white volunteers for the Summer Project. By December 1963,
when it was more apparent that the Summer Project would become a
reality, Charlie proposed that it include the Freedom Schools, the creative
parallel vehicle for supplementing the inadequate black schools.

I also perceived differences between the committed, experienced
SNCC field secretaries and other blacks who came in for the Summer
Project. I believe they were SNCC employees, but they were not SNCC
veterans with the discipline that others in the organization had. I felt that
I was becoming more militant but also hoped that I could still see many
sides. I accepted that the blacks knew more than I did and were in charge
but was conflicted in my judgment when I thought they were lazy. We
had a big job to do and wanted everyone to work at it. But some of these
guys seemed unwilling to go out into the rural counties to work in the
more dangerous areas. Their work ethic did not impress me, but I had
to give them their due. They did not have the same deal I had: "It's an
amazing test—they don't want to work and have to worry about us ignorant white folk who have and will get such a better deal, can leave any-
time we want to," I wrote in a letter home. They thought the Freedom
Schools should not have white teachers because they felt it so important
for young blacks to have black role models.

In addition to my letters home, I wrote a great deal to friends and
remembered my obligation to write to congressmen and senators. As a
volunteer, I could communicate the oppression, economic servitude, and
intimidation that we saw. If people only *knew*, I believed they would pressure the federal government to enforce federal laws and protect the right

to vote. I'm not sure exactly what I said, but on July 6 I wrote my two senators from New Jersey to urge federal protection. Despite the disappearance of the three civil rights workers, which was receiving national attention, the Justice Department remained adamant that the federal government could do nothing because there was no national police force.

Senator Clifford Case, a moderate Republican, thanked me for my letter and said I could count on his "continuing efforts to secure greater Federal participation in Mississippi."[38] He was more specific in his response to my father's letters, telling him, "[Y]ou can certainly take pride in your daughter's readiness to stand up for her convictions. Her action reflects great credit not only to her but to her parents." He enclosed a copy of the strong statement he sent to President Johnson on June 25: "I believe the Federal government has not only the legal authority, but an inescapable moral obligation, to provide a Federal presence on a full-time basis to make clear the Federal intention to prevent unlawful violence and intimidation and to prosecute those who interfere under color of law or otherwise with persons seeking to assert their Constitutional rights."[39]

Senator Harrison Williams, a Democrat, told me that he too had urged the federal government to "use all its resources to protect the individuals in Mississippi." He referred to my letter as describing some of the conditions in Mississippi and stated, "You deserve the admiration and respect of every American for the courage and dedication you have demonstrated in volunteering for the Mississippi Summer Project."[40] In this instance, for a change, the Republican impressed me more than the Democrat.

After the early weeks, I spent little time with the Freedom School teachers and did not visit the schools with the exception of the time singer and songwriter Judy Collins was in Mississippi. She said she wanted "to be a part of the revolutionary summer."[41] So after singing in Jackson, traveling by VW bus with the Eastgate Singers, she stopped first in Greenville on August 3. I took a break to hear them sing at one of the Freedom Schools and in the evening at Friendship Baptist Church. They entertained COFO staff and volunteers from 10:00 p.m. to 1:00 a.m. after the evening performance. We couldn't get enough of the great music, and Judy Collins led us in freedom songs. She later wrote that her audience in Greenville was neither terribly large nor enthusiastic, but they sang their "heads off for the staff." Collins assessed Greenville as "quiet," with people "just not interested enough in what is going on to really care about getting the vote, or joining the Freedom Democratic Party."[42] Judy Collins continued singing in the Delta through Indianola, Ruleville, Drew, and Clarksdale, understanding that what she was doing was dangerous. She was struck by the dedication of the people working in the movement and appreciated the security offered her in the black neighborhoods. She met Fannie Lou Hamer, who left a deep impression on her. Mrs. Hamer had seen hardship and terror but was not afraid, telling Judy Collins, "I have my faith."[43]

When I think about what we did just for fun, I try to remember. I was at my happiest when I joined a compatible, interesting group for conversation. At those times, usually in a café over a meal with a quart of beer or in the kitchen at the Brittons' house, we talked about the movement. We all had ideas and concerns to share about freedom coming to Mississippi. Playing games with local children, driving tours, and singing folk songs with a volunteer playing the guitar are not part of my story.

We did have one informal, fun, purely social occasion: swimming in Hodding Carter's pool. Dorothy Jones, a maid at Hodding Carter's house and an MFDP supporter, invited me to come and stay overnight because she was nervous staying with the baby alone in the fourteen-room house when the Carters went away. I wrote home on August 7 about what she said and what I did: "Bring a couple people out and we could swim if we got there soon after 4, the hour the Carters were leaving for Greenwood. Eventually the Carters knew (would approve it) so it wasn't sneaky and a young reporter who lives out there was there before he left town at 8. From 5 to 7 the whole project was swimming in that private pool—just imagine how delightful that was! I didn't stay but a couple others did, because I had to get back for another delegate's workshop."

We didn't have bathing suits with us in Mississippi and would not have gone out to buy them; we must have just gone in the pool in shorts and T-shirts, happy to relax and cool off. As Pat Vail said, it was "very exciting," although she "kept one eye on the gate waiting to see the police come."[44] She thought the young reporters with the *Delta Democrat-Times*, John Childs and Foster Davis, had invited us. Barbara Mutnick wrote her parents that because we never met together socially, relationships "have often been tense and stilted," but we all laughed and had fun

Former COFO office at 901½ Nelson Street in Greenville, 1964. Photo by Lisa Anderson Todd, June 1994.

in the pool that day, playing Keep Away, getting dunked, and knocking ourselves out. We "needed" the fun; she called it "[s]ort of a purgation."[45]

The swimming party broke up when three men on horseback, like a scene out of the Wild West, rode through the high vegetation surrounding the property into the backyard. Pat thought that was "something she had imagined,"[46] but others have confirmed my distinct memory of such an unexpected sight. We speculated that the horsemen were neighbors protective of the Carters who couldn't imagine that we were invited guests. I find it hard to believe now that I was so dedicated to work that I passed up a new, interesting, comfortable place to sleep overnight. Barbara and Nancy Schieffelin, wise enough to accept the invitation, told me how surprised they were to see "a revolver in the drawer of the nightstand in the guest room."[47] It would not be my choice, but apparently the Carters felt it wise to arm their guests for their protection against intruders. Barbara noted that "the Carters are certainly prepared for anything. That place is like an arsenal. Guns all over—ready for use."[48]

We all hoped that by the end of the summer Mississippi blacks would receive the recognition they deserved and that political, economic, and social justice would follow. The volunteers' views of race relations expanded during the summer as we confronted each other and came to understand fears experienced by both staff and local black residents— even though we could not share that reality. I continued to find the jail-house treatment, racial discrimination, and subtle harassment hard to believe and marveled that blacks could still somehow lead meaningful lives. As we got to know our peers and worked together, we learned many lessons for the future. We faced whatever lay ahead more determined to bring the races together.

With the office on the second floor at 901½ Nelson Street finally ready for us, I went to work.

9

My New Politics

> We all recognize the fact that if any radical social, political and economic changes are to take place in our society, the people, the masses must bring them about. In the struggle we must seek more than mere civil rights; we must work for the community of love, peace, and true brotherhood. Our minds, souls, and hearts cannot rest until freedom and justice exist for *all the people.*
> —John Lewis, speech at the March on Washington, 1963[1]

I was the only white female volunteer assigned to voter registration in Greenville—a special status given presumably because of my experience the previous summer. I felt privileged because of the opportunity to meet local people in their homes as we urged them to register to vote. Some of the other girls were envious of me because they spent their days inside and saw fewer local people in the Freedom Schools.

In 1964, few blacks were registered to vote in the Delta where I was working.[2] Thirteen of the twenty-four counties in the Second Congressional District had less than one percent of voting-age blacks registered. In neighboring Sharkey County, only three blacks were registered voters, and in Issaquena County there was none. But in Greenville the percentage of blacks registered was higher: 2,563 of 20,619 blacks eligible to vote, or 12.4 percent, were registered in Washington County. COFO gave us a paper entitled "Outline of Mississippi Project Areas" that said, "Psychologically, Greenville is a difficult town to work (apathy as well as fear) but certainly there is plenty of mobility to work." The reputation the town had for tolerance and this mobility made me feel during most of the summer that there was much that could be done.

After the disappearance of the three civil rights workers on June 21,

COFO changed its ambitious plans for statewide voter registration but remained fully committed to continuing the Mississippi Summer Project to bring educational and political opportunity to Mississippi's blacks through the planned programs, as it told the parents of summer volunteers. As a precaution, though, it would limit work to a small area around each project center.

What I did in Greenville was to canvass in black neighborhoods door to door asking people to go to the county courthouse to register if they were not already registered. It was a slow process. At times, I would take a half-hour to draw out a person to speak his mind, to learn why he had not already registered. Then I could urge him to go with his friends to the courthouse.

After checking the map in our office to identify the specific neighborhood assigned, a black partner and I would walk door to door on those sweltering summer days. We all went out in integrated pairs in hopes of getting a thoughtful response. If a black went alone, the resident could act dismissive, not taking the request seriously; if a white went alone, the resident might feel compelled to obey authority and agree to register. We stayed as long as we could, hoping that the resident fully comprehended what we were saying and was interested and willing to register and participate. I wanted to avoid going in the middle of the day, when the temperature was in the nineties or higher, and the hours of 4:00 to 7:00 p.m., when it was still light outside, were more conducive to my enthusiasm for the task. I felt personally safe in black neighborhoods during the day. We were noticeable, everyone knew who we were, and I never expected any trouble from blacks, but it did seem wise to be out of those neighborhoods and back home before it got dark. Carrying my clipboard and keeping track of where we went and what we found, we reported back to the office on Nelson Street.

I noted large economic disparities among the small frame houses and their inhabitants: some very poor, some poor but careful to maintain a neat-looking home, and some middle class. I saw very young children with bellies distended from malnutrition playing nearly naked in front yards, which were sometimes only dirt, sometimes raked, but not grass. A child seeing us coming might call back into the house, "Mamma, Mamma, Freedom Rider coming!" Residents usually remained at the front door to

Residential street in Greenville, 1964. Courtesy of Nancy Schieffelin.

greet us and were always polite. It felt special when I was invited inside a home and could see how a family lived. I appreciated even more the offer of a drink of water—always cold—which I would gratefully accept; every refrigerator contained at least one quart jar filled with cold water. The walls were bare except for some photographs, frequently of Jesus or John F. Kennedy or both. I sat on many a bed by the front door as we talked. In a small house for a large family, beds could be placed anywhere, and often I saw a television set. I had never before encountered the distinct, strong odor of unclean humanity, but I did find that unforgettable smell in some very poor homes. The extreme heat likely added to its overwhelming pungency. I saw large families in crowded conditions and ragged clothing, but at least housing, inadequate as it may have been, seemed to be available for every black family. I saw no one homeless in Greenville.

If we were questioned while canvassing or if we had time, we might give a basic talk about the structure of the federal, state, and local governments. We urged the people to attend the next mass meeting and might hand out a small piece of paper with the date and time and place. We hoped that this information would spread by word of mouth. Meetings took place in the early evenings in black churches that supported the movement. We used the Disney Chapel next door to the Freedom House in the South End, and close to Nelson Street we frequently met in the large Friendship Baptist Church. The pastors of these churches were among the first ministers willing, courageous enough, and able to open their doors to the civil rights movement.[3] The numbers at a mass meeting varied, but I knew that even a small turnout was important to motivate local residents, explain what was going on, encourage registration, assuage the fears, and maintain some momentum. COFO staff or local leaders took charge of the meetings, calling on speakers to encourage others to become active. Freedom singing was part of the event, and a minister would participate with prayers and words of inspiration.

I did not speak at these meetings but did participate in the freedom singing and made myself known by just talking to individuals. We hoped that by getting to know us, the local blacks would come to understand what we were doing and trust us. I thought the best, or at least the most interesting, part of any mass meeting was hearing a local person, who was strong enough to stand up and be willing to "testify." I heard about incredible lifetime experiences or about how some had gone down to try to "reddish" (register). These individuals were the ones who urged, encouraged, and motivated others to join in the freedom struggle. I could only stand by.

Since Greenville was so moderate, my job should have been easy, and our registration numbers should have soared. But it was difficult because the atmosphere in the state as a whole intimidated blacks everywhere. The fear was overwhelming, and I could hardly discount or contradict it, let alone urge them not to be afraid. They did not trust the white man. We were also encountering apathy and laziness, and at times I found that very discouraging. Some blacks were pessimistic and thought it would be futile to participate in the movement. Either they had enough income and possessions, or they did not expect they would be able to get anything more. I tried to tell them that they *could* make a difference in their daily lives.

Blacks in Greenville who had not yet registered to vote appeared satisfied and uninterested in taking risks to register to vote. At a mass meeting in late June that David Halberstam reported in the *New York Times*, Levye Chapple, a middle-class black businessman in the printing business and an active Democrat, did not think the problem was the fairness of the registrar, but "one of apathy among our own Negro people." COFO staff member Jesse Davis charged that the established black leaders were "Uncle Toms" who had "sold out the Negroes to gain a privileged relationship for themselves with the white community" and who misled local blacks, telling them that there was "no need to vote" and that COFO "would just cause trouble."[4] The COFO militants had no time for the moderates in the NAACP.

But the relatively large percentage of registered voters in Washington County was attributable to the NAACP chapter in Greenville, in particular the work of James Carter, who had been active in civil rights since the 1940s. He owned a cleaning business in the Carter Building at 901 Nelson Street, where he rented us our COFO office. After the Freedom Rides, he and a few others in Greenville helped the student activists who came to town, providing them with office space and housing. According to an oral interview, he understood voter registration was "the only salvation for people being respected as citizens" and that "[a]s long as you have some qualified electors—voters—why we can do business."[5] We called him "Baby Face" Carter, the entire community's nickname for him. He took blacks to the courthouse to register at a time when the questions were tough—that is, before the clerk "got kind of liberal" because he didn't want to be tied up in court. Carter received credit for the hiring of the first black policemen, who worked weekends on Nelson Street while they held other jobs. He also influenced banks to use courtesy titles for black women. But I was scornful of moderation in Greenville and wrote about the whole group as the "Carter Klan."

Besides getting more voters registered at the courthouse and working on Freedom Registration, the Summer Project worked to find new voices and develop community leadership among day workers, former sharecroppers, and domestics. They had their traditional advocates, but we anticipated they would be more aggressive in advancing their own interests. Charlie Cobb knew the local political picture from his years of work in the Delta and gave us our mandate: work around the established leadership. We were trying to "encourage the black community to find its own voice" so that "people who were usually spoken for began speaking for themselves in tones loud enough to be heard."[6] I don't remember that we used the word, but movement organizers were "empowering" local people to recognize their own potential for leadership. SNCC and COFO believed in the capability of every individual to identify issues, take responsibility, and create local organizations that could make a difference in peoples' lives, with everyone joining together to represent their common interests.

In Greenville, the existing black leadership organized in the NAACP was relatively affluent, comfortable, and cautious. From the very beginning, we did not hesitate to label these men and one woman I can think of—who were middle-class businessmen, professionals, ministers, and teachers—as "Uncle Toms." By submitting to authority and getting along with the white establishment, they kept their social status and preserved their economic well-being. Many of them had successfully registered to vote, and I presumed they did not vote to upset the powers that be. Content with the status quo as they were, they seemed to have little interest in motivating the less well-educated or poor blacks to join their ranks as registered voters. I perceived, rightly or wrongly, that they opposed everything COFO was doing that summer and believed that they were adversely affecting what we were trying to do. Prominent black businessmen such as Chapple were not going to move when moving meant upsetting the apple cart. COFO was in a hurry: we often shouted, "FREEDOM NOW!"

At the beginning of the summer, numbers in the newspaper showed some positive results in voter registration at the courthouse in Greenville. On July 7, the first group of six blacks went to the courthouse to register, and three completed the test. The registrar said "he would be fair to all who came to his office to register." He would pass those who were "qualified."[7] COFO, however, accompanied blacks who couldn't read or write to register because in its view the state, which had failed to provide them education, should allow them to vote. As Bob Moses wrote in "Constitutional Property v. Constitutional People," the state "couldn't deny a whole people access to education and literacy and then turn around and deny them access to politics because they were illiterate."[8] In mid-July, the project planned to accompany applicants whenever ten or fifteen could be gathered, anticipated to be once a week. On July 13, of thirty blacks, mostly from the neighboring town of Hollandale, the registrar thought approximately half "gave reasonable answers to the interpretation of the Constitution," but the results would not be known until after publication of the names in the local newspapers.[9] Plans for a massive drive on July 16—a Freedom Day—brought out 150–200 blacks in a daylong line of prospective voters.

As the summer progressed and the date for the Democratic National Convention neared, COFO focused more on Freedom Registration. Preparation for the Convention Challenge had been under way even before I arrived in Greenville. At the monthly meeting on March 15, 1964, open to all Mississippi movement supporters in the state, COFO had formally announced the Freedom Registration campaign for a new political party to be established in the tradition of nonviolence as an alternative institution and the Challenge to the Mississippi Democratic Party's delegation at the national convention in August. On April 26, 1964, at the next meeting, COFO established the MFDP. The approximately two hundred local COFO, SNCC, and CORE activists who attended this meeting voted to elect as the party's temporary chairman Aaron Henry, who had been the candidate for governor in the 1963 Freedom Vote.

Only four months remained before the MFDP delegates would go to the Democratic Convention in Atlantic City to carry out what Thelwell called a "bold, dramatic, creative idea" that was also "quixotic" and for many "doomed to failure."[10] The political organizing that would take place in dangerous circumstances is without match in the movement for its high degree of complexity and successful accomplishment. In the spring of 1964, Casey Hayden, a white SNCC field secretary, and Dick Jewitt, a white CORE staff member, began with more research "the mammoth statewide organizing" in their role as program coordinators for the Convention Challenge. They prepared the organizing material needed by staff, volunteers, and community leaders; determined precinct boundaries; located halls for meetings; and found people who would go to the all-white precinct meetings. The scope of the effort undertaken indicated, as Casey Hayden put it, the MFDP's "serious intent toward legitimacy."[11]

Registered voters attempted to attend precinct and county meetings of the state Democratic Party, expecting to be excluded. COFO recorded the precinct activities that took place on June 16: blacks were unable to find any evidence of a meeting, were excluded, or were allowed to attend only as observers. Greenville was unusual in allowing blacks who went to four precinct meetings to vote and to be nominated as delegates to the county convention, although none of them was elected. In Precinct 3, they were able to introduce a resolution "pledging the precinct delegates to support the [national party's] platform and the party's nominees at the National Convention," which was unanimously approved. The COFO report noted that "Greenville is about as representative of Mississippi in regard to race relations as a rose in a weed patch."[12]

Elected black delegates from all-black precincts faced similar exclusion from county conventions on June 23.[13] In Greenville, the location of the meeting was not announced in the newspaper, as required by state law, but nineteen delegates and several observers, including COFO staff member Jesse Davis and volunteers Ray Raphael and Lyn Hamilton, found out where it was and attended. Even so, a white five-man caucus met during the meeting and nominated the county delegation and executive committee, slates that were accepted without debate. Doug Wynn, executive secretary of the Washington County Democratic Party, did not allow consideration of the Precinct 3 resolution, thus encouraging loyalty to the state party because none of the delegates from that precinct was present.

I was among the hundreds of summer volunteers who would canvass to register blacks for the new political party, the MFDP, and to provide local residents who had never voted with information about participation in the political process. The goal in Freedom Registration was to register 100,000 persons by the time of the national convention, which was to be provided as proof of the party's base in the state. The qualifications included being twenty-one or older, residence in the state for at least two years and in the county for one year, and the ability to answer questions on a simple one-page form. There was no literacy requirement. The form could be signed with an X in the presence of two witnesses. Any person who registered as a member of the MFDP would be eligible to participate and vote in the party. The MFDP would elect delegates and alternates to the national convention following the same procedures used by the regu-

Freedom Registration Form

(1) Write today's date:_____

(2) Write your full name:_____

(3) How old are you today:_____

(4) Are you a United States citizen:_____

(5) How long have you lived in Mississippi:_____

(6) What county do you live in:_____

(7) How long have you lived in that county:_____

(8) What is your address now:_____

(9) Are you a minister or the wife of a minister:_____

All of the statements above are true:_____
                                      (signature of applicant)

_ _ _ _ _ _ _ _ _ _ _(do not write below this line)_ _ _ _ _ _ _ _ _ _ _ _

State of Mississippi, County of:_____

Sworn to and subscribed before me by the above named _____

on this, the ____ day of _____, 196__.

_____

_____

_____

_____

Freedom Registration form, 1964. Courtesy of the Wisconsin Historical Society

lar Democrats: precinct meetings, county conventions, district caucuses, and a state convention.

COFO presented the MFDP to the volunteers during our orientation and gave us detailed mimeographed handouts entitled *Mississippi Freedom Democratic Party* and *Mississippi Handbook for Political Programs* to study—both of them thorough, well-written documents. They gave us an understanding of the purpose and goals of the new political party and what we needed to accomplish, but we had to figure out for ourselves what specific steps to take in Greenville. Appendix A, "Challenge of the Mississippi Freedom Democratic Party," which was part of these handouts, describes the MFDP and the Convention Challenge in detail.

I was organizing the MFDP at the grass roots in neighborhoods, one household at a time, in one city in the state. In my canvassing, I would say, "Have you heard of the Mississippi Freedom Democratic Party?" The answer would usually be "no," and I would show the simple Freedom Registration forms I carried on my clipboard. We had to explain the origin of the new political party, its importance, and what it was going to do and to emphasize that no outsider would know if black residents had signed the form. So Mississippi politicians and employers would not be able to use these forms to threaten them, as they used the official state voter registration forms. We returned the signed forms to the office for forwarding to COFO in Jackson, where they were kept locked up for "safe keeping" before the completed Freedom Registration forms would be taken to Atlantic City.[14] The MFDP Convention Challenge's potential for gaining national attention at the end of the summer served as my inspiration to go to work every day. I promoted the MFDP more than official voter registration at the courthouse.

COFO soon realized how far it was from its goal of 100,000 Freedom Registrations. On July 19, Bob Moses sent an "emergency memorandum" that reported that the MFDP Convention Challenge programs were "in very bad shape" and that a "massive job" remained to be done for the party to be prepared for the Challenge.[15] He directed all the volunteers not working in Freedom Schools or community centers to "give priority" to organizing for the Challenge until mid-August. Only 34,477 had signed up as of July 26.[16] I could see how important it would be to argue that the MFDP was truly representative of disenfranchised blacks in the state. Our goal in Greenville was 3,500 registrations a week, which meant 15 per worker per day. To meet this goal, we needed to get more people involved in and working on Freedom Registration and knew that it would be the community people who would have to do it. I got to know Charles Moore, a tall, fit, friendly man who was a World War II veteran and worked in the post office. He acted on his belief that more civil rights progress was needed in Greenville and became an effective addition to the COFO ranks. He could help us in our canvassing without too much fear of losing his job, although an effort was made to fire him. He also used his influence as commander of the local black VFW post, which explains why the VFW held a fund-raising dance for COFO in 1964. I didn't know during the summer that he was responsible for the nice air-conditioned housing I had; he "got Britton to take us in."[17]

COFO welcomed an offer for Martin Luther King Jr. to come to Mississippi to aid in the recruitment efforts. Despite friends' concerns for his safety, King traveled to Greenwood on July 21 to begin a five-day tour of COFO projects in Meridian, Vicksburg, and Jackson. He met informally with residents and addressed mass meetings to energize local black support for the MFDP and to generate beneficial publicity. In Jackson, an overflowing crowd of about 3,000 waited three hours in the Masonic Temple to hear him speak. He urged MFDP registration as "the best way to break down the barriers to official registration of voters."[18] He was "proud" that the summer volunteers, which he called "a domestic Peace Corps," were working through the MFDP "to make democracy a reality."[19] President Johnson heeded warnings that the Klan had vowed to kill King and ordered FBI director J. Edgar Hoover to ensure his protection. He had an escort of four cars of FBI men for the trip. King was unafraid in choosing to go to Neshoba County, where "a palpable fear hung over Philadelphia" after the disappearance of the three movement workers.[20]

By July 27, the apathy and silence (out of fear too) in Greenville, which had become a big and difficult area to work, depressed me. As a result, I did not feel very militant. We were not working to a schedule as I had in Greensboro the previous summer, and less daily discipline made me less productive than I might have been.

But I took some initiative and came up with an idea to improve our morale. I suggested that card tables set up in strategic locations on the sidewalks would attract notice and could expedite obtaining Freedom Registrations, in contrast to going from house to house. When I talked to Police Chief Burnley about our proposal, he told me that he didn't want to interfere with our work but didn't want us to break any laws either. As an alternative to blocking sidewalks, he suggested some private property—perhaps an empty lot with no shade. When I questioned whether he meant us to sit in that hot sun, he suggested maybe he could get us an umbrella and then said we could move into a doorway. Chief Burnley was an atypical Mississippi official, a fair-minded, professional man. We got seven hundred registered for the MFDP this way, many of whom had come into town from nearby Metcalf Plantation on a Saturday for errands on Nelson Street. We also set up downtown on Washington Street in the white part of town, but blacks were less likely to sign the Freedom Registration forms there.

By August 16, an update from COFO on the numbers of Freedom Registrations showed 5,837 registered for Greenville and all of Washington County, which was the second-highest total after Jackson and Hinds County. The total number had reached 56,449 but was still little more than half the stated goal.

One day while walking down the street, I felt a tap on my shoulder. Somehow Ivory Phillips, who had been on the Tougaloo project with me the previous summer, had found me while he was in town on his way home from summer school in California. Charlie gave him Freedom Registration forms for residents of his hometown, Rosedale. We hoped he would become active and really do some work, and I was disappointed not to have time for a good conversation with him.

On another day canvassing, I didn't notice a photographer following us. He took a photograph of me carrying a clipboard of registration forms, pen held in the air, with Pam, the black volunteer from Howard. We were talking to a black couple through the screen door of their home, with several curious young children watching. I later saw the picture in the May 23, 1966, issue of *Newsweek* magazine, illustrating the theory of white female civil rights workers' "white African Queen complex" that I mentioned earlier. Neither we nor the place was identified, and the camera was behind us. You could not tell who we were except that we were one black girl and one white girl. I could confirm I was in the photo by the purse I always clutched under my left arm.

In canvassing, we asked people to register to be a member of the MFDP, to talk to their family and friends, to attend mass meetings, and to come to the precinct meeting that would be the first step in electing the delegates to go to the national convention. In looking for new lead-

Canvassing for Freedom Registration with Pam Trotman. Photo published in
Newsweek, May 23, 1966, and *Freedom* (London: Phaidon Press, 2002). Courtesy of the Estate of Shel Hershorn.

ers, believing that everyone had the potential for leadership, we had high
hopes for Dr. Matthew Page. He was a young doctor who had no involvement with the NAACP. I knew that he had grown up in a poor home
in Greenville, had graduated from Tougaloo and Meharry Medical College in Nashville, Tennessee, and had recently opened a solo practice in
general medicine. His age, professional position, reputation for honesty,
and knowledge of the town made him appear to me the kind of progressive leader who would advance the cause of civil rights. A 1952 college
graduate, he would be coming in new to the movement. When I met
him, he impressed me with his demeanor—a serious young doctor, short
and trim, reserved in his speech but at the same time open and friendly
to us outsider kids who acted as if we knew a lot. He told us, with some
scorn, that the black leadership in town promoted voter registration by
telling the registrar of voters who should pass the test based on how an

individual black's vote would be delivered. Later in the summer, Muriel, our project director; Pam, a fellow volunteer; and I went to see him. In a letter home, I described his position as follows: "He said he was willing to serve [on the MFDP county Executive Committee], but did not want to be in a position out front because then the fight would be harder. No commitment there at all because the committee still hasn't met. He won't do anything without the support of the young men in the VFW." We felt strongly that if he would just agree to be active, he would have the energy and ability to bring change to Greenville.

We held workshops to prepare those who were newcomers to politics before they voted for delegates at the precinct meeting. Although the SCLC Citizenship Education Program had a supervisor in the Greenville area and recruited local black residents for teacher training at the Dorchester center in Georgia, I did not hear about the program or know anyone who had gained an understanding of voting, government, and politics from attending the classes.[21] We were engaged in that process, inviting new people to hold MFDP precinct workshops in their homes. They would be competing against the more politically aware middle-class black businessmen who I believed had not done enough to represent the poor. The movement often found women more responsive and willing to participate than men. They were outspoken, courageous, and determined—some of the most determined representatives of the downtrodden blacks in the state. These new leaders would form the nucleus of what we would leave behind at the end of the summer.

The task was challenging. A map in our office on Nelson Street showed the streets and precinct boundaries in the black neighborhoods where we canvassed. COFO assigned the voter registration volunteers by precinct. Valerie and I canvassed and organized in Precinct 6 in the South End, which made transportation difficult from the Brittons' house, but we managed, knowing we could get a cab ride with a black driver if the distance seemed just too long or the weather too hot. COFO soon assigned Valerie elsewhere, and I took sole responsibility for Precinct 6, a small area bordered by white neighborhoods.

COFO prepared the *Handbook for Precinct Organization*, which would have been useful in my organizing of a precinct, but it was not available to us in Greenville.[22] According to the handbook, ideally—and with an eventual goal of increasing official voter registration—we would assist in getting all adults to an initial meeting, where a chairman could be elected, and finding "some issues that the people feel strongly about" to ensure "a lively discussion" at the first meeting. The people would realize that "the only answer to those problems" was "through the use of political power." Since "the way to get political power is to have large numbers of people voting as a group, the people will themselves see the necessity of building a strong precinct organization." Control would not be in the hands of a few, but the people themselves would run the precinct in a true democracy. The chairman could use block captains with responsibility for one or two blocks to maintain voter record cards. The captains would make sure that all adults were registered to vote, attended precinct meetings, were informed of precinct activities, and got to the polls to vote on election day. The suggested frequency of meetings was monthly. A committee could be formed for "social referral" to find out all the social agencies that might be of benefit to people in the precinct. It would help build the precinct organization when "the people realize[d] the real benefits that can be had from such a political organization." Another committee would be for voter registration because of the importance of having "a large bloc of voters" for "a strong political organization." Block parties for filling out sample registration forms, voter registration workshops, and Freedom Days were suggested methods for increasing voter registration. This committee would also work to get out the vote on election day.

Not having this handbook, I was on my own for the first precinct workshop I organized. Our purposes were immediate: we had to explain the Convention Challenge, which would lead to election of delegates from each precinct to the county convention. I felt personal success in the workshop, despite the low attendance of twelve, in part because new people were becoming active and volunteering to conduct precinct workshops in their homes. I envisioned that they would be setting up a more comprehensive political structure than existed with the middle-class black establishment. I wrote home:

> I asked some people today at 5; 3 of us canvassed the area for an
> hour, I went alone at 7, ate two hamburgers, one woman went

out and hustled up four people and by 8:30 we had 12 in the room. Elected a chairman right away—a young guy, a vice chairman (unnecessary), the hostess became secretary (she's a nurse's aide and he's a chauffeur) and by the end of the meeting the host, Mr. Butler, was the treasurer to get the cokes for the next meeting Thursday night at the chairman's house. Mr. Butler was the strong man and the humorist in the crowd. They all took books for freedom registration and I think some of them will be working. The Butlers gave me a 7-up, Hershey bar, and potato chips to take home and took me home! This'll be the nucleus of some movement—I hope.

Elections in a precinct workshop had no significance other than as a trial run for the precinct meeting. On Wednesday, July 29, the day the precinct meetings were scheduled in nine precincts in Greenville, Mr. James Williams helped me canvass. He was a registered voter who had been president of the local NAACP. I met him at a church in the South End in use for a Freedom School, and we went to the office for a list of voters. After a stop for dinner, we walked around from noon to 7:30. Mr. Williams was fifty-five years old, interested, very quiet, and kindly, but with strong feelings about our organizing efforts because a prominent black in town had foreclosed on his cleaning business. As a result, he wanted to stop the group we were calling "Uncle Toms," although he didn't know quite how to do it. I appreciated that he was eager to learn, and he impressed me that he remembered the points that COFO people made. He demonstrated his leadership ability, and I counted him as a new community leader for COFO.

Twenty-three black neighbors came to my meeting of Precinct 6, held in the Bellegrove Baptist Church on Holmes Street, a good turnout. The meeting went well, with full, active participation on an equal basis. The MFDP voters elected Mr. Williams as precinct chairman and delegates to the Washington County convention scheduled for Friday, July 31.

The precinct meetings sent ten delegates from each of the precincts to the county convention. By the time of our meetings, the traditional, established black leaders had begun to realize that they wanted to be part of the MFDP for their own political power, to make sure they would be able to shape the party's policy and direction and not let others have control. With their political skills, these more educated middle-class blacks could influence other MFDP members, who were inexperienced and accustomed to following them.

At the Washington County convention, headlined in the *Delta Democrat-Times* as marked by "confusion" and "bickering," I watched with dismay as Mr. Chapple, who participated in the regular Democratic Party in Greenville, took over the meeting.[23] First, he got himself nominated to be chairman, and then Willie Rollins, a young guy who was working closely with COFO, nominated a friend of his for chairman. The man sitting next to Chapple moved that the election of Chapple be unanimous because of his experience. Charlie Cobb spoke up to stop this procedure, saying that everyone in the room had a right to speak and vote. He pointed out that the motion that Chapple's ally had made was what the regular Democratic Party does, deciding beforehand that So-and-So should be chairman without holding a real election. Charlie then called for a vote, reading out the young guy's name first, and he was elected. People might have thought they could vote for both nominees, but Charlie's technique got the most votes for the COFO-preferred chairman. The vote did not deter Chapple, who managed, when Charlie was not trying to restrain him, to get himself up front for part of the meeting to assist the new young chairman.

Finally, Chapple managed to control the election of county delegates to the state convention—the important part of the meeting—with a big maneuver that really outraged me. He made a motion that all the precinct chairmen and secretaries who were present automatically be made delegates to the state convention. Looking to their traditional political leader, the precinct-elected delegates assumed that he was doing the correct thing, but it seemed to me that they were suffering from what I called "the ignorance of the crowd as to procedure." So the motion passed, and Chapple thus ensured his own election and also that of Dorothy Edwards, the NAACP leader who was the wife of the funeral home director, but otherwise, as I noted in a letter home, he "got a strange bunch of people in there," which made me think he had made "a stupid move." As it turned out, only two others, elected alternates, were in sympathy with all that he wanted to do.

That evening twenty-four delegates and alternates from Greenville and Washington County were elected to go to the state convention.

I feared Chapple would use his position in his own self-interest, and I was confident that he did not support the MFDP's goal to represent black residents other than the middle-class, well-educated blacks. If he were a delegate and a compromise had to be made at the national convention that provided for seating only part of the delegation, I anticipated that he would manage to get seated because of his position within the regular Democratic Party. I anticipated that he would pull all sorts of strings to keep the MFDP down if the regular Democrats would do certain things for him.

After the meeting, I talked to some people who were very upset, as I was, with what had happened, including Dorothy Jones, Hodding Carter's maid, who had been elected an alternate. I thought, or perhaps wanted to believe, that these people expressed a view that was widespread sentiment within the community. Edna Moreton, one of the local MFDP supporters who was housing a volunteer, put it simply: she resented that "it's the little people who do all the work . . . and then these guys walk in and take it all away for themselves." Chapple had not been working on those hot days to collect registration forms. She was upset that what we were working for, "the benefits, prestige, whatever wouldn't seep back down to those who did the hard work." These two women were part of the grass roots; they had not been active politically before they met the Summer Project volunteers but became our supporters, engaged in our work organizing the MFDP, and exerted effort to influence their neighbors and friends to register to vote, freedom register, and attend mass meetings.[24] Only then would blacks be organized politically to represent their own interests. They believed in the fairness of what we were doing, didn't think it should be so hard to vote, and did not accept the status quo. Edna Moreton was one of many women in Greenville who, with their families, were willing to take the risk and bear the expense of housing volunteers.

We had to prepare minutes of all the meetings in Greenville, but nothing was forthcoming from the MFDP Washington County convention. I felt the urgency of getting our documents sent to COFO in Jackson for forwarding to the Washington office, which was coordinating northern support for the Convention Challenge. Proof that our conventions were held would be important for the legal part of the Challenge. On my own initiative, I paid a call early one morning on Mrs. Edwards, who had been elected secretary of the convention. I sat with her in her bedroom, where she had woken up sick, and took notes as she dictated the minutes of the local convention. We could type them up in the office.

The next step in the parallel party procedure was the MFDP district caucus, with the party districts corresponding to the congressional districts. Greenville was in the Second District, covering the Delta, including Greenwood in LeFlore County, Ruleville in Sunflower County, and Sharkey and Issaquena Counties to the south. It wasn't clear what the MFDP was to do because the memoranda received, one from Jackson and one from Greenwood—where SNCC had moved its headquarters for the summer—were confusing. I called the person listed in the Greenwood memo to ask questions and got it straight. Delegates and alternates to the state convention were to attend the district meeting to *caucus*—to meet and talk about what lay ahead. In each of the state's five congressional districts, the caucus elected both delegates and alternates, "subject to the approval of the upcoming State Convention."[25] It was erroneous, therefore, to call the district meetings "conventions" and thus imply that the election of delegates to the state convention took place there. As an expression of local preference, the district caucuses were "very important and some, at least, had understanding of good convention delegates and good political representation."[26]

We held a delegate workshop in Greenville and visited delegates individually before the district caucus to educate the newcomers about the procedure to be followed and check on their support for the Challenge. I noticed that what I called the "factions" showed up right away—the core of new MFDP leadership and the established middle-class NAACP members were vying for election. I understood the purpose of the workshop as follows, as I noted in my letter home: "The traditional philosophy is to put the experienced leadership in *all* positions of leadership, but this is not the philosophy of the MFDP that we tried to get across in the workshop. Anyone can go to the national convention if he can get himself elected because within the MFDP anyone can vote, even if he is illiterate."

In our individual calls on the less politically sophisticated delegates to get them ready for the meeting, what we wanted to do was to explain procedure and try to draw them out. I knew I was on a very political mission because there was a shrewd political group to struggle against, and those who had never been politically active needed to know the facts. Our discussions were strictly limited to political *procedure,* and I was always careful not to tell local residents how to vote.

On Sunday, August 2, after washing clothes until 11:00 a.m., I got to work preparing for the district caucus in Greenville. It was initially scheduled for Monday, but COFO changed it to Sunday at 2:00 in the afternoon so that more people could come. Some 350–400 people from nineteen of the district's twenty-two counties showed up in Friendship Baptist Church. The meeting started at 3:00, an hour late, and was pretty chaotic. Delegates from the counties elected a permanent chairman of the meeting, four delegates and two alternates to the national convention, three representatives to the state executive committee, a presidential elector and alternate. The election of the six delegates to the national convention was an expression of preference, with the actual election by vote of all the delegates from the counties to happen at the state convention. I noted that "each [of the candidates] had to speak and some were great." Now I was getting excited: I "couldn't sit still to listen and take it all in."

After the meeting, I introduced myself to Mrs. Hamer, reminding her that I had had dinner at her home the previous summer. She greeted me warmly and gave me an all-embracing, soulful hug. She told me about a speaking tour that had just taken her to Baltimore, Westport, Connecticut, Philadelphia, and elsewhere. In a letter home, I noted how far she had come: she was now on the MFDP State Executive Committee but only two years ago had been chopping cotton as Fannie before she went to register to vote. She was now well known throughout the Mississippi movement for her powerful voice, her singing, and her courage. At our MFDP district caucus, she led the freedom singing before the meeting started, and I thought it was the best I'd ever heard.

Now I began to worry about sending our Washington County delegates to the MFDP State Convention in Jackson, scheduled for August 6. Would the Greenville NAACP faction take over? Would the more militant blacks in the community stand up or do as their customary leaders said?

It had not occurred to me that they might not even go to the convention until I asked a few of them about their plans. It seemed that some of the delegates were not as interested in the MFDP Convention Challenge as we thought and might not be willing or able to attend because of a scheduling conflict.

So we made individual contacts with the twenty-four delegates to find out who was going. Dr. Page had been elected, but he couldn't go, and he told us he would also not be able to go to the national convention. I was sad to hear that because he was potentially the strongest black political leader we had identified. I learned much later how he eventually did assume a leadership role in Greenville. When I called Mrs. Edwards, whom I considered a typical NAACP member, she told me she wasn't going and didn't care who her alternate was. But at a workshop that evening, we learned from her colleagues that she had changed her mind. She *was* going and would be driving. I considered it a coup that we were able to arrange for Charlie Cobb to travel with her in her air-conditioned Cadillac. Perhaps he could influence her on the ride, or perhaps I was just glad that he would be there to counter the negative influence she might have on others in the car.

On August 6, hundreds of delegates and observers, mostly black, gathered from forty of Mississippi's eighty-two counties at the Masonic Temple in Jackson. The MFDP held precinct and county meetings in thirty-five counties; additional county meetings were held in Jackson because holding them in the counties themselves would have unduly endangered lives.[27] Reports of attendance varied from 750 to 2,500, but 800, the number stated in SNCC's *Student Voice,* has been repeated elsewhere. One local reporter provided an estimate of 750.[28] As a result of other commitments or lack of interest, only eleven out of twenty-four of our Washington County delegation from Greenville went to Jackson.

It was just two days before the MFDP State Convention that the bodies of Chaney, Goodman, and Schwerner were finally found, buried for forty-four days in an earthen dam. This discovery took the focus from the MFDP's goals, just as the disappearance of the three civil rights workers had affected the news coverage of the opening of the Summer Project.

I wasn't there, but another volunteer said that the convention "was quite impressive, with placards . . . showing where the delegation met,

MFDP State Convention in Jackson, 1964. Courtesy of the Wisconsin Historical Society, Image ID 97924.

and like all conventions it was very noisy, and disorganized."[29] The MFDP made the auditorium look like a convention hall with county signs like the placards a national party convention uses for state delegations. On a hot afternoon in this un-air-conditioned building, the large crowd sat, dignified and happy, as they waited to vote. They were dressed in their Sunday best clothes, conscientious, and ready to attend to serious business at the convention. Also spirited, they clapped and cheered and broke into song—freedom songs.

Joseph L. Rauh Jr., a prominent white liberal Washington attorney who had agreed to be the lawyer for the MFDP at the Democratic National Convention, explained his plans for success in Atlantic City. A founder and former chairman of the progressive Americans for Democratic Action and general counsel of the Leadership Council for Civil Rights, with long-standing influence in the Democratic Party, he was a member of the convention's Credentials Committee. He knew the committee did not have a sufficiently liberal constituency to recommend that the convention seat the MFDP delegation *instead of* the segregated Mississippi Democratic Party delegation, but he mentioned the possibility of seating the MFDP delegation alongside the regular Mississippi Democrats. He also knew at this time that "we had no chance of winning anything from the bureaucracy . . . . [T]hey didn't want to give us anything . . . that was perfectly clear."[30] But he offered his strategy to the MFDP in Jackson: obtain at least eleven supporters on the Credentials Committee—that is, 10 percent of its 110 members—who could vote out their position in a minority report; eight state delegations could then demand a vote of all delegates on the convention floor to win MFDP seating. He believed that *if* the MFDP could get a roll-call vote, there could be a win. He said that "the magic numbers are eleven and eight."[31] He struck the theme of the Convention Challenge—the MFDP was "legally, morally, and politically right"—and emphasized that the MFDP was the group that supported President Johnson, whereas the regular Mississippi Democrats were for Barry Goldwater, the Republican nominee: "we're loyal and they're disloyal."[32] As he described his speech a few years later, where he "got kind of demagogic in front of television," he "kept pounding away at 11 and 8, and they were shouting 11 and 8 before the speech was over, and that was the strategy."[33] This rallying cry made it easy to remember the strategy.

As a Washington insider well connected within the Democratic Party, Rauh knew more than he was telling the MFDP leadership or the delegates at the state convention. His withholding of information was presumably wise, considering the need for enthusiastic optimism from the MFDP newcomers to politics. The delegates at the state convention included a majority of former sharecroppers, farmers, day laborers, and small businessmen who were less formally educated than the average politician. Rauh only hinted at a problem in response to a question about support from President Johnson. His assurance that the MFDP would be seated depended on President Johnson's maintaining "a benevolent neutrality."[34]

Ella Baker, sixty, the wise, energetic, and inspiring senior adviser to SNCC, gave the keynote address. She considered the audience "an assemblage of people who have come through the wilderness of fear, who have come through the beatings, the harassments, the brutalization that are characteristic not only of Mississippi but unfortunately characteristic of too many of our areas in America."[35] This convention, she said, was "saying that the day has come when racism must be banished from the political body politic of our country and people." She mentioned the discovery of the bodies of the three missing civil rights workers as the unfortunate event that turned the country's eyes on the killing that was going on in Mississippi, saying, "Until the killing of black mothers' sons is as important as the killing of white mothers' sons, we who believe in freedom cannot rest."[36]

Ella Baker cautioned the delegates against voting to elect members who would act on their own behalf and not represent the interests of the poor when they got to Atlantic City. She had long experience with men tempted by their arrogance, pride, and self-interest while she maintained a commitment to the poorest, the most disregarded, and those most in need. She wanted the state convention delegates to be "careful lest we elect to represent us people who, for the first time, feel their sense of importance and will represent themselves before they represent you."[37]

This election was the principal business of the convention. The delegates would "ratify" the earlier election of the thirty delegates by the congressional district caucuses and elect the remainder of the sixty-eight delegates to the Democratic National Convention.[38] After seeing the maneuvering of the self-interested at the county convention in Greenville, I wondered whether the state convention would elect someone from Washington County. Conflicts between COFO organizers of the Summer Project and the moderate leadership of the NAACP in any county proved inevitable: the delegation might exclude NAACP members who were too conservative and middle class to represent the vast numbers of poor Mississippi blacks. COFO and Bob Moses wanted "as radical a delegation as you could [get], people who would stand up when they got to Atlantic City."[39] To accomplish its aims, COFO engaged in "old-style politics" to make sure the delegation was "the black majority, the rural poor" by "distributing a slate of delegates to be elected at large."[40] At the same time, Moses recognized the merit in a balanced, representative delegation in Atlantic City, including white delegates, some NAACP delegates, and not many SNCC organizers. Before the convention began, at a "SNCC caucus" at the nearby Pratt Memorial Church parsonage, the interested SNCC field secretaries learned that not all of them could seek election as MFDP delegates.[41] In addition to Mrs. Hamer, Moses considered the following native Mississippians to be appropriate representatives: Leslie McLemore, a recent graduate of Rust College in Holly Springs, Mississippi, who had been working in the MFDP Washington office during the summer; Jimmie Travis, the Jackson native who had gotten shot in the neck in February 1963 while working in Greenwood; and Charles McLaurin, a Jackson native working in Ruleville. The convention elected these SNCC workers, including McLaurin, who was not even present, as MFDP delegates to the Democratic National Convention.[42]

The state convention also elected the leadership of the party and the delegation: Lawrence Guyot would be chairman of the party, to head the state executive committee, and Aaron Henry was elected chairman of the delegation to the Democratic National Convention.[43] Henry was the "logical" choice "since he was so well known and well connected nationally."[44] McLemore was elected vice chairman of the party, and Fannie Lou Hamer vice chairman of the delegation. Ed King and Victoria Gray were elected national committeeman and national committeewoman.

The state convention did not elect anyone from Greenville to go to the national convention, but Unita Blackwell and Henry Sias from our neighboring Issaquena County did become delegates. It was Chapple, the NAACP leader and one of the Washington County delegates I did not trust, who worried me. The Second District caucus had not nominated him, but he managed to get himself nominated by another district. I felt great relief when someone so traditionally savvy about politics failed to get the necessary votes to be a national delegate. I presumed he would only be self-interested and not ally himself with the other MFDP delegates.

The MFDP convention proved to be a rousing occasion—with freedom songs sung and a march of enthusiastic delegates around the hall waving flags and county banners. It was politics at its best. I had no role in advising or working with our delegation from Greenville; the business at hand was theirs to decide. I was back in Greenville writing letters and ironing that afternoon.

I felt good about what our organizing meant for blacks in Mississippi.

The Summer Project volunteers had helped provide an educational experience in political participation. When I imagined TV sets turned on during the Democratic National Convention, I felt that Mississippi blacks would become more active in demanding their civil rights. I was even more excited now. I wrote in a letter home:

> This is what the MFDP means—this is the first time 90% of these people have had *any* political voice. It's an important training ground for leadership and political endeavor—thus this has priority over voter registration. Every time I see a TV set here, and it's often, I see the importance of the Convention Challenge. Mississippi Negroes will see Negroes speaking to the nation for them; somebody will be speaking the truth for them for the first time. This will rouse this 50% of the state to become active, to get an idea of how things can be done.

I summarized the reasons for the MFDP effort:

> Reasons for the whole effort: (1) beginning of political activity for all, (2) organizational structure for the training of local leadership; SNCC or COFO will no longer do everything like lead mass meetings and have all the information, and (3) to use in court cases to strike out the voter registration laws—which are discriminatory because they were passed since 1954 and are already enjoined in Panola and Tallahatchie Counties—and to unseat Jamie Whitten in Congress from this district on the basis that Mrs. Hamer who contested his seat in the primary, the candidate of the MFDP, has more constituents than he does if we can reach the quota, whatever it is. Very exciting to say the least.

Hearing about the enthusiasm of blacks who had not participated in politics before now, I considered the MFDP State Convention a great event. Except for getting more registrations in canvassing, COFO had completed the local process before it would take the Challenge to Atlantic City.

After the MFDP state convention, knowing that we had northern liberal support, I really believed that the national Democratic Party would accept the delegation from the MFDP and require the Mississippi Democratic Party to open its proceedings for black participation. In my last weeks in Greenville in August, I got involved in a different kind of local politics as I began to pay more attention to another project—the need for a suitable community center.

Charles T. Askew, an energetic young black architect from Philadelphia who came to Greenville as a Summer Project volunteer, designed a new community center for the blacks in town. The existing community center, essentially one room, was inadequate for all the programs COFO wanted to conduct in that space. He prepared the plans and sketched the front view for a prospectus we circulated to raise funds for construction. Round and openly inviting, it would include classrooms and a library for continuing the Freedom Schools. MFDP would have space for its political meetings.

We picked the name for the new center—"Herbert Lee Memorial Freedom Center," honoring the first Mississippi black killed for his participation in SNCC's voter registration activities. We used the word *freedom* in the name to distinguish the center from a traditional community center, with its activities limited to recreation. Askew anticipated the need to raise $13,000 to $18,000 for construction, which would include $5,000 for land, $6,200 for the materials (specially processed plywood for a simple A-frame construction), and $6,000 for skilled labor. He said the building could be erected in a short time using local community unskilled labor working under supervision. Construction would begin when an initial $3,000 was available. The community would raise funds, and we heard that citizens in the white community had agreed to match dollar for dollar the funds raised by the blacks. COFO wrote and circulated a prospectus with the floor plan and a short description. The volunteers were to raise money from family and friends back home. The plan was to include a place for political gatherings and to meet fundamental needs for clothing, infant health care, nutrition, and education.

Charlie Askew talked to me about the social and economic class distinctions that can exist in a black community and specifically about the middle-class black leadership in Greenville, which he had researched: "There has been Negro leadership for fifteen years here in cleaning, pub-

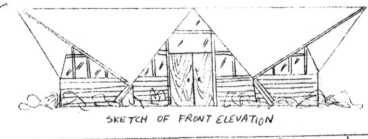

SKETCH OF FRONT ELEVATION

HERBERT LEE MEMORIAL FREEDOM CENTER

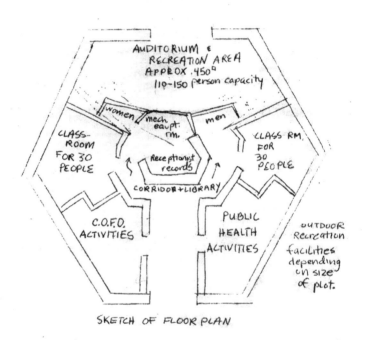

AUDITORIUM &
RECREATION AREA
APPROX. 450□
110-150 person capacity

women

mech.
eaupt.
rm.

men

CLASS-
ROOM
FOR 30
PEOPLE

Receptionist
records

CLASS RM.
FOR
30
PEOPLE

CORRIDOR + LIBRARY

C.O.F.O.
ACTIVITIES

PUBLIC
HEALTH
ACTIVITIES

OUTDOOR
Recreation
facilities
depending
on size
of plot.

SKETCH OF FLOOR PLAN

Plan for the Herbert Lee Memorial Freedom Center. Drawing by Charles T. Askew. Todd Collection.

lishing, funeral homes, doctors, and ministers—but you really can ask the question 'What have they done?'" He objected to how the black leadership operated, explaining to me why they slowed down the progress of the movement: "They have worked all these years *within* the segregated society, and they have gotten certain payments for it—a playground, a new high school as well as personal benefits I believe. When you challenge the whole system, which you do when you ask for CIVIL RIGHTS, these people, call them what you will, will not go along with it. Challenging those in the white community that they work with challenges them too. And so they slow the movement."

We talked disparagingly about the black leadership in Greenville, calling them the "*Negro* establishment"—this was before the country started using the term *black*—or, worse, *Uncle Toms*.

On August 2, I attended a meeting of "essentially the Carter Klan" held in the evening at Dr. Frisby's office to discuss the community center. I remember being the only woman and the only white person there. The group "got hung up in legal matters," I noted in a letter home: whether to organize as a nonprofit corporation, which would require a charter from the Mississippi secretary of state and thus limit any political activity, or a business corporation. As a result, "nothing was accomplished" until a second meeting later that week. Volunteer lawyers, one from Cleveland and another from Pittsburgh, offered a workable alternative. A national corporation such as the NCC could buy the land and lease it to COFO for a dollar. However, only five people showed up at the second meeting, making me fear that the conservative black town leaders were boycotting the project.

At that point, we had a beautiful prospectus, but no publicity. We planned to recruit club representatives from across social and economic class lines to meet and elect a permanent chairman of a new black leadership group that would be responsible for the fund-raising. COFO would collect the funds, and the group chairman and COFO would make withdrawals for expenses. The lawyers were put off by what they called Askew's pushiness, but they were interested in the project and proved helpful. The lawyer from Cleveland particularly impressed me because he was very efficient and seemed to know what he was doing. He reported to us from Jackson that he had talked to people about an NCC financial commitment and willingness to buy the land. I wrote, "Just can't believe that he would call back. Not the way COFO operates; you're never quite sure."

Police Chief Burnley issued a permit for the fund-raising drive to begin August 13, and we hoped to raise $3,000 in the black community and the rest from supporters outside Mississippi. Mrs. Frisby organized a tea, where our Summer Project director, Muriel Tillinghast, talked about the rural areas that were much more active than Greenville and told them many other things they hadn't known in an effort to stimulate fund-raising for the center. I was confident and wrote that groundbreaking would be November 1—regardless. I wanted the contributions I was receiving from individuals and churches in Summit to go to the center, and because funding the center was a responsibility of all the Greenville Summer Project volunteers, I planned to write to those who had left the project early to ask them to raise money. When I learned that the NCC Delta Ministry, a well-financed, long-term program for community development in the Delta, would be opening its headquarters office in Greenville, I was optimistic that sufficient support would become available for a successful project.

The plans for the center and my interest in Greenville kept me committed to my work. I started thinking about persuading my brother Eric to work in Mississippi after his summer in Finland. In the first week of August, I wrote that I had become very political. I was observing things going on that made me think, "There's something you must work against if you don't want to see the whole thing go down the drain!"

We also needed $10,000 to build a community medical clinic in nearby Issaquena County because there were no medical services there, and the people were afraid to go to the doctors in the next county, Sharkey, where it was reported that "the terror is not only real in the minds of Negroes, but . . . a point of pride for whites."[45] I felt that we volunteers should raise the needed funds because Issaquena County had *no* money to donate. I met Unita Blackwell, a dynamic outspoken woman from the small town of Mayersville in Issaquena County. She was a new leader whom I saw when she came to Greenville for MFDP meetings. She impressed me with her dedication and reminded me of Mrs. Hamer. She provided inspiration for me to do my part to meet the county's needs.

Pat and I had begun talking about holding a memorial service for

Chaney, Goodman, and Schwerner, and we helped Muriel and a volunteer minister, the Reverend Everett McNair, the chaplain at Talledega College in eastern Alabama, with the planning. First, we prepared a letter to the editor of the *Delta Democrat-Times* signed by Muriel, Pat, Candy Brown (another volunteer), and me that was published under the headline "We Must All Pray." We wanted Greenville, "progressive and peace-loving" as it was, to acknowledge that Greenville was in Mississippi and that Mississippi was "not free from the travesties of hatred and the malignancies produced by unthinking terrorists" who had murdered Michael Schwerner, James Chaney, and Andrew Goodman. We asked for prayer for those three men and for Mississippi, that "such acts of injustice and inhumanity" not happen again, and that "we, as human beings, care." We asked that Greenvillians come together and pray, "kneel next to each other," that evening at Friendship Baptist Church for the memorial service, concluding the letter, "The Lord will see us through."[46] That evening, "about 200 persons, mostly Negroes," were reported to have attended the event.[47] The MSU planned a memorial demonstration at the Federal Building for the next day. The mayor and the police chief were invited to speak, but they declined to attend. What happened to Schwerner, Chaney, and Goodman was the overwhelming story of the murder of blacks during the summer, but there were other murders that received less attention as well as some disappearances. For instance, on August 1, 1964, Wayne Yancey, a black volunteer who worked in Holly Springs, died in a mysterious car crash, but there was "no fanfare, no FBI investigation, no massive press coverage."[48]

On August 4, I wrote home that I was thinking very seriously about remaining in Mississippi because I thought my work was incomplete. I felt that we had accomplished little in the short period of time we were there but were getting to know the community and building relationships. If only we had more time, we could make a difference. I did not want to abandon people who had become important to me, and the planned community center might never get built if somebody didn't work to raise the funds and rally community support.

I knew that COFO planned to have one hundred volunteers stay in Mississippi. By August 12, I became more forceful with my parents about my staying on. I felt strongly that the Summer Project had just begun: "It takes so long to make people here realize what we are trying to do—they are just beginning to trust us." My thinking was based to a great extent on getting involved with the Herbert Lee Center. I was also influenced by "the strong white liberal support we have . . . the big banker, the newspaperman, *and* the chief of police." I hoped the white community in Greenville would contribute and believed that with more white liberal support for the MFDP at the national level, some real civil rights progress would be made. At the end of my letter, I said, "I'll try to be rational when I come home, but when you see these things and when I see the challenge for myself it becomes much more important than an academic question."

My plans to go to Stanford Law School for the fall had now been disrupted by the desire to stay in Mississippi. Before leaving for the convention, I looked up Marian Wright in her NAACP Legal Defense Fund office near the Masonic Temple in Jackson. She was twenty-five, a Spelman and Yale Law School graduate, put together and attractive, living and working full-time as a black woman lawyer and intending to become a member of the Mississippi state bar. Since there were only three black lawyers in the state who would take civil rights cases, she was making an important contribution. I told her who I was and my conflict: I was wrapped up in the activities in Greenville, and it seemed I should stay down in Mississippi for a year. Or should I go to Stanford Law School in September? She advised me clearly, "Go to law school. Not everyone has that opportunity, and you should take it."

I knew I wanted to go to Atlantic City for the Democratic National Convention, which would be pretty close to home in Summit. Pat and I had been working together on the plans for the new community center and the memorial service, and she shared all my enthusiasms. We planned to depart together for Summit and then the convention.

Some volunteers from Greenville had left early to work on influencing delegates to the Democratic Convention to support the MFDP Convention Challenge. My state seemed covered, and I didn't get involved in talking to delegates or seeking publicity. As the Summer Project activities were winding down, the political forces in the upcoming battle were gearing up. I wasn't hearing about these political developments at the time, but I was fascinated to find out later about all that went on while I was still in Greenville.

10

Early Work on the Convention Challenge

> The first step was investigation, where we did all the necessary research
> and analysis to totally understand the problem. . . . The idea is, decide
> what you need and do it yourself. Take matters into your own hands
> and do it yourself.
> —"The Beloved Community & Philosophy of Nonviolence,
> Remembrance of Diane Nash" (1988)[1]

Preparation for the MFDP Convention Challenge continued while I was
still in Mississippi, but I knew little about what the MFDP advisers, the
civil rights leaders, and Joe Rauh were doing inside and outside the state.
In Jackson, COFO staff were compiling the affidavits of registered voters
who had attempted but were not allowed to attend precinct and county
meetings of the Mississippi Democratic Party as evidence of their exclusion from regular party affairs. They also put together the evidence that the
MFDP had conducted its own precinct and county meetings as well as district caucuses before the state convention that nominated its delegates and
alternates. On behalf of the MFDP, Joe Rauh was to prepare a legal brief
in support of the Challenge for the convention's Credentials Committee.

Nonviolent demonstrations to heighten media exposure and increase
support within the Democratic Party were considered. At an Executive
Committee meeting on July 10, 1964, COFO decided to support demonstrations throughout the country the week before the convention.
COFO also planned "a vigil dramatizing the tragic hell of the daily life
of Negroes living in this country [that would] be held throughout the
convention" until there was a decision on the seating.[2] The committee
considered massive protests, possibly involving civil disobedience if the
MFDP were not seated.

Martin Luther King Jr. saw no choice but to support the Challenge but was hesitant about his role in Atlantic City and participation in demonstrations. Bayard Rustin was concerned that SNCC, the principal organization in COFO, might bring in radicals from the Northeast to demonstrate if the MFDP were not seated. If so, he did not want King involved because "King's reputation was too important to be damaged" by potential violence and destabilization of the national party convention.[3] But SNCC, without involving other groups, would do what the MFDP delegates agreed to do; Bob Moses did not rule out nonviolent direct action. King was on his five-day swing through Mississippi in support of the MFDP when Moses, Jim Forman, Ella Baker, and Ed King discussed their strategy with him, Ralph Abernathy, other SCLC aides, James Farmer, and Rustin at Tougaloo on July 23. Rustin, who had organized participation in the March on Washington, might coordinate a demonstration of 100,000 MFDP supporters outside Convention Hall, but he insisted on having "absolute control of everything outside the state."[4] Ella Baker, who believed that local people in Mississippi were responsible for the MFDP Challenge, was already directing the efforts in Washington, D.C., to obtain resolutions of support from state Democratic conventions. Without Rustin's commitment to local leadership, the discussion of planned, large-scale demonstrations in Atlantic City ended without any decision. The national leaders of the civil rights movement did assure the MFDP of their full support of the Challenge and their presence in Atlantic City.

Rauh asked Moses for research and help writing the brief and said at the end of June that his "confidence in our success remains unabated, though the Goldwater nomination would hurt badly."[5] He had Miles Jaffe, a first-year law student, helping with research on the politics of the Mississippi Democratic Party.[6] Jaffe read state newspapers at the Library of Congress. In response to Rauh's request, Moses suggested that Eleanor Holmes, whom he had recruited for the movement in 1963, could help Rauh with the brief. On July 27, she arrived home in Washington, D.C., straight from Yale Law School graduation and the Pennsylvania bar exam to "supervise" the writing of the brief.[7] When Eleanor arrived, she and Miles did more legal research, driving back and forth in Miles's convertible to the law library in the U.S. Courthouse. As Eleanor said, "We had a great time together."[8] In the end, they wrote the brief, consulting with Rauh in his office in the late afternoon.

From Mississippi, Aaron Henry sent a letter dated July 17, 1964, to John M. Bailey, chairman of the Democratic National Committee, stating that the MFDP would be sending a full delegation to the national convention to assert the right to be seated as the true representatives of Mississippi Democrats.[9] The delegation would be chosen in open meetings in accordance with Mississippi law. The letter requested tickets, floor privileges, badges, housing, and all the rights that accrue to a regular delegation. The MFDP needed to register with the Mississippi secretary of state to file a certificate of standing with the Democratic National Committee that the party had met state requirements to send a delegation to the convention, but the state refused to register the MFDP because of noncompliance with state law, and the MFDP followed an alternative certificate procedure.[10] Guyot, chairman of the MFDP, sent a letter dated August 6, 1964, to the Democratic National Committee, certifying that the delegates and alternates had been elected by the MFDP at the party's state convention on August 6, 1964, that they were loyal to the U.S. Constitution and the national Democratic Party, and that they were the true representatives of Mississippi Democrats and thus entitled to be seated at the Atlantic City convention.

The *Brief Submitted by the Mississippi Freedom Democratic Party* stated the facts of exclusion of blacks from all participation in the Mississippi Democratic Party, the organization and operation of the MFDP, and the operation of the regular Democratic Party—all of which Barney Frank "reviewed for accuracy." He spent "substantial time in Mississippi collecting facts" for the MFDP as a COFO summer volunteer in Jackson.[11] (A copy of the list of delegates in the brief is included in appendix B.)

The *MFDP Brief* argued that the all-white state party wrongfully excluded blacks from participation and thus had no legal, political, or moral right to represent Mississippi Democrats at the national convention.[12] The brief set forth the factual differences between the integrated MFDP delegation and the segregationist regular state party, which had denied black residents voting opportunities and party participation. The Mississippi Democratic Party was illegal because it operated to deny constitutional rights by furthering the state's denial of the right to vote and discriminating against blacks in party affairs in violation of the Fourteenth Amendment. The brief argued that the convention should uphold its progressive positions on civil rights in contrast to the conservative platform of the Republican Party. After enacting the Civil Rights Act of 1964, the Democrats should now endorse the legislative mandate of desegregation and nondiscrimination. The MFDP pledged its loyalty to the national Democratic Party and its nominees. The convention should not favor a disloyal delegation that had adopted a platform at odds with that of the national party and did not plan to support the party's nominees. Moreover, the Mississippi Democratic Party was morally wrong in excluding residents based on race. The MFDP had "an appeal . . . based on truth and justice, which . . . have their own kind of power," focusing on an "illegality, long recognized in our law as offensive to the most elementary principles of fairness, [that] arises from the arbitrary denial of voice and vote."[13] It would be morally wrong for the national Democratic Party to participate in Mississippi's injustice.

On August 18, 1964, Rauh held a press conference to release the brief and urge "benevolent neutrality" from the president.[14] The night before he had sent a copy to presidential aide Kenneth O'Donnell at the White House, pointing out a section in the brief that advocated seating both delegations.[15] Seating both delegations had been the solution in most of the previous cases of seating challenges over the course of more than 120 years. In a footnote to the legal arguments, the *MFDP Brief* included the following rationale: "[T]he seating of both delegations on numerous occasions in the past (see Appendix C) was obviously designed to encourage groups other than the 'regular' group in the hope they would one day help the National Party."[16]

Appendix C in the brief summarized contested delegations to Democratic National Conventions over the 120-year period 1836 through 1960, identifying the action taken in response to a seating challenge. The convention had seated both delegations, splitting the state's vote in thirteen state challenges. "In 1944, both delegations from Texas were seated and they split the vote of the state. . . . Johnson was there at that time and . . . everybody agreed to this. . . . Because nobody was going to vote in the '44 convention." Rauh alerted O'Donnell to this "interesting" information that Johnson himself was part of a challenging delegation that was ultimately seated. He thought "it was pretty good research" to have found this example, which he considered an obvious solution to the current issue of seating the MFDP at a convention when nobody would be voting.[17]

In Atlantic City, Rauh "presented himself as someone who wanted to see the delegation seated."[18] For all his strident advocacy on behalf of the MFDP to be seated, however, the brief forewarns of his willingness to give up on that MFDP goal. If the convention rejected its assertion of legal entitlement to be seated in lieu of the Mississippi Democratic Party, the brief, by including the proposal to seat both delegations, confirmed that the MFDP, too, was prepared to compromise.

Rauh also sent the brief to Walter Reuther, president of the United Auto Workers (UAW) union, who received a copy on August 19, 1964, simply marked "for your information."[19]

In Greenville, I heard or read in the paper that the MFDP was receiving northern state delegation support. In late February 1964, before the party was even officially established, the MFDP received a crucial supporting resolution from the California Democratic Council, a liberal subsection of the state's Democratic Party. Ella Baker, SNCC's senior adviser with extensive political experience and contacts, was in charge of the MFDP Washington office at 1353 U Street, N.W. SNCC field secretaries Walter Tillow, Reggie Robinson, Leslie McLemore, and Frank Smith were enlisting friendly members of the Credentials Committee and getting pledges of state support. On July 8, 1964, the MFDP had resolutions of support from eight delegations, either from a convention or by action of a party executive committee, including the delegations from California, New York, Minnesota, Wisconsin, Michigan, Oregon, Massachusetts, and the District of Columbia.[20] As a result of the SNCC efforts, confidence in getting support for a roll-call vote increased, but the wording of each delegation's resolution differed.[21] For instance, some would vote to unseat the Mississippi Democratic Party, but not to seat the MFDP. The resolutions were support in principle, less than a binding commitment. As Walter Tillow pointed out to me, they were at best a pledge.[22] They would not determine what would occur at the convention. After a sufficient number of states had indicated support for the MFDP, no more were forthcoming. The MFDP did not have time, money, or personnel to send people to all the state conventions.[23] As a result, few state delegations were in reserve if one of those that had pledged its support were to change its mind at the convention. According to Rauh, he knew on Sunday afternoon that he had ten states pledged to support the request for a roll call.[24] The count of ten included Colorado and Washington in addition to the seven states mentioned previously and the District of Columbia.

About the same time I left Mississippi on my way to Atlantic City, the MFDP delegates and supporters from COFO, SNCC, and CORE prepared to leave by bus. They stowed the file cabinets full of Freedom Registrations and affidavits in the luggage compartments at the bottom of the buses.[25] They were enthusiastic that the time had finally come for the long bus ride to the national convention, optimistic that they would unseat the regular all-white Mississippi delegation.

For the most part, they expected to be seated at the Democratic National Convention after their rousing state convention earlier in the month, when Joe Rauh outlined for them a strategy for success—"11 and 8." Although no one was more realistic than he about the chances of success, Rauh also ignored inside information he had received and followed his political instincts to encourage the newcomers to politics when he spoke at the MFDP State Convention. A couple of years later Barney Frank assessed that the "leadership in Jackson did not" anticipate the MFDP delegates would be seated but "expected to be kicked out."[26] Moses did not expect to succeed but thought the process important for consciousness raising and political education of the grassroots rural black people in Mississippi.[27] Ella Baker thought Moses was "among the more hopeful," but she "never expected that we'd be seated."[28] If the people could have a chance to vote, it might happen, but she knew enough about "political chicanery" to know that "if a vote is likely to go against the powers that be, they try to find ways of keeping that thing from coming to a vote."[29] Ed King also said, "We never really thought that anybody would get seated."[30]

Barney Frank observed, however, that the "pessimism of the leaders was not communicated to the rank and file." Using Canton, Mississippi, Annie Devine's hometown, as a typical example, he found that the "people were more optimistic."[31] The optimism was not limited to the less sophisticated, grassroots, rural black delegates but included the young SNCC organizers. Thinking about the "11 and 8" strategy in getting the Challenge to a floor vote, Charlie Cobb could imagine unseating the regular delegation. Although Julian Bond stayed in Atlanta and did not attend the convention, he told me later that he thought, from the support that had been building during the summer, that the Challenge would succeed. He expected support would continue without interference from the president.[32] Judy Richardson, a SNCC staff member who drove to Atlantic City from SNCC's summer Greenwood headquarters as part of the Sojourner Truth Motor Fleet, felt the momentum of "winning" in the events of the summer, with the organization in the D.C. office getting support from state delegations, congressmen, and senators, and so she "absolutely" expected the Challenge to succeed. She suspected that those among the MFDP supporters who later denied that sense of confidence had changed their views with the benefit of hindsight.[33]

To understand that optimism today, it is necessary to consider the context of the times. The political atmosphere in that different time incorporated optimism, hope, and confidence in the institutions of government. Victoria Gray, elected MFDP national committeewoman, whose husband had been fired from his job for her COFO organizing work and supervision of SCLC citizenship education classes, explained why the delegates were so confident. They were "still idealistic enough to believe that . . . the constitutional rights and things were all there to be ours as soon as we met the requirements." They were hopeful and expectant because of

a discovery that there is a way out of, you know, much of that is wrong with our lives . . . and that there is a way to change it and that is through the execution of this vote. . . . We can't get past these people at the state level because they've locked us out, but we, we just know that once we get to the national level, you know, with all of the proof that we have been locked out, and, and the fact that we've had the courage to go ahead and create our own party then there, you know, we [felt] like we were going to get that representation that we'd been denied for so long and participation in the process.[34]

The delegates risked their personal safety, their property, and their economic livelihood in claiming their citizenship rights and planned to tell their stories to members of the Credentials Committee and other delegates about what it meant to become active in the struggle for freedom in Mississippi. Jeri Joseph, a Minnesota delegate on the committee, had advance notice of the MFDP delegation in a ten-page document, "Biographical Sketches of Delegates to National Convention of the Democratic Party—1964." The document reveals, among other facts, that the ages of the MFDP delegates ranged from twenty-one to seventy-two. Their addresses, occupations, years of schooling, whether they were registered to vote, and the "incidents" of white retaliation against them were also recorded. For example, the homes of Hartman Turnbow, a farmer supporting voting rights in Holmes County, and another delegate were "shot into as a result of [their] civil rights activity." Other delegates had been "beaten and jailed," "subjected to bombings," "threatened by phone," "lost jobs," received "three bomb threats," "subjected to bombings, shootings, and threats by phone," "asked several times to leave the state," "shot by sub-machine gun," and "fired from two jobs."[35]

The buses traveling north stopped to pick up Hartman Turnbow, the independent, bold, and energetic leader in Holmes County, and his wife, C. Bell ("Sweets"). In mid-April 1963, Turnbow, in the first organized group of fourteen that had attempted to register to vote, had spoken up to the sheriff and in early May had been targeted by white vigilantes. Nightriders threw firebombs and fired rifle shots into his house. Turnbow grabbed his rifle, shot back, and ran off the intruders. No one was injured, but there was damage from the fire and an ensuing investigation. Not only was Turnbow arrested and charged with arson of his own house, but Bob Moses was arrested for interfering with the investigation. As Turnbow put it, "They thought if they'd burn me out, do around, thought that'd squish it, but that just made it worser. . . . Everybody then was determined to go register. They poured out; didn't care *what* it cost."[36]

Annie Devine, a forty-seven-year-old mother of four who worked as a life insurance agent in Canton and served as secretary of the MFDP delegation, was harassed by police for attending mass meetings, threatened with eviction from the housing project where she lived, and had her rent doubled as a result of her civil rights activity.[37] But when asked, she said she "never really suffered any undue harassment or intimidation" because women never suffer as much as men and because, as she said, "I [have] been very careful, and I've kept myself out of the way of people."[38] The convention would be "extremely exciting" for her as she was "taken with the idea of grassroots groups of people organizing against the establishment, a group of excited people coming together to work toward a common purpose."[39] After the convention, she decided to be a candidate for the U.S. House of Representatives from Mississippi's Fourth District, joining Fannie Lou Hamer and Victoria Gray, who had run for Congress in the June primaries.

Robert Miles, a member of the MFDP Executive Committee, was a fifty-year-old independent farmer from Batesville with a tenth-grade education. He had been active in the Panola County Voters' League before the summer of 1964 and had become a registered voter when a federal court order barred imposition of the restrictive constitutional interpretation requirement for registration. He understood the effect that fear of physical harm had on voter registration. In counties such as Tallahatchie and Sunflower, few people were registered "because of the intimidation, because of the threat, to people . . . and this has been going [on] for the last hundred years. Threatening lives. Not only threat. When I say threat, I just mean . . . people probably shot at you, threat you over the phone, threat your home, threat your home to burn, and things of that kind." Miles himself had suffered as a result of his civil rights leadership: "My home has been shot at twice, it has been bombed a couple of times, and numerous and numerous phone threats."[40]

On August 12, 1964, a Mississippi Chancery Court order temporarily enjoined the MFDP from using the name "Democratic," which was already in the name of another party, and banned ten named persons connected with the party "from acting as representatives, delegates, or officers" due to a "conspiracy," "sham and fraud" on the people of Mississippi because the party had not lawfully organized and "in fact . . . was conceived in the minds of COFO" workers.[41] The order named delegates Aaron Henry, R. L. T. Smith, Edwin King, Fannie Lou Hamer, Victoria Jackson Gray, Annie Devine, Lawrence Guyot, Leslie McLemore, A. Daniel Beittel, and Peggy Connor, a black registered voter who had attended the precinct meeting of the regular Mississippi Democratic Party in June in Hattiesburg. The MFDP did not plan to stop going to Atlantic City even though the elected leadership and the rest of the ten named in the injunction would be subject to arrest and held in contempt of court upon returning to Mississippi from the convention.

The three chartered Trailways buses left from Tougaloo at 10:00 p.m., Wednesday, August 19, carrying about 120 people, black and white, to the convention. Neither Dr. Beittel, a white delegate, who had a scheduling conflict, nor Guyot, chairman of the MFDP, went. When I asked Guyot many years later why he did not go, he explained that he had been arrested during the voter registration campaign in Hattiesburg for disturbing the peace, and two local black residents had put up a property bond for his release from jail. The authorities issued a warrant for his arrest, and if he had not gone to jail, the landowners would have lost their property. Guyot said he was "a political animal" who "fought like hell" and "would have loved" being in Atlantic City, but he was "completely satisfied the way it happened" and "proud" of what the delegates did.[42]

Hollis Watkins, the first Mississippi student to become involved in the SNCC voter registration project in 1961, said it was "real exciting" to be going to Atlantic City as one of the SNCC organizers.[43] SNCC staff accompanied the delegates to give them support and make them feel comfortable. When Charlie Cobb and Ivanhoe Donaldson arrived in Atlantic City in dirty blue jeans and muddy boots, Ella Baker told them they couldn't look like that, and she dressed them up appropriately. I didn't see them, but Jim Forman wrote about them: "the blue jeans twins of Mississippi, . . . the two veterans of the dirt roads and outhouses and grits, all dressed up now in Ivy League outfits . . . suits, button-down collars, striped ties, the works."[44] Handsome, thin, young blacks, toughened by two years of Mississippi experience but still wearing smiles, they were determined to make a good impression on the Democrats who held so much power and could make a big difference for the poor, disenfranchised, previously forgotten people of Mississippi.

The delegates went to the Gem Hotel at 505 Pacific Avenue in Atlantic City, a run-down hotel willing to host an integrated group, available

Union Temple Baptist Church in Atlantic City, New Jersey. Photo by Lisa Anderson Todd, May 2010.

at the last minute and with enough room for the whole delegation. There they would eat their meals, sleep crowded in their rooms, and coordinate lobbying delegates to support the Challenge. I never got to the Gem Hotel but found my headquarters at the Union Temple Baptist Church, the location of the MFDP caucuses, where Pat and I slept among the other supporters on the floor or on pews in the sanctuary.[45]

Virna Canson, a black NAACP activist from Sacramento and a member of the MFDP Credentials Committee, left California the day before her fellow delegates' charter plane. On Friday night, upon her arrival in Atlantic City, she learned the whereabouts of the MFDP delegation and took a cab to the Gem Hotel to see Aaron Henry. She considered him a "wonderful person who is a hard, dedicated worker"; she had known him for three years after meeting him at the Atlanta NAACP convention. He greeted her warmly, and she assured him of her efforts to do all that she could. But she "want[ed] to know their strategy" and "ask[ed] about compromise."[46]

Joe Rauh, an experienced politician and a Democratic Party insider, also left early for Atlantic City, but, unlike the MFDP delegates, he knew what to expect at the convention from his dealings with the White House in August. He understood that President Lyndon B. Johnson, the master of politics, would be in control.

11

Lyndon Johnson

The Formidable President

We can't do it all before breakfast.
—Lyndon Johnson to Walter Reuther[1]

Johnson's consideration of how to handle the MFDP factored in the recent nomination of conservative Barry Goldwater at the Republican National Convention in San Francisco on July 16, 1964. Johnson would have competed with the Republicans for black votes if liberal William Scranton had received the nomination, but now it appeared that blacks would have nowhere to turn but to the Democratic Party. So now Johnson did not need to favor the MFDP to receive black support in the election. Instead he had to concern himself with loss of the southern Dixiecrats in the Democratic Party when the Republicans were appealing to southern white conservatives with Goldwater's candidacy. Goldwater's campaign emphasized states' rights. He had decided to oppose the Civil Rights Act of 1964 based on his view that the federal legislation improperly interfered with the states and the rights of private persons doing business. His opposition to civil rights threatened Johnson's receipt of electoral votes from the southern states. George Wallace, the governor of Alabama who had cried, "Segregation now, segregation tomorrow, segregation forever," and who had stood in the schoolhouse door to block two black students attempting to register at the University of Alabama in June 1963, was also on the national stage opposed to civil rights. Early in the summer of 1964, the first violence from blacks had erupted in riots in northern inner cities. Johnson, the astute politician, began to worry about losing white support with the beginning of a "white backlash" against black demonstrations and job competition. He thought his election would also be affected by loss of these votes if the Democrats paid too much heed to blacks at the convention.

Lyndon Johnson controlled the convention. He had approved selection of the men in charge—"the bureaucracy" of the convention, as Joe Rauh called them.[2] Johnson commanded such loyalty that everyone given authority would do as they were told. He had power to defeat the MFDP. But I was optimistic because we had public support and believed we could get a democratic vote. I was unaware of how the president had prepared for the MFDP Convention Challenge far ahead of time. I have learned what he was doing from reading historians' accounts and listening to his taped telephone conversations, which were released to the public on July 18, 1997.[3]

The call of the convention specified the requirements for the delegation of a state political party to be seated and vote at the convention. Unpledged electors, a southern tradition that gave delegations a degree of political clout to select its nominees, violated the call of the convention. If the Mississippi Democratic Party reserved its votes by this means, its delegation could be considered illegal. Rauh received advice that chances of ridding the convention of the racist Mississippi delegation would be enhanced if "the issue [were] something *other* than civil rights," referring to the use of unpledged electors on the state ballot.[4] Rauh told White House aide Kenneth O'Donnell about a Mississippi law that created uncertainty as to whether Mississippi had unpledged electors or whether its voters would have the opportunity to cast ballots by electors pledged for the presidential and vice presidential nominees. The law might prevent a compromise that would seat both delegations. On July 20, Rauh sent to the White House a draft letter from John Bailey, chairman of the Democratic National Committee, to Bidwell Adam, chairman of the Mississippi Democratic Party Executive Committee, which quoted the call for the 1964 convention and requested that the Mississippi Democratic Party pass a resolution giving assurance of pledged electors.[5]

On July 28, the Mississippi Democratic Party unanimously adopted a resolution at its state convention for a slate of electors pledged to the nominees of the national Democratic Party, with the governor's assurance that a special session of the legislature could "make sure everyone in the state has a right to a choice in November" if the present law were a problem.[6] The delegation thus became legal as constituted.[7] The MFDP was challenging the legality of the Mississippi state delegation but with this resolution lost one of its legal arguments. By writing about this argument to Kenneth O'Donnell, Rauh had intervened on behalf of the Democratic Party and arguably against the interests of his client, the MFDP, while at the same time paving the way for compromise—that is, the seating of both delegations.

Nevertheless, the legality of the state delegation remained an issue at the convention, as the *MFDP Brief* argued. The MFDP did not comply with the state laws to qualify as a political party entitled to send a delegation to the convention, but unconstitutional laws prevented it from conducting required precinct and county meetings in all eighty-two counties in the state. Furthermore, the resolutions of the Mississippi Democratic Party reflected illegality. At its state convention, it resolved to "oppose, condemn and deplore the Civil Rights Act of 1964 as a naked grasp for extreme and unconstitutional Federal Power over private business and private lives" and "urge[d] the Congress to repeal it as soon as possible." Another resolution stated its belief "in separation of the races in all phases of our society."[8]

As the *New York Times* reported on July 20, 1964, the MFDP Convention Challenge represented a potential "embarrassing dilemma for the Democratic National Convention," and President Johnson faced a "politically explosive decision."[9] Seating the all-white segregationist Mississippi Democratic Party would offend the northern liberal voters, and seating the predominantly black MFDP delegation would alienate the white southern electoral bloc. Northern liberals in the Democratic Party favored the campaign for civil rights that had been heating up in the South since the 1955 Montgomery Bus Boycott, the 1961 Freedom Rides, and the 1963 demonstrations in Birmingham and Jackson and that had now culminated in the Mississippi Summer Project with the brutal murders of Chaney, Goodman, and Schwerner. Southern conservatives in the Democratic Party were adamantly opposed to integration and voting rights for blacks. The MFDP was loyal to Johnson, but there was "a very definite Goldwater sentiment . . . [among the regular Mississippi Democratic Party delegates] because of his stand and vote against the civil rights act" and a feeling that he would be the statewide favorite candidate in the general election.[10]

On the same date, July 20, an article by Washington reporters about the MFDP Convention Challenge appeared in a Topeka, Kansas, newspaper, identifying Walter Reuther, head of the UAW, whose picture appeared in the article, and CORE as "in the forefront in the organizing and financing of this explosive undertaking."[11] The article said they were working with Bayard Rustin, who could mobilize CORE demonstrators for the MFDP in Atlantic City and could count on Attorney General Robert Kennedy and California governor Edmund Brown. Both Rustin and Reuther did have an early interest in what would happen in Atlantic City. Rustin was "supportive, even excited, about . . . [the MFDP Convention Challenge] because of its potential to remake political power in the South," but although he had provided assistance to Bob Moses, he was not a *sponsor* of the Challenge.[12] In March that year, when Reuther had learned about the Challenge from Rauh, he was "cooler" in response than Rauh expected. More politically astute than Rauh, he "saw it immediately as a possible confrontation with Johnson" and refused to help.[13] The MFDP would also not be able to count on either Robert Kennedy, about to announce his candidacy for the U.S. Senate from New York, or Governor Brown, a supporter of President Johnson.

The Democratic Party leadership tried to find a solution to the problem the Challenge posed before the beginning of the convention on August 24. On the eve of the MFDP state convention in Jackson, Harold Leventhal, general counsel for the Democratic National Committee, reported his concerns to Bailey and Credentials Committee chairman David Lawrence: "the waters are troubled and they need oil." He had not seen the current Mississippi Democratic Party convention resolutions, but in 1960 they had stated "a belief in the segregation of the races" and included numerous "features hostile to the National Party." He considered the MFPD's credentials weak, but he thought it would be able to make a case against the regular Democrats that would "seem strong and just in many quarters." He proposed "splitting the delegation on a lop-sided basis, say 4 to 1," or proportionate to the membership in the parties. He hoped for an "intermediate solution" that would prevent the Mississippi Democrats from walking out of the convention.[14]

Johnson was discussing the problem with his aides sometime in late July, but he had reached "no final decision on how to resolve it."[15] On July 22, he was in "agony" in a taped phone conversation with his old friend John Connally, governor of Texas, feeling he had no one else to "bother," with every man in the cabinet a holdover from the Kennedy administration. He talked about the selection of a vice presidential nominee and the MFDP Challenge, which he wished he could stop because it was "very bad."[16] With Connally's support, the president soon made his decision in favor of the white southerners. Mississippi had a legal delegation, and, furthermore, southern Democrats would not tolerate "getting on the floor with a bunch of Negroes who were not part of the machinery," as Rauh explained the situation.[17] Johnson did not see any gain in votes from seating the MFDP, only a loss.

Johnson feared the election of Goldwater and believed he needed southern electoral votes to win the fall election. He remembered what had happened in 1948, when three dozen southern delegates had walked out of the Democratic Convention in Philadelphia after Hubert Humphrey, then mayor of Minneapolis, led the delegates to adopt a civil rights plank in the party platform that was unacceptable to the Dixiecrat segregationists. LBJ considered it crucially important to avoid an open-floor fight that would reveal the sharply contrasting views of the party's northern and southern wings and possibly precipitate a walkout. If there were a floor vote, he anticipated that not only Mississippi, Alabama, Louisiana, and South Carolina but also their neighboring states, including his home state of Texas, would walk out. He said he didn't care about Mississippi, Alabama, and Louisiana, but he did not want Mississippi to "run off 14 border states."[18] Motivated by a fear of losing as many as fifteen states to Goldwater in the election, LBJ adopted a policy of "containment."[19] He planned to prevent the civil rights issues from getting to the convention floor. He wanted a display of harmony and unity at the convention in preparation for a landslide victory in the fall. He decided against roll-call votes for nominations. The southern bloc in Congress, with congressmen and senators chairing committees, was needed for legislative programs, and he did not want to antagonize them further. Relations were already strained by his support for civil rights. The evening Johnson signed the civil rights bill, he told his aide Bill Moyers, "I think we just delivered the South to the Republican party for a long time to come."[20] But he was not ready to let it go.

Johnson decided that the MFDP would not be seated for additional reasons that have generally been overlooked. His fear of Goldwater, need for southern electoral votes, and preference for convention harmony over a divisive floor vote or southern delegate walkout are commonly cited as explanation for his decision. These reasons, however, should also be considered in the context of national unrest over civil rights. Public opinion had been sympathetic to the plight of blacks in the South, but a small backlash against civil rights demonstrators had also begun, and it grew after passage of the Civil Rights Act in early July. Blue-collar whites in the urban North feared competing with their black colleagues in a shrinking job market, and it was thought they might retaliate in the voting booth. The first of the urban riots—involving deaths, injuries, arrests, and property damage—occurred in Harlem beginning July 18, then in Rochester, and in early August in northern New Jersey. Johnson's lead over Goldwater shrank from 59 percentage points in June to 28 percentage points by August, and it appeared that race would be "the most emotionally explosive domestic issue" of the fall campaign.[21] After the Democratic National Convention, *Newsweek* reported from an insider: "The only way Lyndon Johnson can lose this election is for voters to cast their ballots on the question of whether or not they like Negroes."[22] Johnson did not want the results of the election to be determined by white Americans' attitude toward blacks. Race should not be the dominant issue before the electorate in the fall.

John Stewart, one of Hubert Humphrey's Senate aides, offered another explanation for Johnson's opposition to seating the MFDP. Considering LBJ's sensitive personality, Stewart projected his thinking: "How could all these people come making all this trouble when I've been the President who got this historic [civil rights] bill through?"[23] Johnson had been labeled "a racist" because he was from the South, a characterization that he considered an unfair stigma. He may have perceived what he considered MFDP's "ingratitude," which he would not have appreciated.

On July 24, after a Midwest governors meeting in Washington, the

Democratic governors visited with the president at the suggestion of Karl Rolvaag, governor of Minnesota, to discuss "the Mississippi problems."[24] Several states had adopted resolutions to prevent seating the all-white Mississippi delegation, but those with Democratic governors now gave assurance that they would "abide by the wishes of the President."[25]

On July 30, the public knew from newspaper reports that Johnson had decided "to seat the regulars and not to seat . . . [the MFDP]."[26] As Rauh admitted later in an interview, he already knew the president's decision when he went to the MFDP state convention in Jackson, yet he did not mention the president in projecting confidence and optimism in addressing the delegation. Once Johnson made his decision, he actively intervened to control the outcome of the dispute.

First, Johnson considered political insider Rauh responsible and pressured him to withdraw the Challenge. Johnson never did acknowledge the individual I knew to be the organizer of the MFDP—Bob Moses— and declined to recognize the leaders among the MFDP delegates— Aaron Henry, Ed King, Fannie Lou Hamer, Victoria Gray, and others. He considered the Convention Challenge to be led by Martin Luther King Jr. and Bayard Rustin.

Rauh knew the president's position from phone conversations he had with White House aides before the MFDP state convention, the number of which only increased after August 6, when MFDP funds, hotel, and buses were arranged. White House campaign leaders did not meet to discuss their strategy and tactics until August 6. They considered the MFDP Challenge "a ticking time bomb," with a known ten to thirteen members of the Credentials Committee possibly initiating a floor fight that would be "fierce and hostile." Jack Valenti, an early Johnson confidant on the White House staff, was dismayed over "the lack of pre-planning that allowed this issue to be so hot."[27] Without any plan, the campaign leaders gave a not very persuasive report to the president. Johnson knew Rauh's strategy from television coverage, and, according to Rauh, the president "realized for the first time that this was serious."[28] The "pressure" on him "to give up, to stop it, and to get out, to quit, resign, and everything else" was "incredible."[29]

Johnson brought in Senator Hubert Humphrey and Walter Reuther to influence Rauh. Humphrey and Rauh were friends and political allies in the liberal wing of the Democratic Party, and Rauh, for whom the UAW had been an important client since 1947, had been chosen general counsel of Reuther's union in January 1964.[30] Rauh, however, distinguished his roles, describing the nature of one conversation with Reuther as follows: "'The president is very angry—Joe, you've got to stop it.' And Walter would be very serious. He'd pound on me, and I'd say, 'Walter, I just can't give up. I believe in this, Walter. After all, I'm an employee of the UAW, but I'm not operating that way here.'"[31]

Reuther even told Rauh that "Lyndon thinks if we seat those people, Goldwater will win," which neither of them realistically expected.[32] Rauh made it clear he was "acting not as your general counsel, but as a citizen," and if he wanted to fire him, he said, "be my guest." Rauh has detailed the calls he received and emphasized that he "never even considered" quitting the Challenge.[33]

Johnson thought that if Humphrey and Reuther had "any leadership," they would get "Joe Rauh off that damn television." On August 9, Johnson called Reuther about Rauh because Rauh was saying he would take the Challenge to the convention floor. Rauh offered to step out, but James H. Rowe, Washington lawyer, former assistant to Franklin D. Roosevelt, and mutual friend of Johnson and Humphrey, advised that he stay in to "not let it get beyond bounds," to "kind of lead them." Johnson instructed Reuther, "Don't let it get out of *your* control." Reuther agreed with Johnson that the regulars should be seated to avoid a southern walkout. He had been against "this maneuver [the Challenge] from the beginning" and predicted that if Rauh were out, it would be "taken over by people out of control."[34]

Johnson told Reuther, "We can't do it all before breakfast." He was "going to do it the right way" if the Freedom Democrats would just wait for four years. "[S]omebody representing views like that will be seated four years from now," he said. He was "going to get these people registered," and he was going to try the Mississippi murderers of the civil rights workers.[35]

Rauh did not intend to resign, but under pressure he made promises to the White House after volunteering to Lee White, the president's special assistant for civil rights, to "pull out of the case," according to a memorandum written by White. On August 11, Rauh professed that the MFDP was "not his idea, and he would be just as happy if it would evaporate." He argued he should not withdraw, though, because "control" would then "pass to communist lawyers." He was referring to William Kunstler and Arthur Kinoy, who were called "communist" because of their membership in the National Lawyers Guild, the bar association with open membership policies and a willingness to provide legal defense to radicals and militant civil rights activists. Rauh was "perfectly willing to stay there and *cooperate completely*" with the president, "consistent with what he believes [is] his responsibility to his clients."[36] Rauh had a conflict of interest between the MFPD's interests and his position as a member of the Credentials Committee, and now he had an additional conflict between his legal representation of the MFDP and his voluntary commitment to the White House.

Rauh, despite his liberal credentials, was very definite in later stating his opinion that "Kinoy was a commie."[37] Shortly after the August 6 MFDP State Convention in Jackson, Kinoy had stopped in Washington at the suggestion of Bob Moses to find out "whether Rauh needed our help in any way in Atlantic City."[38] Ella Baker considered replacing Rauh as counsel before the convention.[39] Kinoy described the visit as "strange," with Rauh uninterested "in opening up any Atlantic City questions with us." Rather "[t]he coldness that had emanated from Rauh was as marked as any I could remember over the years."[40] Rauh has said that the Kinoy visit with Ella Baker and also possibly Bill Kunstler about a month before the national convention was an effort "to oust" him and get him to "withdraw"; they "insulted the hell" out of him. He did not know whether his "primary feeling about keeping the Lawyers Guild out was because of appearances or substance."[41]

In response to LBJ's decision to defeat the MFDP, Rauh proposed his "sensible solution" of seating both delegations and asked that Johnson be neutral in the contest. He proposed to Lee White "the seating of both delegations, not on the merits but on the basis of Party harmony and unity."[42] The votes could be split half and half. If there were "mere benevolent neutrality" on the part of the president, Rauh asserted, that would be enough to assure the MFDP of success.[43] Humphrey, Lawrence, and Bailey, without knowing more from Johnson, also hoped to seat both delegations. On August 10, a Democratic National Committee memo summarizing the arguments expected from the competing Mississippi delegations commented:

> [The Credentials Committee has] authority to determine whether on the face of it a delegation does have a legitimate claim to represent a state at the National Democratic Convention. Both delegations from Mississippi appear to have legitimate claims to represent that state. Therefore, the Committee can readily place both delegations temporarily on the permanent roll with each delegation having the power to cast one-half of the Mississippi votes. This arrangement could continue until changed circumstances dictate another solution, or until the competing delegations can devise another solution which is mutually satisfactory.[44]

Talk of seating both delegations ended when the president's position became known. Johnson did not obtain Rauh's withdrawal, but he could orchestrate alternatives to lessen Rauh's political influence.

Second, Johnson urged NAACP leader Roy Wilkins to stop the Challenge or at least to prevent a roll-call vote. Johnson called Reuther and laid out his problem, asking him how to stop support for what was spreading like "prairie fire." Reuther advised that the black leadership—Wilkins, A. Philip Randolph from the Brotherhood of Sleeping Car Porters, Martin Luther King Jr., and Whitney Young of the Urban League, "the four most stable people"—had to see that they had "nothing to win," be "responsible," and see "the wisdom of avoiding" a roll-call vote. The others in the movement, Johnson said, were "led primarily by members of the Communist Party." Reuther agreed that SNCC and CORE were. Reuther volunteered to call Wilkins; he considered him "the *most* responsible."[45]

Wilkins, however, had an obligation to the NAACP membership. At its fifty-fifth annual convention in Washington, D.C., in June 1964, the NAACP had passed a resolution to call upon Democratic Party delegates to vote to seat the MFDP delegation at the convention. Accordingly, Wilkins sent a memo to all NAACP branches directing them to inform delegates from their states of "the urgency" of the seating because, in part, the white attitude toward the murder of the three civil rights workers added proof that the political system in Mississippi "represents a murderous system, determined to exclude Negro residents from voting and from government." He was emphatic, though, that the NAACP would not participate in any demonstrations in support of the MFDP. Wilkins concluded his directive, "The representatives of this government-by-murder should not be seated at Atlantic City."[46]

When President Johnson called Wilkins, Wilkins sympathized with the president's predicament but stated that his own position would be "untenable" if he publicly opposed seating the MFDP. Johnson understood and was only asking him to think of something, to "scratch his noggin." Johnson said, "I don't know what to do." Wilkins placed the Challenge in context: the "finding of these bodies has taken on so much more emotional load than it had before." Johnson's personal appeal was that "the cause you fought for all your life is likely to be reversed and go right down the drain [if you don't do something to stop the Challenge]." Wilkins wanted to help his president, but he knew he had no influence with the Mississippi civil rights militants and so only offered to talk to a few political people in Michigan and California.[47]

Third, Johnson decided to bolster his sources of information about the MFDP Convention Challenge by requesting FBI surveillance. When he initially had asked for files on the MFDP, he had received nothing because the FBI had "never conducted an investigation of the MFDP and its files contain[ed] no record of it."[48] Now he planned through wiretaps and microphones as well as informants to gather political intelligence in Atlantic City. According to Cartha D. "Deke" DeLoach, FBI assistant to the director, on August 1 Walter Jenkins requested that DeLoach "head up a team to go to the Convention to keep Jenkins advised." Jenkins would then report the information to President Johnson. Jenkins said that Johnson's concern about attempts on his life and the lives of White House staffers and Democratic Party officials provided the FBI jurisdiction for the surveillance. DeLoach expressed reservations, but this presidential assertion was sufficient for Director J. Edgar Hoover to give his authorization. When the Senate Select Committee on Intelligence (the Church Committee) later challenged DeLoach that the FBI was playing politics, he said the agency had followed a presidential directive that came with "a semblance of jurisdiction."[49]

Johnson also wanted to monitor Robert F. Kennedy, then attorney general, because of a "lingering fear that Bobby might yet steal the show and become the recipient of a spontaneous nomination to the vice presidency."[50] DeLoach has insisted that "under no circumstances did the President, Walter Jenkins, or anyone else tell us to keep an eye on Bobby Kennedy or his activities."[51] Johnson's rivalry with the Kennedys, insecurity, and concern that Bobby Kennedy was a more likeable candidate for the 1964 Democratic ticket, however, support the contrary conclusions others have come to about Johnson's purposes for the surveillance. In addition, Johnson speculated to his ally Texas governor John Connally that Bobby Kennedy might have originated the MFDP Convention Challenge.[52]

The administration wanted the FBI to be useful in providing personal protection (normally the role of the Secret Service) in the event of civil disturbances from militant civil rights activists seeking a stronger platform or the seating of the MFDP (the role of the local police). DeLoach considered the assignment "[t]o keep abreast of all serious disruptive plans and activities" because the White House aides in Atlantic City "were particularly interested in suppressing dissent from black groups" to assure a large black voter turnout in the election.[53]

Fourth, and most significant, Johnson investigated whether the MFDP had sufficient support on the Credentials Committee for a minority report that would lead to the divisive roll-call vote on the floor of the convention. What Johnson called "operation one"—making sure that each state filled its two slots on the Credentials Committee with presidential picks—had been unsuccessful.[54] Now Johnson got a reading on all the named, individual, MFDP-supporting delegates on the committee well before the convention. On August 14, in a phone conversation with the president, O'Donnell reported which delegates supported the MFDP and how firm their support was. He was working with John Bailey, calling "everybody we can—directly" to analyze what was needed to prevent the minimum eleven votes for a minority report from the committee. Johnson asked if they were calling the MFDP-supporting delegates themselves. They were not if they could avoid it, O'Donnell responded, acknowledging that "[we] may have to reach that point."[55]

O'Donnell said there were ten MFDP supporters "before we begin the game," counting two from Colorado, two from Washington, D.C., two from Michigan, two from Wisconsin, and two from New York. He said it was "awfully difficult" and went on to list more supporters, specifying which of them were "Negro" or "colored." He added one from California, one from Iowa, and one from Maryland.[56] The count of thirteen was sufficient to file a minority report.

O'Donnell discussed how to persuade the identified delegates to drop the MFDP. Based on the phone calls he was making, O'Donnell classified the delegates as "definitely off" or "they could get" them to support the president. Johnson aides could get John English, a delegate from New York, but they had to count the other New York delegate, "a Negro girl" who worked for New York City mayor Bob Wagner, as "off." Governor Harold Hughes of Iowa told him they could get the Iowa man on the committee, but not the Iowa woman. They might be able to get the Colorado delegates. They could not get the woman from California, Virna Canson, who had "a colored name." Governor Pat Brown had told O'Donnell she was "fine," but O'Donnell did not believe him. They could not get the woman from Maryland, Victorine Adams, because she was a "colored woman." O'Donnell predicted there would be other MFDP supporters, such as the committee members from the Canal Zone and Guam, saying "it's a tough one."[57]

O'Donnell expressed his discouragement. If there were a minority report, that would be "worse than the rest." Considering the problems pretty severe, O'Donnell told Johnson he might go "talk to Joe"—his Democratic political ally in Washington, Joe Rauh.[58] According to Rauh, O'Donnell called him that day, asking, "Why don't we think of something here" because "we ought to do something." In this private discussion, Rauh repeated that "the sensible solution" was to seat both delegations. O'Donnell told Rauh what he already knew: seating the MFDP was unacceptable to the Mississippi Democrats and, more important, to Johnson.[59]

Johnson thought his decision to seat the regulars would be less controversial if they would demonstrate their loyalty to the national Democratic Party by taking the loyalty oath. It was unlikely they would, but Johnson expressed his concern to his friends and former colleagues in the Senate. The 1964 call to the convention required notifying delegates of this condition of eligibility whenever there was a credentials challenge. Johnson hoped a mild oath would be acceptable. Democratic National Committee counsel Leventhal crafted wording that was so mild it required only a formal assurance of an "*intention to* support the Convention's nominees in the forthcoming general election."[60]

President Johnson used his friendship and political leverage with Senator Eastland to influence Mississippi governor Paul B. Johnson to give the Mississippi delegates the freedom to make their own decisions about the loyalty oath. On August 17, Eastland called President Johnson to find out if the Mississippi delegation would be seated. He had heard that if Mississippi put pledged electors on the ballot, it would be. Johnson told him that every state ought to comply with the call of the convention that pledged electors and the names of the party's nominees under the Democratic Party label be on the state's election ballot. He asked Eastland to convince Governor Johnson to let the delegates in Atlantic City decide individually whether to take a loyalty oath that might commit them to support the convention nominees. Johnson would not, however, make any promise of seating and said he did not know what would happen at the convention.[61]

Johnson knew then, as he told the senator, that "there are fifteen" on the Credentials Committee who would vote for a minority report for the MFDP. And he saw "a clear majority" against seating the Mississippi delegation if there were a roll-call vote.[62]

At the same time, however, Bidwell Adam, Mississippi Democratic Party chairman, was predicting that the Credentials Committee would seat its delegation. His reasoning was that Johnson could seat who he wanted to seat, but he would lose big in the South if he did not favor the regulars; it would be "a tremendous political blunder," said Adam.[63]

President Johnson was in control of all these preconvention activities and displayed no interest in negotiating with those who wanted to influence him on behalf of the MFDP. Bayard Rustin, acting as adviser, urged Martin Luther King Jr. to request a meeting with the president to discuss the Challenge. Rauh, too, wanted King to request a White House meeting, for "only if King pushed Johnson forcefully, warning of a direct-action explosion if the MFDP was rebuffed, would there be any chance of the president supporting the joint seating of both contending Mississippi delegations."[64] Rustin, however, did not want King to commit to demonstrations in Atlantic City, for the reasons mentioned earlier and because the civil rights leaders had agreed on July 29 to a moratorium on mass marches, picketing, and demonstrations until Election Day. Roy Wilkins had called for the moratorium because he believed "there could be no real safety in assuming" that Goldwater had no chance of winning the election.[65] SNCC and CORE did not sign that agreement and were thus not prevented from engaging in protests during the convention.

On August 12, King called the White House to follow up on a telegram sent to request a meeting, but he was put off. Lee White did not think a meeting would be helpful, and it would "simply" be "an unnecessary affront to a large number of people at this particular time."[66] On August 13, Rustin called White to press for the meeting King wanted, saying "King really believes his own position is such that he needs to have it known publicly that he has met with and talked to [the president]."[67] Hearing this, White called King to tell him Johnson was too busy for a meeting, but he heard the substance of what King had to say concerning the importance of the MFDP effort to be seated. White conveyed King's arguments to the president that unless there were a suitable compromise, "a disastrous decline" in "the Negro moral[e]" could lead to more riots and demonstrations that would aid Goldwater's campaign, and black voters who could make a difference might "stay at home."[68]

Rustin and White then agreed to a meeting with all the national civil rights leaders.[69] Rauh told King that the president would take the initiative and decline to discuss the MFDP Challenge. The FBI was able to report this information to the White House from a tapped conversation between King and Rustin.[70] On August 19, Wilkins, Farmer, Randolph, and SNCC's chairman John Lewis went to the White House for a meeting with the president at 10:15 a.m., scheduled to be off the record. King sent a telegram of regret that he could not attend, even though he was in Washington to testify to the convention's platform committee. He expected the meeting would be unproductive. By not going, he avoided the need to speak up to the president and threaten the direct-action campaigns Rauh advised. Johnson opened the meeting "by stating flatly that he would not discuss any political questions or the convention." No one brought up the seating of the MFDP, and no attempt was made to negotiate the issues underlying the Convention Challenge. Instead the president discussed "problems of law and order, the FBI investigations that are going on, questions of violence, the demonstrations, unemployment, and retraining."[71] In responding to a letter John Lewis left for the president, Lee White assured Lewis of Johnson's "personal interest and concern" for the situation in Mississippi. White's response letter, dated August 20, stated: "The question of the seating of the Mississippi delegation at the National Convention of the Democratic Party is one that most properly should be considered by the Credentials Committee and I am confident that the points you have made in that connection will be fully considered."[72] The president thus avoided a public position on the MFDP Convention Challenge by asserting that the matter would be properly handled by the convention's Credentials Committee.

Johnson arguably had legal justification for his position. On August 17, Leventhal had submitted a proposal to Bailey and Lawrence that only the regulars who "provided assurance that they will support the ticket of the national convention" would be seated and that the Freedom Democrats would be excluded because they had "no standing" as the Democratic Party.[73] In a subsequent memo, Leventhal explained that the MFDP could not claim standing as the Democratic Party because it could not show that "the delegates chosen by their Convention reflects [*sic*] the true will of the majority of the Democratic voters entitled to participate in the process of selecting delegates to the Democratic National Convention." Leventhal noted that the MFDP constituency was 50,000 (or possibly 80,000), substantially less than the regular Democratic Party of Mississippi. In requiring a loyalty oath of the Mississippi Democratic Party delegates before seating them, the convention would improve the possibility of avoiding a roll-call vote or of winning the vote if there were a roll call. He found this position consistent with the call of the convention requiring a member of the Democratic National Committee to "declare affirmatively for the nominees of the Convention" and precedents. Alternatively, the assurance could be "softened" to an affirmation by the regulars of a "present intention" to support the national ticket.[74]

Johnson knew before the convention began that Democratic congressmen were supporting the MFDP. On August 21, twenty-four Democratic House members from nine states—including William Fitts Ryan (N.Y.), Philip Burton (Calif.), Don Edwards (Calif.), Augustus F. Hawkins

(Calif.), Charles C. Diggs Jr. (Mich.), Adam Clayton Powell (N.Y.), Robert W. Kastenmeier (Wis.), James G. O'Hara (Mich.), and James Roosevelt (N.Y.)—sent a telegram to the president supporting "the concepts" of the MFDP, "the one party" in Mississippi that has "pledged its loyalty, unconditionally, to President Johnson and the principles for which our national party stands." The telegram requested that the president "assure elementary justice" by refusing to seat the regular delegation and making "an accommodation" of the MFDP delegation. The congressmen expressed their hope that the matter could be resolved in the Credentials Committee, but if not that "at least 11 delegates from 8 states . . . file a minority report so that the full convention can work its will."[75]

Rauh, with his White House and Democratic Party connections, was privy to these Johnson-inspired activities *before* the convention. As he has said, he knew when he was in Jackson for the August 6 MFDP State Convention that "we had no chance of winning anything from the bureaucracy . . . they didn't want to give us anything."[76] However, he apparently did not believe he was obliged to provide explanations of what was going on, offer his inside information, or disclose his conflict of interest to the MFDP as the convention date approached.

President Johnson prepared as well as he could for the MFDP Convention Challenge before the delegates assembled in Atlantic City. If the Credentials Committee hearing could have been scheduled earlier, it might have been held with less public attention, but the scheduling could not be revisited.

12

One Woman in Atlantic City

> If the Freedom Democratic Party is not seated now, I question America. Is this America, the land of the free and the home of the brave, when we have to sleep with our telephones off of the hook because our lives be threatened daily, because we want to live as decent human beings in America?
>
> —Fannie Lou Hamer[1]

On Saturday, August 22, 1964, before all the delegates arrived in Atlantic City and before the Democratic National Convention began, Fannie Lou Hamer sat well prepared and well dressed in the large ballroom in Convention Hall, the stage set for the Credentials Committee to hear and decide the MFDP Convention Challenge. To Joe Rauh's credit, he had requested ballroom space for a large audience and nationwide television coverage after President Johnson decided to minimize press attention. The previously assigned room had space for only the committee, witnesses, and pooled television coverage. Rauh, however, wanted the committee and the nation to see what upstanding people the MFDP delegates were.

When UAW president Walter Reuther heard about the dispute over space for the hearing, he advised Johnson to give in to Rauh. If Johnson refused Rauh's request for the larger space, Rauh might get assertive and uncooperative. In Johnson's words, "sometimes when you put the top on the teakettle, it blows off." Granting the request would be "a little encouragement" for getting a compromise. Reuther told Johnson that he had spoken seriously to "Joe" about their long friendship and had threatened Rauh that they would "part company" if, when the chips were down, Rauh did not go along with the president. Reuther was willing to give him a little time but told Rauh, "you won't be my lawyer" one minute after he failed. Johnson reversed his decision on the small room in reliance on Reuther's assurance that Rauh would cooperate if this concession were made.[2]

The Credentials Committee decisions were the first order of business preliminary to the convention because contested delegates could not participate in committee proceedings and would not be able to vote convention business until the committee completed its work. The committee scheduled only an hour for the MFDP because it also needed to hear credentials contests for Alabama, Oregon, Puerto Rico, and Guam. Except for Alabama, which had unpledged electors, these contests involved competing delegations claiming to have been duly selected. At about 3:00 p.m., the elderly committee chairman, "old pro" David Lawrence—formerly governor of Pennsylvania, who had attended every Democratic Convention since 1912, when Woodrow Wilson was the nominee—began the hearing with the full MFDP delegation present.[3] Few of the Mississippi regulars from the state Democratic Party, a hodgepodge delegation of unelected officials, attended the hearing.

Chairman Lawrence said all the right things about the committee's "duty . . . to reach a conclusion that is both legal and proper. . . . [Members were to] resolve the differences brought before us in justice and with reason." He announced that the convention, "in an atmosphere of harmony and unity," would nominate the candidates and adopt the platform by acclamation.[4]

In his opening to the committee, Rauh presented the Freedom Registration forms to show the membership of the new party and summarized the MFDP position in its brief, a copy of which all the committee members had. The MFDP was entitled to be seated—for legal, political, and moral reasons—as the only party loyal to the national party and platform and open to all residents in Mississippi. The potential black voting population in Mississippi was stated in the *MFDP Brief* as 435,000, and COFO had set a goal of 100,000 registrants.[5] More than 80,000 disenfranchised blacks had voted in the 1963 Mississippi Freedom Vote, but only about 63,000 signed in 1964 to register for the MFDP.[6] As a voter registration volunteer responsible for urging MFDP registration, I had thought we did a good job. However, reports of violence during the

summer, including the early disappearance of the three civil rights workers, had intimidated the black residents, and they feared publicity, even
though the newspapers would not have access to their names. That fear as
well as apathy and a sense of futility contributed to individual decisions to
avoid the new and untested MFDP. Rauh supplemented the registrations
with affidavits of residents who had been kept out of the official party's
precinct and county meetings to support his case for seating the MFDP
in lieu of the regulars.

Rauh used his limited time to tell "the story of terror and tragedy in
Mississippi" with an opening statement and an array of witnesses from
the MFDP and the national civil rights leadership. Chairman Lawrence
requested that the witnesses stick to "election machinery and the forms of
election" without going into "the general life of the state of Mississippi,"
but Rauh declined to change the emotional pitch in the hearing room. It
was terror that prevented blacks from voting, terror that kept them out
of the Democratic Party, and he wanted the committee to hear about the
terror that the regular party used against the people of Mississippi. Rauh
asked the Credentials Committee members if they intended to support
the disloyal regulars who were responsible for the violence against the
voter campaigns and throw out the people who wanted to work for Lyndon Johnson.[7]

When Rauh finished, he called the first witnesses at the hearing: Dr.
Aaron Henry, the pharmacist from Clarksdale who was the state NAACP
president and chairman of the delegation, and Ed King, the white chaplain from Tougaloo College who was MFDP national committeeman.
They told how blacks were systematically denied the right to register and
vote with economic reprisals, harassment, and brutality and of the para-
lyzing fear that kept moderate Mississippi whites from supporting civil
rights.

In contrast to these first remarks by two formally educated delegates,
the most moving MFDP message came from one woman—Fannie Lou
Hamer—who used her powerful voice to ask: "If the Freedom Democratic Party is not seated now, I question America. Is this America, the
land of the free and the home of the brave, when we have to sleep with our
telephones off of the hook because our lives be threatened daily, because
we want to live as decent human beings in America?"[8] Mrs. Hamer gave

Fannie Lou Hamer testifying before the Democratic National Convention Credentials Committee on Saturday. Courtesy of A/P Wide World Photos.

a straightforward chronology in the eight minutes she was allotted. On August 31, 1962, she had gone with a group to Indianola to fill out her application to register to vote. The county registrar did not accept any of the group's applications that day. Immediately on her return home, the owner of the plantation where she had lived for eighteen years, alerted to the registration attempt, angrily confronted her with an ultimatum: withdraw her voter application or leave the next day. She answered him: "I didn't try to register for you. I tried to register for myself." She left and stayed with friends in town. White vigilantes soon set out on a shooting spree to get her and to intimidate other blacks from registering to vote. Sixteen bullets intended for her hit her friend's house on the night of September 10, 1962. Having taken precautions, she was sleeping elsewhere that night.

Mrs. Hamer continued with her shockingly graphic memories of the beating she suffered in Winona, Mississippi, on June 9, 1963, when police arrested her group returning from a citizenship workshop. In Mrs. Hamer's words to the committee,

> It wasn't too long before three white men came to my cell. One of these men was a state highway patrolman. He said, "We are going to make you wish you were dead."
>
> I was carried out of that cell into another cell, where they had two Negro prisoners. The state highway patrolman ordered the first Negro to take the blackjack.
>
> The first Negro prisoner ordered me, by orders from the state highway patrolman for me, to lay down on a bunk bed on my face, and I laid on my face.
>
> The first Negro began to beat, and I was beat by the first Negro until he was exhausted, and I was holding my hands behind me at the time on my left side because I suffered from polio when I was six years old.
>
> After the first Negro had beat until he was exhausted, the state highway patrolman ordered the second Negro to take the blackjack.
>
> The second Negro began to beat and I began to work my feet, and the state highway patrolman ordered the first Negro who had beat [me] to set on my feet to keep me from working my feet. I began to scream and one white man got up and began to beat me in my head and tell me to hush. One white man—my dress had worked up high, he walked over and pulled my dress down—and he pulled my dress back, back up. . . .
>
> All of this is on account we want to register, to become first-class citizens.[9]

Mrs. Hamer paused in her testimony and, with tears welling in her eyes, finished with her question: "Is this America?" Her impassioned speech stirred the emotions of many of the traditional politicians on the committee, in particular the women, including MFDP supporter Congresswoman Edith Green from Oregon. Mary McGrory, a Washington reporter, observed that Mrs. Hamer's "recital caused the women to weep and hang their heads."[10] I was moved by how she told her story, and I could imagine the middle-class white women's feelings as they watched and heard this dedicated black woman. She thanked the committee and, after dabbing at her eyes, left the witness table. The MFDP delegation stood up for her when she went to sit down.

Later, Fannie Lou Hamer told a *Jet* reporter, "I felt just like I was telling it from the mountain. That's why I like that song 'Go Tell It on the Mountain.' I feel like I'm talking to the world."[11] As Bob Moses pointed out, she was effective because she "spoke from her heart." He said: "And what came through always was her soul. I mean what you felt when she spoke and when she sang was someone who was opening up her soul and really telling you what she felt and the pain that she had felt and the life that she had lived. And somehow she was able to convey to that, the people, in a way in which we couldn't and I think one of the most beautiful things about the movement in Mississippi was that it was such that it enabled the person like Mrs. Hamer to emerge."[12]

Mrs. Hamer became known to a national audience that day not only with her riveting personal testimony televised live on Saturday afternoon, but also because her testimony was rebroadcast that evening. President Johnson had planned a press conference that would preempt the live broadcast and time the conference to interrupt her testimony. She overheard a man near her tell the cameramen, in her words, to "get that goddam television off them niggers from Mississippi" because, she thought, "the world was hearing too much."[13] Johnson was watching the coverage, and, according to one writer, he "became so alarmed that, on a transparent pretext, he called a televised press conference to divert the country's attention."[14] But in truth Johnson had planned a press conference the day before with TV coverage of a statement to the governors, which would be carried by all the networks. On Friday, August 21, George Reedy, the president's press secretary, told the press that the president would be meeting with as many as thirty-four Democratic governors at 2:30 p.m. the next day and that the press would be called in when he spoke to the governors at about 3:30 p.m. Cameras would be set up in advance, and, as for "coverage[,] there will be sound and film—full coverage." Reporters questioned if he would announce his vice presidential choice or speak about the convention because it sounded like "a fairly large production."[15]

The next day the president's address to the governors started at 4:00 p.m.[16] The cut-away to the White House press room with a personal appearance by the president would normally have happened only for a significant announcement, but the topic of the president's statement was merely an open speech to the governors about "the general situation in the country and the problems facing the nation."[17] He spoke about the tragic day nine months earlier when he had assumed office and said that his pledge then to continue the work of John F. Kennedy had been redeemed. He mentioned that no war had been widened, and the years of prosperity had continued, but he proclaimed a "challenge" that lay ahead to "practice a new politics . . . a new quality of public service, and . . . a new kind and character of partisanship."[18] The lack of newsworthiness of the subject suggests that the primary purpose of the address was to interfere with the live coverage of the MFDP testimony at the Credentials Committee hearing. Johnson was not, however, suddenly reacting emotionally to seeing Mrs. Hamer on TV, as suggested by other accounts.

The next MFDP witness was Rita Schwerner, twenty-two, the strong, sensitive white widow of CORE staffer Michael Schwerner. She spoke about her experience with the Mississippi authorities, who had done nothing to help her following the disappearance of her husband on June 21. A few weeks before the convention, the federal authorities had informed her that his body had been discovered, but the state had not released any official report and not sent her his death certificate. I did not know Rita then but have heard her criticism that no attention was paid to the killing of blacks, that the Neshoba County murders received national and international attention in 1964 and in the years after that because two of the men were white, not because they were civil rights workers who had been killed.

James Farmer, Roy Wilkins, and Martin Luther King Jr. also made statements in complete support of the MFDP. Dr. King thought the Democratic Party should be proud to have the MFDP delegation seated. He wrote later, "For it is in these saints in ordinary walks of life that the true spirit of democracy finds its most profound and abiding expression."[19] Dr. King's words had the same eloquent ring as his famous "I Have a Dream" speech, which I had heard at the March on Washington the previous summer:

Seating this delegation would become symbolic of the intention of this country to bring freedom and democracy to all people. It would be a declaration of political independence to underprivileged citizens long denied a voice in their own destinies. It would be a beacon light of hope for all the disenfranchised millions of this earth whether they be in Mississippi and Alabama, behind the Iron Curtain, floundering in the mire of South African apartheid, or freedom-seeking persons in Cuba. Recognition of the Freedom Democratic Party would say to them that somewhere in this world there is a nation that cares about justice, that lives in a democracy, and that insures [*sic*] the rights of the downtrodden.[20]

The regulars from the Mississippi Democratic Party then presented their position to the Credentials Committee but did little more than deny the assertions that had been made. E. K. Collins, a state senator from Laurel, Mississippi, in his "strategy of denial" said that blacks could participate in the Mississippi Democratic Party precinct meetings and county conventions.[21] In a twenty-five-page brief to the committee, available in sixty copies, the regular Democratic Party argued that it was the one "duly and legally organized" Democratic Party in Mississippi and that its delegates should be seated based on compliance with all the legal requirements for state delegations.[22] For their past loyalty to the Democratic ticket, the regular delegates wanted to be seated without having to pledge loyalty to the current nominees and party platform.

Virna Canson, the black delegate from California who supported the MFDP, asked Collins whether only 20 percent of the population voting to elect the governor of Mississippi was appropriate representation. He said registration was not significant because you cannot make people vote. According to an analysis of the MFDP Credentials Committee debate, when she asked how many members of the delegation were also members of the Citizens' Council, the Ku Klux Klan, or the Society for the Preservation of the White Race, he compared the MFDP to the Ku Klux Klan "as a way to distract from the issues of violence in the state."[23] He said that he could not answer because these organizations kept their rolls secret and operated outside the law. Also in response to a question from Virna Canson, Collins said he would not welcome the

MFDP into the delegation because it is illegally constituted, just like the KKK.

Joyce Austin, the "Negro girl"[24] from New York City whom presidential aide O'Donnell did not expect would change her support for the MFDP, also questioned Collins. She asked whether the state convention was open to blacks and if any attended. He answered that "they were in attendance as observers" but not as delegates because none was elected from county conventions. She also asked whether the party was committed to a segregated society and if its platform urged repeal of the Civil Rights Act. Collins clarified that a resolution, not the party's platform, made repeal a matter for congressional action.[25]

Assistant attorney general Ruble Griffin was a witness on behalf of the regulars to assert the party's purported loyalty to the national candidates and platform. He explained the resolution passed at the state convention that guaranteed that the names of the nominees from the national convention would be placed on the Mississippi ballot in November. He further maintained that the regulars' delegation was the only lawfully constituted delegation of the Democratic Party in the state of Mississippi. The MFDP did not register as required or organize properly and was not recognized in Mississippi. Citing the votes that MFDP candidates received in the June primary election, he said, "These people represent no one."[26]

According to Congressman Robert Kastenmeier from Wisconsin, a supporter of the MFDP on the Credentials Committee, the regulars were "shrewd enough not to say much," but they made "defensive statements that were patently incredible."[27] Theodore White, author of *The Making of the President 1964*, wrote that "though the white delegation was legal, it was morally absurd; it had been elected under laws administered in sin." In contrast, he said, the MFDP's "moral case was impeccable; these were citizens denied the founding rights of Americans."[28] Kastenmeier considered the effectiveness of the moral appeal "the best thing we had going for us."[29]

Rauh highlighted the regulars' unbelievable position in his closing rebuttal statement. He called Collins's statements "a kind of sweet talk here" while they were talking another way in Mississippi, where they vowed to fight for segregation no matter the cost. The Democrats in

Mississippi had called for not returning Kennedy to the White House and had labeled Johnson "a counterfeit Confederate who resigned from the South." Rauh reminded the committee of Mississippi governor Paul Johnson's campaign statement that "the [abbreviation] NAACP stands for Niggers, alligators, apes, coons, and possums." Rauh asked: "Is that the kind of people you are going to seat at this convention?"[30]

Rauh argued that the MFDP was a party, even though it had held precinct meetings in no more than forty of Mississippi's eighty-two counties. The greater threat of violence in some areas of the state limited the MFDP from organizing there. He assured the committee members that "[t]here is no legal problem [because] under law you don't have to do things that are impossible. We did everything humanly possible to follow Mississippi law and even more because there was a grave risk." The MFDP had built a legal party to the extent it could under the discriminatory state laws by registering members, holding precinct meetings and conventions, and pledging loyalty. As a political matter, the national Democratic Party should stand for principle and uphold its progressive positions on civil rights in contrast to the conservative platform of the Republican Party. Rauh also pointed out the Credentials Committee's right to vote the seating of the MFDP: "The law is clear that when there are two groups with substantial membership, and that is what we have here, you have the right to choose those who work for you, those who are for your platform."[31]

As a final point, Rauh maintained that the seating of the MFDP delegation was "legally and equitably right. The liberal principles upon which the Democratic Party has grown great demand that it stand with the Freedom Party at this convention." Mentioning that "the power structure of Mississippi was responsible [for] the death of those three boys" and a vote to seat the regulars would be a vote for the power structure of Mississippi rather than for the people for whom those three civil rights workers gave their lives, Rauh concluded: "Unless we stand up for principle and seat these people who have given so much for our party and our president, what is worse than the fact that we won't win is that we won't deserve to win."[32] Rauh was saying that it would be morally wrong for the Democratic National Party to participate in Mississippi's injustice. Thus, he effectively advocated the legal, political, and moral position of the MFDP in this crucially important forum, which received nationwide televised press coverage.

A greater national feeling of sympathy now arose for the plight of blacks in Mississippi and elsewhere in the South among radio and television reporters and the general public. The impact of the MFDP presentation, especially Mrs. Hamer's testimony, was "awesome . . . the emotions Hamer stirred completely changed the politics of the convention," according to Walter Mondale, at the time Minnesota's state attorney general and a member of the Credentials Committee. Not only Fannie Lou Hamer but also Joe Rauh on national television "captured the momentum at the convention."[33]

Chairman Lawrence sensed the sentiment in the room and declined to ask for a vote on the Mississippi dispute, but not because of "[n]eeding time to overcome the Hamer testimony" or because "Johnson forced the committee to postpone its decision," as was later said.[34] He knew the credentials disputes in 1964 would not resolve themselves quickly, in particular those of Mississippi and Alabama, and the committee's work would not be completed in a day. By telegram on August 13, more than a week earlier, he had sent notice to members of the committee that after "hear[ing] presentations of credentials contests," the committee would adjourn until 2:00 p.m. Sunday and "reconvene in executive session."[35] The hearing recessed after 7:00 p.m. on Saturday, and then it continued into the evening for consideration of the other challenges. The hearing finally adjourned at 11:15 p.m. without a recommendation for the opening session of the convention.

After the hearing, Mrs. Hamer sounded off to her fellow delegates, "fit to be tied because she had been told that she had been thrown off the air" by President Johnson.[36] Back at MFDP headquarters at the Gem Hotel, however, she saw the hearing rerun after the evening news. Knowing that more Americans would be hearing in this broadcast time the full story she told, she cheered up. Americans watching TV also heard Joe Rauh's brilliant, persuasive, and emotional closing statement.

The hearing gave the Challenge momentum and appeared to have greatly improved the MFDP's chances for success. What happened—the emotion, the television coverage, the arguments, and the authenticity of the clear moral message from Fannie Lou Hamer—elevated the spirits of all the MFDP delegates and supporters. A night of celebration began at the Gem Hotel. Rauh joined the MFDP delegates and SNCC staff, happy to celebrate his performance.

However, MFDP strategists still needed to collect from members of the Credentials Committee the required eleven votes for a minority report, a task that proved difficult. MFDP strategists attempted to nail down supporters as committee members took a break from the extended hearing on Saturday night, but no more than seven were willing to sign a statement. Virna Canson was considered "very likely" to commit to a minority report but would have to consult with the California delegation first.[37] Charles Diggs, a liberal black congressman from Detroit, who should have been a powerful supporter of the MFDP, wanted to evade the request. A proposal short of the MFDP's public position—seating the MFDP delegation in place of the Mississippi regulars—soon developed. Representative Edith Green suggested that all delegates taking a loyalty oath of support for the national nominees and platform be seated, with the votes to be split among them. Despite some despair expressed by Fannie Lou Hamer that the Democratic Party would consider seating the regulars, "[i]t was made clear that this [new proposal] was acceptable to the Freedom Party."[38] Thus, the MFDP indicated its willingness to compromise early in agreeing to the Green proposal.

Those of us who were in Atlantic City to support the MFDP sensed that the Freedom Democrats were winning. Overwhelming public support came in the form of telegrams to the White House and delegates in Atlantic City. Of 417 telegrams, all but one favored seating the Freedom Democrats. President Johnson, overseeing these events, might have to do more than he planned to have a harmonious, unified convention that would ensure his election in the fall.

13

Sunday in Atlantic City

We have no right to pick their delegates.

—Lyndon Johnson[1]

President Johnson's plan was to stall the issue of the Mississippi creden-
tials, "procrastinate and make no decision" long enough that seating the
MFDP would become academic. Johnson got another idea from Kenneth
O'Donnell that would be "a backstop": the members of the Credentials
Committee supporting the MFDP could vote not to seat the regular Mis-
sissippi delegation but decline to sign a minority report.[2]

On Sunday, August 23, the MFDP delegates and SNCC staff, along
with some volunteers, continued to lobby the members of the Credentials
Committee to secure and confirm their support for seating the MFDP
delegation. COFO prepared a small seventeen-page primer addressed to
the MFDP convention delegates and worded in simple terms that would
be useful to the less formally schooled delegates in their lobbying. It
explained who they were, with profiles of Fannie Lou Hamer, Aaron
Henry, A. Daniel Beittel, Victoria Gray, and Hartman Turnbow. A final
section described the "lily-white" delegation the Mississippi Democratic
Party had sent to the convention. The primer offered the MFDP delegates' availability for discussion, stating, "It is up to you to decide which
group should be seated."[3] According to Joe Rauh in an oral interview, the
MFDP delegates were "magnificent advocates" for seating the MFDP as
they spread themselves among state delegations, giving "the impression of
sincerity and oppression that couldn't have been better," and Bob Moses
did "a superior job in marshalling his forces" to attend state delegation
caucuses.[4] Worksheets listed the delegates on the Credentials Commit-

tee by name, state, hotel, and hotel phone number for easy contacts with potential supporters.[5] According to a biography of Fannie Lou Hamer, they had a "systematic and efficient" procedure, using worksheets for recording assessments of a delegate's support as "strong," "definite," or "sold us out."[6]

SNCC staff had assignments, but I knew no one who organized the summer volunteers for similar assignment to particular delegations or delegates. Ella Baker, slated for the job, decided it needed a younger person and turned the responsibility over to Eleanor Holmes to direct "the nonstop work." Not only did Eleanor coordinate the assignments, but she took on anyone volunteering to help and "educated her lobbyists."[7] Marian Wright, the new NAACP Legal Defense Fund lawyer in Jackson, assigned Joyce Ladner, a Hattiesburg native and seasoned SNCC organizer, to go with Hartman Turnbow and his wife to lobby the Oregon delegation. Joyce remembers time spent with Congresswoman Edith Green, who was a staunch supporter of the MFDP.[8] I'm sure the congresswoman appreciated Joyce's authoritative, knowledgeable, friendly company. Joyce tells the story of lobbying with "Sweets" Turnbow, who always carried a brown paper sack and always in that sack was her pistol.[9] Charlie Cobb attempted to influence Governor Endicott Peabody from his home state of Massachusetts, reminding him that Mary Peabody, his seventy-two-year-old mother, had been arrested for her support of civil rights in St. Augustine, Florida.[10] Governor Peabody "felt the Freedom Democrats were right but . . . politically he couldn't support them."[11]

Mendy Samstein, a twenty-six-year-old white New Yorker who had left graduate school to join SNCC in Mississippi, and white summer volunteer Marshall Ganz took an assignment to lobby the California delegation, which meant confirming the support of Virna Canson. Samstein understood her to be "a Pat Brown favorite in terms of Negroes" and "part of the upper crust Negro community." He reported the "very strong rumors" that her husband, the president of the local NAACP in Sacramento, was in line for a federal judgeship. He went to see her first thing Saturday morning for breakfast, taking along Fannie Lou Hamer and Annie Devine. He let them do all the talking. Virna Canson "didn't have any question about what is right or wrong, she knew it was right," and she was "very responsive," having asked questions at the Credentials Committee hearing based on notes he passed to her.[12]

Johnson, at this point not entirely confident about his stall strategy, knew that the regulars might go ahead and walk out or that the MFDP might threaten a roll-call vote. And so he prepared an alternative. On the Friday before the Saturday Credentials Committee hearing, Johnson approved a proposal that could be offered the MFDP for a compromise of the dispute. His stipulations were: (1) the Mississippi delegation would have to agree to support the nominees of the convention; (2) the Mississippi delegation would be seated, but there would be a resolution that the convention would never again seat delegations that exclude people on account of race, and (3) although they had "no legal right," "the others"—the MFDP delegates—would have no vote but would be given privileges and badges to sit on the floor of the convention as representatives of the people who can't vote in Mississippi. Johnson pointed out that there wouldn't be any voting, so that part of the plan was simply academic, and the loyalty oath that the Mississippi Democrats would have to sign would be mild. He presented these details to Walter Reuther, instructing him, "You put that over, Walter."[13]

On Sunday, August 23, the *New York Times* reported that after the Credentials Committee hearing, the chairman of the committee had delayed voting to "work out a formula" that would avoid a floor fight; "the chances for such a compromise were believed to be fairly good" as of Saturday night. The *Times* outlined the "formula under discussion" as (1) accreditation of the regulars; (2) seating of the entire MFDP delegation on the floor, meaning they would be treated as "honorary guests" of the convention; (3) a statement commending the MFDP; (4) a loyalty oath for the regulars; and (5) guidelines for changing the convention rules so that in the future "deliberate discrimination in party affairs would be a basis for challenging the acceptability of a delegation."[14] This formula originated in the White House and is called here the "Johnson offer."

On Sunday morning, while people were reading in the newspaper about possibly considering the MFDP delegates as honorary guests of the convention, part of the Credentials Committee met, according to notes taken by Harold Leventhal, to consider Johnson's offer. Attending this morning meeting were Congressman Robert Kastenmeier from

Wisconsin; Congressman Al Ullman from Oregon; Virna Canson, the black delegate from California; and Congresswoman Edith Green from Oregon. MFDP support by Ullman, "point man for the administration" and said to be "in LBJ's pocket," was less than total.[15] The members discussed alternatives to Johnson's offer: seating both delegations or, if a loyalty oath were refused, neither delegation. Virna Canson spoke up: "Give them [the MFDP delegates] some seats—some votes."[16] Ullman offered an alternative proposal for a compromise. Both delegations could be seated, the MFDP could have two votes, and the regulars could have the balance of Mississippi's twenty-six votes.[17] Edith Green had another substitute: "Ask both [to take the loyalty oath]—seat all who will sign." Rauh was not there. He said later that he was "working on making sure we had . . . our necessary eleven. That was the job that morning."[18]

At 11:00 a.m., Martin Luther King Jr. held a brunch to recruit and confirm support from members of the Credentials Committee. The previous night they had been reluctant. MFDP strategists targeted twenty potential delegates to be invited to hear from Dr. King. Virna Canson was unable to attend, and Congressman Diggs continued to be a questionable supporter, but coming out of the brunch were at least eleven supporters who would attend the afternoon meeting of the Credentials Committee. Some gave support to add to the MFDP's "bluffing power in terms of some [eventual] compromise" but were not prepared to take the dispute to a floor fight.[19]

At about 1:00 p.m., Leventhal showed Rauh the Johnson offer, which Rauh found to be "pretty thin," "really dreadful," with nothing for the MFDP delegates and only "some vague thing about the future." He said it was "a pile of crap. They gave us nothing. . . . It was a lousy offer."[20]

At the scheduled 2:00 p.m. Sunday meeting of the Credentials Committee, Chairman Lawrence, applying parliamentary procedure, tried to obtain a majority report that would recommend seating the regulars according to the Johnson offer and to ensure that the MFDP supporters would not file a minority report. As Rauh had informed the MFDP in Jackson on August 6, he knew that the MFDP could not win a majority vote because the Credentials Committee was not sufficiently liberal but, as he said later, "filled up with Southerners, party hacks."[21] Chairman Lawrence called on a delegate from Wyoming to make a motion to adopt the Johnson proposal, which, under the rules, could have only one amendment before voting. Thus, the initial offer became known as "the Wyoming proposal." Before the meeting, Rauh requested recognition so he could propose an amendment that both delegations be seated. He felt entitled to speak, but the chairman ignored him, turning to Ullman. In Rauh's view, the proceeding had been set up unfairly against him. As Rauh recalled, Ullman proposed what he had suggested that morning: an offer to MFDP of "two votes . . . [to] be shared by the whole delegation, as part of the Mississippi vote," in addition to the guest seats. Ullman recommended "seat[ing] a token number of the Freedom Democratic Party—perhaps two, perhaps the Chairman and Chairwoman of the Party."[22] This proposal included votes that would be specifically for Mississippi, not at large, a seat for a woman, and both seats for elected MFDP leaders. Rauh objected to it on the basis that Ullman was unreasonably reducing the MFDP demands before negotiations even began. Edith Green countered with her suggestion of "seating all members of both contesting delegations who would take loyalty oaths and dividing Mississippi's 26 votes equally among them."[23] Her proposal also included voting that would be for Mississippi, not at large.

Both Rauh and Edith Green believed they had ample support on the Credentials Committee for a minority report. Rauh counted seventeen supporters and, to his credit, prevented the committee from voting at this time. Edith Green counted eighteen supporters who would sign a minority report for the MFDP. Mrs. Hamer's story had touched her, and she was "serious," acting as "a threat" to Johnson's effort to resolve the Challenge. She was considered "a player," an effective advocate. She refused to disclose the names of the supporting members of the committee but "said she had the votes."[24]

The Ullman amendment split the MFDP supporters on the committee. Ullman was "positive that Green had the votes," and he was against a floor fight.[25] He believed that he could swing seven votes against a minority report if there were a "deal that helped the Freedom Party in Atlantic City." Kastenmeier considered an offer of two seats "enough of a concession . . . politically to undercut our [the MFDP's] position." The MFDP had "won a point."[26] The Johnson offer granted the MFDP only honorary guest seating, not seats that would represent, if only symbolically, the

voting and participation that the MFDP was seeking. Now the committee seemed willing to add to the Johnson offer and give the MFDP two
seats. Rauh counted again, found that he still had the required eleven
supporters for a minority report, and continued to object on behalf of
the MFDP. He used the threat of a minority report in public posturing
on Sunday afternoon.

The chairman could not call for a committee vote until he knew the
outcome would not include a minority report and would satisfy President Johnson. Several members of the committee, including Walter Mondale, suggested a subcommittee to find a compromise.[27] Mondale was
Humphrey's protégé, a young man at age thirty-six, on the rise in the
Democratic Party, nearing the end of his second term as Minnesota's
attorney general, and attending his first national convention. Based on
Humphrey's advice, the chairman selected Mondale to head the subcommittee. Humphrey had warned Mondale that the Mississippi credentials
contest could become "a national flashpoint" when the Credentials Committee would be forced to choose a slate.[28] The whole country was alert
to the civil rights battles and would be watching the televised hearing.
A Humphrey aide had alerted Mondale "to stay in close touch" with
Sherwin Markman, an attorney from Iowa, who was also on the Credentials Committee.[29] Mondale had a "passion for racial equality and instinc-
tive concern for society's outcasts," but now he felt he was "representing
Humphrey and he did not want to let him down."[30] He was "the perfect
choice" because he was a Humphrey ally, well known as a liberal in Minnesota and a member of Americans for Democratic Action. The nucleus
of the northern support in the Democratic Party, this organization had
passed a political policy resolution at its May 1964 convention urging
the Democratic National Committee to seat the MFDP.[31] Americans for
Democratic Action was "leading the fight in a real sense."[32] Mondale
took the assignment because it might serve him well in his political ambi-
tion; he was "very conscious" of the implications for his career. He hoped
for appointment by Minnesota's governor to Humphrey's vacant Senate seat after election of a Johnson–Humphrey ticket. He knew, however, that he would have little discretion to reach a compromise since the
sitting president was "watching every step of the proceedings from the
White House."[33]

The subcommittee included Markman, who "was really representing the Administration";[34] Charles Diggs, the liberal black congressman from Michigan; former Texas governor Price Daniel; and Irving Kalter from Georgia. Mondale could break any North–South tie. Tom Finney, a thirty-eight-year-old Washington lawyer, formerly with the CIA, was a partner of Johnson's friend Clark Clifford. He was labeled the president's "chief agent" and served as adviser to the Credentials Committee and the subcommittee.[35] Active at the 1960 Democratic National Convention in an effort to draft Adlai Stevenson and stop Kennedy, Finney was well acquainted with the Johnson inner circle. He had some familiarity with the MFDP, or at least with Mississippi, from accompanying Allen Dulles, CIA director, to Jackson at the time of the federally coordinated search for the three missing civil rights workers.[36] Mondale as tie breaker would be "representative of the dominant faction of the party."[37] Members of the subcommittee went off to "begin improvising," as Mondale put it, and the Credentials Committee adjourned.[38]

SNCC field secretary Mendy Samstein called the committee's Sunday maneuver "a delaying action until they could knock down our eleven people" needed for the minority report. Johnson aides had already begun to "muscle" at least some of the MFDP support to less than eleven.[39] Mondale viewed the adjournment as "an excuse to get negotiations going."[40]

After the committee adjourned, Walter Jenkins, assigned to be in Atlantic City with Bill Moyers, reported to the president by telephone before 4:00 p.m. He described the substance of Ullman's proposal as adding two seats to Johnson's offer. Johnson's reaction suggested that he did not know about the two-seat idea. Jenkins proposed that Chairman Lawrence could put a new offer of seating two MFDP members as "a token of appreciation and esteem" to a vote in the Credentials Committee. Ullman was confident of enough votes to avoid a minority report, but the votes were not yet lined up. Delay would be required. Delegates from New York, California, and Oregon were continuing problems. Governor Brown of California might help. From New York, John English was supporting the president, but the woman representative on the committee, Joyce Austin, the black woman working for Mayor Wagner, was uncertain. That left Oregon, presumably a reference to Edith Green. The administration was counting thirteen MFDP supporters.[41]

At this time, Johnson objected to the idea of two seats for the MFDP, saying, "We have no right to pick their delegates." Moreover, he felt that seating *any* blacks from Mississippi would cause offense to the southern bloc. Governor Connally of Texas had reportedly used the crudest language—calling the MFDP delegates "those black buggers"—in advising Johnson against allowing blacks on the floor of the convention as delegates.[42] The Mississippi regulars did not want the predominantly black MFDP recognized as legitimate. Just as they would not choose to sit down and eat with blacks, they did not want to sit next to black MFDP delegates at the convention. Johnson listened but did not change his offer.

Johnson had planned how he would micromanage the dispute at the convention, but the MFDP had showed more political strength than expected and had refused his idea of honorary guest seating. The Credentials Committee had to come up with new ideas to keep the issue off the convention floor. And Rauh was no longer to be trusted. LBJ told Jenkins, "If he [Rauh] plans to play with us, then it [the issue] can't get out on the floor. . . . Don't you tell him," Johnson commanded.[43] Rauh had not been getting the president votes, except for the support of English from New York. O'Donnell or Jenkins were ordered to speak to him about that.

The Mondale subcommittee needed to find a solution that would be acceptable to Johnson. Determining what the regulars would agree to that would also satisfy the MFDP proved difficult. According to Mondale, "We had more train wrecks than you could count on two hands."[44] Markman called it "a very, very painful negotiation." The MFDP "wanted their remedy right now," and the southerners wanted the status quo.[45] The Mississippi regulars were actually not very concerned about the MFDP Convention Challenge. Hodding Carter III told me they were "quite clear" that they didn't care: "to be seated, or unseated or anything else, because they didn't believe the party had the guts to do the only important thing, which was to strip the congressional delegation of seniority. All the rest of it was essentially irrelevant."[46]

The MFDP wanted voting participation on an equal basis—nothing less than 50 percent of the votes for Mississippi.[47] The MFDP delegates adopted Edith Green's proposal as their consistent position on compromise. Shared voting according to the number of delegates, both regulars and Freedom Democrats, who agreed to take the loyalty oath represented both a gain and a loss for the MFDP delegates. Most important, they would gain equal political power in official recognition and the votes they deemed critical. But they would have to give up their demand that the Mississippi Democrats be excluded from participation in the affairs of the national Democratic Party. By seating the all-white segregationist Mississippi Democrats, the national Democratic Party would be recognizing the status quo—the legality, political power, and moral legitimacy of the racists. The Democrats would not be criticizing or condemning the Mississippi Democratic Party for excluding black residents from participation in party affairs and for preventing blacks' voter registration. The black victims of racism and discrimination who were elected MFDP delegates would not find it easy to sit in the same seats with the whites. The MFDP wanted *inclusion* in the national Democratic Party processes but, in the interest of compromise and a fair settlement of the Challenge, would no longer demand *exclusion* of the Mississippi Democrats. They did not want to *share* voting power with racists but would agree to compromise to sit with them as convention delegates and vote for the interests of all Mississippi citizens.

On Sunday, the White House knew from its FBI surveillance that Martin Luther King Jr. would be sending a telegram on behalf of the MFDP early that evening.[48] He called for seating *only* the MFDP and reminded the president that the MFDP had been asking for his "benevolent neutrality" in the credentials dispute. The issue was not "a routine political one" but involved "a fundamental moral question . . . whether the Democratic Party will stand for fair political representation, against violence and oppression, and for those people who are denied the right to vote in Mississippi." Only the president would be able to make clear the Democratic Party's position on the MFDP. King noted the support on the Credentials Committee to fight for the MFDP on the floor of the convention and asked the president to join with them.[49]

The telegram upset Johnson, considering it "a major challenge to his authority," and talked about it to his friend Senator Richard Russell from Georgia. Johnson even considered that the MFDP was "getting ready to take charge of the convention" and speculated that the telegram was part of a plot hatched by Bobby Kennedy, that it was "Bobby's trap."[50]

On Sunday evening, black Democrats from state delegations, all experienced politicians, caucused at the Deauville Hotel about seating the MFDP. According to a report by Charles Sherrod, SNCC's first field secretary who worked in southwestern Georgia, some MFDP delegates and supporters managed to attend this caucus without invitation.[51] Congressman Charles Dawson from Chicago, "the black dean of politics," commanding the attention of the others, emphasized adherence to President Johnson and the national party.[52] That notion angered Annie Devine, the secretary of the MFDP delegation from Canton, who spoke up: "We have been treated like beasts in Mississippi. They shot us down like animals. We risk our lives coming up here . . . politics must be corrupt if it don't care none about people down here. . . . These politicians sit in positions and forget the people who put them there."[53] She pleaded that the politicians not forget them after the treatment they had received in Mississippi, but her words had little effect. Knowing what Johnson wanted, the black politicians at this meeting individually affirmed their party loyalty, letting the MFDP know that it could no longer count on their support for the Challenge.

That night and late into the morning hours, "discussions" took place for a compromise of the MFDP Challenge. Mondale became the "central figure," and Rauh, who had been named a special adviser to the Mondale subcommittee, appeared before the informal sessions of the group.[54] The significant meeting took place in Dr. King's suite at the Claridge Hotel, when Credentials Committee supporters wanted to discuss with MFDP leaders, their strategists, and Bob Moses what the MFDP would be willing to give up in a settlement. Moses was late; he arrived with some of the MFDP delegates. He had been speaking to an MFDP caucus at the church to help the delegates understand that they were in a battle with Johnson, who was using political pressure against them, rather than in a legal dispute. A number of MFDP delegates who went to the meeting in King's suite listened from the hallway, consistent with Bob Moses's idea that they should hear the discussions to be able to make their own decisions.

According to Arthur Waskow, an MFDP strategist from the Institute for Policy Studies, who wrote up the events in Atlantic City, the possibility of two votes for the MFDP came up. One option would be seating both delegations with full rights, except that there would be no decision as to voting rights until the convention faced an issue that required a vote. The MFDP conjectured without knowing for sure whether nominations and other actions might be carried by acclamation. A second less desirable option was "the notion of giving two votes to the Freedom Party," which Waskow said was "not totally unacceptable."[55] Bob Moses later disputed a claim that he indicated he would accept two votes.[56] At this time, the two-votes proposal was understood as the Ullman substitute introduced on Sunday afternoon at the Credentials Committee meeting: two votes would be given to MFDP leaders and would not be at large, but part of the Mississippi vote in general.

During this Sunday night session, Rauh and Congressman Diggs, a member of the subcommittee, were emissaries who would carry the MFDP views on compromise to the Mondale subcommittee and relay information from the subcommittee to the MFDP group. However, they took nothing helpful back to the MFDP group before the end of the evening meeting. With regard to the possibility of seating both delegations, with voting rights deferred, Rauh reported back from the Mondale subcommittee that the "notion . . . [was] scoffed at on the grounds that there would indeed be actual roll calls at the convention."[57] Johnson, however, had no desire for divisive roll-call votes, and the chairman's opening of the Credentials Committee hearing had confirmed that actions would be taken by acclamation. Rauh said that the subcommittee was negotiating with him and others, but that "nothing much [was coming] out of that."[58] According to Rauh, the subcommittee had nothing to offer, and there was nothing for him to present on behalf of the MFDP. Since the Mondale subcommittee put nothing out for consideration, negotiations did not take place. The idea of two votes was in the air—thrown out as a "trial balloon"—but not on the table.[59] Rauh had heard talk of two delegates "from the day [he] got [to Atlantic City]," but he had no response to this idea for the subcommittee.[60]

Rauh had wanted both delegations seated as a compromise, which was his "sensible solution."[61] He knew a two-seat offer was being talked about. He could have considered it with the MFDP and used it to engage in negotiations. Instead, he claimed the MFDP did not *receive* an offer, which absolved him from making any counteroffer of an alternative that the MFDP delegates might have found acceptable. Rauh had a different style of negotiating: every night through Monday night he stopped in to visit with his friend Humphrey and told him, "You've got to give more."[62] He engaged in his own form of private negotiations, of which Aaron Henry might have been privy, but he was not sharing with the MFDP delegation what he was doing.

No one else was attempting negotiations through direct contacts with the Mondale subcommittee on the basis of the Green proposal. The White House and the Credentials Committee deemed Martin Luther King Jr. to be the principal proponent for the MFDP, and he "dominated the media," but Bob Moses found it difficult to "get information as to what was actually happening." King did not have a strategy that he would sit down and consider with the MFDP; there was "[n]o communication. No coordination." At a historic moment like this convention, people did not "rise above their own interests" and look at the decisions to be made for the long-range. Instead, "everyone was busy with their own personal agendas."[63] Sunday night, when the Mondale subcommittee was searching for a compromise, the parties came closest to negotiating, but there were no competing offers that could be mediated to a compromise.

When the discussions ended at 3:00 a.m., Rauh told the group, as reported in the press, "I think we better get some sleep because I think we'll have a floor fight tonight."[64] At this point, Rauh was misleading the MFDP in talking about a floor fight even though he knew that President Johnson would not allow this to happen. A member of the Credentials Committee, he served the interests of the Mondale subcommittee as a special adviser and cooperated with the White House, while he still, without any regard to his conflict of interest, claimed his status as counsel to the MFDP, advising them of what they wanted to hear.

On Sunday, the MFDP believed it was in a strong position to gain its desired goal of voting participation in the convention that would begin the next night. And so its strategists planned "for what looked definitely to be a floor fight on Monday."[65]

But the decision on the Mississippi credentials was in the hands of Mondale, and his subcommittee had to satisfy the president. Johnson had decreed that there would be no floor fight and that the Mississippi regulars were legally entitled to be seated. The Johnson offer gave no more than honorary guest status to the MFDP. Something more was required. There was talk, but no offer of two seats.

Now President Johnson would use an important ally of the civil rights movement in Atlantic City. Hubert Humphrey had a major role to play on Monday.

14

Humphrey's Pleading on Monday

Well, Mr. Humphrey, do you mean to tell me that your position is more important to you than 400,000 black people's lives?
—Fannie Lou Hamer[1]

On Monday, August 24, Senator Hubert H. Humphrey, the long-serving liberal senator from Minnesota, civil rights warrior at the 1948 Democratic Convention, and Senate majority leader, who had played a crucial role in the recent passage of the Civil Rights Act of 1964, was Lyndon Johnson's man in charge. When Humphrey arrived in Atlantic City on Saturday, he declined to speculate on the outcome of the credentials dispute but told reporters that he had "doubts" that there would be a floor fight. He hoped there would be "an amicable and just settlement" because the "Democratic Party doesn't need a fight."[2]

In early July, Humphrey had alerted Johnson to the "potential dangers" of the convention credentials fight heating up between the two Democratic groups from Mississippi, but Johnson had seemed to pay little attention.[3] Joe Rauh, Humphrey's friend and ally in Americans for Democratic Action and the Democratic Party, did not want him to get involved in the credentials dispute because he thought it was "the stupidest thing that he could do."[4] Humphrey agreed, but in early August the president directed him to get into it, and he had no choice. On August 14, Humphrey had called Johnson to assure him that he was seeking the agreement that Johnson wanted; he had "been at it," working hard. He said that the Freedom Democrats were talking about seating both delegations, even seating all the delegations that had contests, so it would be a unified convention without issues. But Johnson quickly said no. As a friend of the national civil rights leaders, Humphrey would be the one to explain to them the circumstances of the coming election and persuade them to accept Johnson's reasons for not seating the MFDP delegates.[5]

Humphrey was known to be Johnson's front runner for the vice presidential nomination. Robert Dallek, a Johnson biographer, has explained the choice as follows: "[Johnson] and Humphrey had good relations dating from the 1950s when they had created a bridge between conservative and liberal Democrats. More important, Humphrey's presence on the ticket would give the country a competent second-in-command and would strengthen Johnson's electoral appeal in the Midwest and industrial Northeast."[6] His appeal for Johnson also lay in "his open, ebullient nature and his unswerving loyalty," according to historian Doris Kearns Goodwin.[7] Johnson was not straightforward, however, about selecting his running mate and made Humphrey nervous when he floated trial balloons of possible candidates. On July 30, he had ruled out *all* of his cabinet appointees, including Robert McNamara, Orville Freeman, and Adlai Stevenson, to avoid popular support arising for Bobby Kennedy, who still served as attorney general and was an object of his open dislike. Then he narrowed his choices to Senator Eugene McCarthy from Minnesota, Senator Thomas Dodd from Connecticut, and Humphrey.

Humphrey "aspired to the vice-presidency, and from there he hoped to move on to the White House" but could not campaign directly.[8] William Connell, his administrative assistant, instructed the senator's staff to contact all Humphrey supporters as they came in to the convention that the senator did "*not* want a high-pressure pro-Humphrey effort mounted" or even to "create the appearance of pressure on the President" to select Humphrey. They would need to be "content to await the President's decision."[9] Humphrey was popular with every party faction, and the staff would work quietly to persuade political leaders throughout the country that he would be the strongest nominee for vice president.

Johnson wanted to maintain secrecy about his choice, however, in part as "an exercise in creating interest in what would otherwise be a cut and dried Democratic convention." He "played the game for all it was worth, since it provided the only apparent drama for the convention."[10] He also wanted to get the widest possible support for Humphrey within the Democratic Party. The suspense might appear to build until the last moments of the convention, but many knew that Humphrey would be Johnson's choice.

Johnson wanted a yes man in the vice presidency whom he could control. Jim Rowe, who was a mutual friend of both Johnson and Humphrey, met with Humphrey several times on behalf of the president to obtain his pledge of loyalty to Johnson.[11] Johnson asked Humphrey to get his friend Rauh to withdraw the Challenge, but if that was not possible, to resolve the MFDP Convention Challenge through agreement with MFDP leaders. In any event, Humphrey was to ensure there would be no public turmoil that would stem from a vote on the convention floor. If Humphrey did not do a satisfactory job with the MFDP Convention Challenge, Johnson made plain through Rowe that Humphrey would not be the vice presidential nominee.

Johnson was upset seeing Rauh on television night after night. Humphrey thought he could "force his [Rauh's] hand," but Rauh refused to quit the MFDP.[12] Humphrey worked hard but did not satisfy the president. If the regulars were to be seated, Humphrey suggested, according to a mid-August taped phone conversation, the convention should establish "a commission within the party" to "take a look at this whole business."[13] He obtained Johnson's consent to adding a provision for future reform and thus contributed a significant part of Johnson's proposal for compromise announced in the Sunday papers: deliberate discrimination in party affairs would be established as a basis for challenging the acceptability of a delegation in the future.

While Humphrey acted out his role in Atlantic City, the president used another friend of the civil rights movement as he monitored the convention from the White House. Walter Reuther called President Johnson before 9:00 a.m. Monday morning and told him what "we ought to do."[14] Reuther had become head of the UAW in 1946 and had built it into one of the largest, most politically powerful unions in the country. The UAW, which had a large black membership, had provided major support for the 1963 March on Washington and gave financial support to national civil rights groups, including Martin Luther King Jr.'s SCLC. As it happened, the UAW also employed Rauh as its general counsel. Reuther was acclaimed as a reform-minded, liberal leader ahead of his peers in using labor's political influence in the forefront of the civil rights and social justice movements. Lyndon Johnson, wanting labor support when he suddenly ascended to the presidency after the assassination of President Kennedy, gave Reuther his personal attention and quickly created a loyal ally.

In early August 1964, Johnson had asked Reuther what to do about Rauh and how to end support for the Challenge and had given him a mandate not to let the situation get out of his control. Now Reuther talked with party men he "respected" who had a plan of delay for avoiding a floor fight the opening night of the convention. The Credentials Committee could issue a partial report to the convention covering the contested delegations but state that the Mississippi issue was receiving further study in a subcommittee. Reuther considered the subcommittee "very good" because its members were "under control." The best approach would be for the convention to use the subcommittee for delay so that the dispute would "get lost in the shuffle of the convention." Although Johnson saw some danger of walkouts in four days of delay, he agreed to the plan to avoid a floor fight "as long as possible." He thought not only that ten to twelve southern state delegations would walk out of the convention if the convention refused to seat "a legally elected delegation" and that repercussions would follow in the South, but that "we're going to hurt ourselves materially in other places in the country . . . it's going to hurt us in New York City." The frequent explanation for Johnson's position was his fear of a southern walkout, but here he referred to the more serious consequence of a nationwide "white backlash" to a display of black militancy at the convention. In his early Monday morning phone conversation with the president, Reuther reassured Johnson about Rauh, saying that he "is perfectly willing to break with these fellows."[15]

Meanwhile, 5,260 delegates and alternates were arriving in Atlantic City for the opening of the convention that evening. The MFDP delegates and their supporters continued to lobby members of the Credentials Committee and to attend state delegation caucuses, with even more urgency now that Rauh said there would be a floor fight that night. SNCC organizer Courtland Cox compared their activities to "trench warfare" as they confronted the forces of political power lined up to oppose them.[16]

Both Rauh and Edith Green thought it a good idea to make the Green proposal known to the delegates, and a press release asked all convention delegates to vote for "the Green Resolution," the minority report including the provisions that each Mississippi delegate—from both parties—"affirm unequivocally . . . support and work for" the nominees of the convention, give assurance that voters will be able to cast their ballots for Democratic Party nominees, and support the platform adopted by the convention before being seated as a delegate to the convention. The votes of the Mississippi delegation would be "divided proportionately amongst the delegates seated," including the regulars and the MFDP. [17]

I was in Atlantic City with my friend Pat Vail. We spent our time outside on the boardwalk, walking around, seeing SNCC staff and talking to other summer volunteers, keeping our ears open to hear what was going on with the Challenge. We might have been looking for televisions reporting the news or just waiting for word from supporters on the Credentials Committee, but in any event it was "hard to get information." [18]

That Monday morning, the Credentials Committee reconvened and discussed the Green proposal, which would seat members of both delegations who took a loyalty oath and divide the votes among them. [19] According to Democratic National Committee counsel Harold Leventhal, the committee could not seat the MFDP delegation or its members because it was illegal: it had not held conventions in every county as required. The majority on the committee objected to conferring legal standing on the MFDP and setting a precedent of recognizing an insurgent delegation that had not fully complied with party rules. Members further believed that acknowledgment of the MFDP would anger the regulars and cause the feared walkout. No votes would be taken at the convention, so the number of votes to be given to the MFDP, according to the committee, was immaterial. Official interest in the Green proposal died early. The committee again made no progress and left matters to Mondale's subcommittee.

Humphrey was in charge on Monday, but only nominally in that President Johnson retained control. The president instructed him to present the Johnson proposal to the MFDP and obtain an agreement. It was the same meager offer that Rauh had disparaged on Sunday: seating the regulars, provided they took a loyalty oath; honorary seating for the MFDP delegates; and a rule to bar future seating of segregated delegations.

Humphrey, however, had no authority to negotiate with the MFDP but was limited to selling what Johnson wanted.

The first meeting in Humphrey's suite that day included Dr. King; Roy Wilkins; Bob Moses, Aaron Henry, Ed King, Fannie Lou Hamer, and Victoria Gray from the MFDP; Edith Green and Allard Lowenstein, the white, politically well-connected, liberal activist; and other MFDP supporters.[20] White House associate Tom Finney also attended. Lowenstein is reported to have facilitated this meeting for the MFDP.[21] The timing of the meeting is unclear, but it is evident that Humphrey was following instructions to obtain agreement from the MFDP.

Humphrey began the meeting by urging the challengers to back down because he could only go so far. He pleaded that his chance to become vice president hung in the balance. He talked about what he would do if nominated and elected with respect to race relations, poverty, education, health care, and peace in Vietnam. In other words, if Humphrey did not win his arguments, he—the champion of civil rights—would not be in the White House, and so the long-term cause of civil rights would suffer. The meeting was not for "honest negotiation," but only for Humphrey to find "some credentials committee settlement that would be accepted by the convention without a debate and floor fight," regardless of the MFDP needs and opinions.[22]

Moses wanted the entire MFDP delegation present and able to listen as the others talked. *All* the delegates should share the same information and learn firsthand from their participation in the political process at the national level. His view was in keeping with an important goal of the Challenge to give black Mississippians a political education in the workings of both local and national politics. Because the MFDP, like SNCC, operated without a top-down, leader-directed hierarchical structure, the delegates had to be present for negotiations to be able to reach a decision on "whether to accept any compromise."[23]

Fannie Lou Hamer, not intimidated by established politicians, confronted Humphrey about his personal ambitions versus standing up for the social causes that the Democrats professed. She was delighted to meet him but later remembered him, as she said, as "a little round-eyed man with his eyes full of tears." His plea "amazed" her and provoked her to ask, "Well, Mr. Humphrey, do you mean to tell me that your position is

more important to you than 400,000 Black people's lives?"[24] She was crying when she left the meeting. Having confronted Senator Humphrey,
she understood why the powers that be in the Democratic Party would
bar her from further discussions.

At the Union Temple Baptist Church, where the MFDP delegation
held its meetings, Rauh "got a message to come to a meeting . . . [with
Humphrey] at one o'clock."[25] Congressman Charles Diggs requested
that Humphrey call this second Monday meeting and was able to ask
what was supposed to be a small group to attend.[26] He included Bob
Moses, Dr. King, Andy Young, Fannie Lou Hamer, Al Lowenstein, Joe
Rauh, Edith Green, other MFDP-supporting members of the Credentials
Committee, and others. Moses remembers a meeting with Humphrey
that had "a lot of people there . . . as many as twenty . . . it was packed."[27]
Lowenstein's presence surprised Rauh. He claimed ignorance as to how
Lowenstein could be invited to attend and get through the extremely difficult security to Humphrey's suite. Rauh described "a great discussion,
but nothing was really moving." About the time Virna Canson arrived
at 2:00 p.m., Edith Green walked out of the meeting "insulted."[28] She
said Humphrey was using undue pressure to get an agreement, which
led Humphrey to complain that members of the Credentials Committee
didn't even need to be at the meeting; he wondered why they were there.
She let the waiting press know how angry she was that Humphrey was
pressuring the MFDP to accept the Johnson offer.

Virna Canson made her "pitch" at this meeting that the Johnson offer
"skirted the real issue . . . it's as if we had come right to the edge of the
water but refused to go in. We need to take the big step and that is to
extend the vote to the Freedom delegation." She said she was not concerned whether to give the MFDP one vote or enough votes for the
entire sixty-eight-member delegation because the vote in this case was "a
symbol of good faith on the part of the party" and "a symbol to the regular Mississippian that tradition had indeed been broken." She expressed
her "deep concern over a floor fight." The political fact of life was that
"some vote must be given" to the MFDP. She felt that that message had
gotten across and that the leadership of the MFDP accepted "compromise" as "the other political fact of life."[29] But then Bob Moses broke
the silence after she spoke, causing her "anger and frustration" when he

took a "hard line," saying: "The time has come for Negroes to speak for Negroes, for Negroes to represent Negroes. The Freedom Democrats can accept no less than equal votes at the convention." The MFDP's consistent position in any upcoming negotiations for a compromise would be that others should not be speaking for the black MFDP delegates, but they should have "equal votes at the convention." The statement angered Humphrey, who responded that Moses's position could not be true if democracy is to be real in a society where we can all live in peace as brothers.[30] In a harmonious society, Humphrey envisioned groups that would not only advocate for themselves but also speak for each other. The *Minneapolis Morning Tribune* reported on Tuesday that "Humphrey's unity conference" with Edith Green, Martin Luther King Jr., Aaron Henry, and others was "a failure."[31]

Leaving the meeting, Virna Canson let Moses and Dr. King know her view that a floor debate, which she did not think could be won by the MFDP, would have professional politicians fighting like animals. The public response to the Credentials Committee hearing was positive, but forces *against* rather than *for* the MFDP would be unleashed in a floor fight. Her notes reveal that she told them on Monday afternoon that if they were going to "push for an untenable position, count me out."[32]

Rauh was concerned about a Credentials Committee meeting scheduled for 2:00 p.m. that day and the opening of the convention that evening. He asked Humphrey to get a postponement of the meeting. Some of the others left the meeting with Humphrey and returned with word that Chairman Lawrence had postponed the meeting. Rauh wanted submission of the committee report to the convention delayed past the Monday opening night because he had no prestigious, politically important, influential members of Congress or senators lined up and willing to speak on behalf of the MFDP to the full convention. Contrary to Rauh's version, Virna Canson was walking with him to the Credentials Committee meeting two hours late when they saw Bailey and Lawrence coming toward them to find out what was delaying them. Soon they were surrounded by news reporters. She said they ducked the reporters for Bailey and Lawrence to handle the questions. Rauh has related a conversation in which he threatened his "11 and 8" strategy to get the delay, unaware that the White House also wanted a delay. He learned that Lawrence had decided to put off voting the committee's recommendation on the Mississippi credentials for another day. In his lecture at the Atlantic City Revisited symposium in 2000, Mondale said that "part of what we were doing in our subcommittee was buying time to keep the dispute off the convention floor"—just as Reuther had proposed to Johnson on Monday morning.[33]

Humphrey is reported to have had a third meeting in the late afternoon to continue his pleading with the MFDP. Joe Rauh, Edith Green, Robert Kastenmeier, Dr. King, Bayard Rustin, and Ed King are said to have attended. Again, no progress was made.[34]

Humphrey gave his assessment of the day's meetings to Jenkins, who reported it in a 4:30 p.m. phone call to the president. Humphrey had told Jenkins, "I'm a hell of a salesman. I walked into the lion's den, I listened patiently, I argued fervently, I used all their heartstrings" but "made no headway." Humphrey advised that unless the MFDP got at least "some votes," they would try for a floor vote. If the Credentials Committee report on Mississippi were delayed past Monday night, there might be "more hope." Humphrey was relying on Dr. King, who was "more moderate," and Aaron Henry, "quite intelligent" and "more reasonable than some." Racking his brain for what might be done next, he thought maybe President Johnson could invite some MFDP representatives to Washington, but he did not recommend an invitation. Johnson told Jenkins he did not want to "see them or have anything to do with them." Jenkins told the president that members of the committee were "restive" and that Chairman Lawrence did not think the issue could be avoided for the full convention, so some conclusion needed to be reached by the next evening. Johnson thought the MFDP should go ahead and agree to the offer, but he could do nothing; it was up to the chairman of the convention. All he could say was that they should see if Reuther could talk to them, "settle this two vote thing," "bury it in subcommittee," or just "go on and take the compromise Rauh proposed." Concerning the last suggestion, Johnson sarcastically added that if they wanted Goldwater, they could have Goldwater. Jenkins understood from Johnson that now they should "go ahead." Johnson sounded discouraged.[35]

Walking up and down the boardwalk near the Convention Hall with Pat, I knew what we were supposed to do—talk directly to delegates for their support in a roll-call vote to seat the MFDP. That meant figuring out who was an official delegate—with a vote—and who wasn't.

Among the middle-aged men—some serious, some smiling—all dressed up in suits but wandering aimlessly on the boardwalk, we looked for badges. All the delegates had them but didn't always wear them. The badge tipped us off that a guy was official. We peered at a badge to see the state the delegate was from to decide whether he was a known friend, a maybe, or someone from the South who we could anticipate would oppose our plea. We would ask them where they were from if we couldn't see the name of the state on the badge. We expected that a vote would be held Monday night, that all the delegates would be able to vote on the seating question on the convention floor, and we were optimistic that when that happened, we would win the vote.

If one of these delegates looked curious or his wife took an interest, he might ask *us* what it was like to be a civil rights worker in Mississippi. That would be the fun part, to get in a discussion with these middle-aged men and women. Were we scared? Did we know Andrew Goodman? Did we see any violence? What was it really like to live with the local "Negroes"? I found it challenging to describe what it was like to be in Greenville all summer, but I did the best I could to give them a picture of how bad the situation was in Mississippi. I also wanted to convey my dedication to the registration work I did and how wonderful the local black people were whom I knew. We gained confidence in our pitch when we ran into delegates from the states we knew had promised during the summer to support the MFDP, glad that some delegates were on our side. With someone from Oregon or California or Michigan, we knew we were talking to a friend. I didn't get any hostile or sarcastic responses from anyone, though, and felt very positive about what we were doing—or *trying* to do. Both Pat and I wanted to be persuasive, but most of the delegates we approached were noncommittal, and we were probably not changing any minds.

On Monday evening, spirits were high within the MFDP and among its supporters in a turnout of a thousand demonstrators and several thousand spectators at a rally at 7:00 p.m. outside Convention Hall. Aaron Henry led the demonstration, which had been organized by SNCC and CORE to increase enthusiasm and support for the issuance of a minor-

Martin Luther King Jr. addressing a boardwalk rally outside Convention Hall in Atlantic City on Monday. Courtesy of George Ballis/Take Stock.

ity report and a roll-call vote the next evening. He said that twelve state delegations supported a convention floor vote. The press reported that Henry had firmly rejected the Johnson offer that Humphrey had presented during the day's meetings, calling it "back-of-the-bus treatment" that was "completely unacceptable."[36] Mickey Schwerner's parents and James Chaney's younger brother Ben were there. Other speakers at the two-hour rally included Senator Wayne Morse of Oregon, whose delegation had voted to take the issue to the floor of the convention, and Congressman Philip Burton from California.

The main speaker, Martin Luther King Jr., condemned the Mississippi Democratic Party as the party of racism that was responsible for the death of Chaney, Goodman, and Schwerner. He had warned the national Democratic Party, which was expecting blacks to work for Johnson registering voters and getting them out on election day, that "Negroes may just go fishing on election day" if they did not throw out the lily-white delegation and replace it with the Mississippi Freedom Democrats.[37] About the national Democratic Party, he said, "This is the Democratic Party's moment of truth. It must decide whether to take the low road of racism or the high road of justice."[38] Dr. King's speech in support of seating the MFDP seemed to raise the chances of success even higher.

Jenkins gave Johnson another report listing more than eight states that would go to the floor for a vote. When Johnson asked what he meant, he clarified that they were states in favor of a roll-call vote, not states with members on the Credentials Committee who supported the MFDP. There would not be a walkout on Monday because the issue would not go to the convention until Tuesday night. He told Johnson that Rauh's position in support of the MFDP was firm.[39]

Convention chair Bailey opened the convention Monday night at 8:45 p.m. Convention authorities gave all the contending Mississippi delegates official guest passes on Monday night for the opening of the convention. Because no one had official credentials yet, the MFDP delegates sat in the gallery, not on the floor, and the regulars stayed away, some ten blocks from the convention activity in the Chalfonte Hotel, more upscale than the MFDP quarters at the Gem Hotel. The Mississippi seats were empty. Mr. Lawrence presented the report of the Credentials Committee, identifying which contested delegates and alternates from Alabama, Oregon, Puerto Rico, and the Virgin Islands had been accredited, stating that the committee had "not yet made its determination with respect to the contest in Mississippi," and requesting leave to submit its report thereon at a later time.[40] The convention did adopt the party platform recommended by the platform committee. No controversy erupted over the civil rights plank in the platform, which applauded "the efforts of the Administration to provide full and equal civil rights for all Americans" and called the Civil Rights Act of 1964 the "high point of achievement in this effort" and "landmark of our Democracy."[41] Appealing to southern sensitivities, the Democratic platform's promise of "fair, effective enforcement" of the act was in fact milder than the corresponding Republican pledge of "full implementation and faithful execution."[42]

That first night President Johnson watched the convention coverage with his friends Washington lawyers Abe Fortas and Clark Clifford, worried that a divisive roll-call vote would take place the following evening.[43] Reuther called and told Johnson he had a charter plane available. As soon

Empty Mississippi delegation seats at the Democratic National Convention, Monday night. Library of Congress, Prints and Photographs Division, Washington, D.C.

as he finished negotiation meetings between the UAW and the three U.S. automobile companies, he would be able to arrive in Atlantic City about 3:00 a.m. to "get in there" and do his best on behalf of Johnson.[44] This account is contrary to Rauh's understanding that "Johnson order[ed]" Reuther in, despite Reuther's being "actually in negotiations" on behalf of the UAW.[45] Johnson told Reuther that he, Fortas, and Clifford were "distressed beyond words" and appreciated Reuther's offer. In the taped phone conversation, Reuther said he thought the blacks were being "completely irrational" and seemed not to understand that next time there could be no discrimination against them. Johnson was concerned about the reaction coming in from northerners that blacks were "taking over the country," according to the way they appeared on television, and he worried about losing the northern white vote as well as the southern vote. He informed Reuther that the number of Credentials Committee

MFDP supporters was down to thirteen, counting two from Michigan, and he thought it could be brought down further. He gave Reuther that assignment and made it clear that he did not want to be quoted.

Rauh spent the first convention session "trying to round up speakers for the Tuesday night thing," saying he "still had 11 and 8" because the Credentials Committee had not acted on the Ullman offer of two votes.[46] He was discouraged because he could not find leaders of large northern or western states or senators or congressmen who would speak for the MFDP on the convention floor. He claimed later, "I was *beginning* to wonder. . . . I began to wonder really whether I could really pull it off *anymore*."[47] With his knowledge and experience, however, he must have had serious doubts about a floor-vote victory for the MFDP long before this point.

On Monday night, Reuther talked to Jenkins and Finney about what could be done to end the Challenge and learned that the state delegations that the MFDP needed for a roll-call vote included the territories of Puerto Rico, the Virgin Islands, and Guam. Reuther contacted Governor Carl Sanders of Georgia, the chairman of the Rules Committee, and soon a new rule stipulated that only delegations from states could ask for a roll-call vote.[48]

Humphrey had failed to get MFDP agreement to the Johnson offer of honorary seating on Monday, but he had not lost everything. The many delegates who favored his nomination had been hearing since they had arrived in Atlantic City that it was jeopardized by support of the MFDP. Now the word was specific: the president didn't want the seating of the Mississippi delegation to be an issue threatening a possible divisive floor vote. The minority report, which was still thought to have the votes of more than eleven delegates on the Credentials Committee committed to sign, required eight state delegations to get to the floor for a roll-call vote. Humphrey proceeded to check on what the state delegations would do if there were a minority report. He wanted to make sure the vice presidential nomination was more important to the delegates than the MFDP.

At least seven of Humphrey's staff contacted more than thirty-five state delegations on Monday and checked with some again on Tuesday to find out whether they had voted in their caucuses to support the president on the "Mississippi problem."[49] The staff turned in their reports, listing the persons they had relied on for information within the delegation, and someone typed them up in a uniform format. Most were dated August 24, 1964, which was Monday. The staff also checked on the position of Credentials Committee members who were MFDP supporters. They contacted twelve western states and noted the position of Washington, where Marjorie King, "a Negro," had signed the minority report but had nearly been "repudiated" by her caucus. She was "suffering a conflict of conscience, but would probably go along" with what the state's caucus considered an acceptable offer to the MFDP. The Oregon caucus, which included Al Ullman and Edith Green, adopted a resolution that would unseat the Mississippi regulars. Requiring a loyalty oath they might not take would allow for seating the MFDP with "a compromise" under which the MFDP delegates would be seated and "share the vote." But Edith Green was "militant for *all or nothing*." The sense of the Oregon delegation was that "the issue should be negotiated in the Credentials Committee." The nine reports from midwestern states noted that the Wisconsin and Iowa Credentials Committee members supported the MFDP. The Wisconsin delegation supported Humphrey's unity proposal, allowing an exception for Congressman Kastenmeier if he wished. Mrs. James Dunbar, the Iowa woman on the Credentials Committee was planning to vote to seat the MFDP, but not sign the minority report. Governor Hughes wanted Humphrey to talk to her, but President Johnson thought this plan was a good alternative when he heard the idea on Sunday morning.

Reports from six eastern states indicated a 75 percent estimated support for the minority report in the New York delegation and that problems would arise in the Pennsylvania delegation if there were a floor vote because so many elected officials were up for reelection. Humphrey's staff also concerned itself with the southern states and the border states that Johnson didn't want to have "run off." If they were inclined to walk out of the convention, they could cause the unpleasant divisiveness that would harm Humphrey's chances for the nomination. These delegates intended to stay in the convention, but some professed their backing of the Mississippi regulars. Alabama didn't matter, and no one even contacted LBJ's Texas.

The truth was that most of the delegations were waiting for the Credentials Committee to render a decision because they would "back a majority of the committee" or, as with Colorado, might "lean toward" the MFDP "but would go for a workable compromise," not wanting a floor fight. Indiana, facing pressure to vote with the majority of the Credentials Committee, was an exception that planned to vote to take the minority report up on the floor. Some delegates reported that they "would support the President." Missouri simply had "[n]o position or interest in the Freedom delegation problem." Nevada also was "not especially interested" but hoped there would be no floor fight. Puerto Rico troubled the staffer with a rumor that "if the minority report is stifled, it is because Senator Humphrey has gotten the word from the President and is working to do this." The staffer emphasized being alert to any such reports "because they could backfire."

Where a delegation was divided, voting could be delayed. Ella Baker, SNCC's politically savvy senior adviser, believed that the delegations "had no opportunity to vote over anything" because of "a party maneuver to keep the issue from coming up." She considered it a "great loss" that people at the convention had no opportunity to participate in any decision-making.[50] The California delegation—divided between strong supporters of the MFDP from the liberal California Democratic Council, which had been the first to endorse the MFDP Convention Challenge, and Governor Pat Brown, an ally of President Johnson—delayed voting until the Credentials Committee acted.

Humphrey was reassured by the staff reports that state delegation votes were insufficient for the MFDP to get a roll-call vote when the convention reconvened on Tuesday. Whether the Challenge would end in a victory or defeat depended on how the leading actors played their parts during the day. Walter Reuther volunteered to take the key role in Atlantic City on Tuesday.

15

Reuther's Manipulation on Tuesday

Now ram that damn thing through.
    —Lyndon Johnson to Hubert Humphrey and Walter Reuther[1]

Before I heard anything about Walter Reuther, I was waking up on the church pew Tuesday morning thinking Pat and I should do more of what we had done Monday—wandering the boardwalk trying to talk to delegates about why they should vote to seat the MFDP that evening. When Pat was ready, we headed for Convention Hall to find our allies. Not a delegate yet in sight. We were excited that finally that night the convention would hold the roll-call vote on seating the Mississippi delegation. It looked as though it would happen. Why else would there be a delay?

Even President Johnson thought a roll-call vote was inevitable. John Bailey, the dominant figure in Connecticut politics and chairman of the Democratic National Committee, called Johnson early Tuesday morning to offer whatever he could do, assuring him of his loyalty but unable to commit support from congressmen and senators in the Connecticut delegation.[2] They needed black votes in urban areas in upcoming elections and could not afford to oppose the MFDP. Johnson anticipated that a sweeping convention vote for the black delegates would look as though the Democrats were letting the blacks take over. The campaign strategy "dictated against making civil rights the pivotal issue," not wanting "voters to cast their ballots on the question of whether or not they like Negroes."[3]

Johnson was in deep despair for the rest of the day and claimed that he did not want to go to Atlantic City and was ready to withdraw his candidacy. He was preparing a statement for his press secretary, George Reedy, to release. In the transcript of a phone conversation between Johnson and Reedy that appears in *Taking Charge,* Michael Beschloss's record of the Johnson tapes, Reedy discouraged Johnson from withdrawing, pointing out that it would "throw the nation into quite an uproar."[4]

After lunch on Tuesday, Johnson retired to his room with the shades drawn and made many phone calls. He did not sleep. Lady Bird Johnson recorded in her diary that when they talked in the afternoon, "He did not want to accept the nomination. He did not want to go to Atlantic City." She wrote him an encouraging letter later in the day, telling him that he was "strong, patient, determined . . . [and] brave." Statements have been made about Johnson's "depression" or "mental breakdown" during the convention, and some have said that he was miserably conflicted, wanting to do the right thing and support black voting rights, yet fearing loss of the election to Goldwater if he did. More than a single issue probably caused his despair. He talked to Lady Bird about "burdens," and she wrote in her diary that "it was the same old refrain" and how hard the hours were for her to endure.[5]

That night he was still in despair, asking Reedy to walk with him on the White House grounds at midnight. According to Reedy, "They'd seated that Mississippi delegation that came up with strange credentials. He'd [Johnson] straightened out a number of those various delegates."[6] Thus, the Mississippi credentials dispute had been resolved, and Johnson no longer feared a floor fight, yet he continued seeking sympathy. For about an hour that night, he was vehement about not wanting to go to Atlantic City to accept the nomination. Reedy found him "terribly convincing," even though his "reasoning bore only the faintest resemblance to reality."[7] Reedy tried to talk him out of it. Johnson responded, "Fuck 'em, they don't want me anyway. . . . I'm going to tell them I'm not going to accept the nomination." He had threatened to resign before, but Reedy was worried that he was serious this time. Reedy attributed the threats to a combination of Johnson's wanting to "get people to beg and plead with him not to," "to confuse the situation," and "to play games with people."[8]

There was no doubt that the MFDP Convention Challenge put pressure on Johnson, but he had also just dealt with the August 7 congressional Tonkin Gulf resolution that authorized his escalation of the war in Vietnam. When Johnson kept wailing for sympathy, Reedy's view, as he

said in a 1990 oral interview, was that Johnson was "only seeking attention and reassurance" in "a childish temper tantrum," either "genuinely
conflicted about his ability to unify and lead the nation" or "limitlessly
manipulative."[9] In an earlier memoir about LBJ, Reedy had concluded
that this behavior was to bolster Johnson's own self-esteem, that "the
major part of it was the desire to build a stunted ego."[10] Throughout
the summer of 1964, according to Doris Kearns Goodwin, Johnson had
"continued to alternate between periods of elation, excitement, and self-
confidence and periods of severe depression, inhibition, and doubt."[11] So
the episode on Tuesday has no single explanation.

I mark Walter Reuther's arrival in Atlantic City—presumably at 3:00
a.m. Tuesday morning, as he had planned—as the beginning of what Bob
Moses called the "complete manipulation" of the MFDP.[12] According to
Joe Rauh, Johnson *ordered* Reuther to come, to pressure Rauh in person,
but the record indicates that Reuther was a ready, willing, and able volunteer, eager to support the president in the final phase of their plans to
prevent MFDP disruption of the convention with a roll-call vote.[13] Rauh
said Reuther told him later that he had been very busy and did not want
to go to the convention, but Johnson had "insisted," "absolutely forced
him to come."[14] Reuther knew exactly what Johnson wanted; he had told
Reuther earlier to "put this over," not trusting Humphrey to succeed in
negotiating an acceptable solution.[15] It looked as if Reuther would bring
to town the idea of or at least Johnson's consent to some modification
of his original offer, which appeared necessary to get a settlement of the
dispute. Reuther was a strong ally and financial backer of the civil rights
movement, a skilled negotiator, and he could exercise the political power
that Johnson had now decided to use on Tuesday.

Monday night and into Tuesday morning, Mondale and his subcommittee were still working on finding a solution, something that could be
added to the Johnson offer that would satisfy the MFDP and its supporters on the Credentials Committee. Rauh had been "with [the subcommittee members] . . . for several hours Monday night," but he had
nothing to propose on behalf of the MFDP.[16] He did not offer to bring
anyone from the MFDP with him to the subcommittee meeting, and
there is no indication that the subcommittee asked to hear directly from
Bob Moses or any MFDP delegates.

After Reuther's arrival in Atlantic City, the subcommittee came up with the addition of two delegates at-large with votes to the original Johnson offer. Mondale explained the addition as "a new recommendation: to symbolize the [national] party's commitment to integration and to affirm the justice of the Freedom Democrats' cause. . . . [It] would urge the convention to seat the co-chairs of the Freedom delegation, Aaron Henry and Ed King, as delegates-at-large with full voting privileges."[17] Actually, Henry and Ed King were *not* cochairs of the delegation. Ed King was the national committeeman. If cochairs had been named, Fannie Lou Hamer, who was the vice chair of the delegation, would have been the choice, a better one in many people's opinion, including mine. But the subcommittee wanted one black and one white person as a symbol of integration. By making them delegates at-large, this addition wouldn't take votes from the regular delegation. By excluding Fannie Lou Hamer, who was not considered a "proper" spokesperson for the Democratic Party, the committee ensured that she would not have the speaking privileges of a delegate.

Sherwin Markman, a thirty-five-year-old Yale lawyer from Iowa, claims credit for the new idea. He later explained the addition as recognizing the denial of voting rights as a national problem: "The problem of the Negro in Mississippi was a national, rather than a parochial problem. And therefore, why don't we . . . rather than giving them two seats from Mississippi—that since it was a national problem and a symbolic problem—why don't we create two additional seats, out of the entire flag so to speak, from the Union, and give it to them, not taking it away from anybody, but just adding two delegates."[18]

I understood in Atlantic City that the White House originated the final offer, that Johnson gave instructions to Reuther, and that Reuther flew in to Atlantic City to present the solution to the Mondale subcommittee. From what others said later, Reuther played a key role in resolving the dispute on Tuesday with a new proposal, but it is unclear whether he was carrying specific orders from the president to Atlantic City. *Newsweek* reported after the convention that White House associate "Finney had a new twist" after discussions with friendlier leaders of the Georgia and South Carolina delegations, who agreed with the new concessions to the MFDP.[19] David Broder, a Washington political col-

Democratic Party officials looking happy early Tuesday morning. *Right to left:* Credentials Committee chairman David Lawrence, Democratic National Committee chairman John Bailey, Michigan congressman Charles Diggs, and Oregon congressman Al Ullman. Courtesy of A/P Wide World Photos.

umnist, wrote at the time that Reuther's "exact role in devising and selling the settlement" was a mystery, but that he played "a vital part" in averting a floor fight. Broder reported that the offer came from a breakfast meeting.[20] Mondale has explained that "a group of us" came up with the new offer during "a long night" Tuesday morning.[21] A journalist's later account was that after arriving in Atlantic City, Reuther "huddled" with Humphrey and Mondale "charting a new proposal" that would offer the MFDP two at-large seats with voting rights.[22] Washington columnists Rowland Evans and Robert Novak, writing in their biography of Johnson in 1966, were more specific: "When Reuther arrived, he joined Humphrey, Finney, and Jenkins in a meeting in Jenkins' suite lasting the rest of that long night. Stunned by rejection of their first compromise effort, they decided that a true compromise was now impossible. . . . [I]nstead of *compromise,* the requirement now was for a final *solution"* that would satisfy the MFDP and, more important, the liberal delegates who were supporting the MFDP.[23] Humphrey was "not sure just who initiated it."[24] Markman was clear that "the idea on seating" the two at-large delegates was his "own contribution"; the idea was "knocked down a dozen times, [but] finally sailed, and it was done."[25] Humphrey was generally given credit for a job well done, but the new terms needed Reuther, and thus they came to be referred to as the "Reuther–Johnson offer."

Mondale writes in his memoir *The Good Fight* that he "took [the offer] to Hubert, who liked it."[26] He discussed it with Humphrey, Reuther, and Lawrence at an early breakfast meeting, when they considered how to present the Reuther–Johnson offer for acceptance by the regulars, the MFDP, and the Credentials Committee and how to put it in the best light for press coverage.[27] They barred all discussion of the solution with MFDP officials.[28] The subcommittee voted after breakfast, and Mondale got a majority vote, with opposition from the two southerners, who thought the proposal handed too much to the MFDP. The group that came up with the solution spent the morning briefing powerful political leaders in the party and informing them that "this was it, whatever the MFDP did."[29] Mondale then prepared a report to the committee for voting and approval without a minority report.

Sometime on Tuesday when I heard that Reuther was in town and learned about him, I wondered whether Rauh would continue to advocate for the best interests of the MFDP or now feel he needed to please Reuther and agree with President Johnson's proposal. If he followed Reuther's advice, he would retain his legal business with the UAW. The conflict of interest was obvious to me even before I went to law school and took any courses in ethics. I thought Rauh had to choose between conflicting forces, but he never did. *Rauh tried to work both sides.*

Long before the convention, Rauh had agreed to cooperate with the White House, not to make trouble, and to keep the MFDP under control.[30] Reuther had ordered Rauh to withdraw the Challenge early in August, and now he was in Atlantic City to force Rauh to get the MFDP to accept the Reuther–Johnson offer. Rauh had told Reuther that he did not have to take orders from him because this did not involve UAW business and that he should be free to support the MFDP. On Saturday, he had fought well for the MFDP at the Credentials Committee hearing. Would he continue the good fight?

When Arthur Waskow talked to Rauh on Tuesday, Rauh "was convinced there would be a floor fight that night."[31] Rauh does not acknowledge meeting Reuther when Reuther came to Atlantic City, but it is difficult to imagine that he didn't know what was coming generally, if not specifically. Rauh said he awoke exhausted on Tuesday morning, in a daze, and didn't know where to go or what to do. He wandered over to the MFDP caucus, fearing the reaction of the MFDP delegates if they perceived that the Challenge was lost. The delegates were considering all the alternatives that had been thrown out as "trial balloons." Bob Moses, wanting the delegates fully informed, was "trying to get those issues across to people, what was at stake, what role the President was playing."[32] When Aaron Henry called on Rauh to speak, he reported that as late as 6:00 a.m., presumably from his stopovers to visit Humphrey in his room, "the President won't budge from his initial [position]." He was "using all the pressure he could, threatening in every way." Rauh said he "made a plea for tolerance . . . for people to understand each other and not have bitterness come out of this." The delegates did not believe Humphrey was supporting them, but Rauh defended him, saying he was "doing all he could." The MFDP had "made a great impact," and "if we went to the floor, if they offered us nothing, we were going to the floor. If we won, fine. If we lost, let's not hate." Rauh was pleased with the applause he received from the delegates, but Ella Baker "turned on" him and, as he said, "just cut me to ribbons." She said she didn't care about "traitors like Humphrey deserting their liberal trend" and implied that Rauh didn't care about poor people, oppressed people.[33]

Rauh was uncertain, but he thought something was going to happen at the afternoon Credentials Committee meeting. He told the MFDP delegates that he did not have "the vaguest idea" what was in the offer he expected to receive. He knew "the big shots," as he called them—Lawrence, Humphrey, Mondale, Reuther—but they did not consult him.[34] On Sunday afternoon, Johnson had instructed them, "Don't tell him," for fear that Rauh's communications with the MFDP would cause the

MFDP to raise otherwise avoidable objections.[35] When asked about Mondale's role in thinking up the Reuther–Johnson offer, Rauh didn't know; "there was kind of an Iron Curtain over that crowd." The MFDP authorized him to settle only on the basis of the Green proposal for shared voting. He knew, however, he no longer had any choice, his "11 and 8" strategy was not holding up, and he would now accept the terms of a new offer. But he told the delegates that he was going on to "fight" for them in the meeting. He left the church for the afternoon meeting of the Credentials Committee with enough time to get a hot dog and stop for "a shot of booze."[36] The delegates dispersed to continue their lobbying Tuesday afternoon.

Humphrey and Reuther assigned Bayard Rustin to make the Reuther–Johnson offer to the MFDP. According to Charles Sherrod's paper on the events at the convention, "It was reported that a group from the MFDP had gone to talk with representatives of the White House and a report was given: it was the five-point compromise. . . . There were now seven hours left" for the MFDP delegation to "examine the compromise, think about it, accept or reject it," and take the appropriate action before the convention session that evening.[37] His statement places receipt of the information at about 1:00 p.m. Tuesday, after Rauh had left the church. Rustin may have made an informal presentation of the new proposal to some of the SNCC organizers when, according to Walter Tillow, he showed up at the church about noon.[38] He may have also talked to Bob Moses. Moses remembers "walking up to" a meeting "with Bayard, Bayard saying he was in ecstasy at being at the very center of the history making process."[39]

Pat and I were out on the boardwalk and didn't know when the MFDP heard about this proposal. We were still looking for delegates to tell them to vote that evening to seat the MFDP. The more we thought about it, though, the more interested we became in managing somehow to get into Convention Hall. That was where we thought the action was.

In the early afternoon, Rauh arrived for the closed Credentials Committee meeting, which no one from the MFDP could attend. His story is that he *first* heard about the Reuther–Johnson offer when he was on his way into the meeting. Congressman Diggs told him to call Reuther. Rauh has said that this offer was the "only one offer" the MFDP received.[40] Fearing that the committee would go ahead without him, Rauh asked Chairman Lawrence for a brief delay so he could make the call. As Rauh recalled in an oral interview, Reuther told him about "the decision": a loyalty oath for the regulars, two MFDP delegates, and "a pledge they'll never seat lily-white delegates again."[41] Reuther called it "a tremendous victory," and Rauh agreed that it was "a great proposal." Rauh understood that "the decision" was "what he [Reuther] and Johnson had agreed to."[42]

Reuther got tough about Rauh accepting the decision, but Rauh said he first had to consult with Aaron Henry, chairman of the MFDP delegation. The delegation had given him his instructions about the Green proposal in the morning, so there was really no reason to consult. He had, however, promised Henry that he would not take any offers without talking to him. As an attorney, Rauh could consider consent from the head of the organization, the individual presumably authorized to act for the organization, sufficient for him to reach an agreement binding on the organization. He had no thought of consulting with the entire MFDP delegation, as Moses would have wanted. He apparently did not understand the MFDP position that the entire delegation should participate in deliberations before reaching a decision. He did not acknowledge the need to talk to Bob Moses or to involve the entire delegation. He may also have ignored full consultation because he expected a rejection by the MFDP, but not by Aaron Henry, and he wanted to vote for the proposal and obtain a unanimous Credentials Committee majority report.

Reuther told Rauh that Henry was in a meeting with Humphrey that was about to begin. Rauh wanted the Credentials Committee meeting postponed to give him time to get Henry's agreement. Reuther agreed that he would get an adjournment. But when Rauh asked the chairman for the postponement, Lawrence told Rauh he had "his orders": orders for an adjournment would have to come from the White House. Rauh told Lawrence that he would oppose the committee action on the subcommittee report until he could talk to Henry. Mondale arrived to present the subcommittee recommendation that the committee adopt the Reuther–Johnson offer, and he, too, said the Credentials Committee meeting could be adjourned for Rauh to speak to Henry. Someone allied with the White House, however—"a little punk" named Sherwin Markman, the subcommittee member from Iowa, according to Rauh—said the decision had been made, "we're going to put it through right now."[43] There could be no further delay.

Johnson wanted consensus on the Mississippi credentials issue. When Reuther got to Atlantic City, he was to sit down with Humphrey and all the key Democrats to work out agreement to a resolution of the issue. In the early afternoon on Tuesday, Humphrey called the president to report his "progress" and present the details and the rationale for the proposal under discussion. The regular delegates' legal prerogatives would be preserved by seating them, provided they took a loyalty oath, and a declaration of openness would provide for full participation of all in the future. Humphrey took credit for the new addition in the Johnson proposal: two MFDP delegates, "one white, one colored," would be seated with votes. Granting these votes to the MFDP would be an expression of the Democratic Party's concern for "the right to vote" and "political participation." This "recognition of the right to vote" he considered a "show of conscience." Humphrey assured the president that votes would not be taken away from the Mississippi delegation. Reuther explained that they could avoid a floor fight and unify the party with this proposal, which would "harmonize moral obligations with legal problems."[44]

Humphrey scheduled a meeting at 3:30 p.m. with Dr. King and "this fellow Henry"—not to negotiate, but to recommend the strong position that had been taken. Johnson asked twice, "Have you talked to them?" He received only a vague response to the effect that the talking was not formal. According to the taped phone conversation, Johnson saw a "good solution" despite a danger in only "recognizing a symbol." The Democratic Party might be confronted with the same problem again in the future, but he hoped that the declaration of an open party through the provision for future barring of segregated delegations would take care of the potential danger. Johnson advised that they now "ram that damn thing through." He warned them to act independently and deny talking to him.

Referring to his choice for his running mate, Johnson reassured Humphrey that he was "fair" and "not a sadistic person." Humphrey could rest more easily now that he had completed his assignment and his vice presidential candidacy was no longer in jeopardy.

On Tuesday afternoon, there were two simultaneous meetings in different locations, without communication between them: the Lawrence–Mondale–Rauh Credentials Committee meeting and the Reuther–Humphrey meeting.

The Reuther–Humphrey meeting included a third key person, Bayard Rustin. When Rustin "show[ed] up at the Convention, he show[ed] up there with Reuther."[45] Rustin asked Ed King and Aaron Henry to come immediately to the Claridge Hotel "for an important discussion," but not to bring anyone else, specifically not Mrs. Hamer and not Al Lowenstein, and "to tell no one else about this session." Rustin did not want Bob Moses, who was not a member of the delegation, to come, but Ed King protested that he and Henry "were not going anywhere without Bob."[46] The careful and deliberate scheduling, which one reporter called "skillful maneuvering," kept the MFDP principals occupied behind closed doors, away from telephones and access to news and reporters during the Credentials Committee meeting.[47] It also kept Rauh from communicating with the MFDP. Henry was available in the Humphrey meeting with Reuther, who knew Rauh wanted to talk to Henry, but Reuther did not put them in touch with each other. The afternoon was "filled with maneuvering and manipulation calculated to keep [the MFDP representatives] away from Rauh and force [their] acceptance."[48]

Bob Moses went to the Reuther–Humphrey meeting expecting negotiations and a new proposal that would be more favorable to the MFDP.[49] Ed King assumed that the purpose of this meeting was to discuss blacks' participation in large-scale demonstrations on the boardwalk, which had been considered in the Tougaloo meeting on July 23.[50] Because Rustin had not wanted Moses at the meeting, King was suspicious about what the subject would be.

Ed King was surprised to find Humphrey at the meeting. Martin Luther King Jr. and Andrew Young were also there. Rustin presided and introduced Reuther, who was present on behalf of President Johnson to get an agreement from the MFDP. The details of the new offer—"the first time it was officially presented" to the MFDP—seemed known to everyone else in the room.[51] There would be no negotiations—a decision had been made. Rustin stressed that "everyone in the room agreed that this present settlement was good and that this was absolutely the last time that we could discuss the matter." Moses and Ed King were angry that Dr. King, present and seemingly okay with the new proposal, could "presume to speak and negotiate for us." Humphrey said that Henry and Ed King had to agree and that it was up to them to force the delegation to accept the offer. Ed King raised questions and concerns about the terms of the Reuther–Johnson proposal, even though the previous pronouncements had made clear that nothing would change through discussions.[52]

Advocates for the new proposal relied on the importance of Humphrey, the best candidate to run with Johnson, serving as a liberal vice president to support social change and to influence President Johnson in civil rights matters. They tried to make the new proposal appear to be a victory for the MFDP. Because the loyalty oath requirement would mean that most of the regulars would walk out, the MFDP would still effectively unseat the regulars. The MFDP representatives raised several objections: (1) the "at-large" designation did not give the MFDP representation for Mississippi and should be changed to "MFDP seats"; (2) the unit rule operated unfairly to give the MFDP only two votes, whereas the few regulars who did not walk out would have all twenty-six Mississippi votes for the sixty-eight delegates; (3) the location of the at-large MFDP seating was unknown and might not be as close to the Mississippi standard as it should be; and (4) the two at-large votes might not actually be cast and seen on TV as MFDP votes. Ed King offered to give up his seat, even though others in the room wanted the delegation integrated, and alternatively suggested that the two at-large seats be split into half-votes with four representatives elected by the MFDP, not selected by others. Ed King thought the MFDP group might consider this item negotiable. If the delegation could name who would take the two seats, *maybe* the offer would be acceptable. Humphrey knew, however, that this was the absolutely final plan and that he could not go back to the White House to suggest changes.[53]

The discussion focused on the provision for naming the delegates for the two at-large seats. Bob Moses pointed out that the Democrats were selecting the leaders for the blacks as white people had always chosen the spokesmen for blacks. They talked about who would be chosen because of an indication that this might be changed. When Fannie Lou Hamer's name was mentioned, there was a remark about whether she was a "proper" spokesperson. Bob Moses remembers that Martin Luther King Jr. said something about how "she splits her infinitives."[54] Humphrey said that the MFDP was not allowed to vote to select delegates, and adding seats after a vote of the MFDP delegation could not be considered because it was likely that Fannie Lou Hamer would be elected.[55] The Democratic Party leadership considered her persona non grata, not worthy of speaking for the campaign, and did not want to include her in any discussions with Humphrey after the initial meeting. They adopted the view Roy Wilkins had of her. After the Credentials Committee hearing, Wilkins had told Fannie Lou Hamer that she was "ignorant" and didn't "know anything about politics." He asked her, since the MFDP had made its point, why she didn't "pack up and go home."[56] The party establishment thus neglected the political weight Mrs. Hamer carried in the MFDP as well as the esteem in which she was held in the eyes of her fellow delegates, MFDP organizers, and volunteers such as myself.

If Mrs. Hamer had been a delegate, she would have had the powers of any delegate in the convention, including the right to speak. Although Johnson had said earlier that the national Democrats could not pick delegates for Mississippi, now the preselection seemed aimed at preventing Mrs. Hamer from taking a seat and appearing on the convention floor. Mondale has said, "Obviously, Johnson's biggest nightmare was the thought of Fannie Lou Hamer leading a debate on the Mississippi challenge on national television from the convention floor."[57] Democratic leaders, Ed King noted later, were now "afraid of the power of Fannie Lou Hamer, power that came from speaking and living the truth."[58]

The naming of the two delegates was the most insulting aspect of the Reuther–Johnson offer. The Democratic Party leadership wanted not only to limit MFDP participation in the convention but also to choose who would represent the MFDP *and* to veto people the MFDP might want to represent it. Moses and Ed King were outspoken as to the unacceptability of this provision in the proposal. They understood that some thought Mrs. Hamer would be a poor speaker, using bad grammar and not expressing herself well, which would not look good on national TV for the MFDP, "the Democratic Party, or the Negro cause in general." Mondale and Rauh later acknowledged that the selection of the MFDP representatives was a mistake.[59] Rauh asserts that the mistake was made because no one had consulted him on the naming of the two delegates. By leaving out Fannie Lou Hamer and favoring black urban professionals, the Reuther–Johnson proposal ignored the strong faction of sharecroppers, domestic workers, and farmers who formed the rank and file of the MFDP delegation.

Voting was the issue in Mississippi, and now it was also the issue in Atlantic City. The MFDP was demanding votes in settlement of the Challenge, but it seemed that the Democrats in power were not truly concerned about the right to vote. Humphrey confirmed that only voice votes would be cast at the convention. Offering the MFDP two seats when votes would not be cast or counted therefore had only symbolic meaning.

While Ed King was engaging Humphrey in an analysis of the terms of the Reuther–Johnson proposal, Moses spoke of the violence and injustice in Mississippi and government failure to protect civil rights workers and local blacks in voter registration drives and to enforce federal law.[60] Humphrey and Reuther could see that they had not gained the critical support of Moses, a man of recognized power and integrity. The discussion revealed that the MFDP could not accept the proposal "on any grounds of logic, morality, common sense, or good politics." Humphrey and Reuther then gave up their persuasive efforts and "became desperate." They turned to the subject of their own "morality, righteousness, and courage" and wanted to make sure that everyone in the room understood their perspective. They cited the dangers they saw in the possible election of Goldwater, arguing that the MFDP should not initiate a floor fight or massive demonstrations, which would jeopardize Humphrey's nomination and the election of President Johnson.[61]

What Rustin said at the beginning of the meeting Humphrey confirmed as it neared an end: according to Ed King, "it was all we were going to get. This was it and there was little point in further talk about the Green proposal or anything else." Humphrey expected the leaders in the meeting to get agreement from the MFDP delegation. The MFDP representatives promised to present the offer to the delegation as fairly as possible. Moses said he would respect the delegation's decision but thought the MFDP should go to the floor for a vote. Rustin commented that "the MFDP could not possibly win the floor fight and that a public defeat would be bad for the MFDP" and the movement. Dr. King spoke up for the first time, "strongly agreeing with Rustin at this point," when it was becoming clear the MFDP would reject the Reuther–Johnson proposal. Although Dr. King knew that parts of the proposal were unacceptable, he thought it should be carefully considered rather than hastily rejected. Rustin added that a floor fight would be bad for the Democratic Party in a crucial election and could endanger Humphrey's chance to become vice president.[62]

Not knowing how weak Rauh's position had become, the MFDP representatives boasted that they would get Rauh to pull the convention supporters together for a floor fight. Reuther then made his threats. He pointed his finger at Martin Luther King Jr., telling him to "remember who pays for you," referring to the fact that the UAW had supplied crucial money to Dr. King and the SCLC in crisis times, particularly in Birmingham in 1963 to get hundreds of kids bailed out of jail.[63] Reuther was clearly threatening to cut off money to Dr. King if he did not do what Reuther wanted. Reuther's financial threat may have influenced King, but it would have no effect on the MFDP.

In his book written with Constance Curry, *The Fire Ever Burning*, Aaron Henry expresses the opinion that Reuther used "poor strategy," putting "figures on the table" about money given to the SCLC when Dr. King needed it.[64] According to Ed King, Reuther was telling Dr. King that "favors done for them in the past now called for repayment." He "outlined the thousands of dollars that the UAW and other Northern liberals had put up to finance bail money in Birmingham and other campaigns."[65] Henry thought the approach was "almost ridiculous." He knew that the threat to Dr. King had no influence on Moses and the MFDP. As Henry put it, "[Dr.] King could not claim to represent the feelings of Mississippi Negroes who had never felt the results of Reuther's good will—they didn't owe him anything."[66] It was "incredible," commented Ed King later. "They really put it to Martin King . . . about the money."[67] From what Rauh heard, the Humphrey meeting "got pretty rough."[68] Martin Luther King Jr., MFDP's most powerful supporter, would now tone down his rhetoric.

Henry mentioned that he would like to discuss the offer with Rauh.

Reuther said there would be no need to do that because the MFDP should not expect further help from its attorney. If Rauh did assist the MFDP with a floor fight, he would "have Joe Rauh fired from his job."[69] Reuther did not need to threaten Rauh with loss of his job again during the convention, but now the MFDP was learning of the threats that had begun weeks earlier.

Reuther had a central role not only in planning the maneuvering, but also in using his financial clout against the MFDP Challenge. Rauh has recognized that there is "no question" that Reuther was "the central figure in the compromise."[70] Humphrey agreed later that "the main efforts" came from Reuther, who was brought in because he "was always a good negotiator."[71]

Johnson was well aware of what was going on in Atlantic City because he was receiving regular reports from Jenkins and Moyers as well as from FBI wiretaps, bugs, and informers. Assistant to the director of the FBI Cartha D. "Deke" DeLoach ran the surveillance operation, including "a squad of twenty-seven agents, one radio maintenance technician, and two stenographers." The FBI also secured press credentials with the cooperation of NBC News for agents who went out onto the convention floor, posing as newsmen. The second floor of the old post office accommodated a control center. By intercepting conversations among Dr. King, Rustin, and others; conversations at the storefront office at 2414 Atlantic Avenue used primarily by CORE; and MFDP two-way radio conversations, and by using informers and undercover agents, the FBI had the ability to communicate MFDP strategy to the White House. Two black undercover agents, who "penetrated" the MFDP headquarters at the Gem Hotel and the Union Temple Baptist Church used for its "strategy meetings," had an exclusive telephone line to provide information to the control center.[72] DeLoach sent fifty-two pages of daily summaries of intelligence data to Jenkins and kept Jenkins and Moyers "constantly advised by telephone of minute-by-minute developments."[73] Because of this work, the White House "knew exactly where they [the significant players working for the Challenge] were and what they were doing."[74] After the convention, Johnson asked Jenkins to express his appreciation to Hoover for the work that kept Jenkins and Moyers "constantly alerted to the actions of certain personalities and groups who, if left unchecked, would certainly have proved far more disruptive."[75] Jenkins said the president thought the job done at Atlantic City was "one of the finest he has ever seen."[76]

Meanwhile, at the simultaneous Lawrence–Mondale–Rauh Credentials Committee meeting, the chairman denied a recess, knowing what the White House wanted and fearing that his responsibility to implement the Reuther–Johnson proposal would be derailed. In his presentation, Mondale laid out the terms of the new proposal, emphasizing that it was a compromise that did not go as far as the MFDP wanted it to go or as far as the white southern delegations wanted it to go. Although admitting the existence of discrimination and intimidation in Mississippi, he argued that the MFDP was "a protest movement not a political party" and therefore its "claim under the call of the Convention is not so clear."[77] In a skillful piece of advocacy, he was "flattering" Rauh. Rauh said Mondale "made [the proposal] sound so favorable to us, and he would interject all the time about how much I had won, and that made it harder to fight." According to Rauh, Mondale did an "eloquent" job, making "a most magnificent presentation" of the subcommittee report. Rauh pointed out that "Mondale made it brilliantly and he interspersed it with his own liberalism and his own belief in civil rights. . . . I mean it was an absolutely perfect report. It was the right thing. Everybody felt [it]."[78]

Mondale did not include assurances that either side would accept the terms of the Reuther–Johnson proposal in the subcommittee report. George P. Mahoney, a Dixiecrat delegate from Maryland, said that Aaron Henry and Ed King were "satisfied and happy about this situation."[79] A newspaper account stated that "someone came in [just before the vote] and said two Freedom Party leaders had agreed by phone to accept at-large delegate status."[80] These assertions were plainly incorrect because none of the leaders had heard the proposal, but Mondale did not label them false, thus misleading the committee members in their voting. Rauh never challenged them either.

Rauh was in a dilemma: favoring the Mondale report, which he believed was the maximum the MFDP could get but also feeling unable to vote for it without Henry's authorization. He could not get a delay because about a hundred members of the committee were "shouting 'Vote, vote, vote!'"

Rauh mentioned "a mob psychology,"[81] whereas Mondale remembered it "as being more civilized than that."[82] The chairman proceeded without learning the MFDP's position. Rauh easily voted "no," based on not knowing Aaron Henry's position. He also knew that his vote would be without effect.[83]

Rauh observed that "only a few" voted with him in the voice vote; he was unsuccessful in getting a roll-call vote in committee. He said "eight of us voted . . . no . . . a ragtag eight."[84] He called what was left a "few remnants," who did not include delegates from states such as California or New York that might have been influential in gathering more support for the MFDP. He knew he had eight and "could name six who voted no": the two from D.C., two from Colorado, the guy from the Canal Zone, and the guy from Guam.[85] For some unknown reason, he omitted Edith Green and, presumably, Robert Kastenmeier. The result was that the committee chairman got his majority vote approving the Mondale subcommittee report as its recommendation to the full convention. Edith Green reserved the right to file a minority report, which the chairman allowed, provided the report had the required number of eleven signatures. Rauh judged that the MFDP could not win a vote on the floor. The proposal was more than anyone expected, and the convention delegates would think they had given the MFDP enough.

What had happened to so many of the eighteen MFDP supporters on the committee who did not vote for a minority report? Delegates had been changing their minds since Sunday afternoon after the idea of two votes came up and as they heard appeals to support Humphrey for vice president or be loyal to President Johnson. Broadcast of the final offer, called a "compromise," circulated around the convention with news that the MFDP had *accepted* the offer.[86] Hearing that, some MFDP-supporting Credentials Committee members apparently felt they did not need to attend the last meeting, considering that the MFDP no longer needed their votes.

Although these reasons were factors, the most often mentioned cause of the decline in support was the irresistible pressure that Democratic leaders put on individuals to change their positions. Rauh explained that the MFDP lost the eleven of its "11 and 8" because "the Administration was really giving us the business."[87] On Monday night, according to Jenkins's report to the White House, thirteen delegates still supported a minority report for the MFDP. When that number dropped below eleven, the committee could call for a vote. On Tuesday morning, the FBI reported that Jenkins "concedes they currently have 13," but he was attempting "to have various Democratic heads talk to various members of the Credentials Committee and have them change their vote to not bring this question to a fight on the floor." He was "of the opinion that he may be able to succeed."[88] The "talking to" was more than just that. According to Mondale later, "Johnson's handling of the Freedom Democrats' challenge walked a thin line at times between hardball and over-the-line tactics."[89]

Moses wanted to expose these tactics because it was important for the MFDP delegates to understand that "we're fighting Johnson and not some vague uncertainty that the delegates have about the legality of this." But Rauh "wanted to hide the role of the President." He argued that "tactically it [emphasizing Johnson's role] was a bad thing to do because then you antagonize the President even more," although Moses thought Johnson was already as antagonistic as he could possibly be.[90] The press made it look as if the issue were being decided by the Credentials Committee, but the outcome was more dependent on power politics: whether the MFDP could hold its "11 and 8" against the president.

The White House was not sure on any given day who on the Credentials Committee was still committed to the MFDP, but it had obtained a list from SNCC that provided some help in deciding which delegates to target. On Sunday night, Congressman Diggs of Michigan asked Bob Moses and Courtland Cox for names of supporters on the committee. He told them he would give the list to Lawrence "to show him we have the strength to pull a minority vote on the floor." Moses was reluctant, but Cox pressed him to give the list to "show that we had some clout."[91] Thelwell recalls that there were fourteen names on the list.[92] Cox believes that the list made "a huge difference" because it "allowed Lyndon Johnson to target the delegates with bullying and bribery."[93] I believed the same thing when I was in Atlantic City. Cox and Thelwell thought that the White House staff was *able* to make threatening calls when they *learned* who was on the list Moses gave to Diggs. But Johnson had already known from his aides' research in mid-August who the supporters were and had analyzed their vulnerabilities. He knew how the list was going down in number as the convention progressed. The turning over of the list was important only if "the names kept changing," as Thelwell asserted to me,[94] but White House aides in Atlantic City were keeping close track of the delegations and had other sources for the same information.

Pressure was applied, and threats were made to individual delegates on the committee, which changed some votes. We heard the rumors in Atlantic City. Mendy Samstein and Marshall Ganz, who lobbied the California members, related the story of Virna Canson to others in Atlantic City as they knew it. They knew on Sunday that her support was questionable when she started to "hedge," talking about compromise, and could not attend Dr. King's brunch. She has been the principal example of Johnson pressure that dried up MFDP support on the Credentials Committee.[95] In her notes, she recorded a Tuesday morning breakfast meeting with Winslow Christian, a member of Governor Brown's cabinet. He told her that Johnson had just asked the governor what Virna Canson was going to do, that he did not want her to be the eleventh person to sign the minority report. She refused to make a commitment but said she would "make every effort to comply."[96] A woman told her later that "her [Canson's] husband's desire to be a judge" could be in jeopardy if she remained loyal to the MFDP.[97] During the convention, Canson talked to her husband and told Mrs. Hamer how happy she was that he understood. He told her to "do whatever I think is right" and not worry about him.[98]

Virna Canson wanted the MFDP delegates to have a symbolic vote at the convention and find a compromise that would avoid a floor fight. When the subcommittee report encompassed what she considered essential, she refused a request to sign the minority report before leaving the Credentials Committee meeting. Nick Kotz, who contacted the Canson family years later and received thirty-seven pages of handwritten notes from Virna Canson's daughter Faythe, wrote in a footnote in his book *Judgment Days:* "Her husband did not receive the [state] judicial appointment. He and his family were convinced that his wife's show of independence, which he supported, had killed the appointment. In her diary, Verna [*sic*] Canson described the pressure she was under but claimed that she had approved the final compromise on its merits."[99] According to her notes, her final position was consistent with her desire for no more than a symbolic win for the MFDP that would avoid a floor fight. By holding out as long as she did, she served to pressure Johnson to give the MFDP at least some delegate seats that represented votes.

Rauh received information about pressure placed on other delegates. The man from the Canal Zone had his job with the U.S. Army threatened, but he decided to continue his support of the MFDP, anyway. Rauh also talked about other delegates getting pressured: Victorine Adams from Maryland dropped out early "by attrition," as did Joyce Austin, Mayor Wagner's secretary in New York.[100] It is less convincing that other threats were actually made: continued support of the Freedom Democrats might mean the loss of a government contract that the delegate's firm was seeking or the loss of a poverty program in someone's congressional district or denial of a prospective loan.[101]

The taped phone conversations confirm contacts that Johnson did make or arrange for others to make. He called Governor Hughes of Iowa and gave him a "stern lecture," warning that an Iowa delegate on the Credentials Committee would only hurt Senator Humphrey's chances of getting the vice presidency if she carried out her threat to sign a minority report.[102] He called the publisher of the *Denver Post* to ask for assurances that the Colorado delegates would not sign a minority report.[103] He discussed with Jenkins whether to try to reach New York mayor Wagner when they hadn't "moved the New York woman" and to have Michigan governor Mennen Williams "get Reuther to the Michigan people."[104] Victorine Adams, a black member of the Baltimore City Council, received "relentless pressure from both the White House and state officials in Annapolis."[105] Johnson representatives were "working" on Washington delegate Marjorie King until she was "leaning toward" the president's position, and they guessed that she would go along with him.[106] Abe Fortas called an associate to influence the delegation from Puerto Rico to decline support.[107]

Johnson "believed every man has his price" and that he could obtain support by directing his aides to use "muscle" on Rauh and the delegates on the Credentials Committee known to be supporting the MFDP and ready to submit a minority report.[108] Based on Rauh's statements and on

documents that show which delegates Johnson targeted, the last thirteen supporters by Monday night appear to have been two from Colorado, two from the District of Columbia, two from Michigan, one from
Oregon, one from Wisconsin, one from New York, one from California,
one from Iowa, one from the Canal Zone, and one from Guam.[109] Two
in this list of thirteen, who remained supporters of the MFDP until the
very end, were independent black women: Virna Canson and Joyce Austin. Another on this list of thirteen was either Rauh or Diggs, neither of
whom would present a problem for the president. Some of the thirteen
were "bluffers" who held to support of the MFDP until the last minute,
when they decided they would not sign a minority report.

Mondale announced the results of the Lawrence–Mondale–Rauh Credentials Committee vote to the eagerly waiting press. He told the press
that the regulars would be seated under the terms of a compromise that
the Credentials Committee had approved. The timing of the committee's
vote and Mondale's announcement have been "sources of controversy"
ever since.[110] If Mondale had said the committee approval was "unanimous," it would have been clear that Rauh had abandoned the MFDP
and voted for the Reuther–Johnson offer. If Mondale had said that the
MFDP had agreed and accepted the offer, the MFDP Challenge would
be ended.

Mondale bears responsibility for the announcement of the Credentials
Committee decision that affected later events, but what he actually said
was less important than what the press reported: the regulars would be
seated under the terms of a compromise that the Credentials Committee
had *unanimously* approved, and "the compromise had been accepted"
by the MFDP.[111] With the use of the term *compromise*, the implication
was that the MFDP had agreed to the proposal. Reporters were given
the impression that the terms were acceptable to the MFDP and that the
vote was unanimous. Rauh claimed Mondale "filibustered a little bit . . .
savoring his victory . . . [and] having a good time talking." Rauh waited
impatiently for fifteen minutes, he said, to take over the microphone to
announce that the MFDP had *not* agreed to the proposal and that he
had voted against it. He was still suggesting the possibility of going to
the floor—"we may try to get enough votes."[112] But he was too late.

Spokesmen acting on behalf of the president were letting the delegations and members of the Credentials Committee know that the MFDP had accepted the final offer, the so-called compromise.

The word *compromise* spread quickly in Atlantic City and influenced further developments for the MFDP. President Johnson's unilateral decision—aided by Reuther, Humphrey, Mondale, and the convention managers and implemented by the Credentials Committee—became known as "the compromise." This term appears in most accounts of the MFDP Convention Challenge. However, it is inaccurate and misleading. A compromise involves *consent* reached after discussion involving mutual concessions. There was *no mutually agreed resolution* of the MFDP Convention Challenge.

John Connally and Carl Sanders, governor of Georgia, were helping Johnson keep southern states from joining a walkout in sympathy with Mississippi. Johnson took a call from Sanders late Tuesday afternoon to hear how upset he was that two MFDP delegates at-large were being given the status of official delegates when they had no legal right to sit in the convention. He alarmed Johnson, projecting "complete havoc" with a wholesale walkout. Johnson defended the terms that had been worked out; he said he "didn't raise it [the final decision]" but had been told in the morning about it. Mississippi was seated, there was a resolution to take care of the problem in the future, and two people were recognized, but that was "symbolic," not depriving Mississippi of anything or hurting anybody, and there wouldn't be any votes anyway. Johnson went further to say that despite violation of the civil rights laws, they had won and were getting seated with all their votes. "They got to let them vote." The MFDP had "a legitimate case to be made," but he didn't want to make it.[113] As shown in Michael Beschloss's excerpt of the conversation in *Taking Charge*, Johnson was feeling "harassed to death" and said, "Mississippi's seated! She gets every damned vote she's entitled to. She oughtn't to be seated. She wouldn't let those nigras vote. And that's not right."[114] Johnson recognized the validity of the MFDP cause here, but he never did so publicly.

About an hour later, Walter Jenkins called Johnson to tell him that members of the Credentials Committee who might be MFDP supporters had been told not to sign a minority report and that "she," meaning

Edith Green, did not have more than ten votes. Johnson asked if Reuther could "straighten out" Rauh and was assured not only that Rauh would be okay, but that Jenkins thought the MFDP would withdraw, that the proposal was not what they wanted, but they would accept. Johnson still seemed nervous: "[A]re you sure you have the votes?" Yes, but in any event, a roll call was impossible, and if there were one, Jenkins projected that they would have 98 percent of the vote. Johnson advised that it be brought up at the beginning of the convention session and "ram it right on through" before reporters could generate a fight. Now Johnson wanted Jenkins to "work on the South" to prevent a walkout.[115] The next call assured Johnson about other southern delegations not liking the proposal, but not planning to leave.[116]

The broadcast of the Credentials Committee vote on television interrupted the Reuther–Humphrey meeting as it was nearing its end. Humphrey had presented the proposal to Dr. King and the MFDP leadership for acceptance—not negotiation—*while* the Credentials Committee was ramming it through as Johnson directed, and, except for the MFDP objections, everything had gone according to the plan Humphrey had described to Johnson by phone early that afternoon. It is, therefore, difficult to credit reports that Humphrey was surprised by the news report. For example, "Humphrey could not believe what he was seeing. He thought there was still time to talk, but now he realized he had been used by the administration to stall the MFDP that afternoon while it ensured that the Credentials Committee accepted the compromise."[117] Ed King claims that Humphrey did look surprised. He does not believe that Humphrey participated in what he called "Mondale's deceitful scheme of holding us in conversation while keeping us away from the real action."[118]

In Atlantic City, we knew little about Mondale, a newcomer to national politics, and viewed him with skepticism, unlike Humphrey and Reuther, who were well-known friends of the civil rights movement. While the MFDP leadership was kept away from the crucial Credentials Committee meeting, he reported the subcommittee's proposal to the committee and has been considered by some to be the one responsible for the scheming and manipulation. Ten years later Wally Roberts, a Freedom School coordinator in Shaw, Mississippi, in 1964, wrote about Mondale as "the hatchet man who executed the orders to deny . . . [the MFDP] power."[119]

The news report of the Credentials Committee vote astounded the MFDP representatives, propelling them into action. Bob Moses is reported to have said to Humphrey, "You cheated!" or "You tricked us!"[120] Perhaps he did yell at Humphrey, but it's hard to imagine the mild-mannered Moses yelling. That would have been totally out of character since he usually never raised his voice. But Moses himself has written that he slammed the door in Humphrey's face and was "furious."[121]

Moses raced by taxi to the church where the MFDP delegation held its meetings and was the first to arrive with the news that the Credentials Committee had decided to seat the regulars and give only two seats to the MFDP. In another taxi coming from the Reuther–Humphrey meeting, Dr. King, Andrew Young, and Ed King discussed what should happen after the MFDP delegation learned about the Credentials Committee's decision to seat the regulars. Young thought it important that the MFDP accept the decision and argued that position to Dr. King. If Aaron Henry and Ed King could take their seats, that would be "more than Mississippi black folks had won before." Both Young and Dr. King took the Goldwater threat "very seriously" and did not want to jeopardize Johnson's election. Young said later, "This was not protest politics, but real politics, and a lot was at stake."[122] At the same time, Ed King, sitting to Dr. King's left in the backseat of the cab, was trying to influence Dr. King against using his powerful oratory to influence the delegates to accept the decision.[123]

As the word spread, delegates and supporters, Pat and I included, went to the church as soon as we could. If the vote was indeed unanimous, Rauh had betrayed the MFDP. Some in the MFDP believed, as Charlie Cobb told me he did, that Rauh had known what would happen in the Credentials Committee when he had spoken to the MFDP that morning and promised that he would accept no less than the Green proposal.[124] The MFDP did not know what Rauh did inside the closed meeting of the Credentials Committee but thought that he had made a deal the night before, that he was "dishonest" in not telling the morning caucus about the offer, and that he was not going to "really consult with the caucus." People felt he "sold out."[125] Moses was off meeting with Humphrey, and he, too, was under suspicion for having sold out the delegation.

The principals arrived at the church: Dr. King, Aaron Henry, and Ed King from the Reuther–Humphrey meeting and Rauh, Edith Green, Kastenmeier, and some other supporting committee members from the Lawrence–Mondale–Rauh meeting. The question for the MFDP delegation was whether to accept what the Credentials Committee would report to the full convention that night, the second day of the convention: the Reuther–Johnson offer that the Credentials Committee had *adopted* without hearing from the MFDP.

The emotional pitch in the room was high: the MFDP delegates and supporters were realizing that, after all the positive signs they had seen the previous night, they would not be seated at the convention. There was confusion because no one knew for sure what was going on. John Dittmer in *Local People,* his 1994 history of the Mississippi civil rights movement, describes an air of "frustration and anger" in the room: "This proposal had been sprung on them after the fact, and now the outsiders who had supported their Challenge—Rauh, Rustin, and Dr. King—appeared to have sold them out."[126] The frustration and anger found its target in Rauh for his reported vote against the MFDP in the Credentials Committee meeting.

The meeting began about 5:00 p.m. Rauh spoke first, explaining the terms of the decision and how the support for the MFDP on the Credentials Committee had fallen away until there were no longer sufficient votes for a minority report.[127] I felt that he had not been open and honest in representing the MFDP. I didn't know exactly what he was doing, but he was friends with Humphrey, and Reuther's UAW was important to Rauh's law firm and livelihood. No one had authorized him to agree to the Reuther–Johnson proposal, but he must have *agreed* to it because we heard that the vote was unanimous. In this atmosphere, Rauh could not persuade the MFDP that he had voted no. I was astounded when he went on to tell the delegation that the decision was just fine. He *recommended* that the MFDP accept it. Once he was for the decision, the betrayal appeared clear.

Edith Green spoke against the Reuther–Johnson proposal. Dr. King wanted to speak, but the audience shouted him down because they believed he, too, had a hand in the decision. Rauh thought this afternoon caucus "got to be an awful shambles." He claimed later that Bob

Fannie Lou Hamer, upset about the final decision of the Credentials Committee on Tuesday. Courtesy of George Ballis/Take Stock.

Moses spoke after Edith Green and caused all the "hysteria" that was in the room.[128] I have been confident for years (right or wrong) that Bob Moses said not a word. I remember waiting for him to speak and feeling disappointed that he did not. Aaron Henry wanted to postpone taking a vote because the delegates were "furious," "there wasn't a cool head in the delegation," and "calmer heads might prevail" later, but, according to him, Moses was "irreconcilably opposed to postponing a decision," knowing that "the delegation would reject the proposal if an immediate vote was taken."[129]

Back in Washington shortly after the convention, Rauh complained to Arthur Waskow about "the manner of the [MFDP's] rejection of the 'compromise'" on Tuesday afternoon, which he called a "steamroller."[130] A year later he said his criticism of the MFDP included its "failure to hold a rational discussion of the compromise" on Tuesday and its use of words such as *sell-out* and *double-dealing*, which he denied had taken place. Democrats in very difficult roles, he argued, had acted with "a very high degree of integrity."[131]

On that late Tuesday afternoon, the MFDP delegates did not understand why they should now accept only two at-large seats when they wanted votes for all the delegates. What was going on? The MFDP delegation and people like me wondered why it had lost its support for a minority report on the Credentials Committee. It was soon rumored that Johnson had applied pressure on individuals with overnight telephone calls, threatening them personally if they did not withdraw their support from the MFDP. We thought it must have been overnight because the momentum for a floor vote had been so strong on Monday night. Irresistible pressure on individual members of the Credentials Committee appeared to be the only reason the question of seating would not go to the floor of the convention for a roll-call vote by all the delegates.

Rauh presented a decision to the MFDP delegation that we saw as offensive, undemocratic, and underhanded because it seemed to have been made in secret. We didn't know, however, that the politicking had been going on for weeks—working on relationships, offering, trading, and withdrawing favors among powerful men anxious to serve their own self-interest. We saw threats. In truth, what happened at the last minute—the decision rammed through the Credentials Committee—only concluded those ongoing efforts, as anyone more politically aware than most of us would have known.

The MFDP voted to reject the Credentials Committee decision, hoping for a roll-call vote Tuesday evening. According to Aaron Henry, "seventy percent opposed it." Probably more voted against the decision in this first vote by a show of hands as there was little reason to accept it on Tuesday. The delegates had a little time to "round up eleven members of the committee who would be willing to sign a minority report." They had nine, according to Aaron Henry, but other supporters, including Diggs, were not to be found that afternoon.[132]

I did not understand then that there was still time to prepare a minority report and submit it to the convention. I thought there was no longer any chance of an MFDP victory. The remaining supporters on the Credentials Committee met in another part of the church to agree on a statement to the waiting press. Rauh announced their belief that the delegation should have been seated in full, but "a tremendous advance has been made."[133] They met in a closed session and agreed that their deliberations would be kept secret. Rauh never reported any differences of opinion in the group.

Although Bob Moses wanted him to, Rauh did not look for additional supporters. He later called the remaining group of supporting Credentials Committee members "an awful rag-tag thing" without California, Michigan, or any black delegates other than Gladys Duncan from D.C. He concluded that "there was no power to the eight that were left." He had no interest in a roll-call vote because the supporters remaining were "the rummiest crowd you can think of," a "rump operation." The MFDP delegation had been dignified to this point, so Rauh did not want "what had been a beautiful and marvelous operation to become a shabby thing."[134] Some of the last supporters had dropped the MFDP as they decided to avoid attending the afternoon Credentials Committee meeting when the vote would be taken. The loss of support was due in part to getting "word from the convention managers that the President didn't want the issue aired publicly any more—that he didn't want [the MFDP] seated in place of the regular Mississippi delegation."[135] Some delegates might have signed a minority report if they had not heard on the news that the MFDP had agreed to the proposal.

The Mississippi regulars also rejected the final proposal. Giving anything to the MFDP was unacceptable, and they took offense at being
asked to take a loyalty oath. They were only being asked to declare
their *intention* to support the convention's nominees, but they felt
that even that was too much to promise. They found the final proposal
"unbelievable" and protested "[the] seat[ing] [of] an outside pressure
group with no legal claim to delegate status."[136] Only four of their delegates—led by Doug Wynn from Greenville—took the loyalty oath.[137]
Wynn's wife's father, Ed Clark, a powerful figure from Texas, was close
to Lyndon Johnson, and Johnson was godfather to the Wynns' daughter. Wynn's more liberal politics and this personal relationship with the
president resulted in Wynn's serving as the main contact between White
House aides and the regulars delegation. Fred Berger of Natchez and
Randolph Holladay of Picayune, also lawyers, joined him in supporting the national ticket, taking the oath and their seats in the Mississippi
section on Tuesday night. A fourth regular, Mrs. Mildred McMullin of
Newton, secretly signed the loyalty oath late Wednesday but did not
take her seat.

The convention session opened at 8:43 p.m. Tuesday evening, with temporary chairman Senator John Pastore of Rhode Island presiding.[138] Aaron
Henry and Ed King went in with an escort or guest passes and took seats
although they had no official "delegates at-large" credentials. As the first
order of business, the convention took up the Credentials Committee
report on Mississippi, which Governor Lawrence read. Members of the
delegation of the regular Democratic Party of Mississippi were declared
duly accredited delegates who had signed a declaration of their "intention
to support the Convention's nominees" in the general election. Included
in the call for the 1968 Democratic National Convention would be the
undertaking of an assurance by a state party that voters, "regardless of
race, color, creed, or national origin," would have the opportunity to
participate fully in party affairs. Members of the MFDP delegation were
"welcomed as honored guests" of the convention. Dr. Aaron Henry and
the Reverend Edwin King were accorded "full delegate status, in a special
category of delegates-at-large," but this status was granted "wholly apart
from the question of the contest as to the delegates from Mississippi,"

Convention Hall during the 1964 Democratic Convention. Courtesy of the LBJ Presidential Library.

"in recognition of the unusual circumstances presented at the hearing," and "without setting any precedent for the future." There was no minority report, which would have been presented first. A voice vote ended with a slam of the gavel and a declaration that the report was approved. Although the nays were much louder than the ayes, the chairman did not recognize the liberal and southern opposition, quickly overriding the noise of dissenting voices.[139]

The timing of the vote at the opening of the convention session took Edith Green by surprise. By her count, there were still more than eleven supporters who could file a minority report, which she intended to do that evening. She had told John McCormack, the convention chairman, of her plan. The convention agenda that had been distributed to all the delegates had included the Credentials Committee report on Mississippi as the *last* item of business, so the Oregon, California, and New York delegations, thinking they had time, were out caucusing, considering whether to support a roll-call vote. Edith Green would soon have the three additional signatures required for a minority report, but a slam of the gavel ended the issue.[140]

In letters written shortly after the convention, Rauh referred to Credentials Committee MFDP supporters "who got off the train early" and to "the underground railroad" on Tuesday night.[141] What he meant is only the subject of speculation: some Credentials Committee supporters were still working on a minority report that the MFDP wanted. Rauh thought Gar Alperowitz, one of the MFDP strategists, was behind this effort, but he later apologized for implicating Alperowitz in an anti-LBJ campaign. Rauh did not report what Edith Green planned after the secret meeting of MFDP Credentials Committee supporters at the church. She has been credited as a strong, effective recruiter of other convention delegates as MFDP supporters, and she alone independently maintained the courage of her convictions throughout the convention.

In the end, the power of the convention chairman to change the agenda at the last minute was sufficient to outmaneuver delegate support for the MFDP. Presiding chair Senator Pastore exercised his discretion, knowing the wishes of the White House and the declining political support for the MFDP among delegates. Edith Green judged the convention maneuver "a very unfair exercise of power for the chairman of the convention, to change the order of the agenda—call it up while they knew the states were out caucusing on that very, very matter." She said that the 1964 convention was "one of the most disillusioning experiences" she had ever had "in terms of the pressures that were put on by the powers-to-be to change the minds of the minority on the Credentials Committee."[142]

I had expected a debate followed by a democratic vote, but the slam of the gavel was the final action. Only the president had the ability to use political power to stop a groundswell of public opinion over three days that had favored the Mississippi black disenfranchised. Johnson and his supporters appear to have spent three days arriving at their resolution, but their plans had been at least two weeks in the works. Rauh knew what the outcome would be, but not exactly how it would play out and how it could be made to look like a victory for all concerned. Jim Forman looks at it another way in his book *The Making of Black Revolutionaries*: "For three full days, poor, working-class people and one middle-class preacher

. . . brought the great convention to a standstill."[143] Through complete manipulation, Reuther's maneuvering on Tuesday ended the Challenge without a fair fight within the Democratic Party. The MFDP Convention Challenge had failed.

According to Rauh, at the end of the Tuesday convention session he returned to the convention managers at the podium the credentials issued to Aaron Henry and Ed King, which they had rejected.[144] However, the Democratic National Committee did not issue credentials for the delegates at-large until Wednesday, the day after the convention had adopted the Credentials Committee report. The committee letter stated that two seats were provided adjacent to the Alaska and Arizona delegations. Rauh claimed that he was surprised to discover eleven signatures on a minority report filed with the convention some time before the end of the evening. Five people had signed it when it no longer made a difference. They looked like civil rights supporters, but in fact they had been loyal to President Johnson.

Perhaps the eleven needed for the minority report had been there all along, but by Tuesday evening Rauh knew that if a minority report were submitted to the convention, he could not get eight state delegations to demand a roll-call vote. This second hurdle would have been just as decisive in causing the Challenge to fail. The chairman of the convention could ignore a cry from the floor for a roll-call vote, with the supporting territories no longer qualified to demand a roll-call vote, and Rauh did not have behind him the political leaders of eight major states, such as California, New York, and Michigan, who could demand to be recognized. A minority report lost its significance without political support to get it to the floor of the convention for debate and a roll-call vote.

The MFDP had come a long way before its Convention Challenge failed. Still undaunted, the Freedom Democrats had more to do.

16

The Mississippi Freedom Democratic Party Turns to Protest

> We didn't come all this way for no two seats 'cause all of us is tired.
> —Fannie Lou Hamer[1]

Angry about the Credentials Committee decision, MFDP delegates decided on Tuesday evening to make their grievances known through nonviolent direct-action protest. Since Sunday night, supporters had maintained an around-the-clock vigil, with as many as four hundred young people sitting on the boardwalk.[2] Others walked silently up and down with MFDP placards as a reminder of the conditions in Mississippi that had resulted in the murders of Chaney, Goodman, and Schwerner. The large portraits of them were prominently hung or carried by the demonstrators for all to see. In his book *Ready for Revolution*, Stokely Carmichael describes the vigil as "unusually powerful and moving." He stayed on the boardwalk "talking to the people . . . who stopped by" and did not attend any meetings.[3] One of the people he spoke to was Hodding Carter III, who was covering the MFDP Convention Challenge for the family newspaper, the *Delta Democrat-Times* of Greenville, Mississippi. As Carter told me, he had assumed the pose of a liberal northerner conducting interviews on the boardwalk, but Stokely recognized him and yelled out, "That's not who he is. He's Hodding Carter from Greenville, Mississippi!"[4]

Once the Tuesday evening session began, the convention decision that the MFDP delegates would not be seated provoked more picketing outside. The Mississippi regulars' boycott of the convention gave the MFDP the opportunity for a sit-in inside Convention Hall. The MFDP

Stokely Carmichael *(facing the camera)* protesting on the boardwalk in front of Convention Hall. Courtesy of Nancy Schieffelin.

knew from news accounts that the seats in the Mississippi section would be empty because most of the regulars refused to take the loyalty oath and were leaving town. Courtland Cox presented the idea of the sit-in in a discussion with Bob Moses about what to do next. The whites had walked out, and he said, "Why not take the seats?" Bob thought it was "a good idea."[5] Bayard Rustin had been concerned that SNCC would bring in radicals who might provoke violence, but SNCC intended to involve only the MFDP delegates without recruiting large numbers of student activists.

Sharlene Kranz, the young SNCC volunteer coordinator of the delegates' transportation, told me she heard "[i]t's over."[6] She shut down the MFDP operations at the Gem Hotel and headed to Convention Hall to join an assembly of disappointed MFDP delegates and supporters. Aaron Henry wanted to calm the crowd. He urged that it was time "to approach the situation positively." He wrote, "I tried to convince them that we should be thankful that we had come as far as we had and that this was not the time to stop." He wanted the newsmen to stay focused on the MFDP and its goals, fearing that they would pay more attention to radicals engaged in civil disobedience and threatening disruption of the convention.[7]

About five hundred supporters were in a picket line in front of Convention Hall.[8] Some joined hands around three of the MFDP delegates who initially forced entry into Convention Hall. After that most of the delegates entered with loaned badges or guest passes. In a letter, one of the summer volunteers described arranging "a system of runners" that he found "really exciting": someone would get badges inside and carry them to a person outside, who would pass them on to waiting MFDP delegates.[9] Barred by guards despite their credentials, small groups used different side entrances, which were more open. Five Freedom Democrats were the first to enter with these badges: State Stallworth Sr. of Moss Point, Mrs. Emma Sanders of Jackson, Robert Lee Stinson of Laurel, Mrs. Pinkey Hall of Hattiesburg, and Reverend Merrill W. Lindsay of West Point.[10] They took the empty Mississippi seats, and by doing so they made a public statement of their entitlement to represent both blacks and whites in Mississippi.

State Stallworth, a thirty-one-year-old International Paper Company employee from Moss Point, was outside when a fellow came up to him and asked him if he was from Mississippi and whether he wanted to go into the convention. If he got Stallworth credentials, would he go in and take a Mississippi seat? Stallworth said he would. The man came back with New York credentials and went in with him; his end seat was across the aisle from the empty, roped-off Mississippi seats. At a signal, Stallworth stepped across to sit under the Mississippi banner, and, as he said, "Whew. The news media swarmed on me like a swarm of vultures. They wanted to know who I was; where did I come from; how did I get in there; what was going on; what was my name. . . . Whoa, man. Good gracious. Whew." The seats were bolted to the floor, and when the marshals tried to throw him out, he hung onto his chair and stayed. He continued, "The news media come over there and start[ed] putting the camera on them. If it wasn't for that, they'd have threw me out." The marshals retreated because the cameras were on, and then other MFDP delegates came to take the seats; it was "a big excitement." Stallworth learned later that the man who had offered him credentials was Senator Wayne Morse from Oregon.[11]

At 10:12 p.m., the sergeants-at-arms asked the MFDP delegates "respectfully to leave" the seats, but none of them moved.[12] Force was ordered to remove them. Abraham Washington, a twenty-five-year-old college graduate from Phelps, was lifted to his feet and escorted out of the hall. But when they went to remove Hazel Palmer of Jackson, she refused to stand up despite two officials tugging at her. Cliff Carter, a White House aide working closely with Jenkins and Moyers, countermanded the initial order to remove the delegates.[13] Instructions to let the people already seated remain but not to permit other delegates to join them avoided more scenes of the eviction on television. Politically, "a televised eviction would be worse than the sit-in."[14] The scene was one of "pushing, shoving turmoil," but it was caused by the reporters and spectators, not by the "orderly" demonstrators.[15]

Aaron Henry and Ed King left the seats they had taken to join the demonstrators. They are reported to have announced: "They wanted us at-large but we want our section in Mississippi. The seats are here and we are here."[16]

When the Freedom Democrats arrived, the three Mississippi regular delegates who had taken their seats "[b]y an incredible coincidence" were called off the convention floor to visit a friend, and all the seats were vacant. The regulars returned, but they decided not to make "a physical effort to regain possession of their places" and found seats under the podium.[17] The convention managers gave new instructions to the guards, and admission for the MFDP delegates became less difficult. Once they were in the hall, no one objected to their taking the seats. As a SNCC announcement proclaimed at the time, "Reporters and cameramen flocked around the Mississippi section to find 21 Freedom Democrats in the seats."[18]

At some point during the protest, when Fannie Lou Hamer had the chance to talk to reporters, she summed up the Challenge in a statement often repeated as an explanation of the rejection of what the Democratic Party offered the MFDP. As her biographer Kay Mills writes, she "boomed," "We didn't come all this way for no two seats 'cause all of us is tired."[19] By the second part of that statement, often omitted, she meant

MFDP delegates taking the Mississippi seats left empty by the white Mississippi Democratic Party delegates on Tuesday, surrounded by reporters and security guards. Courtesy of George Ballis/Take Stock.

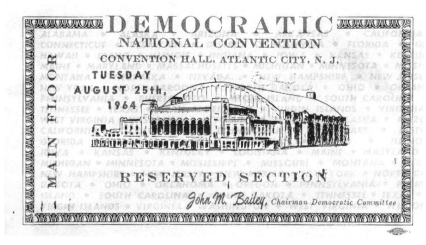

My guest pass to the 1964 Democratic Convention. Todd Collection.

that all the delegates wanted chairs; they needed to sit down and rest their weary feet.

Pat and I had managed to get guest passes and anticipated that Tuesday night would be particularly exciting. It was stirring just to be *inside* to see the masses of people, signs, patriotic paraphernalia, and the hustling newspaper and television reporters and cameramen in the old gigantic Convention Hall. Not having watched prior conventions on TV, I didn't know what to expect. I saw a chaotic sea of overweight Americans wearing silly hats and dressed in red, white, and blue as we picked our way over the jumble of electrical cables and wires all over the floor in the back of the hall. Looking for some action and without seats to go to, I felt I was challenging myself to look as if I belonged and knew what I was doing. I wanted to be near a reporter interviewing delegates on the convention floor—not to be seen on TV, but to try to figure out what momentous, historic events might happen before my very eyes. I recall that we were in the back of the hall on the left, far from the Mississippi section, which was closer to the front on the right. We ventured forward in our aisle but didn't stay long because we were tired of standing on our feet or afraid of getting caught or for some other weak reason. Others who got in with borrowed credentials couldn't stay long because they had to return the badges to the delegates they had been issued to, but my guest pass entitled me to entry for the entire evening. Maybe Pat and I left the convention just knowing we would feel more comfortable outside participating in the demonstration.

Believing fervently that the MFDP had been wronged, we joined the picket line for a while and the group that congregated near the entrance to Convention Hall to sing freedom songs. This went on until late that night.

By late Tuesday, August 25, 1964, the Mississippi credentials dispute was resolved, but President Johnson and his political advisers were still not satisfied. At the conclusion of its final meeting on Tuesday afternoon, the Credentials Committee had announced that a compromise had taken place. The convention adopted its recommendation. Everyone in Atlantic City was talking about the "compromise," even though no such thing had happened. The Democratic liberal politicians thought it would be better for the fall campaign if the MFDP delegation *accepted* and *agreed* with the so-called compromise, and so they would launch a new effort of persuasion on Wednesday.

The convention managers sought to bar the MFDP delegates from entering the hall for more protests on the convention floor Wednesday night.[20] Guards at all the entrances tried to prevent their entry, but with borrowed credentials they again managed to get into Convention Hall and resumed their demonstration. Judy Richardson remembered gaining access by "borrowing uniforms" from the Young Citizens for Johnson and mixing in with the girls running errands on the convention floor.[21] During the day on Wednesday, the janitors had removed the chairs from the Mississippi section, except just enough seats remained for the three regular delegates and the FBI and Secret Service agents who surrounded them for their protection. Kept out of the seats they had peacefully occupied the night before, the MFDP protestors had to stand in the aisles. The "One Man, One Vote" placards held high conveyed the message for the audience, reporters, and TV-viewing public. When about nine MFDP delegates entered the front row of the Mississippi section, they had to stand, but both the nearby Michigan and North Dakota delegations offered the standees seats.[22] Len Holt, a civil rights lawyer and author of one of the first books about the project, *The Summer That Didn't End,* describes the MFDP delegates standing near the Mississippi section as proud black and white men and women from Mississippi: "[T]hey looked beautiful."[23]

On Thursday night, reserved for an emotional tribute to the fallen President Kennedy and including the traditional nominating speeches for the presidential and vice presidential nominees and the nominees' acceptance speeches, the MFDP sit-in continued. Not comfortable with sit-ins, Aaron Henry "had disappeared," presumably to go back home.[24] The rows in the Mississippi section had been placed closer together, and sergeants-at-arms guarded each row at both ends, leaving the MFDP representatives no recourse but to stand in the aisles again.[25] At one point, about seven protestors formed a circle in the middle of the aisle near an intersection and stood silently as if in prayer.

The MFDP had claimed legal entitlement to the seats at the convention, and after that was denied, the sit-ins logically continued the Challenge in Convention Hall as a nonviolent demonstration of the delegates' position. The sit-ins were important because they "carried through with a principle that these were the seats that belonged to the people of Mississippi, the black people of Mississippi, as well as the white people. It was a kind of creative disruption and civil disobedience carried into the middle of politics. We had had civil disobedience everywhere else, so it belonged in politics, too." Unlike the back-room politics that had decided the Challenge, the MFDP protests were "honest, open civil disobedience."[26]

Martin Luther King Jr., the leading advocate of nonviolence in the southern struggle for freedom, agreed. Bob Moses specifically asked him "whether the nonviolent demonstration held . . . on the convention floor was appropriate in his mind as a nonviolent response" to what had happened.[27] King agreed, going on record as approving this form of response by the MFDP delegation. The sit-ins should be understood as a creative response to the tension and "feelings of deep bitterness and frustration" that existed and could have otherwise exploded into attempts at disrupting the convention.[28]

Journalists, however, disagreed with the MFDP's nonviolent approach in politics. They criticized the demonstrators as "undisciplined, mistrustful Freedom Democrats" and found them to be "unable or unwilling to yield even an inch in the name of compromise" because they were "committed to protest as a way of life."[29] Arthur Waskow answers this charge in his book *From Race Riot to Sit-In* in discussing the use of "creative disorder" in politics: "[Objections were] based on the belief that orderly and disorderly politics could not mix. To many of the national [civil rights] leaders, this belief means that when 'protest' movements entered party politics they must and should give up their 'protest' style and their purity of conviction, and must be prepared to compromise."[30]

Critics saw the MFDP as an immature, outmoded protest group unprepared to compromise and unwilling to participate in the give and take of the political process. The MFDP, however, had an obligation to the disenfranchised Mississippi blacks it was representing in Atlantic City. Again, Waskow explains its response well: "[I]n all sorts of politics some kinds of compromise were necessary, but . . . effective politics, even in the political-party arena, required a refusal to destroy or abandon for the sake of compromise the minimum moral basis upon which one's own constituency had been built. . . . [T]hey argued that acceptance of the Administration offer would have been seen among Negro Mississippians as precisely such an abandonment."[31] The protest had a purpose, but few people were prepared at the time to understand the role of nonviolent demonstrations in politics.

17

Wednesday

Persuasion Fails

> I do not think the word *compromise* is the correct one. The delegates
> of the FDP felt that it was not a compromise, but rather a decision
> which was handed down to them. If it was a compromise then the FDP
> would have had a chance to save something. They were not consulted.
> The Democratic Party said, "Here, take this, it's all we will give you."
> —Stokely Carmichael to Robert Penn Warren[1]

The White House wanted the MFDP to accept the Credentials Committee's decision that was adopted by the convention in order to restore
convention harmony and improve Johnson's election prospects. The
Democrats did not like protests from its black constituency: "The sight
of black Mississippians engaging in acts of civil disobedience against the
party of Lyndon Johnson made liberal Democrats uncomfortable."[2] In
agreement with the wishes of the White House, chairman Aaron Henry
assembled the delegates in their meeting place at the Union Baptist Temple Church at 10:00 a.m. on Wednesday to reconsider the vote that had
rejected the decision the previous day. In an alternative account, Henry,
in favor of the decision and wanting the delegation to reconsider its rejection, "invited" Dr. King, James Farmer, Bayard Rustin, and others to
address the delegation.[3]

In the first meeting with Humphrey on Monday, Bob Moses had been
concerned that the whole delegation was not present to decide whether
it agreed with what was being offered. He has said, "We agreed that
anyone who wanted to talk to the delegation to persuade them, should
have access to them . . . that the whole delegation should be able to sit

down and listen through all the arguments."[4] The talking and the listening would now continue all day. I woke up on that hard pew in the church and planned to stay for the meeting.

In the Wednesday meeting, the MFDP delegates were not considering an offer, refusing to negotiate, and declaring unwillingness to compromise. The convention had made its final decision. The outcome of the MFDP Convention Challenge was clear and unchangeable.[5] The only question was whether the MFDP delegates would acquiesce or continue to object to the terms. No negotiations had taken place. The Credentials Committee had not sought their views *before* its vote, and the convention did not hear the MFDP's views before it adopted the committee's report.

Pat and I went to the meeting. The room was crowded, and we had to stand in the aisle. Being there, in the presence of political leaders and warriors in the civil rights movement, was the high point of my Mississippi summer. I didn't know how what the outcome of the meeting would be. Maybe something would change. The powers that be had summoned articulate, influential, political giants to persuade the black former sharecroppers, farmers, and day laborers who were new to politics. These speakers would try to make them understand, just as Humphrey had tried to influence the MFDP leadership, that the election of Lyndon Johnson would be good for the Democratic Party and for the advancement of civil rights and social welfare legislation in the future and that it would be good for the movement to stop protesting against the convention's decision.

Henry explains in his book *The Fire Ever Burning* that his "main interest" was in having the delegates listen to the civil rights leaders who wanted to address them. He believed the MFDP owed them the "common courtesy of listening to what they had to say." Furthermore, the MFDP should not alienate them and be left without their advice in the future: "[W]e were not in a position to get on the bad side of anybody who was basically sympathetic with our goals. If we alienated these civil rights leaders who had helped us get this far, we would go back to Mississippi and have no one left to turn to for advice in national dealings in the future."[6] Personally, Henry found it difficult to refuse to cooperate with the president of the United States. He favored the convention's decision but *said* he was also "wavering" about the acceptance or rejection. He told the delegates, "I'm with ya'll, whatever ya'll decide I'm with ya'll. . . . I'm not for it or against it."[7]

Ed King did not want a swift, unconsidered, outright rejection but took a strong position that the delegates "must be allowed to talk about it." As a white, middle-class, urbanized member of the delegation, he had been selected for seating as a safe symbol of integration. Henry wanted to take his own at-large seat, and Ed King was understood to be in favor of accepting the convention decision, although he has told me that he "voted against accepting the compromise." He expected that most of the MFDP delegates would again reject the convention decision but wanted a full discussion. He "had more faith in their basic wisdom than many of the SNCC staff present."[8]

Pat and I listened to the morning speeches and heard the comments from delegates and others in the audience. The MFDP delegates voted a second time to reject the decision, this time "by an overwhelming majority," but not unanimous. The voting split along socioeconomic lines, a division in the Mississippi movement that would continue after Atlantic City. Several of the professional, middle-class blacks thought it wrong to go against the wishes of the leadership. They wanted to express their loyalty to the Democratic Party and the president. They did not want to offend liberal friends in the Democratic Party by rejecting what the experts, with a better understanding of politics, had carefully worked out. Besides, it "might be dangerous to make an enemy in the White House." Some in SNCC feared these professional blacks would force their opinions on the poorer, less experienced, grassroots majority of the delegation, but in fact the moderates had "little influence" on the rest of the delegation.[9]

To my surprise, Henry wanted everyone to convene again after lunch. According to him, the delegates agreed to reconsider the convention decision (what he calls "the compromise proposal") in an afternoon meeting. He implies in his book that no vote was taken at the end of the morning session.[10] As I recall, the meeting continued into the afternoon based on the belief that new speakers would present more persuasive and effective arguments to change the MFDP vote. Fannie Lou Hamer said, "They began to corner us. You know they kind of shoved this down our throats."[11]

In the Wednesday meetings, liberal Democratic Party members and national civil rights leaders who had supported the Challenge all summer were now saying "the compromise" was a good thing. Dr. King thought it offered hope for political progress, but in general he took a neutral position. He advised the delegation to make its own decision. In his autobiography, he states: "[The compromise] was a significant step. It was not a great victory, but it was symbolic, and it involved the pledge of high party officials to work with the Freedom Party for the next four years to gain registered voters and political strength in Mississippi. . . . Had I been a member of the delegation, I would probably have advised them to accept this as an offer in good faith and attempted to work to strengthen their position."[12] He thought the movement needed a victory at the time, and it would be especially important for blacks and the rest of America to see the MFDP win. According to Ed King, accepting the decision would mean "strength for him, help for him in Negro voter registration throughout the South and in the North."[13]

Bayard Rustin was the strongest advocate for acceptance. He argued for change in the militant politics of the movement, saying the delegates "must broaden their outlook from moral protest to political alliance."[14] I found him eloquent in his speech, strikingly handsome in his bearing, and forceful, giving what has been labeled "a brilliant talk," but he did not persuade me. Rustin upset his audience.[15] He had been a mentor to young black students who joined the movement as full-time SNCC field secretaries, and it was disappointing, to say the least, that now he was advising less militancy and more compromise. Mendy Samstein shouted, "You're a traitor, Bayard, a traitor! Sit down!"[16]

Rustin highlighted the future reform provisions of the decision, in which the MFDP and its leadership had little interest. In his biography of Rustin, John D'Emilio summarizes Rustin's position as follows: "By choosing to move beyond demonstrations and participate in mainstream politics, [Rustin] argued, they were entering a world where the give-and-take of negotiation was the way an agenda moved forward. Johnson's offer might not in some abstract sense be just, but it recognized the rightness of the MFDP's cause by promising to change forever the rules of the party."[17] Rustin wrote his views in "From Protest to Politics: The Future of the Civil Rights Movement," an article arguing for politics rather than for continued protest in the civil rights movement that was published in the February 1965 issue of *Commentary*. He discussed demands for changes in the socioeconomic order, where society had failed to meet not only black needs, but human needs generally. Only through political power, which required a coalition strategy with others, could blacks hope to succeed with radical programs for full employment, reconstruction of the educational system, urban renewal, and abolition of poverty. He faulted those within the movement who lacked "a realistic strategy" for achieving fundamental change and substituted militancy, which he called "a matter of posture and volume and not of effect." He credited the leadership of Bob Moses for a tactical shift to bid for political power in "a strategy calling for the building of community institutions or power bases" that was more than voter registration. But then he faulted the MFDP for its "tactical error in spurning the compromise." Regardless of the MFDP action, Rustin recognized that it had "launched a political revolution . . . within a major political institution." He acknowledged that it was, after all, "part of a coalitional effort."[18]

In advising the MFDP, Rustin had his own self-interest to consider. A. Philip Randolph, Rustin's longtime senior mentor and friend, had proposed a new organization, the A. Philip Randolph Institute, intended "to strengthen those alliances which are either already formed or beginning to be formed between groups whose basic interests are democracy and equality for all people."[19] Rustin would serve as executive director. Reuther was "pleased to join in this very worthwhile project" with a UAW contribution of $25,000.[20] Thus, the new opportunity cemented Rustin's alliance with Reuther and helps to explain his position on the Challenge decision.

James Farmer, national director of CORE, conflicted between "his conscience and what pressure was forcing him to do," spoke "neither for nor against" but pledged that "CORE is with you no matter what you decide."[21] Whereas Jim Forman found it "a decent statement," Ivanhoe Donaldson found it "the most shocking" that Farmer lent support to the decision when so many CORE people had worked hard with SNCC in Mississippi. In Ivanhoe's words, "[Farmer] took a neutral position at a time when people thought that he had the responsibility to take a more decisive role, one way or the other. . . . But instead, he sort of threw his hands up and was unable to deal with the situation."[22] On July 29, 1964, Farmer had angered President Johnson with his dissent from the civil rights leaders' agreed moratorium on mass demonstrations that NAACP executive director Roy Wilkins had requested "to avoid helping Barry Goldwater in the November presidential election."[23] Perhaps as a seasoned politician, Farmer was considering CORE's future relations with the administration and did not see it in CORE's interest to anger Johnson further. After the fact, he stated that the MFDP's stand rejecting "tokenism" was correct: it was "a principled stand rather than one of practical politics," as he put it, and the MFDP delegates could not accept at-large seats, nor could they tolerate the convention's choosing the two people who were to take the seats.[24]

The NCC had actively supported the movement, conducting the Oxford orientation for the volunteers and recruiting ministers for the Mississippi Summer Project, but it "eventually . . . supported the majority compromise."[25] Robert Spike, executive director of the NCC Commission on Race and Religion, was not at this Wednesday meeting because he had injured himself tripping over an obstacle on an Atlantic City street and was hospitalized, but the commission's legal counsel Jack Pratt spoke, urging support for the president's position.

Few of the delegates there to listen spoke up in the open meeting. Most of them were probably thinking: Why were the civil rights leaders suddenly settling for less than they had been trying to help the MFDP get? What had happened that the delegation did not know about? The political maneuvering, the secrecy, and rumors that their leadership had agreed to the two seats made them feel betrayed. They were getting a look at how things *really* worked and were receiving an education in politics. Barred from most of the discussions, the MFDP delegates demanded an explanation. Why hadn't the Democrats asked *them* what they wanted if there were going to be a compromise?

There were other speakers—an "array of power that the administration" had lined up—to urge the MFDP to accept "the compromise," according to Jim Forman.[26] Senator Wayne Morse from Oregon, who had provided credentials for the MFDP delegates to get into the convention hall the previous night, categorically said that the MFDP had won a "victory" and that it should be accepted.[27] About Senator Morse, Henry

wrote that, "though very circumspect, [he] seemed to be slightly leaning" in the direction of acceptance of the offer.[28]

Even Edith Green's position may have changed before the end of the
convention. On Tuesday, she had apparently advised Humphrey's staff
that she "accepted the unity proposal," the Johnson offer, on the "Mississippi Problem."[29] She was of two minds on compromise in American
politics. Later she stated her views on maintaining one's position on principle: "[A]t times I feel it is entirely possible to win more by refusing to
compromise your original position, if it is a true reflection of worthy val-
ues, than by accepting the unacceptable in consolation for a battle well
fought. To do less breeds disrespect in your opposition and as a result you
may never fully win any battle." But she also believed that "if there is one
rule of American politics, it is that compromise is better than nothing at
all, i.e., the art of compromise, the art of the possible,—half of a loaf is
better than none. It is a necessity."[30]

Bob Moses thought the decision should be rejected, but he believed
that the decision was for the MFDP delegates to make. The delegates
knew his views, which had circulated during the meeting the previous
day. I didn't observe what SNCC staff were doing during the meeting,
but some discussed informally the merits of the decision with individual
MFDP delegates. Some were reportedly adamant in urging rejection to
more moderate members of the delegation inclined to go along with
President Johnson.[31] But Willie Peacock has reported the SNCC staff's
restraint in not attempting to influence the delegates: "[I]t was [the delegates'] decision, based on all of what everybody had said. That was their
decision. And it's not that I wasn't in agreement with it, because to hell I
sure was. But I sure kept my mouth closed and didn't try to influence it.
That's the restraint that SNCC organizers did. That was the restraint."[32]

The MFDP delegates listened and rejected the advice of the traditional civil rights leaders. They wanted more than the token two seats,
which was a very small representation of Mississippi's sixty-eight delegates. To be heard, they said, it was necessary that the country talk to the
people and listen to them, not to a handpicked few "leaders" selected by
the opposition. The "at-large" designation did not give the MFDP representation for Mississippi. Despite the MFDP arguments, the convention had seated and recognized the regular Mississippi Democratic Party

delegation without condemnation of its racism and denial of the right to vote to a significant proportion of the state's population.

The provision for future reform in the offer was insufficient to change the MFDP vote. In truth, the national Democratic Party offered the MFDP nothing for the future in terms of permanent recognition, program, official status, or guarantee of participation in the 1968 convention. For the next convention, in 1968, the right to challenge state delegations that discriminated applied only to exclusion of black *registered* voters. Black voters might be able to attend a party meeting, which would be an "open" state party, but there was no guarantee that they could participate in decision making. The committee set up to review matters for 1968 had no official status or power. Furthermore, as Edith Green noted, "no anti-discrimination resolution passed by this convention could be binding on the 1968 convention."[33]

The convention decision was an effort by the White House, led by President Johnson, to prevent a floor vote and avoid controversy over the issue of racism. The MFDP had gone to Atlantic City demanding full rights for themselves and others but would have accepted any honorable compromise between reasonable people. The MFDP tested the Democratic Party to accept the Challenge it presented, a test the convention failed. The MFDP did not have to accept political realities. Furthermore, in any fair and open negotiations they should have been consulted and given time to deliberate their choices. The decision instead came from back-room secret negotiations among the power brokers. The MFDP called it dictation. Mondale, however, denied later that "machine politics" was involved. He said a "collection of very gifted and thoughtful and decent Americans" was "genuinely trying to wrestle with a tough problem in a way that would help civil rights and help the Democrats."[34]

The speakers' dramatic words on a momentous, historic occasion fascinated me. I waited and waited to hear from Bob Moses, who I thought would present the case so clearly and say to the assembled MFDP delegates what I was thinking. He had worked so hard for recognition of the MFDP, and I knew he would be the most effective speaker of all of those heavyweights, but basically he remained silent. He was infuriated by what had happened, but he was not going to tell the MFDP delegates what to do. In meeting with Humphrey, he had refused to accept any proposal "without the delegation discussing it and deciding whether it was something that it could accept."[35] Moses respected the ability of everyone, rich or poor, educated or not, to know his or her own interests. Now he was leaving the question for the MFDP delegates to decide. That was his philosophy; that was his nature.

Although I was there and have been confident that Bob never spoke, my research indicates otherwise and has told me what he said. One recorder of the events said that he "quietly and simply explained [to the assembled delegates] why the compromise was bad."[36] Another reported that he said, "The Freedom Party must determine its views on the basis of Mississippi and its own hopes and desires, not on the basis of trying to please the liberal civil rights establishment nationally in the United States; . . . it must remember its constituents."[37] Forman wrote that although Moses did not want to, he was expected to speak on Wednesday and did. He reported that Moses said "we had to bring morality into politics. That's what was wrong with the country now. There is no morality in politics; otherwise we would not be here."[38] One historian concludes, "When he finally spoke he only announced his resolution 'to remain out of the controversy' because the decision was the delegation's to make."[39] Moses did not express his view that the MFDP must continue to reject the two seats.

Late in the afternoon, the MFDP delegation met privately in a separate room for a final vote on whether to accept or reject the decision. Henry, chairing the meeting, excluded everyone else: the prominent leaders of the civil rights movement who had just spoken, SNCC staff, outside supporters such as myself, observers who had gained entry, and an FBI undercover agent who had "successfully penetrated . . . the . . . strategy meetings."[40] The press was not present but had been left outside for all the discussions. We waited, not knowing what was happening in the smaller room where they had assembled. Finally, someone came out and announced another resounding rejection of the decision. That was just what I wanted to hear.

Several MFDP delegates have spoken about what happened in the final closed meeting. Mrs. Hamer strongly opposed reconsidering and accepting the decision: "They only gave us two votes at large 'cause they knowed we wouldn't have had nothing"; after which she said, "We just didn't come here for just that." She had asked Bob Moses, Jim Forman, and Ella Baker if the delegates should accept the decision and was told the same thing by all of them. You're "the people living in Mississippi, and you people know what you've experienced in Mississippi . . . you make your own decision."[41] She had some doubts, but with support from the leaders she respected and other strong women in the delegation, she spoke up and held out for rejecting.

Henry Sias, a quiet, strong eighty-three-year-old farmer, "a great man" who was also a teacher, didn't understand not being able to register to vote.[42] He was from Issaquena County, just south of Greenville. He said he was squelched by Annie Devine and Fannie Lou Hamer after he spoke to recommend acceptance. He explained how they shamed him into changing his vote: "When they got through talking and whoopin' and hollerin' and telling me what a shame it was for me to do that I hushed right then . . . I changed my mind right there . . . Those two women opened my eyes."[43] SNCC had been empowering blacks in Mississippi since 1961, and COFO volunteers had spread themselves throughout the state during the Summer Project with the same purpose: to give confidence to the delegation that they could make their own decisions about what was in *their* interest. Blacks had been saying yes to the white man, accepting what was handed them when their leaders told them it was the right thing to do. This time the MFDP delegates stood up and in their own voice said, "No."

The MFDP's third and final vote "certainly was not unanimous" but was quickly labeled "unanimous."[44] The MFDP delegates, in secret, "overwhelmingly rejected" the decision of the convention.[45] Aaron Henry said the vote remained the same, with "seventy percent opposed," but Waskow's contemporaneous account recorded the understanding that "there was a 60–4 vote against reconsidering the rejection."[46] After the all-day session ended, Aaron Henry, with Fannie Lou Hamer and Ed King by his side, announced the results to the press. Mrs. Hamer told Henry he could not go out and tell the press that the MFDP reconsidered and accepted "the compromise"; he could not water down the MFDP statements or "try to get in good with the Party liberals" because "she would attack him" if he did.[47] As she said, "We almost fought there at one time. Because I told Dr. Henry [that] if he didn't tell them better that we wasn't going to accept no compromise, I, you know, would do something to him." She stood between him and Ed King, looking larger than Henry and holding her cane. "If Henry had said compromise, the country would have thought today that we had compromised. But that's one time they weren't going to hear that word, not out of Henry. I've never carried no weapon, but I would have hit him so hard, he wouldn't know what had happened."[48] He had no choice: he announced a unanimous decision, despite his reservations. The delegation acted with extraordinary self-discipline, not indicating that a few wanted to accept the decision. Delegate Charles McLaurin, a SNCC organizer from the Delta, explained it to me: "No one would vote against Mrs. Hamer."[49] Before leaving for Mississippi, to the credit of all these individual delegates and their grassroots leadership, "people didn't break ranks."[50]

The MFDP delegates held to their conviction that they should have received the right to participate in the convention proceedings, select their delegates, and represent Mississippi after fair and open negotiations. The civil rights leaders and politicians did not persuade them to the contrary. After the convention, the MFDP sent a four-page report on the Convention Challenge to friends of the MFDP in response to "concern and confusion" regarding the rejection of the decision.[51] This delegation was more than just an alternative black political party. As an integrated party that grew out of the civil rights movement, the MFDP asked for participation on a fair and equal basis and an end to racism in the Democratic Party and in Mississippi. The MFDP delegates were not comparable to other political party delegates. For a black to participate in political activity made him "automatically a rebel against the segregated society." The black delegates went to Atlantic City "in immediate and grave danger" of losing jobs, homes, even lives. In its report, the MFDP stated: "Many of those who represented the FDP at Atlantic City have suffered the most brutal and continual reprisals ever since they began working for their political rights. This lends a peculiar and unique air to their efforts to attend the convention, and means that they were *literally gambling their lives* against the right of being seated in Atlantic City."[52]

The MFDP understood that its loss resulted from "massive pressure from the White House, through the mediation of Hubert Humphrey." Popular support for the MFDP seating had appeared present, and many supporters, if not most, believed that a roll call on the floor would have resulted in a victory. The MFDP called the decision the kind of "dictation" that blacks had always faced in Mississippi. Now these courageous delegates were learning to stand up against what white supremacists had always been deciding for them.

The report on the Convention Challenge provided specific, well-stated reasons for the rejection. (1) The MFDP wanted to stop accepting "token recognition"—the two, not sixty-eight, seats, which were acclaimed for their "symbolic value." For the people to be heard, the MFDP needed to "make the country talk with and listen to them," not to a few handpicked representatives. (2) The MFDP went to Atlantic City to unseat the regular Mississippi Democratic Party, but that party was nevertheless "fully seated and recognized," even though it did not represent the people of Mississippi. (3) According to the party's promise, states would not be permitted to interfere with black participation in the Democratic Party if states wanted their delegations to be seated at the 1968 convention, but this reform provision had little significance in Mississippi. Only registered voters would participate in state party politics, and only about 6 percent of blacks in Mississippi were registered. (4) The MFDP went to Atlantic City to represent the blacks in Mississippi, as other delegations represented people in their states. It was "unreasonable" to give two at-large seats to the MFDP and ask that it represent all the blacks in the country. (5) The final offer was "a completely one-shot affair." The MFDP received "nothing in the way of permanent recognition, patronage, official status, or a guarantee of participation in the 1968 convention." (6) A committee intended to review open participation for the 1968 convention had "no official status of power." (7) The MFDP went to Atlantic City "to raise the issue of racism, not simply to demand recognition," and would not accept a decision designed to prevent a floor fight and avoid the issue of racism.

According to the report, the MFDP "would have accepted any honorable compromise between reasonable men." The delegates wanted equal participation. They would have accepted a proposal on a fifty–fifty basis, but the White House did not allow for discussion and negotiation of what the MFDP considered a fair solution.

The MFDP discussed why it rejected the committee's decision in its

Primer No. 1, *The Convention Challenge and the Freedom Vote,* the first in a series of educational and organizational booklets for MFDP activists and students in the freedom schools. The booklet summarized in simpler terms: "The offer was not good enough. . . . The Freedom Democratic Party said it was tired of tokens. It wanted 68 votes, not two votes. It wanted to vote for Mississippi. And it wanted to choose its own leaders."[53]

The MFDP delegates refused to accept the decision that had been handed them, but they did not reject the Democratic Party. When the convention was over, Ed King, the MFDP's national committeeman, along with Victoria Gray, national committeewoman, as the elected MFDP representatives, requested membership on the Democratic National Committee. They saw Harold Leventhal shortly before a committee meeting on Friday, August 28, 1964, and asked, "trying to be helpful, not obstructive," that they be allowed to address the committee or, if not, that a letter they presented be read to the committee. Leventhal said no, "there wasn't time." The committee met and called the roll with no answer received from Mississippi. Leventhal advised the committee of the MFDP offer to cooperate and assurance of its intention to support the ticket. He again said no after the meeting when the MFDP repeated its request for representation. But he did appreciate an MFDP offer to aid registration drives and travel to campaign for the ticket. The MFDP offer raised a question of "a single channel within the Committee for dealing with the Freedom people," which Leventhal called "a ticklish assignment."[54] William Higgs, a white Mississippi attorney for the MFDP who had left the state after a February 1963 conviction on a so-called morals charge, was living in Washington and would be "bad news" in such a role, according to Leventhal. Leventhal stated his preference that Aaron Henry be "the *sole* contact with the Freedom Party."[55]

When the White House learned of the MFDP's final rejection of the convention decision, President Johnson decided to travel to Atlantic City on Wednesday, a day earlier than scheduled, to announce his selection of Senator Humphrey for vice president and thus take attention away from the Mississippi story, which was dominating the news.[56] Lyndon Johnson found the whole affair unpleasant. He was a liberal supporter of civil rights but wanted to support the movement on his terms.

18

Victory or Defeat

I will revisit one of the pivotal events in the civil rights struggle—
the saga of the Mississippi Freedom Democratic Party. In 1964, this
group of courageous people fought to open up the political process in
Mississippi to black citizens. They took their cause to the Democratic
National Convention in Atlantic City, where they forced the party to
confront the ugly segregation in its midst. What happened there permanently and profoundly changed both the Democratic Party and
American politics.
—Walter F. Mondale, February 11, 2000[1]

The MFDP Convention Challenge ended in victory or defeat depending
on how you view the story and when you pass judgment on what happened. The name "Atlantic City" now has historic significance in the civil
rights movement because it represents the events of five days in August
1964 that changed the course of the movement and the Democratic Party.
For civil rights veterans like me, it has been much more than a resort town
featured for gambling on the New Jersey shore, providing names in the
board game *Monopoly,* and hosting the Miss America pageant.

My view of what happened in Atlantic City had been based on the
information I had in 1964. The MFDP delegates, SNCC and CORE
organizers, national civil rights leaders, COFO volunteers, politicians,
reporters, commentators, observers, and historians held their own views
and developed their opinions as to whether the Challenge was a victory
or a defeat for the new political party. My view and perhaps the views
of others were slanted. Looking back at the MFDP's legacy from the
events that followed the convention's decision and learning from pri-
mary-source research that tales of the Challenge have been confused, I
have moved away from the views I held in 1964 and reached new conclu-

sions. In 1964, my only thought was that Atlantic City represented a devastating defeat. Because it had a major impact on the course of my life, I have wanted to examine it further.

But this story is about *them*. The MFDP delegates made the Challenge possible. They decided to claim their constitutional rights and, despite violence, intimidation, and harassment, formed a new political party. They risked their lives to register to vote in Mississippi and travel beyond the borders of Mississippi to ask for political participation on an equal basis in the Democratic Party. How did they react to the symbolic two seats the Democratic National Convention handed them?

The MFDP delegates returned to Mississippi defeated, but with "defiance and a certain pride."[2] On August 29, several hundred people attended a rally in Jackson and heard how close the MFDP had been to getting a floor vote. Aaron Henry was not present, and he was to resign from the MFDP as required by the NAACP soon after, but he offered a statement. He asserted that the MFDP came within one vote in the Democratic Party's Credentials Committee. But Lyndon Johnson had controlled the vote for "purely political" reasons. Nevertheless, the MFDP "victory on moral and legal grounds was overwhelming."[3] Regardless of what had happened in Atlantic City, the MFDP campaigned for the Johnson–Humphrey ticket pursuant to its promised loyalty to the Democratic Party, knowing the importance of a Democratic victory in November.

Back home in Ruleville, Fannie Lou Hamer gave "a high-powered, oft-times bellowing account" of "how disillusioned she was to find hypocrisy all over America." She said that "King, Roy Wilkins, Bayard Rustin, James Farmer, and Aaron Henry had been willing to sell out the FDP by their willingness to accept" the final symbolic offer. She insisted that the MFDP would have been prepared to split the votes with the regular Democrats, but that "two votes at large was no deal."[4] Linda Davis, a volunteer who went to Ruleville after her sophomore year at Oberlin, remained on site until August 1965. She remembers Mrs. Hamer was "still steaming" when she arrived home.[5] Nevertheless, Mrs. Hamer campaigned for the Johnson–Humphrey ticket in the fall, as she also campaigned for her own candidacy for Congress from the Second District.

Unita Blackwell, an MFDP delegate from Issaquena County, did not feel defeated. The MFDP had unseated most of the regulars, drawn national attention to the MFDP and problems within the Democratic Party, and learned about "politics—practical politics—and how political parties operate."[6] She had seen "a moral situation that had to be righted" and "not just a political something to get away with . . . and negotiate." She recognized that an important goal of the Challenge was to provide black residents with a political education in the workings of the Democratic Party on both the local and national levels. The MFDP created new leaders, and she was one who could now share the benefit of the education received in Atlantic City. The MFDP could "teach the lowest sharecropper that he knows better than the biggest leader what is required to make a decent life for himself."[7] The convention had served as a classroom—or, as Bob Moses put it, a "theater for empowerment."[8]

The Reverend Clifton R. Whitley II, an MFDP delegate from Rust College, considered the MFDP rejection of the convention decision "a tremendous accomplishment."[9] Tokenism from white society would no longer work as blacks were beginning to define their own goals. He told Joanne Grant, reporting for the *National Guardian*, "By accepting them [the two votes] we would have sanctioned America's notion that men of any degree of integrity can be manipulated or bought."[10] "Had we accepted the compromise then," he said, "our action would have reinforced the white man's notion that he can deal with the Negro successfully in a half-hearted sort of manner and that he could reduce the tensions that the conditions under which the Negro lives and the possible life that he is federally constituted created by tokenism."[11] For delegate Robert Miles, the Panola County farmer whose home was shot at and bombed more than once for his activism, the final offer was not enough:

> We were not allowed our seats in the convention; we were told that we could compromise with two seats . . . they would point out clearly who was going to cast our ballots for us. That was Rev. Ed King, Aaron Henry. . . . We thought we had sense enough to choose who we wanted to cast the ballots for us, or cast the vote, or whatever it was. Then we rejected . . . the two seats because this was what we'd been used to all our lives. Just a little measly bite. . . . Now why would we go way to Atlantic City and get the same thing that we had at home? That wasn't what we wanted.[12]

Thus, the offer didn't matter to some delegates. Charles Graves, elected delegate from Tibbee in Clay County, said, "I'm glad we didn't accept the two seats, because it wouldn't have met [*sic*] nothing to us. Those two seats wouldn't have meant any more to us than what we had already, and we didn't have nothing to start with."[13]

Peggy Jean Connor, a delegate from Hattiesburg, returned home "disappointed, but that didn't stop us," she said. She campaigned not only in Mississippi, but also went to New York. She continued to be active as an officer in the MFDP: "We were determined to show the Nation that the Mississippi Freedom Democratic Party was not a one-shot organization that would fade away."[14] The Challenge was certainly not a total loss for the MFDP.

MFDP chairman Lawrence Guyot even considered it a success: "Despite the Convention's decision, Atlantic City was for us a great victory, because for the first time it told our story to the country and demonstrated our growing strength."[15] Guyot told me, "In Mississippi, the hardest, the most recalcitrant, the most committed to terror, the most socially acceptable uses of terror in America, we were able to fight every political institution that existed—on our terms. We were able to fight to such an extent that we forced Lyndon Johnson to stop us. Lyndon Johnson spent time and energy and effort to stop the Freedom Democratic Party."[16]

Others believed that they *had* gotten something. They had forced the president and the nation to take notice, and most of the official white delegates for Mississippi hadn't taken the seats they were awarded. Delegate Charles McLaurin went back to his SNCC work in Sunflower County thinking victory because "they had to get something."[17] As Margaret Block, a Mississippi native and early SNCC field secretary in Tallahatchie County, who was unable to go to the convention, told me, "I think we came out pretty good."[18] At age eighteen, she was handing out voting rights pamphlets in Charleston, where people would "close the door [before she came]. They were really afraid." Threatened by a Klansman with a knife "right in front of the courthouse," she was protected by a Justice Department agent, and, on another occasion, she was sped out of the county in the back of a hearse after receiving a death threat.[19]

I like to imagine the reaction of the MFDP constituents at home in rural Mississippi who watched the Credentials Committee hearing on Saturday and saw one of their own, Mrs. Hamer. Surely they were proud in the end that their people rejected the token handout and stood *opposed* to the government that had not treated them fairly. The black Mississippians were "energized and encouraged, even by the defeat in Atlantic City, just the sense that there was some power to it."[20]

However, the empowered MFDP back in Mississippi did not find acceptance among the urban, well-educated, middle-class blacks in Mississippi. The traditional black leaders refused to work with the MFDP as a "class barrier" developed. They seemed to have been replaced, and there was "bitter resentment" toward the lower-class, rural, poor blacks.[21]

Journalists saw the outcome as a remarkable victory for the MFDP. A *New York Times* editorial said that the MFDP "made a serious mistake in rejecting the compromise" and that the "subsequent seizure" of the empty Mississippi seats "accomplished nothing. On the contrary, it dimmed the clear moral and symbolic triumphs they had already achieved and provided new fuel for those who argue there is no 'satisfying' the Negro militants."[22] Murray Kempton said in the *New Republic* that the MFDP delegates "had forced themselves farther than anyone could have imagined upon the conscience of a political party. But . . . [t]o them their victory was a defeat, and the sophisticates among them were . . . [too tired] to know what they had won."[23] Anthony Lewis, writing in the *New York Times*, called the outcome "a remarkable victory for the Freedom group" and regretted that the "emotions of the civil rights movement" were not channeled "into the ordinary political process."[24] Lucille Komisar, a former editor of the *Mississippi Free Press*, said that when the MFDP delegates "continued to refuse the 'at large' seats, most observers asked incredulously, 'But don't they know they've won?'"[25]

The SNCC organizers who accompanied the MFDP delegates to Atlantic City and lobbied on their behalf returned to Mississippi with an attitude distinctly different from the local residents. They left Atlantic City angry, bitter, and distrusting.[26] Courtland Cox commented that they were also "exhausted."[27] Joyce Ladner has said that she left Atlantic City "terribly, terribly disappointed and in pain" when the MFDP actually lost after all that work.[28] When I met her in Washington, D.C., in 2001, I told her I thought the vote represented a loss of faith in our government. She said it was "a loss of innocence."[29] SNCC could no longer trust liberal whites.

SNCC had been working for reform, expecting support from outsiders once the facts of Mississippi were brought to national attention; then, they thought, the federal government would have public support to be able to act to make necessary changes. Without sufficient press coverage, few knew the extent of the oppression and brutality that blacks were suffering in Mississippi. Before my month at Tougaloo in 1963, I had heard about segregation and discrimination against blacks in the South but did not fully appreciate what was going on there. It would take more than passive knowledge to activate concern even among well-meaning, middle-class, white northerners. As Guyot and Thelwell wrote in 1966, SNCC held "a confidence in the ultimate morality in national political institutions and practices."[30] When grievances were exposed, an appeal to the nation's conscience would rectify the centuries of wrongs.

But this strategy to bring change to Mississippi on behalf of disenfranchised blacks failed. The MFDP encountered the Democratic establishment, which refused to share power in Atlantic City with poor, less formally educated, rural black citizens. The Democratic Party leaders did not know these oppressed blacks from Mississippi, many of whom had been marginalized and isolated from mainstream America and were not ready to welcome these strangers into their midst. Fannie Lou Hamer had a style that was foreign to the middle-class, white, suburban politicians used to dealing with each other in their back rooms and to speaking the same way. They did not understand these independent people and did not have the means to control them in the traditional give and take of politics, in which the MFDP delegates were not schooled. The Democrats in Atlantic City alienated the dedicated young activists and demoralized the Mississippi civil rights movement. The student organizers called the decision "an insult."[31] And so Cleveland Sellers wrote the SNCC response in his autobiography, *The River of No Return*: "After Atlantic City, our struggle was not for civil rights, but for liberation."[32] According to Charles Sherrod, the white majority that controlled the decision-making process did not trust blacks with "a share in power." As he wrote, "We want more than 'token' position or even representation. We want power for our people."[33]

SNCC staff, the volunteers, and the grassroots delegates would have been more equipped for events in Atlantic City if someone had been able to provide them with more preparation for entry into national politics. During the summer, there had been no "development program" to provide "a kind of political education for the staff itself about the internecine political strategies of the party structure," as Bob Moses has put it. In addition to the hands-on introduction to local politics and the analysis of Mississippi and of how it got where it was, what the MFDP meant for the Democratic Party structure and the state and "what we were up against," according to Moses, would have made a difference for many going to Atlantic City.[34]

Not only did SNCC feel defeated, but its former allies dropped their support, and the civil rights coalition that had supported COFO, the Mississippi Summer Project, and the MFDP splintered. On September 18, only three weeks after the Atlantic City convention, the NCC called a meeting of national civil rights leaders and their white liberal allies in "the God box" in New York City.[35] The stated purpose of the gathering was to "discuss ways of cooperating in Mississippi in the future."[36] The whites, who were in the majority at the meeting, included Joe Rauh and Al Lowenstein, the meeting hosts Bob Spike, Jack Pratt, and three others from the NCC. Other attendees represented the NAACP, the NAACP Legal Defense Fund, the SCLC, and CORE. The NCC invited SNCC to the meeting, held at a time when Bob Moses and Jim Forman were in Africa on a journey sponsored by Harry Belafonte designed to repair and rebuild the wounded warriors. SNCC staffers Courtland Cox and Mendy Samstein went to "sit there" and "know what was going to be said" at what they anticipated would be a "hostile meeting."[37] They took notes as they heard the criticism of SNCC operations in Mississippi: confusion about how decisions are made in COFO; Bob Moses "dictates and we must take it or leave it"; Bob Moses and SNCC want "a single-line approach" when they must have "understanding of strategic complexity."[38] Pratt accused SNCC of "railroading" the MFDP delegates into rejecting the final outcome of the Convention Challenge, but Cox said it was the delegation that had made the decision.[39] In discussion of the Credentials Committee decision, Moses and Forman had spoken to present the SNCC position to the MFDP only after Rustin, King, and others had advocated accepting the decision.

Mississippi was "no longer a local problem," and the national organizations wanted to structure a new decision-making body that would "make Mississippi susceptible to national influence" and to which COFO would submit. Lowenstein proposed "a new central body that will be regulated and democratized and broadened in its base . . . [with responsibility] for handling money and making other decisions." Lowenstein wanted "structured democracy," not "amorphous democracy."[40] Lowenstein knew SNCC operations well from his initial foray into Mississippi in mid-1963 and his work on the Freedom Vote, when he saw the possibilities of change in the Democratic Party, but SNCC had cast him aside over fundamental philosophical differences before the summer began. Gloster Current, director of branches and field administration for the NAACP, considered the MFDP "a delusion" that caused "confusion among local people," the underclass that he called "the underbrush." When freedom democrat groups formed, they were associated with "suspicious characters."[41] Cox and Samstein saw "a campaign to undermine or neutralize SNCC by the liberal–labor Establishment and its brokers."[42] The meeting in the God box ended with talk of SNCC leadership being asked to attend another meeting of the group, but that meeting never took place. Thus, one of the outcomes of the Challenge was what Roy Wilkins called "a lasting sense of grievance [that] did terrible damage to relations between white liberals and black organizers in the South."[43]

For Stokely Carmichael, "the major moral" of Atlantic City was that "black people in Mississippi and throughout this country could not rely on their so-called allies. Many labor, liberal, and civil rights leaders deserted the MFDP because of closer ties to the national Democratic Party." And so, for Stokely, "Black people would have to organize and obtain their own power base before they could begin to think of coalition with others. To rely on the absolute assistance of external, liberal, labor forces was not a wise procedure."[44]

The MFDP Convention Challenge is historically significant for its impact on the civil rights movement. Writing in 1998, Congressman John Lewis stated in his memoir *Walking with the Wind:* "[T]his was the turning point of the civil rights movement. . . . That crisis of confidence, the spirit of cynicism and suspicion and mistrust that infects the attitude of many Americans toward their government today, began, I firmly believe, that week in Atlantic City."[45] Moses concluded that Atlantic City was a "watershed in the Movement because up until then the idea had been that you were working more or less with the support of the Democratic party, or certain forces within the Democratic party."[46]

Atlantic City was one among many factors affecting SNCC in the early fall of 1964: confusion over its program, the absorption of more than one hundred white volunteers who stayed in Mississippi after the summer, organizational and personnel issues that became highlighted at the Waveland retreat in November, and the decision to send Stokely and others to organize a new political party in Lowndes County, Alabama. SNCC lost confidence in northern labor–liberal support and shifted away from nonviolence, the Beloved Community, the goal of racial integration, interracial cooperation, and expectations of the federal government and began "moving in a nationalist direction [after] the 1964 convention."[47] On June 16, 1966, the cries of "Black Power! Black Power!" that went up in Stokely's chant with Willie Ricks on the Meredith March in Greenwood symbolized this change. Press coverage of racial injustice in Mississippi gradually shifted to white fear of violence, black nationalism, black racism, black supremacy, and conflicts among Martin Luther King Jr. and other leaders of the previously united civil rights movement. The fact that Stokely's "nationalism never precluded effective working relations with whites" escaped recognition.[48] In a May 1967 meeting, SNCC expelled whites from the organization. In 1968, it adopted a new name, the Student National Coordinating Committee, replacing "Nonviolent" with "National."

Bob Moses found the whole Convention Challenge experience unsettling. Giving two symbolic seats represented "the wrong way of thinking" when the MFDP was asking for equal treatment.[49] The admission of only two delegates was similar to society's attitude toward school integration: a few select individuals could join, but not the majority of school children equally entitled to a quality education free of segregation. The MFDP wanted its share of political power, not tokenism. As Moses told me, the Democratic Party had "no energy" to do more than "limited assimilation, just a few at a time."[50] The rejection of the MFDP meant that the Democratic Party had time to "set up a group of people in Mississippi who were more to their liking . . . a coalition . . . to whom political power could be passed on."[51] He believed that as a result the Democratic Party lost a program for the entry of poor blacks into the party, and soon the cities erupted in rebellions and riots. Moses was surprised at how weak the support was for the MFDP. "You turned around and your support was puddle-deep. It wasn't any real support."[52] Even the far Left backed away out of fear of the Goldwater threat and of the possibility that the demonstrations would set off a reaction that would prevent Johnson's election. In his book *Radical Equations,* Moses defends the MFDP as the proper delegation to represent Mississippi:

> [T]he MFDP has been . . . accused of ignorance, and if you think knowledge is book knowledge, they were. They hadn't been through the schools; they hadn't been processed in the ways in which most of the delegates to the convention were processed. Their knowledge was about life, not books, especially about life in Mississippi. And they understood the relationship of the politics they were trying to challenge to the life they wanted to lead. They were as cognizant of *that* as anyone needed to be. They were relying on this knowledge, plus the ability to speak directly to the truth, to qualify them for admission as the proper delegation.[53]

A few months after the 1964 convention, Moses also defended the legality of the MFDP Convention Challenge. The Democrats said that "legally" the MFDP could not be seated because it didn't abide by the laws of Mississippi, but those laws were illegal; they "[didn't] abide by the laws of the U.S."[54] For Moses, it was a question of power: the Democratic Party leadership had it and didn't want the MFDP to have it.

Ella Baker was less disappointed and did not consider the Challenge to have ended in defeat.[55] The experience had mobilized a solid core of Mississippi activists and provided political lessons for organizers. They now understood the possibility of functioning through the national Democratic Party.

I believed that the MFDP had suffered an enormous defeat in Atlantic City, which I felt personally. I left disillusioned that the Democratic Party had not lived up to its ideals. Pat said she was "vastly disappointed" and "really angry about it" but also proud of the MFDP delegates, who had "done so much, put their lives on the line, their jobs, their families, and . . . made a statement . . . [they] let everybody know that they were there, they had a voice and they intended to be heard."[56] In contrast, Stephen Bingham, a Yale student who volunteered for ten days to help with the Freedom Vote in the fall of 1963 and was a voter registration volunteer in Holmes County in 1964, did not agree with the MFDP decision. The outcome seemed to him "such an extraordinary victory in so many, many ways, that whatever might have been lost by accepting compromise as a solution would have been gained by the immeasurable increase in the status nationally, not only of the 'radical,' direct-action oriented southern civil rights movement, but of the national civil rights movement."[57]

Another white volunteer who was in Holly Springs for the summer, Chude Pam Parker Allen from Pennsylvania, went to Atlantic City and considered the MFDP Challenge a failure of the system. For her, "it was the end of . . . any integrity or credibility that the political system had." Calling herself "a little idealist," she "saw the system as bankrupt."[58] I had never thought of myself as "a little idealist," but my view from my studies included an expectation that the Democratic Party would accept the poor and the unemployed. The Democratic Party had sponsored welfare legislation during the Depression and had just led passage of the Civil Rights Act of 1964 in Congress. But in August that same year it sidestepped the rules when society's blacks—poor, powerless, and excluded—were about to win political voice through a democratic vote. That is, they might have won such a voice if they had been allowed the support for a minority report to get to a roll-call vote. But the ruling national Democrats, led by the formidable Lyndon Johnson, wouldn't let the vote get to the floor. During the summer of 1964, Mrs. Hardin and Mrs. Britton, black women in Greenville, had befriended and cared for me, and I had been working with men and women just like the MFDP delegates in organizing the MFDP to go to Atlantic City. I wanted them to be recognized and rewarded. Instead they were rejected.

"What should I do now?" I wondered. "Keep trying? Support Democratic politicians? Drop out?" I didn't have to decide those questions because, although I had been ambivalent, I was going to law school. I felt troubled before leaving for school but occupied myself in seeing friends and getting ready to drive cross-country with what I would need for the school year. In early September, I accepted an invitation to speak about the Mississippi Summer Project at the Central Presbyterian Church, one of the largest and most prominent churches in my hometown, Summit, New Jersey. It was not my church, and I did not know the minister, but he had sent me a donation early in the summer and wanted his congregation to learn more about our work and support it. We requested that any donations be sent to Greenville for the Herbert Lee Memorial Freedom Center project. Six hundred people attended and contributed nearly $2,500 for the center. Nathan H. Schwerner, father of Michael Schwerner, one of the freedom workers killed, talked about "what motivated his son to go to Mississippi and what others can do to help in the cause of racial equality."[59] My fellow Summit volunteer Charles ("Chips") Sowerwine, who was in Drew, Mississippi, for the summer, and I spoke on different subjects. I was a better public speaker after the summer, more sure of myself and less nervous. I talked about canvassing for Freedom Registrations, community organizing in Greenville, and the purpose of the MFDP Convention Challenge. What I understood of Lyndon Johnson's not wanting a divisive roll-call vote was limited, but no one challenged me or asked me any questions.

In general, I had difficulty talking about what had happened in Atlantic City. Anger welled up in me as I started from the beginning to describe the hostility and random violence against blacks seeking the vote in Mississippi, to explain the MFDP goals and why this party was needed as an alternative organization set up to parallel the segregationist Mississippi Democratic Party, and to recall the national Democratic Party's treatment of black Mississippians. Not liking to argue and frustrated that my family and friends, northern liberals, just did not understand, I clammed up, preferring to say nothing. That was better than stumbling over my words as they tumbled out, garbling my arguments, raising my voice, interrupting, hearing my voice wavering with emotion, repeating myself, and giving up, exasperated when I was unable to state my message clearly and gain understanding and acceptance of my point of view. So I stopped trying to describe the events I had witnessed in Atlantic City and how I felt. At the end of the Mississippi Summer Project, those events represented the goal I had worked so hard for, and I was dismayed by defeat.

My hopes for more civil rights legislation that would change the situation of blacks in Mississippi were dimmed. I couldn't talk to others, and I could not explain to myself what had really happened. I felt bad and just stopped thinking about Atlantic City.

So I withdrew from the experience. Asked about the Mississippi Summer Project, which became an infrequent question as time passed, I just summarized what I did as a voter registration volunteer and sometimes mentioned organizing for the MFDP's Challenge at the Democratic National Convention in Atlantic City. Meeting blank looks, I would explain that 1964 was "Freedom Summer," the summer that three civil rights workers were killed. The conversations ended quickly. For more than forty years, I did not volunteer to new friends or acquaintances the information that I had been a civil rights worker in Mississippi that fateful 1964 summer. But I didn't forget. I bought numerous books about the Mississippi civil rights movement, read them as time allowed, and was never satisfied that I understood why the MFDP Convention Challenge met defeat. I decided to write a book about the Challenge, and after I retired, I did.

As I remembered, read, and wrote, Theodore White surprised me with the following assessment in *The Making of the President 1964*: when "the compromise" was read on the convention floor on Tuesday evening, August 25, and accepted with "a single bang of the gavel," he said, "a *victory* had been achieved."[60] His book about the 1964 election was so important and interesting that I did not understand: How could *he* use the term *victory* to describe what had happened to the MFDP Convention Challenge?

With my blinders on back in 1964, I had missed all the descriptions of the decision in response to the Challenge as a victory. Newspapers and magazines carried the major story of the 1964 Democratic Convention's final decision—always called "the compromise"—that prevented a disruptive floor fight. The majority reform wing of the Democratic Party called it a success even though neither side accepted its terms. Governor Lawrence told the *New York Times* it was "a turning point" for the Democratic Party, which had been influenced by all-white southern delegations in the past.[61] Rauh considered it a significant gain and more than he had initially hoped for. I was not absorbing these accounts but instead read the press coverage as dismissive of the MFDP delegates: their refusal was "morally right, but politically naive."[62]

I can now understand Rauh's point of view. After the final decision was approved by the convention, Rauh said it was "a great, great, great victory" when he urged its acceptance by the MFDP.[63] Knowing that the MFDP was not satisfied, he said publicly, "Nobody ever gets all they want," but he mentioned privately his "inner torment over the settlement."[64] Rauh had wanted reform and realignment of the Democratic Party as a progressive party and a movement of the Dixiecrats to the conservative Republican Party in the South. His interest in the Challenge was more in political action on a national scale and less in the political education for the black disenfranchised in Mississippi and the opening of that closed society. Rauh thought the MFDP "squeezed" as much as it could out of the convention, and he had "hope" that guidelines were set for the future to open up the Democratic Party to blacks, women, and Hispanics.[65]

Bob Moses and Rauh had a "misunderstanding" about what the intention of the Challenge was in Atlantic City. Moses understood that Rauh's "intention was to gain whatever it was possible to gain, and [that Rauh had] made a decision that what was possible to gain were the two seats."[66] But this understanding was not based on any conversation between them after the confrontation at the Reuther–Humphrey meeting on Tuesday. Rauh wanted to clear up the misunderstanding and went to visit Moses in 1977. According to Thelwell, "He saw, conducted, and described himself as an 'honest broker.'"[67] Now he wanted to make clear to Moses, for whom he had a great deal of admiration, that he had not "sold out" the MFDP.[68] Rauh explained that Moses believed in "community organization as the role of blacks and not political action." He left the meeting feeling, "we are friends," "we understand each other," and no one did "anything that wasn't highly ethical and moral in the fight between Moses and me."[69] Moses told me that he believed that the Democratic leadership "kept him out of the loop." He also provided his "generous interpretation" that Rauh "was in over his head" despite his credentials with the national party reform wing, the D.C. party structure, and the UAW.[70]

Walter Mondale, who had the responsibility of arriving at a resolution through the subcommittee of the Credentials Committee, has said that there was no solution that would satisfy everybody, but he believed that "the result that . . . [they came up with] was a good one." What Mondale wanted was change in the party that would guarantee integrated delegations. As he said, "What really counted [was] the objective of an integrated Democratic party . . . both whites and blacks participated. . . . I wanted to set up a set of rules and an incentive for people from Mississippi and elsewhere, to go through that door of the political party, and build a political party, just not a quadrennial delegation that showed up with no significance to the public life of the state."[71] Mondale did ultimately think that the final proposal "failed" the Freedom Democrats on two "important" points: they went to the convention seeking recognition not just as Democrats, but as Democrats from the state of Mississippi with the right to choose their own representatives, and "[c]ertainly the Freedom Democrats were entitled to a decent interval to consider our proposal. I am not proud of how this was handled."[72]

History should now recognize the MFDP Convention Challenge for what it accomplished, and the delegates should be applauded for risking their lives to make Mississippi a better place. Energized and organized after the Convention Challenge, the MFDP launched the Congressional Challenge to the seating of the five Mississippians elected to the House of Representatives.[73] At the opening session, a House resolution barred the Mississippi congressmen from taking the oath of office, allowed the MFDP and its attorneys to conduct depositions in Mississippi, and kept the issue of voting rights before the Congress. When voting rights legislation passed, the MFDP would no longer be able to complain of discrimination in congressional elections.

The long-standing efforts to obtain voting rights in Mississippi proved successful in time with SNCC's campaigns beginning in 1961, the 1963 Freedom Vote, and the Mississippi Summer Project, in particular the latter's focus on organizing the new MFDP for two national political challenges. All of this work heightened awareness in the country of the treatment of blacks as second-class citizens and led to a moral imperative to enforce the right to vote granted by the Fifteenth Amendment to the Constitution. Thus, the MFDP should be credited for its role in the passage of the Voting Rights Act of 1965, which prohibited states from imposing voting qualifications to deny the right to vote on the basis of race or color and included effective federal enforcement mechanisms applicable to states with a history of discriminatory voting practices. By 1970, 67.7 percent of Mississippi's eligible black population were registered voters.[74] President Johnson deserves praise for proclaiming "we shall overcome" in his March 15, 1965, speech to Congress when he proposed the legislation.[75] He could have noted then the MFDP challenges that protested voter discrimination as contributing to public support for the legislation, but he never recognized the MFDP contributions to passage of the Voting Rights Act enacted on August 6, 1965. Instead, history accords Dr. King's efforts in Selma, Alabama, as the crisis that provided the momentum for the legislation. Johnson does not acknowledge the MFDP in his memoir *The Vantage Point: Perspectives of the Presidency 1963–1969.*[76] Doris Kearns Goodwin also does not mention the MFDP in her 1976 biography of Johnson but quotes Johnson remembering Atlantic City as a "place of happy, surging crowds and thundering cheers. To a man as troubled as I was by party and national divisions, this display of unity was welcome indeed. . . . As I stood there warmed by the waves of applause that rolled in on us, touched to the heart by the display of affection, I could only hope that this harmonious spirit would endure times of trouble and discouragement as well."[77]

Under the chairmanship of the "headstrong and combative" Guyot, the MFDP pursued its goals of becoming the Mississippi Democratic Party and increasing political consciousness among black Mississippians.[78] MFDP activities included candidate campaigns in the fall Freedom Election, organizing in counties that had active, committed, local leadership, and litigation to oppose dilution of the black vote. However, not long after the return of the MFDP from Atlantic City, professionals in charge of the national Democratic Party began the creation of a new party in Mississippi so that they would have the type of delegation they could support in 1968.[79] The Loyal Democrats, formed in June 1968 under the leadership of Hodding Carter III and Aaron Henry, included representatives from the MFDP, but the coalition was largely the Young Democrats, the NAACP led by Charles Evers, Prince Hall Masons, Mississippi

AFL-CIO, and Mississippi Teachers Association. At the new party's state convention, the moderate faction consisting of liberal whites and urban, educated, middle-class blacks was in control and, without participation by the MFDP, developed a slate of delegates for election to the national convention that included only ten members of the MFDP. The Loyal Democrats, half black and half white, unseated the all-white Mississippi Democratic Party at the Democratic National Convention in Chicago in 1968, but the victory did not indicate "the achievement of political power for poor, black Mississippians, the Freedom Democratic Party's core constituency."[80]

Nevertheless, the MFDP did help elect black officials in Mississippi. In 1964, when only 6 percent of the black voting-age population was registered to vote, there were six black elected officials in the state. By 1987, Mississippi had 803 black elected officials, more than any other state. Unita Blackwell, the MFDP delegate from Meyersville in Issaquena County, was the first elected black woman mayor in Mississippi, serving her town from 1977 to 1997. In 1967, Mississippi voters elected their first black state legislator since the 1890s, Robert G. Clark, a school teacher from Holmes County, where the MFDP has remained an organized political force and continues its meetings to date. In 1986, Mike Espy became the first black congressman elected from Mississippi since post–Civil War Reconstruction, and in 1993 Mississippi elected Bennie Thompson, a black civil rights activist and graduate of Tougaloo, to the House of Representatives. He served as the chairman of the House Committee on Homeland Security from 2007 to 2011.

Perhaps most important, the MFDP Convention Challenge in 1964 opened up the Democratic Party. In 1986, Mondale called it "the civil rights act for the Democratic party, an act that the Republicans have yet to adopt these many years later." He further described the historical significance of the Challenge: "From then on out at every convention, the people that were discriminated against, if they were, could make that a legal grounds of challenge. And in fact, if you look at national Democratic delegations from the South and elsewhere now—since that convention, they are now fully integrated delegations. So it was a very, very profound change in the Democratic party that took place in the rules adopted at the '64 convention, and I'm proud of it."[81] The Challenge not only ended discrimination against blacks in state delegations but also led to other reforms. At the Democratic Convention in Chicago in 1968, Democrats imposed new rules for state delegations' future eligibility. George McGovern chaired a commission that specified for the 1972 convention that delegations be more representative through primary contests that would elect a proportion of blacks and a proportion of women. This rule increased diversity at the national conventions and made the selection process more democratic than it had been in the past with behind-the-scenes deals.

The 2008 candidacy of Barack Obama can be traced through such gradual changes starting with the 1964 MFDP Convention Challenge. He could not have made his successful run for president without the support of a major political party. In an interview on Inauguration Day 2009, Bob Moses noted that "the crucial thing [about Obama's election] . . . was the 1964 challenge of the Mississippi Freedom Democratic Party to the National Democratic Convention, because that was where the stage was set that allowed this to happen, because . . . that action more than anything else . . . opened up the national party structure."[82] The promises made to the MFDP and kept "made the election of Obama possible."[83] Roger Wilkins, distinguished black civil rights activist, lawyer, journalist, and history professor, has said there is "no doubt" that Obama would not be president "but for the Mississippi freedom movement."[84]

Lyndon Johnson's legislative accomplishments after his election mark his reputation today as a president who knew the Congress and had the persuasive skills to implement a progressive agenda that included not only voting rights, but also Medicare, Medicaid, and the War on Poverty. What he did at the 1964 Democratic Convention, however, has been obscured because few historians have paid adequate attention to this chapter of civil rights history. Johnson is known for his political skills in influencing others to obtain desired results through the twisting of arms and his larger-than-life personality. His conduct with respect to the Convention Challenge can be seen as politics as usual, of which he was a master and better at than his competitors—or beyond the pale, as Mondale has suggested.

In Atlantic City, those of us who worked to make the Convention Challenge possible created an understanding needed to explain the sudden change of events on Tuesday afternoon. I have found more to the story of the defeat than what I believed at the time in Atlantic City. Looking back now, I see how divided the two sides to the dispute were, the difficulties of reaching agreement, and the remarkable decision for the future that the Democratic Party made. But the MFDP demands were reasonable; its delegates were willing to compromise, and they were entitled to be respected and heard in the attempt to reach a settlement. The Democratic Party was not prepared to accommodate them; it was too much to ask.

Lyndon Johnson achieved a landslide victory in the fall election, taking what was then the greatest popular majority in history, more than 61 percent. His margin in the Electoral College was 486–52. He lost only six states: Mississippi, Alabama, Louisiana, Georgia, South Carolina, and Goldwater's home state, Arizona. In Mississippi, 87 percent of the vote went to Goldwater.[85] The Freedom Election conducted for the disenfranchised Mississippi blacks who wanted to participate in politics favored the Johnson–Humphrey ticket with 63,839 votes and only 17 for Goldwater–Miller.[86] The lower participation, compared with the 1963 Freedom Vote, is attributable to intensified white resistance to black political participation.

The MFDP is due more credit than it has received. The bold, creative, and well-prepared plan to replace the all-white segregationist Mississippi Democratic Party delegation at the convention, the determined insistence on participating in Democratic Party politics on an equal basis, and the courageous refusal to acquiesce in symbolic tokenism led to major advances in political participation of the underrepresented. Brave men and women who were willing to risk their lives worked tirelessly to right centuries of wrongs.

I lived among them only a few months in the summer of 1964, receiving what they generously gave to summer volunteers like me. I pay tribute to those dedicated and determined people who struggled for freedom and justice and hold them up as examples for all of us, including the next generation of new leaders to follow. Any citizen can now participate, vote, and take a stand in pursuit of what is right. As the *National Guardian* put it in August 1964, "The surprise—perhaps the real victory—of the convention is that a combination of 20-year-olds and rural Mississippi

Negroes, who have been 'kept in their place' for so long by terrorism, could so clog the well-oiled parts of a powerful political machine and could force the country—nonviolently—using the politician's own weapons and techniques, to confront racism face to face."[87]

Epilogue

[The teachers are] the nurturers and encouragers of all the dreams, all the seeds deep in all the hearts where the future of a redeemed and rescued land now dwells.
——Vincent Harding, *Hope and History*[1]

I changed after my summer in Mississippi, and so did Greenville. SNCC and Mississippi also went through major transformations following Atlantic City. And, as Walter Mondale said, the courageous people in the Mississippi Freedom Democratic Party "permanently and profoundly changed both the Democratic Party and American politics."[2]

The Mississippi Summer Project in 1964 was a milestone among the many historic events in the civil rights movement. For a short period of time, young people, black and white, banded together in a shared commitment to better the lives of black residents throughout the state of Mississippi. With limited resources, we used our goodwill, our energy, and our wits in a common purpose aimed at freedom, justice, and hope for a better society and an improved democracy. New resources arrived in black communities, and the project established the right of integrated groups to work in Mississippi.[3] Our success was also marked by the evolution of new leadership in communities beginning to stand up for themselves, despite a lack of formal education, minimal financial resources, and long-felt fears of brutality and economic repercussions. The college-age volunteers—of different backgrounds, with all types of personalities, and from all walks of life—became future leaders of new movements for social change and professionals in careers dedicated to public service. Experiences in Mississippi radicalized many young college students and made them regard the government and the political establishment with skepticism.

The MFDP delegates who went to Atlantic City returned to Mississippi and, undaunted, continued their struggle for freedom and the right to vote. SNCC veterans Charles McLaurin, Leslie McLemore, Jimmie Travis, and Hollis Watkins went home to Mississippi and stayed. They remained committed to what they had learned in the civil rights movement as they made new contributions in the following years. Aaron Henry and Fannie Lou Hamer stayed in Mississippi and received acclaim for their leadership. Other MFDP delegates are still at home there or died there largely unsung, except in their local communities. Many, many more blacks in Mississippi who remain anonymous also risked their lives in the struggle for freedom. And a number of blacks in Mississippi whom no one has been able to count disappeared and are presumed to have been murdered.

After the 1962 bloody insurrection at Ole Miss, when the admission of James Meredith as the first black student required federal marshals, and after passage of the Civil Rights Act of 1964, which ended legal segregation, the events of the Summer Project were added reason for the white establishment in Mississippi to begin opening their closed society and accepting association with blacks on an equal basis. White Mississippians could be released from themselves, their history, their racism, and their past, if they so chose.

For me, the summer was a transforming learning experience—as I became more aware about racism in politics and gained from dealing with all people impartially. My attitude toward minorities changed. I had had no interaction with people of color in suburban New Jersey and knew very few blacks in college in the early 1960s. Our candidates for Freedom Registration were adults far older than I, a situation that taught me about communicating with older people and made me appreciate the wisdom of my elders. I gained a comfort factor with black people as a result of working and living with them in 1964.

Law school at Stanford did not turn me into a political conservative, nor did it turn me away from the heart of the civil rights effort. In April 1965, I wrote a friend that I had "changed—the militancy has worn off, but I don't want it to wear off completely or I become a stodgy middle class citizen and what's worse (IF) a lawyer."[4] I told her my plans to participate in the Law Students Civil Rights Research Council. I applied for an internship in Mississippi for the summer of 1965, wanting to see "the whole situation with a new perspective." I received an assignment to the

Lawyers Committee for Civil Rights under Law, which was opening a new office on Farish Street in Jackson, but that internship was not to be. I met with two Palo Alto lawyers on a late Friday afternoon for what I thought was conversation but was really an interview. They were going down to Jackson for a month, and I got upset with what I called their "naivete."[5] My comment at the time was that it "definitely takes patience to cross the generation and lack of experience line, but I'm all for working on it."[6] Before leaving Stanford, I received notice that the Lawyers Committee decided they needed one less law clerk and that I would be reassigned in Jackson. I learned later that the Palo Alto lawyers decided to eliminate me because I was "a Movement person" and they wanted to remain apart from the movement and because I was "childish and immature."[7] That judgment really didn't seem to fit me, but I did sound more militant on the issue of civil rights than they expected.

Going back to Mississippi in the summer of 1965 to my new assignment with the National Lawyers Guild got Mississippi out of my system for years. I worked with Claudia Shropshire, a Detroit attorney assigned by the Guild for a year to coordinate its project involving litigation pursuant to Title III of the Civil Rights Act of 1964 to open public facilities in twelve Mississippi counties. I had a good summer living in Tougaloo with Claudia and meeting the Guild volunteer lawyers who came down for a week, but somehow I lost my fury and diligence that summer. I knew none of my fellow volunteers who were still in Mississippi after the summer of 1964, and, lacking sufficient initiative, I made no effort to find and visit with any local black leaders during the week I spent in Greenville.

I did look up Mrs. Britton, the woman I had stayed with at the end of the summer in 1964, visiting her at the drugstore at Nelson and North Streets. In a 1977 oral history interview, she said every one of us wrote to her when her husband died suddenly that fall. She mentioned me specifically, remembering my name as "Liza," because I had come back to Greenville after studying law and visited her in the store. She said I was "well-dressed and everything," which I apparently "wasn't" "the first time [I was in Greenville in 1964]."[8] Sufficient progress and promises had made Guild-sponsored litigation unnecessary in Washington County.

In the summer of 1966, I clerked for the Office of Economic Opportunity, the new antipoverty program, at its headquarters in Washington, but after graduation I found job opportunities in civil rights and poverty law limited. In the fall of 1967, I became a staff attorney in the office of general counsel of the United Planning Organization (UPO), the local community action agency in Washington, funded by the Office of Economic Opportunity and other federal agencies. For two years, I primarily wrote contracts with delegate agencies operating antipoverty programs in the metropolitan Washington area.

The MFDP Convention Challenge was not uppermost in my mind or activities, but it affected me indirectly in my career. With the rise in black nationalism that followed from Atlantic City, whites were resigning from UPO, and the agency became increasingly staffed by blacks. High employee turnover, promotions from within, and a change in atmosphere made me gradually feel alien in a culture that was not my own. Interracial cooperation seemed to end for me, and I felt no longer effective in making my own contribution. I also wanted more challenge in my legal career.

For these reasons, I resigned from UPO in 1968 without having another job. I quickly rejected my family's suggestion that I return home to Summit and instead pursued private practice in Washington, D.C. After years of private corporate law practice in D.C., where I specialized in litigating government contract disputes, which are generally heard by an administrative board or in the U.S. Court of Federal Claims, I qualified to be selected for one of the few judicial positions on a federal agency Board of Contract Appeals. In 1983, the National Aeronautics and Space Administration (NASA) had an opening on its board, and the agency head appointed me as an administrative judge. In 1993, NASA elected to have its contract disputes heard by the Department of Defense and made arrangements for me to become an administrative judge on its Armed Services Board of Contract Appeals. I served there for more than twelve years, managing my caseload, hearing trial-type testimony, and writing findings of fact and conclusions of law for three-judge panel final decisions subject to review by the U.S. Circuit Court of Federal Appeals. As a federal employee, I was sworn to uphold the Constitution of the United States and faithfully fulfill the duties of my office. For me, that oath meant providing a full and fair hearing to contractors who appealed to the NASA or the Armed Services Board a decision made by an agency contracting officer, particularly when the contractors proceeded without an attorney. My obligation was to decide each case based on the applicable federal law and provide a reasoned, clearly written decision for the understanding and benefit of the parties. The cases varied, and the work was both challenging and interesting as I did my best to render justice.

All this time, though, the Mississippi movement stayed with me as I watched for new books and purchased them even though I did not always read them immediately. When I did read them, I was interested in the explanation of the events at the 1964 convention, but what happened was confusing. I was never satisfied that I knew why the MFDP met its defeat.

In 1994, I went with my fellow Greenville summer volunteers Pat Vail and Nancy Schieffelin to Tougaloo College for the thirtieth anniversary of the Mississippi Summer Project. The well-planned program included seminar presentations and entertainment from the Freedom Singers. We drove up to Greenville just to look around and found a very different city. I couldn't get my bearings at all, not even remembering the downtown levee, that high green landmass designed to keep the Mississippi River out of the nearby downtown streets. Two big casinos that had arrived with gambling sometime after 1992 dominated the riverside. Boarded-up buildings, graffiti, and young men hanging around on Nelson Street, our old main street, discouraged me. I imagined violence, crime, drugs, teenage gangs, and mayhem. The lifestyle of the 1970s and 1980s replaced what had been a vital commercial section of town. The Civil Rights Act of 1964 allowed blacks to patronize all stores and restaurants, and as part of the nationwide trend the downtown Greenville stores moved out to strip malls on Highway 82.

Pat, Nancy, and I drove down to the South End to hunt for the Freedom House but couldn't remember the address. We thought we found the street and guessed it was a house next to the Disney Chapel. Pat volunteered to ask the neighbors but told Nancy and me to stay in the car so that *three* white women would not intimidate elderly blacks sitting on their nearby front porch. Pat asked if they remembered the "Freedom Riders," and after a while they acknowledged that the Freedom House had been on their street and confirmed its location. We went back to the

Greenville summer 1964 volunteers *(left to right):* Virginia Steele, Lisa Anderson Todd, Nancy Schieffelin, Candy Brown Gonzalez, Pat Vail, and Barbara Mutnick in Jackson, July 1994. Todd Collection.

Tougaloo meetings in new Greenville T-shirts and found other volunteers who had also spent the summer in Greenville in 1964: Virginia Steele, Candy Brown, and Barbara Mutnick.

When I started writing this book in 2006, I wondered about our plans for the new community center to be built in Greenville. Was the Herbert Lee Center ever built? It may seem strange that I knew nothing about it and never inquired, but that's how disassociated I became from my 1964 summer. My first information came in a book about the Delta Ministry, which stated that its staff had been invited to send "two representatives to the executive board of the Herbert Lee Memorial Community Center—a coalition of a number of Negro organizations—and [Delta Ministry] gave

$2800 toward remodeling the center."[9] I was disappointed that the organizers hadn't named it "Freedom Center" as we had planned.

In 2008, when I went back to Mississippi for a conference, I learned more about Greenville from my visit there. A chain had taken over the formerly luxurious Downtowner Motel, and the nearby casinos were attracting tourists. I was happy to see strict legal segregation gone, with blacks and whites working together, greeting each other on the street, and eating at the same restaurants, including whites at black restaurants. I found the Freedom House at 940 Sidney Street looking much the same as I had seen it in 1994. It made me sad to see just green grass on the whole block of Nelson Street between Harvey and Muscadine Streets, where the Carter Building, which housed the COFO office, had been torn down. I started my research at the library and planned to meet people from my past.

My first call was to Dr. Matthew Page, whom we had unsuccessfully tried to recruit for the MFDP in 1964. All I knew when I called was that he had offered, with two other blacks, to integrate the Mississippi Democratic Party sometime after 1964. He graciously invited me to his home for the interview, where I met his wife, Vivian. He had not anticipated that the Mississippi Summer Project would work, but he felt that it had. It got people to thinking seriously, and folks with the same ideas started talking among themselves. The local black ministerial alliance decided it was time for the ministers of small black churches to do something; they were no longer afraid that a minister could lose his church for being active in the civil rights struggle. Because the repercussions for speaking out were decreasing in Greenville owing to the movement activities that summer, more people were willing to take personal chances.

Local people involved in the MFDP in Greenville remained active after I left, and new people became Freedom Democrats, but Dr. Page thought "really it [the MFDP] was based in Jackson."[10] He "didn't do very much [with the MFDP], but [he] contributed." In his opinion, the MFDP was "basically a party of [the] poor . . . [the grass roots] led by longhairs, whites from other areas." He did not criticize that it was made up of the grass roots but "detested somebody else directing me." He appreciated people coming in to help, but when the question of control came up, he would say, "You're welcome to help us, but I'm not going to allow you to control me and anything that I have."[11] Hodding Carter III agreed: "Matt was a guy who could not have been more in support of everything that was going on and more resentful of it being done by outsiders and not internal black leadership." Page did not resent the infusion of outsiders in 1963 and 1964 but "welcomed them with reservations": rather, he objected to the summer volunteers "in effect questioning the leadership of the black middle class."[12]

Matthew Page had been an outsider himself while he was away from Greenville for college, medical school, and service in the air force, not returning to start his medical practice until 1959. He was not ready to assert himself during the Summer Project but became much more directly involved by the end of the 1960s and thereafter through the Herbert Lee Center, the first Child Development Group of Mississippi Head Start program and its successor the Mid-Delta Education Association, the Mississippi Humanities Council, and the Mississippi Advisory Committee to the U.S. Commission on Civil Rights.

After Dr. Page told me he was a delegate to the 1968 convention in Chicago, I was delighted that this young, capable, respected leader finally got involved on behalf of the people we were trying to get participating in politics in 1964. It was Guyot who told me—to my surprise—that Matthew Page was not part of the MFDP but allied with Hodding Carter III in the coalition of Loyal Democrats of Mississippi. At least six people from Greenville were Loyalist delegates to the 1968 convention. In making my assumptions, I did not think about relationships in Greenville. Hodding Carter Jr., the first publisher of the local *Delta Democrat-Times*, had been Page's mentor, helping to finance his education and medical practice. In 1960, he had written a feature article in the *Saturday Evening Post* about how this promising young black had overcome obstacles to become a doctor.[13] Dr. Page continued to be politically active through the 1972 Democratic National Convention in Miami, but "things just got a little too exciting . . . and uncomfortable" for him.[14] At that convention, he "lost [his] faith in the political system in the country" and bowed out of local and state politics.[15]

When I mentioned Doug Wynn, one of the regular delegates of the all-white Mississippi Democratic Party who had agreed to take the loyalty oath in Atlantic City in 1964, Dr. Page told me that he had grown up

Church at 639 Bellayre Street, formerly the Herbert Lee Community Center, in Greenville. Photo by Lisa Anderson Todd, March 2012.

with Wynn in the same neighborhood: Wynn in the big house on Main Street and he in the "shotgun house" a few blocks away. The black and white children played together, and the black mothers or the white mothers' maids would fix a sandwich or cup of soup for them and provide a pallet for them to take naps. But there were "limitations." They couldn't go to school together, and, as he said, "We couldn't—well, when we met each other downtown, we had to act like we didn't know each other."[16]

I asked him about the Herbert Lee Center. The center was primarily sponsored by the Delta Ministry, which was able to bring in expertise and get foundation funding. The local community raised an unprecedented $5,000 and bought an old church for conversion into a community center. Our plans for a community-controlled meeting place were realized, even though the architect's plans for new construction were not needed. Fannie Lou Hamer came over from Ruleville to speak there at MFDP meetings. Dr. Page was a founder and the president of the center. The

Herbert Lee Center no longer existed in 2008, but the abandoned building was at 639 Bellayre on the corner of Bellayre and Cately Streets. The Pages kindly gave me a tour to show me the location. Four or five years after the center opened, more blacks were registered to vote, the MFDP was less active, and its Head Start program had to move to a larger facility. The center sold the building to a church, which used it for about three years, and another church acquired it recently.[17]

I also asked about Charles Moore, another potential leader COFO had identified in 1964 and someone I knew from his help canvassing for Freedom Registrations. Dr. Page called him "a unique individual . . . my comrade and friend."[18] They shared a lot of things together, and Moore made quite a contribution serving on the Greenville City Council. Moore had died, but I learned more about him from "Civil Rights of the Sixties," a paper he wrote that is in the Greenville Museum, as well as from the transcript of an oral history interview he did, which I found in the library. Moore was elected vice president of the Herbert Lee Center, which he described as an umbrella organization of the Delta Ministry, COFO, and the NAACP leaders. As his widow told me, "He never let up"; he was always working to make things better for his children.[19]

The 2006 tributes in Moore's obituary told me that he was an inspiration to the community, serving on the city council for twelve years before retiring in 2002. The mayor remembered him "for his tenacity and overall willingness to say what was on his mind and do what was right for all the people of Greenville."[20] Moore had believed in what he stood for and was direct and to the point with his opinions, at the same time remaining approachable and keeping an open mind. It was not until December 10, 1973, that voters elected a black to the city council. Sarah H. Johnson ran as an Independent for an at-large seat and was elected. Charles Turner, who had been a leader of the MSU in 1964, was also elected to the city council.

Another person I wanted to find in Greenville was Bern Keating, who had put a picture of me in the July 5, 1964, *New York Times Sunday Magazine*. I thought he might have more photographs from the first week of our project. Hugh McCormick, a historian and owner of the McCormick Book Inn, told me that Keating had died and gave me the home phone number for his wife, Franke Keating. Mrs. Keating was friendly and apologetic when I called, telling me that she was ninety-one, had broken her hip, and could not get to the storage area where the photos might be. When I asked her whether she thought the Summer Project was a good thing, she said, "Oh, absolutely. Both my husband and I thought things needed shaking up."[21]

I thought better of Bern Keating when Franke Keating volunteered the story of how her husband, visiting at our Nelson Street office in mid-summer 1964, where there was no air conditioning, saw a young black man working on a design for a community center.[22] He told the man, "That's an unreasonable place to work. Why don't you come out to my house?" He put him in his wife's studio, and every day he would pick him up at 8:00 a.m., take him back to the Nelson Street office at noon, and then return him to the house for further work the rest of the afternoon. When Keating realized how ridiculous all those back-and-forth trips were, he suggested that the man have lunch with them. Mrs. Keating sounded amused and not at all offended that she then had to fix *another* toasted cheese sandwich every day for our volunteer architect Charles Askew. On a later trip I took to Greenville, she invited me to her home, where we had a most enjoyable visit, and she gave me a poster for the book *Mississippi*, which the Keatings had published in 1982, with her photographs and his text. As a professional photographer, member of the Greenville Arts Council, and resident in the city since 1946, she had promoted many projects to bring cultural and educational events to the Delta before her death in 2011.[23]

Others in Greenville agreed that the Mississippi Summer Project had a positive impact in changing the way people looked at things. When I saw Johnny Frazier at a reunion, I introduced myself and asked him if he was from Greenville and had been in Jackson the summer of 1963. He gave me a grateful bear hug and said, "You did so much." He called Greenville "a sleepy town" but said that the Summer Project made it possible for someone like him to begin the pursuit of his successful career.[24] His story included expulsion from Coleman High School for wearing a black armband because the school desegregation mandate of *Brown v. Board of Education* was ignored in Greenville, an act that had prompted an editorial in the paper from Hodding Carter Jr. In a panel presentation, I heard him describe his arrest on August 26, 1960, for sitting in the front of a bus from Atlanta to Greenville, subsequent jailing, and loss of "consciousness during the beating" by a sheriff and deputy sheriff on the way to jail.[25] That had happened in Winona, Mississippi, a few years before Fannie Lou Hamer was beaten in the same jail. When Hugh McCormick introduced me to Bob and Betty Jo Boyd, who happened to be in the bookstore when I was, I asked them if the Summer Project was a good thing for Greenville. He said, "Absolutely," and she said, "Oh yes."[26]

Dr. Page called James Carter "the black mayor of Greenville,"[27] as he was known even though he had no such official position. He told me that Carter had taken many chances all of his life but had never faced white retaliation. He was able to take people to the courthouse, stay until they signed the papers, and get them registered to vote. Later he would take them to vote, waiting until they actually voted. Dr. Page sounded more admiring of this process than when he had told me about local voter registration in 1964.

Over the years, the civil rights veterans have realized the importance of preserving our history and sharing our stories to inspire young people to become involved in today's pursuit of human rights and struggle for freedom, justice, and a humane society. We are reminders of what ordinary young people can do when joined with others. Today's students need to believe that if they engage in struggle in their communities, they, too, can achieve change. On April 10, 2014, President Obama, in his remarks at the LBJ Presidential Library Civil Rights Summit, warned us not to be complacent. He said, "Securing the gains this country has made requires the vigilance of its citizens. Our rights, our freedoms—they are not given. They must be won. They must be nurtured through struggle and discipline, and persistence and faith." He hoped that his daughters and young people everywhere would learn that "with enough effort, and enough empathy, and enough perseverance, and enough courage, people who love their country can change it."[28] I believe that expectations should be high.

My story is just one of many. Others are to be discovered. Original documents are archived in numerous places in the South and elsewhere, and some have been digitized for the Internet. Extensive resources are available on the Civil Rights Movement Veterans website (www.crmvet .org) and elsewhere. Issues are discussed on the SNCC listserv (https://

lists.virginia.edu/sympa/info/sncc-list). The Veterans of the Mississippi Civil Rights Movement, a 501(c)(3) nonprofit organization founded by Jimmie Travis, a SNCC veteran, and Owen Brooks of the Delta Ministry, has sponsored annual conferences in Jackson, Mississippi, that welcome students with the message "Empowering the next generation—passing it on to carry it on." An important purpose of these conferences has been to energize youth to move forward for social justice.

Fifty years after Freedom Summer, issues of racism remain. As Michelle Alexander explains in her stunning recent book *The New Jim Crow: Mass Incarceration in the Age of Colorblindness,* we should not think that we do not care about race or aspire to being colorblind: "The colorblindness ideal is premised on the notion that we, as a society, can never be trusted to see race and treat each other fairly or with genuine compassion. A commitment to color consciousness, by contrast, places faith in our capacity as humans to show care and concern for others, even as we are fully cognizant of race and possible racial differences."[29] Each of us is challenged to recognize racial differences and to show the same care and concern for all. Alexander maintains that a new system of racial control has replaced slavery and Jim Crow since 1965 in the criminal justice system, which has legalized discrimination against an astounding percentage of the black community. She describes today's indifference to the operation of mass incarceration and compares it to our historical attitudes toward legal segregation and discrimination. Her book is a compelling reminder that the business of the 1960s civil rights movement is unfinished. We all have a responsibility to speak out against racism and injustice.

The goals of the civil rights movement have yet to be achieved. As Pinkey Hall, an MFDP delegate from Hattiesburg, said in 1995, "We've come a long ways, but we got miles and miles and miles yet to go."[30] In addition to continuing racism and its invidious effects, issues of economic disparities and poverty remain to be addressed in an effective way. But, as Vincent Harding has advised, a new generation will "do the job the way they discover what needs to be done" in an agenda for "the expansion of democracy in America."[31]

The MFDP Convention Challenge could have and, I continue to believe, should have happened differently. We can only speculate on the course of history if the Democratic Party had opened its doors to the

MFDP and provided a route for blacks—rich and poor, rural and urban, southern and northern—to travel to personal satisfaction, good citizenship, and prosperity. But at the very least we can understand what happened in 1964 and the forces that actually shaped our history.

When Howard Zinn wished me "the best of luck" in writing this book, he said the MFDP in Atlantic City was "certainly an idea worth pursuing because that moment in history cast so much light on many things other than the specifics of the MFDP challenge."[32] I have wanted to clarify what others have written and share my perceptions of that historic event as only a participant–observer can. I cannot claim a perfect memory, but I have made every effort to present an accurate account.

Acknowledgments

I have dedicated this book to my parents, who met in Grantsburg, Wisconsin, and moved to New York City after they completed their education and married. I am grateful that they always understood and supported me, including my choice to serve as a volunteer on the 1964 Mississippi Summer Project. They also complied with my request to save the letters I wrote during the summer.

Numerous friends have listened to the story of this book, given me encouragement, read portions of the manuscript, and offered their editing. They include Maureen Beck, Tansy Howard Blumer, Karl Flaming, Susan Hand, Anne Sonnekalb Iskrant, Emily Meschter, Brenda Niemand, Michael Popkin, Sandy Powers, Sylvia Reed, Hal Witt, and Anne Harding Woodworth. The course I took with Natalie Wexler at the Writer's Center in Bethesda, Maryland, was useful. During the summers, I joined Writer's Workshop, which met weekly at the Saltmarsh Center in Nantucket, Massachusetts. I thank the late Judy Shure, who warned me that I was "latinating"; Marta Allen, who cheered me with her enthusiasm for the excerpts I read; the late Elaine Winer, who entertained my husband and me at her Surfside Nantucket home and advised me to write more dramatically, as she did in her novel *The Seagull's Wife;* David Kopko, a fellow Cornellian and year-round island resident who held the group together; and Mary Kenny and Jan Glitzenstein, who shared their wisdom, unfailing kindness, and many bits and pieces of helpful advice.

In looking for a literary agent, I found encouragement from Nina Graybill and Ron Goldfarb in Washington, D.C., and when I turned to find an editor, I was pleased with the courtesy provided by Karl Weber, a member of Consulting Editors Alliance, who believed I had a book that was publishable. He referred me to his colleague in the alliance, Arnold Dolin, who edited an early draft of the book. He asked me many good questions and advised me to delete extraneous material of little interest. Lynn Golbetz, formerly with the Stanford University Press, was both friendly and professional in significantly improving portions of the manuscript.

Many librarians and archivists assisted in my research. I traveled to several locations to find information, as indicated in my notes. Individuals were helpful on site and responded to later requests for information, in particular Allen Fisher at the Lyndon Baines Johnson Presidential Library, Michael Edmonds at the Wisconsin Historical Society, my college friend Joan Karliner Leighton at Stanford, Christine Gibbons McKay at the Schomburg Center of the New York Public Library, and Brenda Fulton-Poke at the William Alexander Percy Memorial Library in Greenville. Thanks go to Jan Hillegas for retrieving documents and helping me use the resources of the Mississippi Department of Archives and History. I am grateful to Lincoln Thurber, head reference librarian at the Nantucket Atheneum, for giving me similar service in retrieving, copying, and providing books and documents. I want to thank my former secretary Nancy Simmons Brown for taking on the difficult job of transcribing some of my interviews. At the University Press of Kentucky, I have appreciated the welcome by Steven Lawson, professor emeritus, Rutgers University, and his willingness to look at my draft manuscript as well as the support provided by acquisition editors Anne Dean Dotson and Bailey E. Johnson and by editing supervisor Iris A. Law.

John Dittmer, professor emeritus, DePauw University, has given me enormously helpful advice on the book. Since March 2008, he has been considerate and friendly in providing several detailed reviews of my drafts, which have been invaluable. James T. Campbell, Edgar E. Robinson Professor in U.S. history at Stanford University, who specializes in African American history, met with me when I was at a Stanford reunion and at the Mississippi Department of Archives and History, shared his views of the Mississippi civil rights movement, and read a draft of my manuscript with great care, giving me useful suggestions for revision. I am also grateful to Wesley Hogan, director of the Center for Documentary Studies at Duke University, for her prompt review and thoughtful comments on an important chapter at a particularly busy time in her career.

Mary King has been unfailingly kind and attentive in serving as my principal mentor and adviser on all aspects of my project. Having her companionship at the SNCC fiftieth anniversary celebration in Raleigh in April 2010 and her introductions to many civil rights veterans solidified our friendship. Hodding Carter III took an interest in my project, offered his time and advice when we compared notes about Greenville in his office, and gave significant and encouraging comments on an early draft of the chapters about the convention. I have enjoyed conversations with presidential historian Robert Dallek about Lyndon Johnson and about writing books at various gatherings featuring our grandchildren, who are friends and neighbors. During a Cornell reunion weekend, Professor Theodore J. Lowi, John L. Senior Professor of American Institutions at Cornell, answered my question about the legacy of the MFDP in a single word, "Obama." He offered me a helpful incentive to create a deadline for myself to finish the book. I thank Ed King for sharing his stories of the Mississippi civil rights movement and his account of the MFDP Convention Challenge in his personal papers as well as for answering by email my numerous questions. My fellow volunteers—in particular Pat Vail, Nancy Schieffelin, and Barbara Mutnick—and the SNCC veterans gave me important information. As indicated in my notes, they include Margaret Block, Joan Browning, Charlie Cobb, Courtland Cox, Connie Curry, Ivanhoe Donaldson, the late Lawrence Guyot, Dorie Ladner, Joyce Ladner, Judy Richardson, Betty Garman Robinson, Charles Sherrod, Frank Smith, Ekwueme Michael Thelwell, and Dottie Zellner, to whom I add CORE veteran Dave Dennis.

I thank the Reverend Karen Brau, pastor of Luther Place Memorial Church, for listening to me over the past five years and encouraging me in this project. Pastor Robert Holum, her predecessor, was always interested in my civil rights stories and regretted being too young to volunteer in 1964. His wife, Binnie, an accomplished artist, performer, and writer, told me about Anne Lamott's *Bird by Bird*, which gave me valuable early advice about writing. Retired Pastor John Steinbruck gave me reason to be drawn to Luther Place years ago.

I am grateful to my family; my brother Eric, who asked frequent questions about "the book" and congratulated me for my perseverance; and my brother John, who has been similarly interested, along with his daughters, Cynthia and Linnea. Cynthia has shared her knowledge of writing in the academic world and graciously hosted me in Austin, where she received her Ph.D. in linguistics from the University of Texas before becoming a professor at Grinnell College. Our daughter, Alexandra, and grandchildren, Emily and Matthew, allowed me time away from babysitting, puzzle making, biking, and other family activities to get the book written. My husband, David, has been my mainstay throughout, and I am grateful for his tolerance, good judgment, and humor while waiting to share with me other activities.

Appendix A

Challenge of the Mississippi Freedom Democratic Party

The following document, "Challenge of the Mississippi Freedom Democratic Party," is a COFO handout that was originally distributed at the orientation of volunteers for the Mississippi Summer Project in June 1964 (available at the Wisconsin Historical Society, MFDP records, 1962–1971, folder 1, box 1 and microfilm 788, reel 1; and copy in Lisa Anderson Todd's files).

CHALLENGE OF THE MISSISSIPPI FREEDOM DEMOCRATIC PARTY

* * * * * * *

I. DEVELOPMENT OF THE MISSISSIPPI
FREEDOM DEMOCRATIC PARTY

Three basic considerations underlie the development of the Mississippi Freedom Democratic Party and its plans to challenge the seating of the delegation of the Mississippi Democratic Party at the 1964 National Democratic Convention. They are:

1. The long history of systematic and studied exclusion of Negro citizens from equal participation in the political processes of the state grows more flagrant daily.

2. The Mississippi Democratic Party has conclusively demonstrated its lack of loyalty to the National Democratic Party in the past, and currently indicates no intention of supporting the platform of the 1964 Democratic Convention.

3. The intransigent and fanatical determination of the State's political power structure to maintain the status-quo clearly demonstrates that the "Mississippi closed society," as Professor James W. Silver of the University of Mississippi asserts, is without leadership or moral resources to reform itself, and hence can only be brought into the mainstream of the twentieth century by forces outside of itself.

A. PARTY DISCRIMINATION:

The Mississippi Democratic Party controls the legislative, executive, and judicial branches of the government of the State. All 49 senators, and all but one of the 122 representatives are Democrats. Repeatedly, the State legislature has passed laws and established regulations designed to discriminate against prospective Negro voters. The 1963 gubernatorial campaign was largely directed towards restricting the Negro vote. The state convention is being held in the Jackson Municipal Auditorium and the Heidelberg Hotel, both of which are segregated. In its devotion to racism and suppression of minority expression, the Mississippi Democratic Party prevents Negro Democrats and white Democrats who disagree with the party's racist stance from participating in party programs and decisions.

B. PARTY DISLOYALTY:

Mississippi citizens who desire to do so cannot support the National Democratic goals by joining the Mississippi Democratic Party. The Mississippi Democratic Party has declared in public speeches and printed matter that it is NOT a part of the National Democratic Party. The campaign literature for the election of Governor Paul B. Johnson, in November 1963, is a case in point, as the following exerpts show: ... "Our Mississippi Democratic Party is entirely independent and free of the influence or domination of any national party" ..... "The Mississippi Democratic Party, which long ago separated itself from the National Democratic Party, and which has fought consistently everything both national parties stand for........"

2

In 1960 the Mississippi Democratic Party failed to honor its pledge to support the nominees of the National Democratic Convention. Immediately after the convention the Mississippi party convened a convention and voted to support unpledged electors in an effort to defeat the nominees of the Democratic National Convention.

C. THE CLOSED SOCIETY:

"It can be argued that in the history of the United States democracy has produced great leaders in great crises. Sad as it may be, the opposite has been true in Mississippi. As yet there is little evidence that the society of the closed mind will ever possess the moral resources to reform itself, or the capacity for self-examination, or even the tolerance of self-examination." from Mississippi: The Closed Society, by James W. Silver.

Civil rights groups working in Mississippi are convinced that political and social justice cannot be won in Mississippi without massive interest and support of the country as a whole, backed by the authority of the Federal government. As the political leadership of Mississippi feel threatened by the winds of change, they devise new and more extensive legal weapons and police powers. Police preparations were made all through the spring to harass, intimidate, and threaten the educational and political programs now being carried on in Mississippi. Five new bills, prohibiting picketing, banning the distribution of boycott literature, restricting the movement of groups, establishing curfews, authorizing municipalities to pool police manpower and equipment, and increasing penalties that may be assessed by city courts, were hurriedly signed into law. Other similar bills are still pending.

II. ORGANIZATIONAL STRUCTURE OF THE
FREEDOM DEMOCRATIC PARTY

The Mississippi Freedom Democratic Party was conceived to give Negro citizens of Mississippi an experience in political democracy and to establish a channel through which all citizens, Negro and white, can actively support the principles and programs of the National Democratic Party. The Council of Federated Organizations (COFO), a confederation of all the local civil rights and citizenship education groups in Mississippi, is assisting local citizens to develop the Mississippi Freedom Democratic Party.

This party is open to all citizens regardless of race. It was officially established at a meeting in Jackson on April 26th; the approximately 300 delegates present elected a temporary state executive committee, which will be responsible for setting up precinct and other state meetings. These meetings will parallel those of the Mississippi Democratic Party, and every effort will be made to comply with all state laws which apply to the formation of political parties. Registered voters in the Freedom Democratic Party have already attempted to attend precinct and county meetings of the Mississippi Democratic Party, an experience which only offered further proof of the racial discrimination rife within this party and of its disloyalty to the National Party (See Appendix).

The Mississippi Freedom Democratic Party is presently engaged in three major efforts: (1) Freedom Registration; (2) Freedom Candidates; and (3) The Convention Challenge.

A. FREEDOM REGISTRATION:

Official registration figures show that only some 20,000 Negroes are registered in Mississippi as compared to 500,000 whites. This represents less than 7% of the 435,000 Negroes 21 years of age in the state. The Freedom Registration is designed to show that thousands of Negroes want to become registered voters. By setting up registrars and deputy registrars in counties across the state, some 100,000 or more persons may be inscribed on the Freedom Registration books by the time of the Democratic Convention. Last November some 83,000 Negroes voted in a mock gubernatorial race, in which COFO President Aaron Henry ran against Gov. Paul B. Johnson.

The Freedom registrars will use simplified registration forms based on voting applications used in several Northern states. Any person who registers in the Freedom Registration will be eligible to vote in the Freedom Democratic Party conventions and to participate in party work.

B. FREEDOM CANDIDATES :

The four candidates who qualified to run in the June 2 primary in Mississippi were nominees of the Freedom Democratic Party. The Freedom Candidates plan to run again in a mock election under the auspices of the Mississippi Freedom Democratic Party in November. This will help to establish the fact that thousands of Negroes are deprived of citizenship participation because of the racist character of Mississippi's voter registration procedures.

The four candidates are Mrs. Victoria Gray, opposing Senator John Stennis; Mrs. Fannie Lou Hamer, opposing Rep. Jamie L. Whitten; the Rev. John Cameron, opposing Rep. William M. Colmer, and Mr. James Houston, opposing Rep. John Bell Williams.

The Platforms of the candidates of the Freedom Democratic Party articulate the needs of all the people of Mississippi, such as anti-poverty programs, medicare, aid to education, rural development, urban renewal, and the guarantee of constitutional rights to all. This is in sharp contrast to the lack of real issues in the campaigns of the candidates who won in the primary. Senator Stennis did not even bother to campaign in the state.

C. THE CHALLENGE TO THE DEMOCRATIC NATIONAL CONVENTION:

Delegates from the Freedom Democratic Party will challenge the seating of the "old-line" Mississippi delegation at the Democratic National Convention this August in Atlantic City, New Jersey. All steps necessary to preparing and formally presenting the challenge of the Freedom Democratic Party are being taken. Several State Democratic Conventions have alrealy passed resolutions in support of the challenge. BUT WE NEED YOUR COOPERATION AND HELP!

1. We need convention delegates to champion the cause of representative government in Mississippi.

2. We need people who will speak out in the credentials committee and on the convention floor.

3. We need hundreds of Democrats - individuals and organizations - to instruct their delegates, petition their representatives, party leaders, and the President to face up to the fact that only a renegade Democratic Party exists in Mississippi - a party which enjoys the benefits of national affiliation, but spurns all responsibilities. Such a party can only continue to bring disgrace to the National Democratic Party.

Appendix B

Mississippi Freedom Democratic Party Delegates

The following document, "Mississippi Freedom Democratic Party Delegation," was first published in *Brief Submitted by the Mississippi Freedom Democratic Party for the Consideration of the Democratic National Committee, Credentials Committee of the Democratic National Convention, Delegates to the Democratic National Convention*, 70–71 (available at the Civil Rights Movement Veterans website, http://www.crmvet.org/docs/6408_mfdp_brief.pdf, and copy in Lisa Anderson Todd's files).

70

MISSISSIPPI FREEDOM DEMOCRATIC PARTY DELEGATION:

National Committeewoman: Mrs. Victoria Gray
National Committeeman: Rev. Edwin King
Chairman of the delegation: Mr. Aaron Henry
Vice-chairman of the delegation: Mrs. Fannie Lou Hamer
Secretary: Mrs. Annie Devine

Delegates:

Mrs. Helen Anderson
Dr. A. D. Beittel
Mrs. Elizabeth Blackwell
Mrs. Marie Blalock
Mr. Sylvester Bowens
Mr. J. W. Brown
Mr. Charles Bryant
Mr. James Carr
Miss Lois Chaffee
Mr. Chois Collier
Mr. Willie Ervin
Mr. J. C. Fairley
Mr. Dewey Green
Mr. Laurence Guyot
Mrs. Winson Hudson
Mr. Johnny Jackson
Mr. N. L. Kirkland
Miss Mary Lane
Rev. Merrill W. Lindsay
Mr. Eddie Mack
Mrs. Lula Matthews
Mrs. Yvonne MacGowan
Mr. Charles McLaurin
Mr. Leslie McLemore
Mr. Robert Miles
Mr. Otis Millsaps
Mrs. Hazel Palmer
Rev. R. S. Porter
Mr. Willie Scott
Mr. Henry Sias

Alternates:

Mr. C. R. Darden
Mrs. Ruby Evans
Mr. Oscar Giles
Mr. Charlie Graves
Mrs. Pinkie Hall
Mr. George Harper
Mrs. Macy Hardaway
Mr. Andrew Hawkins
Mr. William Jackson
Mrs. Alta Lloyd
Rev. J. F. McRee
Rev. W. G. Middleton
Mr. Joe Newton
Mrs. M. A. Phelps
Mrs. Beverly Polk
Mr. Henry Reaves
Mr. Harold Roby
Mrs. Emma Sander
Mrs. Cora Smith
Rev. R. L. T. Smith
Mrs. Elmira Tyson
Mr. L. H. Waborn

71

Delegates:

Mr. Robert Lee Stinson
Mr. Slate Stallworth
Mr. E. W. Steptoe
Mr. Joseph Stone
Mr. Eddie Thomas
Mr. James Travis
Mr. Hartman Turnbow
Mr. Abraham Washington
Mr. Clifton R. Whitley
Mr. Robert W. Williams
Mr. J. Walter Wright

Notes

Abbreviations

CRDP	Civil Rights Documentation Project, University of Southern Mississippi, Hattiesburg
CRMV	Civil Rights Movement Veterans
DNC Series	Democratic National Committee Series, Lyndon Baines Johnson Presidential Library, Austin, Tex.
LAT	Lisa Anderson Todd
LBJL	Lyndon Baines Johnson Presidential Library, Austin, Tex.
LOC	Library of Congress, Washington, D.C.
MDAH	Mississippi Department of Archives and History, Jackson
MHS	Minnesota Historical Society, St. Paul
RTCM	Recordings and Transcripts of Conversations and Meetings, Lyndon Baines Johnson Presidential Library, Austin, Tex.
TC	telephone conversation
UNC	University of North Carolina, Chapel Hill
USM	University of Southern Mississippi, Hattiesburg
WHCF	White House Correspondence Files, Lyndon Baines Johnson Presidential Library, Austin, Tex.
WHS	Wisconsin Historical Society, Madison

1. In Atlantic City for the Democratic Convention

1. Pat Vail and Lisa Anderson Todd (LAT), telephone conversation (TC), August 5, 2013.

2. Drew Pearson, "Washington Merry-Go-Around," *New York Post,* August 30, 1964.

3. Cleveland Sellers, *The River of No Return: The Autobiography of a Black Militant and the Life and Death of SNCC* (New York: William Morrow, 1973), 108; Mary King, *Freedom Song: A Personal Story of the 1960s Civil Rights Movement* (New York: William Morrow, 1987), 343; Stokely Carmichael and Ekwueme Michael Thelwell, *Ready for Revolution: The Life and Struggles of Stokely Carmichael (Kwame Ture)* (New York: Scribner, 2003),

404; Sharlene Kranz, interviewed by LAT, Washington, D.C., May 22, 2010. I remember seeing the car on display and believing it was the actual 1963 blue Ford Fairlane station wagon as others have written. Some scholars have considered that impossible because the FBI would have had custody of the vehicle. The FBI reported that "a flat-bed truck with a burned car on it" appeared in Atlantic City on August 23, 1964, which was "falsely alleged to be the automobile of the three murdered civil rights workers in Mississippi" (H. N. Bassett to Mr. Callahan, memo, January 29, 1975, Folder 8, "1964 DNC Inquiry FBI File," Box 17, Nick Kotz Papers, Wisconsin Historical Society [WHS], Madison). The playwright Lorraine Hansberry had given the station wagon to CORE. FBI and local authorities prevented its being taken to Atlantic City, saying it was being held for evidence (David J. Dennis Sr. to LAT, emails, February 7, 2014).

4. These freedom songs are printed in full in Guy Carawan and Candie Carawan, eds., *Sing for Freedom: The Story of the Civil Rights Movement through Its Songs* (Montgomery, Ala.: New South Books, 2007); see also Pete Seeger and Bob Reiser, *Everybody Says Freedom: The Civil Rights Movement in Songs and Pictures* (New York: Norton, 1989).

5. Andrew Young, *An Easy Burden: The Civil Rights Movement and the Transformation of America* (New York: HarperCollins, 1996), 308.

6. Andrew Young, telephone interview by LAT, May 21, 2010.

7. Pat Vail, interviewed by LAT, Washington, D.C., June 12, 2008.

8. Sally Belfrage, *Freedom Summer* (Greenwich, Conn.: Fawcett, 1965), 247; reprinted in 1990 by the University Press of Virginia.

2. My Life before Mississippi

1. Frederick Buechner, *Beyond Words* (New York: HarperCollins, 2004), 112.

2. For the mid-twentieth-century civil rights movement in the United States, I use the dates 1955 to 1965, following Mary Elizabeth King, "Civil Rights Movement (USA): Methods of Nonviolent Action," *International Encyclopedia of Peace*, 318–23 (New York: Oxford University Press, 2009). The major events of these years are the events I learned about in my studies and in Mississippi. They include the accomplishments of interracial organizations committed to nonviolent direct action. My brief summary is intended to give the general reader a framework for understanding the time that coincides with my coming of age in this book, which actually ends in 1964. I am aware of criticism of the "dominant narrative" of the civil rights movement, which is dated from 1954 to 1965 or 1968, marked at each end by the *Brown v. Board of Education* Supreme Court decision in 1954 and either the pas-

sage of the Voting Rights Act in 1965 or the assassination of Martin Luther King Jr. in 1968 (Jacquelyn Dowd Hall, "The Long Civil Rights Movement and the Political Uses of the Past," *Journal of American History* 91 [2005]: 1233–63). Certainly the movement did not begin suddenly, nor has it ended. In Mississippi, it was preceded by black resistance, political mobilization, increased black voter registration, and citizenship education, which Charles Payne describes in *I've Got the Light of Freedom: The Organizing Tradition and the Mississippi Freedom Struggle* (Berkeley: University of California Press, 1995), 21–77. See also John Dittmer, *Local People: The Struggle for Civil Rights in Mississippi* (Champaign: University of Illinois Press, 1994), 13–14, 29–35, 55–59. The movement can also be marked by organizational protest from Montgomery to Selma or in Mississippi by reactions to the Emmett Till murder on August 28, 1955, and the final decision made by the MFDP delegates at the Democratic National Convention on August 26, 1964. In the summer of 1965, blacks held a major demonstration against proposed state legislation in Jackson, and political organizing continued in local communities. New generations should not deem the civil rights movement to have come to an end. They need to continue our nonviolent interracial efforts to guarantee freedom, justice, and equality for all.

3. Cited in Payne, *I've Got the Light of Freedom*, 54.

4. Cornell University has renamed these colleges the College of Agriculture and Life Sciences and the College of Human Ecology; see http://www.cornell.edu/academics/colleges.cfm. I was in the College of Arts and Sciences.

5. For more information on direct-action protests in Mississippi, see Mrs. Medgar Evers, with William Peters, *For Us, the Living* (New York: Doubleday, 1967), 235–36; M. J. O'Brien, *We Shall Not Be Moved: The Jackson Woolworth's Sit-In and the Movement It Inspired* (Jackson: University Press of Mississippi, 2014), 25–26.

3. Mississippi, 1963

1. Beginning in the 1950s, EVS sponsored work camps throughout the world for young Protestant volunteers to engage in construction and community-service projects. Projects were generally located in Europe, the Middle East, and Asia. Scholarship in the early 1960s on the role of the church to "discern God working in the secular world," the preaching of Martin Luther King Jr. to white northern churches, the Birmingham campaign, and King's *Letter from a Birmingham Jail* led to the NCC's formation of the Commission on Religion and Race on June 7, 1963. This group would focus on racial concerns, send white ministers to participate in Hattiesburg's Freedom Day

in February 1964, sponsor orientation for the Mississippi Summer Project in Oxford, Ohio, send volunteer ministers and campus lay leaders to Mississippi during the summer of 1964, and establish the long-term community-development ministry of the Delta Ministry, which opened its headquarters in Greenville on September 1, 1964 (James F. Findlay Jr., *Church People in the Struggle: The National Council of Churches and the Black Freedom Movement, 1950–1970* [New York: Oxford University Press, 1993], 30–34, 111). There were other EVS projects in the United States, but my project was unique for correlating difficult physical work with the civil rights movement. John and Margrit Garner, familiar with the EVS from the work camp in Byblos, Lebanon, where they met during the summer of 1960, wrote a proposal to the World Council of Churches for funding, possibly with some help from Tougaloo, noting "the college's need for assistance with some routine maintenance and the college's commitment to the civil rights movement in a sea of segregation" (John Garner to LAT, email, September 24, 2013).

2. See John R. Salter Jr., *Jackson, Mississippi: An American Chronicle of Struggle and Schism* (Hicksville, N.Y.: Exposition Press, 1979; reprint, Lincoln: University of Nebraska Press, 2011); O'Brien, *We Shall Not Be Moved.*

3. Buechner, *Beyond Words*, 352–53.

4. See James W. Silver, *Mississippi: The Closed Society* (New York: Harcourt, Brace & World, 1964), 98–99, for the details of the charges.

5. Chris Rice, "Reconciliation as the Mission of God: Christian Mission in a World of Destructive Conflicts," Duke Divinity School Center for Reconciliation (2005), 20, quoted in Adam Taylor, *Mobilizing Hope: Faith-Inspired Activism for a Post–Civil Rights Generation* (Downers Grove, Ill.: IVP Books, 2010), 169.

6. Quoted in Ellen Levine, *Freedom's Children: Young Civil Rights Activists Tell Their Own Stories* (New York: Puffin Books, 1993), 110; see also Pat Watters and Reese Cleghorn, *Climbing Jacob's Ladder: The Arrival of Negroes in Southern Politics* (New York: Harcourt, Brace & World, 1967), app. I, "The Winona Incident," for a June 13, 1963, interview with Fannie Lou Hamer and Annelle Ponder.

7. Quoted in Levine, *Freedom's Children*, 111.

8. Quoted in Jerry DeMuth, "'Tired of Being Sick and Tired,'" *The Nation*, June 1, 1964.

9. Charles Marsh, *God's Long Summer: Stories of Faith and Civil Rights* (Princeton, N.J.: Princeton University Press, 1997), 22.

10. Quoted in King, *Freedom Song*, 351.

11. In "Fannie Lou Hamer Conversation with SNCC Worker, Dale Grunemeier, Ruleville, Mississippi, 1964," in "References by Fannie Lou Hamer,"

Civil Rights Movement as Theological Drama, Project on Lived Theology, University of Virginia, at http://archives.livedtheology.org/view/references/all/Fannie%20Lou%20Hamer.

4. On to Greensboro, North Carolina, and Back to Cornell

1. Martin Luther King Jr., *The Autobiography of Martin Luther King, Jr.*, edited by Clayborne Carson (New York: Warner, 1998), 222.

2. In the 1950s, the AFSC established its Southeast regional headquarters in Greensboro. AFSC staff there worked primarily on hiring blacks in nontraditional jobs. In 1957–1958, they focused on school desegregation, conducting human relations workshops for teachers (William H. Chafe, *Civilities and Civil Rights: Greensboro, North Carolina, and the Black Struggle for Freedom* [New York: Oxford University Press, 1980], 30, 34, 75, 113). The AFSC had identified racial tensions as a source of underlying injustice and had begun working on civil rights issues as early as 1925. The AFSC established a work camp program in the mid-1930s and made efforts to integrate these groups at several work camp sites in the South (Jack Sutters, "AFSC's Civil Rights Efforts, 1925–1950," September 2001, at https://afsc.org/story/afscs-civil-rights-efforts-1925-1950). After moving to Atlanta in 1960, Constance Curry directed the National Students Association Southern Student Human Relations Project and served on the SNCC Executive Committee. In 1964, she became the AFSC southern field representative for grassroots implementation of rights under the 1964 Civil Rights Act and the 1965 Voting Rights Act. She worked with white women in Jackson, Mississippi, who had formed Mississippians for Public Education for peaceful school integration. In the fall of 1964, she coordinated a task force formed by the NAACP Legal Defense and Educational Fund and the AFSC to "encourage enrollment of black children and to document the difficulties they faced." In 1966, she became the administrator of the AFSC Family Aid Fund, which, with the support of the Ford Foundation, made loans and grants to individuals and community groups harassed for exercising their civil rights. In 1968, Connie Curry was the AFSC liaison to the planning of Dr. King's Poor People's Campaign. In 1975, as a result of a decrease in cases of individual harassment, Ford terminated funding, and, although keeping the regional office open, the AFSC could no longer justify the position of southern field representative. See Constance Curry, "Wild Geese to the Past," in Constance Curry, Joan C. Browning, Dorothy Dawson Burlage, Penny Patch, Theresa Del Pozzo, Sue Thrasher, Elaine DeLott Baker, Emmie Schrader Adams, and Casey Hayden, *Deep in Our Hearts: Nine White Women in the Freedom Move-*

ment (Athens: University of Georgia Press, 2000), 25, 27–28, 31–32; Constance Curry to LAT, email, September 14, 2013.

3. See Chafe, *Civilities and Civil Rights,* 119–47.

4. Charles Euchner, *Nobody Turn Me Around: A People's History of the March on Washington* (Boston: Beacon Press, 2010), 110–11.

5. King, *The Autobiography of Martin Luther King, Jr.,* 222.

6. Avon Rollins Sr., "August 28th, 1963—the March on Washington," August 5, 2003, revised June 14, 2008, at the Civil Rights Movement Veterans (CRMV) website, http://www.crmvet.org/info/mowrolin.htm.

7. John Lewis and Michael D'Orso, *Walking with the Wind: A Memoir of the Movement* (New York: Simon & Schuster, 1998), 219.

8. Ibid., 217.

9. Martin Luther King Jr., "I Have a Dream," August 28, 1963, at http://www.archives.gov/press/exhibits/dream-speech.pdf.

10. Ibid.

11. Quoted in William P. Jones, *The March on Washington: Jobs, Freedom, and the Forgotten History of Civil Rights* (New York: Norton, 2014), 151.

12. Quoted in ibid., 169.

13. Lisa Anderson, "AFSC Voter Registration Project, Greensboro, N.C., August 9–30, 1963," summary report, 10, copy in LAT's files and in Box 13, Ella Baker Papers, Manuscripts, Archives, and Rare Books Division, Schomburg Center for Research in Black Culture, New York Public Library.

14. Randolyn Johnson Story, interviewed by LAT, Franklin, Tenn., March 22, 2008.

15. Lisa Anderson, letter to the editor, *Summit Herald,* September 5, 1963.

5. Planning for the Summer Project

1. Lawrence Guyot, oral history interview, September 7, 1996, Civil Rights Documentation Project (CRDP), Center for Oral History and Cultural Heritage, McCain Library and Archives, University of Southern Mississippi (USM), Hattiesburg.

2. Frank R. Parker, *Black Votes Count: Political Empowerment in Mississippi after 1965* (Chapel Hill: University of North Carolina Press, 1990), 17, 31; Neil R. McMillen, "Black Enfranchisement in Mississippi: Federal Enforcement and Black Protest in the 1960s," *Journal of Southern History* 43, no. 3 (1977): 352.

3. John Doar, on the panel "The Societal Response to SNCC," SNCC 50th Anniversary Conference, April 15, 2010, Raleigh, N.C.

4. Margaret Block, interviewed by LAT, Cleveland, Miss., March 16, 2009.

5. Quoted in David J. Garrow, *Bearing the Cross: Martin Luther King, Jr. and the Southern Christian Leadership Conference* (New York: Perennial Classics, 1986), 625.

6. Howard Zinn, *SNCC: The New Abolitionists* (Boston: Beacon Press, 1964), 216. For more information about SNCC, see Clayborne Carson, *In Struggle: SNCC and the Black Awakening of the 1960s* (Cambridge, Mass.: Harvard University Press, 1981), and Wesley C. Hogan, *Many Minds One Heart: SNCC's Dream for a New America* (Chapel Hill: University of North Carolina Press, 2007).

7. Bob Moses, interviewed by LAT, Cambridge, Mass., April 16, 2013; John Dittmer, "The Politics of the Mississippi Movement, 1954–1964," in Charles W. Eagles, ed., *The Civil Rights Movement in America* (Jackson: University Press of Mississippi, 1986), 78–79; Dittmer, *Local People*, 212; Watters and Cleghorn, *Climbing Jacob's Ladder*, 46–47, 61–62.

8. "Freedom Democratic Party Given Boost," *Mississippi Free Press*, July 25, 1964.

9. Charles Cobb, oral history interview, October 21, 1996, CRDP.

10. Hollis Watkins, oral history interview, October 23, 29, and 30, 1996, CRDP.

11. Quoted by Frank Smith in a conversation with LAT, Washington, D.C., June 20, 2013.

12. Richard Woodley, "It Will Be a Hot Summer in Mississippi," *The Reporter*, May 21, 1964, in "Register of the Mississippi Freedom Democratic Party Records, 1963–1971," WHS microfilm, Reel 1, Item 2, General Papers 1963–1965 (MFDP Papers), available in Reel 2646 at Mississippi Department of Archives and History (MDAH), Jackson.

13. Doug McAdam, *Freedom Summer* (New York: Oxford University Press, 1988), 40.

14. Dottie Zellner, telephone interview by LAT, September 27, 2008.

15. Walter Tillow to LAT, letter, February 24, 1964.

16. Penny Patch, "Sweet Tea at Shoney's," in Curry et al., *Deep in Our Hearts*, 154.

17. COFO, *Mississippi Summer Project*, brochure, copy in LAT's files.

18. See James W. Silver, *Mississippi: The Closed Society* (New York: Harcourt, Brace & World, 1964).

19. Quoted in Matt Horton, "White Identity & Perception: The Experience of White Student Nonviolent Coordinating Committee (SNCC) Staff & Friends (1960–1967)," M.A. thesis, American University, 2009, 164,

citing Daniel Levine, *Bayard Rustin and the Civil Rights Movement* (New Brunswick, N.J.: Rutgers University Press, 2000), 156–57.

20. Quoted in Garrow, *Bearing the Cross,* 332.

21. John D'Emilio, *Lost Prophet: The Life and Times of Bayard Rustin* (New York: Free Press, 2003), 380.

22. Ibid., 386–87.

23. "Council of Federated Organizations Civil Rights Action Program in the State of Mississippi," *Congressional Record,* 88th Congress, 2d sess., House of Representatives, June 16, 1964; "Democratic National Convention 1964 MFDP Literature," Democratic National Committee (DNC) Series I, Box 77, Lyndon Baines Johnson Presidential Library (LBJL), Austin, Tex.

6. Orientation

1. Quoted in Belfrage, *Freedom Summer,* 16.

2. Claude Sitton, "Students Warned on Southern Law," *New York Times,* June 19, 1964. The same article notes the presence of seventy-five full-time workers from SNCC and similar organizations involved in the project.

3. McAdam, *Freedom Summer,* 66.

4. Quoted in Nicolaus Mills, *Like a Holy Crusade* (Chicago: Ivan R. Dee, 1992), 88. For more information about Bob Moses, see Eric Burner, *And Gently He Shall Lead Them: Robert Parris Moses and Civil Rights in Mississippi* (New York: New York University Press, 1994), and Laura Visser-Maessen, "A *Lot* of Leaders? Robert Parris Moses, SNCC, and Leadership in the Production of Social Change during the American Civil Rights Movement, 1960–1965," Ph.D. diss., University of Leiden, 2013.

5. Charles (Chips) Sowerwine to Friends and Helpmates, letter, July 20, 1964, Charles (Chips) Sowerwine Papers, McCain Library and Archives, USM, copy in LAT's files.

6. Elizabeth Sutherland, ed., *Letters from Mississippi* (New York: McGraw Hill, 1965), 15; reprinted as Elizabeth Martinez, ed., *Letters from Mississippi: Reports from Civil Rights Volunteers & Poetry of the 1964 Freedom Summer* (Brookline, Mass.: Zephyr Press, 2007).

7. Nancy Schieffelin, interviewed by LAT, Jackson Heights, N.Y., April 5–6, 2007.

8. Quoted in Belfrage, *Freedom Summer,* 16.

9. Quoted in Robert W. Beyers, "September 1964, Why They Went South," cited in Brad Herzog, "100 Years Our Back Pages," *Cornell Alumni Magazine,* July 1968; see also Seth Cagin and Philip Dray, *We Are Not Afraid: The Story of Goodman, Schwerner, and Chaney and the Civil Rights Campaign for Mississippi* (New York: Macmillan, 1988), 30.

10. Marian Wright Edelman to LAT, email, April 8, 2013. The other black Mississippi lawyers were Jack Young and Carsie Hall. Edelman became the fourth when she passed the Mississippi bar in 1965.

11. Quoted in "Civil Rights: The Invaders," *Newsweek*, June 29, 1964.

12. Quoted in Claude Sitton, "Students Briefed on Peril in South," *New York Times*, June 17, 1964; see also Milton Viorst, *Fire in the Streets: America in the 1960's* (New York: Simon & Schuster, 1979), 257.

13. Vincent Harding, "Freedom Summer Orientation Briefing," Mississippi Summer Project orientation, June 1964, Western College for Women, Oxford, Ohio, available at the CRMV website, http://www.crmvet.org/docs/harding.htm.

14. Quoted in Claude Sitton, "Novices Irk 'Pros' in Rights Course," *New York Times*, June 18, 1964; see also Dittmer, *Local People*, 243.

15. Freedom Walk script, Miami University, Oxford, Ohio; Ann Elizabeth Armstrong to LAT, email, October 26, 2009. See also Jane Adams's notes from Freedom Summer Training, June 17–26, 1964, Mississippi Freedom Summer Digital Collection, Miami University, Oxford, Ohio, and Sutherland, *Letters from Mississippi*, 28.

16. Dorie Ladner, conversation with LAT, Washington, D.C., November 17, 2009.

17. Sitton, "Students Briefed on Peril in South."

18. Sutherland, *Letters from Mississippi*, 18.

19. Carmichael and Thelwell, *Ready for Revolution*, 301. The description was later amended to "a band of brothers and sisters."

20. Gene Roberts and Hank Klibanoff, *The Race Beat: The Press, the Civil Rights Struggle, and the Awakening of a Nation* (New York: Knopf, 2006), 259.

21. Sutherland, *Letters from Mississippi*, 12.

7. June 21, 1964

1. Sutherland, *Letters from Mississippi*, 27.

2. The quoted phrases are from the *Jackson Clarion-Ledger*, June 28, 1964; see also Shirley Tucker, *Mississippi from Within* (New York: Arco, 1965), 32–33.

3. Quoted in Bob Herbert, "Changing the World," *New York Times*, October 27, 2009; search "Andrew Goodman postcard" on the Internet to see the image.

4. Barbara Mutnick, interviewed by LAT, Jackson Heights, N.Y., April 5–6, 2007.

5. "William Alexander Percy," *Mississippi Writers and Musicians*, at http://mswritersandmusicians.com/writers/william-percy.html.

6. Curtis Wilkie, *Dixie: A Personal Odyssey through Events That Shaped the Modern South* (New York: Simon & Schuster, 2001), 58, 187.

7. Hodding Carter III, interviewed by LAT, Chapel Hill, N.C., March 30, 2009.

8. Charles Moore, oral history interview, June 20, 1977, Oral History Project: Greenville and Vicinity, William Alexander Percy Memorial Library, Greenville, Miss., and MDAH.

9. Charles L. Moore, "Civil Rights of the Sixties," Greenville History Museum, Greenville, Miss.

10. Matthew Page, interviewed by LAT, Greenville, Miss., March 25, 2008.

11. Sutherland, *Letters from Mississippi*, 25; see also Taylor Branch, *Pillar of Fire: America in the King Years 1963–65* (New York: Simon & Schuster, 1998), 361.

12. Schieffelin interview, LAT.

8. Living as a Volunteer in Mississippi, 1964

1. Charles E. Cobb Jr., interviewed by LAT, Tougaloo, Miss., March 21, 2013.

2. John Frazier, oral history interview, March 21, 2004, CRDP.

3. James E. Carter, oral history interview, August 3, 1978, Oral History Project: Greenville.

4. "Leslie T. Turner to The Powers That Be," weekly report, July 10, 1964, Jackson, Miss., Box 38, James Forman Papers, Manuscript Division, Library of Congress (LOC), Washington, D.C.

5. Week's activities report, July 12, 1964, signed Morton Thomas, Box 38, Forman Papers.

6. Morton Thomas, interviewed by LAT, Cambridge, Mass., August 10, 2009.

7. Ibid.; COFO, "Mississippi Summer Project Running Summary of Incidents," June 16–August 26, 1964, copy in LAT's files and at http://www.crmvet.org/docs/64_fs_incidents.pdf.

8. Louis Grant to Charles [Cobb], memo, July 9, 1964, Box 38, Forman Papers.

9. Sutherland, *Letters from Mississippi*, 79; Mutnick interview. Barbara Mutnick has identified the anonymous letter as hers.

10. "Federal building demonstration. No harassment," report from Greenville, Miss., June 25, 1964, in COFO, "Running Summary of Incidents."

11. Quoted in "COFO Denies Link with MSU," *Delta Democrat-Times,*

June 30, 1964. For a study of the editorials and news articles by Hodding Carter III and the *Delta Democrat-Times* covering the Mississippi Summer Project in 1964, see Susan Weill, "The Press Challenge of Social Responsibility in Times of Political Upheaval: Hodding Carter III and the *Delta Democrat-Times* Respond to Freedom Summer in 1964," *Journal of Mississippi History* 72, no. 4 (2010): 367–400.

12. Mutnick interview, LAT.

13. Carmichael and Thelwell, *Ready for Revolution*, 308.

14. Sara Evans, *Personal Politics: The Roots of Women's Liberation in the Civil Rights Movement* (New York: Vintage, 1980), 87.

15. Joyce Ladner called Evans's book "totally rubbish"; Evans did not interview the people who could have told her what really happened, so her use of the statement was both "pathetic" and "ridiculous," said Ladner when she participated in the 1988 SNCC reunion conference (edited transcript in Cheryl Lynn Greenberg, ed., *A Circle of Trust: Remembering SNCC* [New Brunswick, N.J.: Rutgers University Press, 1998], 144; see also Joyce Ladner, "Remembrance of Women in the Freedom Movement, 1988," at the CRMV website, http://www.crmvet.org/nars/ladnerj.htm).

16. King, *Freedom Song*, 452.

17. Joyce Ladner, edited transcript in Greenberg, ed., *Circle of Trust*, 145.

18. Carmichael and Thelwell, *Ready for Revolution*, 431–35.

19. Mills, *Like a Holy Crusade*, 86; McAdam, *Freedom Summer*, 75, 77 (three hundred Freedom School teachers and community center volunteers attended the second week of orientation; additional volunteers continued arriving for a brief orientation in Jackson, with an estimate that "probably never more than 600 or so volunteers [were] in the state at any time"). The frequently stated number of 1,000 volunteers is not the number of college-age volunteers but includes professionals who spent far less than two months on the Mississippi Summer Project.

20. Quoted in "Roselle Woman in Mississippi; Mother 'Worried' but Proud," *Elizabeth Daily Journal*, June 25, 1964.

21. Rev. Russell E. Swanson, Faith Lutheran Church, Murray Hill, N.J., to LAT, letter, August 10, 1964.

22. Sutherland, *Letters from Mississippi*, 18.

23. Bern Keating, "Youth Corps in Mississippi," *New York Times Sunday Magazine*, July 5, 1964.

24. Mrs. Lamar Britton, oral history interview, February 6, 1977, Oral History Project: Greenville.

25. Tracy Sugarman, *Stranger at the Gates: A Summer in Mississippi* (New York: Hill and Wang, 1966), 93.

26. Alvin Pouissant, "The Stresses of the White Female Worker in the Civil Rights Movement in the South," May 13, 1966, at the CRMV website, http://www.crmvet.org/docs/poussaint.pdf.

27. "'African Queen' Complex," *Newsweek,* May 23, 1966.

28. King, *Freedom Song,* 215.

29. Mary Aickin Rothschild, *A Case of Black and White: Northern Volunteers and Southern Freedom Summers, 1964–1965* (Westport, Conn.: Greenwood Press, 1982), 58; COFO, "Mississippi Summer Project Running Summary of Incidents." Other than the June 25, 1964, demonstration, only one Greenville incident was reported on June 30: on June 19, a black porter at the Greenville General Hospital was beaten by a policeman there and charged with resisting arrest and disturbing the peace.

30. Polly Wynn Allen to LAT, email, February 17, 2014. The NCC later selected Greenville for headquarters of the Delta Ministry because of its relatively progressive white civic culture and the groundwork laid in the white community during the summer.

31. Quoted in King, *Freedom Song,* 8. For an understanding of how SNCC aspired to the Beloved Community and implemented the philosophy of nonviolence, see Diane Nash, "The Beloved Community & Philosophy of Nonviolence," in Greenberg, ed., *A Circle of Trust,* 18–23, and at the CRMV website, http://www.crmvet.org/nars/nsah88.htm. See also Charles Marsh, *The Beloved Community: How Faith Shapes Social Justice, from the Civil Rights Movement to Today* (New York: Basic Books, 2005).

32. Quoted in William McCord, *Mississippi: The Long, Hot Summer* (New York: Norton, 1965), 61–62.

33. King Center, "The King Philosophy," at http://www.thekingcenter .org/king-philosophy#sub4, accessed May 31, 2013. For more information about Martin Luther King Jr.'s concept of the Beloved Community, see his book *Stride toward Freedom: The Montgomery Story* (New York: HarperSanFrancisco, 1958), 101–7.

34. Martin Luther King Jr., "The Negro Is Part of That Huge Community Who Seek New Freedom in Every Area of Life," *Challenge,* February 1, 1959, available at http://mlk-kpp01.stanford.edu/index.php/ encyclopedia/documentsentry/the_negro_is_part_of_that_huge_community_ who_seek_new_freedom_in_every_area.

35. Marsh, *The Beloved Community,* 104.

36. In this book, I don't write about limitations because of my gender. I didn't have experiences dealing with men that made me angry, resentful, or disappointed that I was being treated differently because I was a girl. I was among the independent-minded people in the movement, participating on an

equal basis in confronting the hostility of the white racist society. Joyce Ladner has explained her thinking as follows: "It was within SNCC that this beloved community operated for a while, and it was within that context that I thought I was equal. I thought I was a full participant. Because all of us came with a stronger sense of our own identity, a stronger sense of purpose, I believe. Most of us did" (edited transcript in Greenberg, ed., *A Circle of Trust*, 144).

37. Quoted in Howell Raines, *My Soul Is Rested: The Story of the Civil Rights Movement in the Deep South* (New York: Penguin, 1977), 247.

38. Senator Clifford Case to LAT, letter, July 21, 1964, LAT's files.

39. Senator Clifford Case to Carl M. Anderson, letter, July 21, 1964, LAT's files.

40. Senator Harrison Williams to LAT, letter, July 23, 1964, LAT's files.

41. Judy Collins, *Singing Lessons: A Memoir of Love, Loss, Hope, and Healing* (New York: Pocket Books, 1998), 129.

42. Ibid.

43. Quoted in Judy Collins, *Sweet Judy Blue Eyes: My Life in Music* (New York: Crown Archetype, 2011), 162.

44. Vail interview, 2008, LAT.

45. Barbara Mutnick to her parents, letter, n.d., Folder 11, Box 1, Jim Kates Papers, McCain Library and Archives, USM.

46. Vail interview, 2008, LAT.

47. Mutnick interview, LAT.

48. Barbara Mutnick to her parents, letter, n.d.

9. My New Politics

1. Quoted in Zinn, *SNCC*, 217.

2. Statistics from the *Congressional Quarterly*, week ending July 5, 1963, p. 1091, in "Negro Voters by District and County," n.d., copy in LAT's files; see also Folder 9, Box 3, Michael J. Miller Civil Rights Collection, M368, McCain Library and Archives, USM.

3. Rev. D. R. Royal of Friendship Baptist was an early supporter of civil rights who hosted Medgar Evers as a friend of the family when he came to Greenville. The Royals invited Virginia Steele, an older professional volunteer who was the library coordinator for the state's community centers, to stay at their home for the summer. She exchanged visits with Mrs. Lilly B. Royal after becoming good friends over the summer; the Royals' son told me they were "so close" (William M. Royal, telephone interview by LAT, April 9, 2014; see also Martinez, *Letters from Mississippi*, 127, 368).

4. Both Chapple and Davis quoted in David Halberstam, "Negroes Dispute Voter Drive Plan," *New York Times*, June 28, 1964.

5. James Carter interview, Oral History Project: Greenville.

6. Charles Cobb Jr., "Empowering Communities," *Brookings Review* 20, no. 4 (2002): 29.

7. Quoted in "First Negro Group Applies for Registration Test Here," *Delta Democrat-Times,* July 8, 1964.

8. Robert P. Moses, "Constitutional Property v. Constitutional People," in Theresa Perry, Robert P. Moses, Joan T. Wynne, Ernesto Cortes Jr., and Lisa Delpit, eds., *Quality Education as a Constitutional Right: Creating a Grassroots Movement to Transform Public Schools* (Boston: Beacon Press, 2010), 83.

9. Quoted in "Summer Campaign Registers 30," *Delta Democrat-Times,* July 15, 1964.

10. Ekwueme Michael Thelwell, interviewed by LAT, Amherst, Mass., August 11, 2009.

11. Casey Hayden, "Fields of Blue," in Curry et al., *Deep in Our Hearts,* 356.

12. COFO, "Mississippi: How Negro Democrats Fared," MFDP Papers, Reel 1, Item 2, General Papers 1963–1965, available in Reel 2646 at MDAH.

13. COFO, "Mississippi: How Negro Democrats Fared," Part II, MFDP Papers, Reel 1, Item 2, General Papers 1963–1965, available in Reel 2646 at MDAH.

14. "Freedom Democrats Challenge Old Order Politics," *Mississippi Free Press,* August 1, 1964.

15. Bob Moses to All Field Staff and Voter Registration Volunteers, memo, July 19, 1964, "re: High degree of probability that we will not be prepared for the National Democratic Convention," copy in LAT's files.

16. "Freedom Registration," document dated September 26, 1964 [*sic*], in "MFDP Challenge 1965," Box 4, Betty Garman SNCC Files 1961–66 Mississippi, Schomburg Center; see also Hayden, "Fields of Blue," 357–58. Only 63,000 signed the Freedom Registrations (Joseph L. Rauh Jr., Counsel, Mississippi Freedom Democratic Party, before the Credentials Committee of the Democratic National Convention, August 22, 1964, in Susie Erenrich, ed., *Freedom Is a Constant Struggle: An Anthology of the Mississippi Civil Rights Movement* [Montgomery, Ala.: Black Belt Press, 1999], 309).

17. Bernadine Young, interviewed by LAT, Greenville, Miss., March 20, 2009.

18. Quoted in "Freedom Democratic Party Given Boost," *Mississippi Free Press,* July 25, 1964.

19. King, *The Autobiography of Martin Luther King, Jr.,* 250.

20. Garrow, *Bearing the Cross,* 342.

21. Annelle Ponder to R. Hunter Morey, letter, October 8, 1963, Folder 4, Box 3, R. Hunter Morey Papers, MSS 522, WHS.

22. COFO, *Handbook for Precinct Organization*, Folder 8, Box 3, Morey Papers.

23. Foster Davis, "Confusion, Bickering Mark FDP Convention," *Delta Democrat-Times*, August 1, 1964.

24. I mention Dorothy Jones and Edna Moreton as only two women activists, in addition to my hosts, because I remember them specifically. Other local black women who were leaders in the civil rights movement in Greenville were Thelma Barnes, hired as staff secretary by the Delta Ministry when its headquarters office opened on September 1, 1964, and Bernadine Young, who worked in Head Start after she moved back to Greenville. The highly capable Thelma Barnes quickly became part of the program staff of the Delta Ministry, ran for political office, and continued active in race-related work within the Methodist Church after the decline of the Delta Ministry in 1974 (see Findlay, *Church People in the Struggle*, 111, 118, 119, 129, 155; Polly Greenberg, *The Devil Has Slippery Shoes* [Washington, D.C.: Youth Policy Institute, 1990], 726–27, 774; and Thelma Barnes, interviewed by LAT, Greenville, Miss., March 29, 2010). In June 1963, Thelma Barnes served as secretary of a new organization formed to represent blacks in response to a call from the Greenville City Council for a biracial meeting in the wake of integration demands by the Greenville Student Movement chaired by Jacob Allen Byas ("Greenville City Council Asks for Bi-racial Meeting," *Mississippi Free Press*, June 1, 1962). Bernadine Young was a member of the Washington County Employment Committee formed in the fall of 1964 to end discrimination in hiring women by Greenville's largest factory, Greenville Mill, and led three months of picketing against the mill (Mark Newman, *Divine Agitators: The Delta Ministry and Civil Rights in Mississippi* [Athens: University of Georgia Press, 2004], 91–93; Bruce Hilton, *The Delta Ministry* [London: MacMillan, 1969], 49–53). She started her career as a community activist in 1964 to end discrimination against women of color and began work in Head Start in 1965, serving on the board of directors of the Herbert Lee Community Center. In 1983, she was elected the first black Justice Court judge of Washington County and went to the Democratic National Convention as a delegate in 1976 (Bernadine Young, interviewed by LAT, Greenville, Miss., March 28, 2010, and March 18, 2012; obituary, *Delta Democrat-Times*, April 18, 2014).

25. William L. Higgs, *Mississippi Political Handbook*, April 1962, 12, Folder 6, Box 2, Miller Civil Rights Collection.

26. Ed King to LAT, email, June 3, 2013.

27. *Brief Submitted by the Mississippi Freedom Democratic Party for the Consideration of the Democratic National Committee, Credentials Committee of the Democratic National Convention, Delegates to the Democratic National Convention,* copy in LAT's files and at the CRMV website, http://www.crmvet.org/docs/6408_mfdp_brief.pdf; hereafter *MFDP Brief.*

28. *Student Voice,* August 19, 1964; Carson, *In Struggle,* 123; Kelso Sturgeon, "'Freedom Party' Makes Plans for Challenge at Convention," *Jackson Daily News,* August 7, 1964.

29. Joel Bernard to Mrs. Louise de Seyes, aerogramme, August 15, 1964, Folder 1, Box 1, Jacqueline Bernard Papers, MSS 230, WHS, at http://cdm15932.contentdm.oclc.org/cdm/ref/collection/p15932c0112/id/3559.

30. Joseph Rauh, interviewed by Anne Romaine, June 1967, Folder 63, Subseries 2.1.2, MFDP, 1964–1990s, Series 2, Professional Materials, 1964–1994, Anne Romaine Papers 1935–1995, Wilson Library, University of North Carolina (UNC), Chapel Hill.

31. Joseph Rauh, on the panel "MFDP and the Atlantic City Convention," Mississippi Summer Reviewed, November 1, 1979, Tougaloo College, transcript at MDAH.

32. Quoted in Ernest B. Furgurson, "Convention Fight Seen," *Baltimore Sun,* August 7, 1964.

33. Joseph L. Rauh Jr., Oral History Interview III by Paige Mulhollan, August 8, 1969, transcript, Oral History Collection, LBJL, at http://web1.millercenter.org/poh/transcripts/rauh_joseph_1969_0808.pdf; Joseph Rauh, interview by Blackside, Inc., May 19, 1986, for *Eyes on the Prize: America's Civil Rights Years (1954–1965)* (Blackside, 1987–1990), all transcripts at Film and Media Archive, Henry Hampton Collection, Washington University Libraries, St. Louis, Mo.

34. Quoted in Richard Corrigan, "Freedom Slate Picked in Jackson," *Washington Post,* August 7, 1964.

35. Quoted in Dittmer, *Local People,* 281–82; see also Paul Good, *The Trouble I've Seen: White Journalist/Black Movement* (Washington, D.C.: Howard University Press, 1975), 170.

36. Ella Baker, keynote address, MFDP State Convention, August 6, 1964, transcription by Daphne Chamberlain from ABC television coverage, May 22, 2012, copy in LAT's files; see also Barbara Ransby, *Ella Baker & the Black Freedom Movement: A Radical Democratic Vision* (Chapel Hill: University of North Carolina Press, 2003), 335.

37. Baker, keynote address.

38. Higgs, *Mississippi Political Handbook,* 13.

39. Quoted in John Dittmer, "The Transformation of the Mississippi Movement, 1964–68: The Rise and Fall of the Freedom Democratic Party," in W. Marvin Dulaney and Kathleen Underwood, eds., *Essays on the American Civil Rights Movement* (College Station: Texas A&M University Press, 1993), 14, citing Clayborne Carson's interview of Bob Moses, Cambridge, Mass., March 29, 1983.

40. Ibid., 15.

41. Leslie McLemore, interviewed by LAT, Jackson, Miss., March 22, 2007.

42. Charles McLaurin, conversation with LAT, Jackson, Miss., March 23, 2012.

43. *Student Voice,* August 19, 1964.

44. Ed King to LAT, email, June 3, 2013.

45. Report from Greenville Office, "re: Medical Situation in Issaquena County," n.d., copy in LAT's files.

46. "We Must All Pray," letter to the editor, *Delta Democrat-Times,* August 9, 1964.

47. "Memorial Set for Three CR Workers," *Delta Democrat-Times,* August 10, 1964.

48. Sellers, *River of No Return,* 103–6; Cleveland Sellers, "Killed: Wayne Yancey," n.d., at the CRMV website, http://www.crmvet.org/mem/sncc50_wayne-yancy.pdf, accessed May 5, 2014.

10. Early Work on the Convention Challenge

1. Edited transcript in Greenberg, ed., *A Circle of Trust,* 21–22, and at the CRMV website, http://www.crmvet.org/nars/nash88.htm.

2. Minutes: COFO Executive Committee Meeting, July 10, 1964, Folder 1, "Administrative and Official Records and Reports," Box 3, Morey Papers.

3. Moses interview, LAT.

4. Ed King, interviewed by Anne Romaine, August 1966, Folder 61, Romaine Papers, UNC; for more information about the July 23, 1964, meeting at Tougaloo, see D'Emilio, *Lost Prophet,* 381–82, and Garrow, *Bearing the Cross,* 341–42.

5. Joseph L. Rauh Jr. to Bob Moses, letter, June 30, 1964, MFDP Papers, Reel 1, Item 1, Correspondence 1964–1965, available in Reel 2646 at MDAH.

6. Miles Jaffe, telephone interview by LAT, June 7, 2013.

7. Eleanor Holmes Norton, interviewed by LAT, Washington, D.C., April 9, 2013.

8. Ibid.; see also Joan Steinau Lester, *Fire in My Soul: The Life of Eleanor Holmes Norton* (New York: Atria Books, 2003), 122.

9. Aaron Henry to John M. Bailey, letter, July 17, 1964, "DNC—Credentials 1964—Mississippi," DNC Series II, Box 102.

10. *MFDP Brief,* 17, 20, 68–69.

11. Ibid., 35.

12. Ibid., 36–61.

13. Ed King, personal papers, Jackson, Miss.

14. Quoted in David Kraslow, "Presidential Neutrality Urged on Mississippi," *Los Angeles Times,* August 19, 1964.

15. Rauh interview, Mulhollan.

16. *MFDP Brief,* 60–61.

17. Ibid., app. C, 72–73.

18. Moses interview, LAT.

19. "Legal Department June–Oct 1964," Folder 117, Box 69, UAW President's Office, Walter P. Reuther Collection, Archives of Labor and Urban Affairs, Wayne State University, Detroit, Mich.

20. "Insurgents Map Mississippi Plan," *New York Times,* July 9, 1964, also available at the CRMV website, http://www.crmvet.org/docs/64_mfdp_resolutions.pdf. In February 1964, the California Democratic Council resolution used the name "Mississippi Freedom Democratic Party" for the first time (Walter Tillow, interviewed by Anne Romaine, September 1, 1966, Folder 57, Romaine Papers, UNC).

21. SNCC organizers traveled and spoke to delegates in the states, but Rauh said SNCC was "not able to get political commitments . . . people who're that far left in attitude cannot get commitments out of politicians" (Rauh interview, Romaine).

22. Walter Tillow, telephone interview by LAT, September 21, 2010.

23. Ella Baker, interviewed by Anne Romaine, March 25, 1967, Folder 65, Romaine Papers, UNC.

24. Rauh interview, Romaine; see also Dittmer, *Local People,* 289.

25. Pinkey Hall, oral history interview, December 13, 1995, CRDP.

26. Barney Frank, interviewed by Emily Stoper, November 11, 1966, for Emily Stoper, *The Student Nonviolent Coordinating Committee: The Growth of Radicalism in a Civil Rights Organization* (Brooklyn, N.Y.: Carlson, 1989), 281.

27. Moses interview, Carson, copy in LAT's files courtesy of Carson.

28. Ella Baker, interviewed by Emily Stoper, December 27, 1966, for Stoper, *The Student Nonviolent Coordinating Committee,* 271; see also Ransby, *Ella Baker,* 336.

29. Baker interview, Romaine.

30. Ed King interview, Romaine.

31. Frank interview, Stoper.

32. Cobb interview, LAT; Julian Bond, interviewed by LAT, Washington, D.C., January 26, 2009. Bond also said, "I didn't think it would work . . . I thought more would result than just this offer of two seats" (quoted in Fred Powledge, *Free At Last? The Civil Rights Movement and the People Who Made It* [Boston: Little, Brown, 1991], 597). Bond has also described what followed his optimism about the Challenge: "The FDP failure in Atlantic City was a crushing blow . . . . *I* personally had thought the convention would seat them. This was probably naïve, but I was very disappointed" (Julian Bond, interviewed by Emily Stoper, n.d., for Stoper, *The Student Nonviolent Coordinating Committee*, 275–80).

33. Judy Richardson, interviewed by LAT, Cambridge, Mass., August 10, 2009.

34. Victoria Gray Adams, interviewed for *Eyes on the Prize*, November 9, 1985.

35. "Biographical Sketches of Delegates to National Convention of the Democratic Party—1964," "Politics: Mississippi Freedom Democratic Party Credentials Controversy," Box 2, Jeri M. Joseph Papers, Minnesota Historical Society (MHS), St. Paul; see also Student Nonviolent Coordinating Committee files, 1959–1973, microfilm, Manuscript Room, LOC.

36. Hartman Turnbow, oral history interview, August 16, 1967, CRDP. For more information on Turnbow, see Sue [Lorenzi] Sojourner, with Cheryl Reitan, *Thunder of Freedom: Black Leadership and the Transformation of 1960s Mississippi* (Lexington: University Press of Kentucky, 2013), 18, 31–33, and Taylor Branch, *Parting the Waters: America in the King Years 1954–63* (New York: Simon & Schuster, 1988), 781–82.

37. For Annie Devine's experience, see Vicki L. Crawford, "Beyond the Human Self: Grassroots Activists in the Mississippi Civil Rights Movement," in Vicki L. Crawford, Jacqueline Anne Rouse, and Barbara Woods, eds., *Women in the Civil Rights Movement: Trailblazers & Torchbearers 1941–1965* (Bloomington: Indiana University Press, 1993), 19.

38. Annie Devine, interviewed by Anne Romaine and Howard Romaine, November 22, 1966, Folder 59, Romaine Papers, UNC.

39. Quoted in Rev. Barbara Devine Russell, "Annie Devine," in Joan H. Sadoff, ed., *Pieces from the Past: Voices of Heroic Women in Civil Rights* (n.p.: Tasora, 2011), 104. This profile by family members does not report incidents of harassment and states that Annie Devine was "not interested in going public with any of the experiences she had during the civil rights movement. She did not want to profit from the work she did" (105).

40. Robert Miles, interview, n.d., KZSU Project South Interviews (SC0066), Department of Special Collections and University Archives, Stanford University Libraries, Stanford, Calif.

41. Quoted in "Freedom Party Banned in Mississippi," *Times Picayune,* August 13, 1964; see also Kenneth Toler, "State Delegates Plan Retaliation," *Memphis Commercial Appeal,* August 19, 1964. The injunction was modified to allow the delegates to go to Atlantic City.

42. Lawrence Guyot, interviewed by LAT, Washington, D.C., October 27, 2011.

43. Watkins interview, CRDP.

44. Ivanhoe Donaldson, interviewed by LAT, Washington, D.C., June 15, 2010; James Forman, *The Making of Black Revolutionaries* (New York: Macmillan, 1972), 387.

45. Union Temple Baptist Church, with an established congregation dating from 1907 and rebuilt in 1959 after a fire, has been recognized for its leadership in the civil rights movement. Reverend Matthew E. Neil, who served as pastor during 1943–1988, generously made the church and its meeting rooms available to the MFDP (Union Baptist Temple, "Church History," at http://www.ubtnet.org/history.html). In April 2011, the Atlantic City branch of the NAACP honored Union Temple Baptist with a church leadership award, noting its participation in the movement and the fact that churchgoers worked to accommodate black delegates shut out of hotel rooms during the 1964 Democratic National Convention (Erik Ortiz, "NAACP Honors Relationship with Atlantic City Churches, Members of Community," *Press of Atlantic City,* April 24, 2010, at http://www .pressofatlanticcity.com/news/pressatlantic_city/naacp-honors-relationship-with-atlantic-city-churches-members-of-community/article_d139ec9a-4ff1-11df-924d-001cc4c03286.html).

46. "Verna [*sic*] Canson Notes," Folder 1, Box 37, Kotz Papers, M2008-043; hereafter "Canson Notes." Canson and Henry met at the Gem Hotel, but the FBI reported that he was staying at the Breakers Hotel (Folder 6, Box 17, Kotz Papers).

11. Lyndon Johnson

1. LBJ and Walter Reuther, TC, August 9, 1964, 9:51 a.m., Citation 4840, Recordings and Transcripts of Conversations and Meetings (RTCM), LBJL.

2. Rauh interview, Romaine.

3. Allen Fisher to LAT, email, March 5, 2010; see also the introduction, "Recordings of Telephone Conversations, White House Series," October 11,

1996, at http://www.lbjlib.utexas.edu/johnson/archives.hom/Dictabelt .hom/dictaintro.asp, for a fuller explanation of the timing of release of the Johnson taped telephone conversations.

4. Letter to David Wolf, undated and unsigned on Oberlin College, Department of Government, stationary, enclosed in David Wolf to Mr. Rauh, note identifying the enclosure as being from Carey McWilliams, Box 86, Joseph L. Rauh Jr. Papers, Manuscript Division, LOC. McWilliams was editor of *The Nation* from 1955 to 1975. Wolf was a COFO volunteer in Jackson, Mississippi.

5. Michael E. Parrish, *Citizen Rauh: An American Liberal's Life in Law and Politics* (Ann Arbor: University of Michigan Press, 2010), 167; Joseph L. Rauh Jr. to Philip K. [*sic*] O'Donnell, White House, letter, July 20, 1964, enclosing "draft letter as requested" from John Bailey to Bidwell Adam, Box 86, Rauh Papers.

6. Quoted in John Herbers, "Misssissippi Democrats Avoid Goldwater Stand," *New York Times,* July 29, 1964; see also Charles M. Hills, "State Democrats Delay Decisions on Candidate," *Jackson Clarion-Ledger,* July 29, 1964.

7. LBJ and Kenneth O'Donnell, TC, August 14, 1964, 3:29 p.m., Citation 4925, RTCM; LBJ and Hubert Humphrey, TC, August 14, 1964, 8:25 p.m., Citation 4938, RTCM.

8. "Resolutions Passed at the 1964 State Convention of the Mississippi Democratic Party of the State of Mississippi," Folder 4, "MFDP and Election Challenges 1964–65," Box 4, Morey Papers; *MFDP Brief,* 11.

9. Claude Sitton, "Democrats Face Mississippi Split," *New York Times,* July 20, 1964.

10. James Baggus, "State's Democrats Keep Silent Guard," *Jackson Clarion-Ledger,* July 30, 1964, quoting Bidwell Adam, chairman of the Mississippi Democratic Party Executive Committee.

11. Robert S. Allen and Paul Scott, "Negroes Oppose Demo Delegates," *Topeka Daily Capital,* July 20, 1964.

12. D'Emilio, *Lost Prophet,* 386.

13. Viorst, *Fire in the Streets,* 254.

14. Harold Leventhal to John Bailey and Governor Lawrence, memo, August 5, 1964, "Democratic National Committee, 1963–65," Box 32, Harold Leventhal Papers, Manuscript Division, LOC.

15. Jack Steele, "Problem of Miss. Delegates in LBJ's Lap," *Washington Daily News,* July 22, 1964.

16. LBJ and John Connolly, TC, July 22, 1964, 5:31 p.m., Citations 4320, 4321, 4322, 4323, RTCM.

17. Rauh interview, Romaine.

18. LBJ and Walter Reuther, TC, August 9, 1964, 8:51 a.m., Citation 4840, RTCM; see also Michael R. Beschloss, ed., *Taking Charge: The Johnson White House Tapes, 1963–1964* (New York: Simon & Schuster, 2007), 510–11, 516.

19. Godfrey Sperling Jr., "Negro Delegation Vexes Democrats," *Christian Science Monitor,* August 23, 1964.

20. Quoted in Nicholas Lemann, *The Promised Land: The Great Black Migration and How It Changed America* (New York: Knopf, 1991), 183.

21. Timothy N. Thurber, *The Politics of Equality: Hubert H. Humphrey and the African American Freedom Struggle* (New York: Columbia University Press, 1999), 150; see also Godfrey Hodgson, *America in Our Time: From World War II to Nixon—What Happened and Why* (New York: Vintage Books, 1976), 214.

22. Quoted in "It's LBJ Week in Atlantic City," *Newsweek,* August 31, 1964.

23. John Stewart, interviewed by Anne Romaine, April 1967, Folder 64, Romaine Papers, UNC.

24. James Rowe to the President, memo, July 21, 1964, attached to James Rowe to Jack Valenti, memo, July 21, 1964, "Gen HU 2/ST 24 7/18/64–8/9/64," White House Correspondence Files (WHCF), Box 38, LBJL; Valenti to the President, memo, July 22, 1964, attached to Karl F. Rolvaag to the President, letter, July 27, 1964, "Ex HU 2/ST 24 7/17/64–11/30/64," WHCF, Box 27.

25. Karl F. Rolvaag to Walter Jenkins, letter, July 27, 1964, attached to Jenkins to Rolvaag, letter, August 5, 1964, "Ex HU 2/ST 24 7/17/64–11/30/64," WHCF, Box 27.

26. Chalmers M. Roberts, "Democrats to Seat Regular Delegates," *Washington Post,* July 30, 1964; see also Watters and Cleghorn, *Climbing Jacob's Ladder,* 290, and Rauh interview, Romaine.

27. Jack Valenti, *A Very Human President* (New York: Norton, 1975), 201–3.

28. Rauh interview, Mulhollan.

29. Rauh interview, Romaine; Rauh interview, *Eyes on the Prize.*

30. Parrish, *Citizen Rauh,* 123; UAW International Executive Board Meetings Collection, Box 14, Reuther Collection.

31. Rauh interview in Henry Hampton and Steve Fayer, *Voices of Freedom: An Oral History of the Civil Rights Movement from the 1950s through the 1980s* (New York: Bantam Books 1990), 197.

32. Quoted in Todd Gitlin, *The Sixties: Years of Hope, Days of Rage* (New York: Bantam Books, 1987), 154.

33. Rauh, "MFDP and the Atlantic City Convention" panel, 30.

34. LBJ and Walter Reuther, TC, August 9, 1964, 8:51 a.m., Citation 4840, RTCM; see also Beschloss, ed., *Taking Charge*, 511.

35. LBJ and Walter Reuther, TC, August 9, 1964, 8:51 a.m., Citation 4840, RTCM.

36. Memorandum for the President, "re: Discussions with Joe Rauh on Mississippi 'Freedom Party,'" August 11, 1964, WHCF, PL 1/ST 24, "Seating Mississippi Delegation at Democratic Convention," Box 81, emphasis added.

37. Rauh interview, Mulhollan; Joseph L. Rauh Jr. to Leon M. Despres, letter, June 9, 1964, Rauh Papers.

38. Arthur Kinoy, *Rights on Trial: The Odyssey of a People's Lawyer* (Cambridge, Mass.: Harvard Univ. Press, 1983), 259; Joseph Rauh, interviewed by William H. Chafe, June 9, 1988, Allard Lowenstein Papers, UNC.

39. Moses interview, LAT.

40. Kinoy, *Rights on Trial*, 259.

41. Rauh interview, Chafe.

42. Memorandum for the President, "re: Discussions with Joe Rauh on Mississippi 'Freedom Party,'" August 11, 1964.

43. "Mississippi Rights Unit Gets Backing," *Baltimore Sun*, August 20, 1964; Kraslow, "Presidential Neutrality Urged on Mississippi"; see also Carson, *In Struggle*, 124, citing Rauh interview, Romaine.

44. Fred Dutton to Bill Moyers, memo, "re: Mississippi Delegation," August 10, 1964, "Gen PL 1/ST 24 11/22/63—8/21/64," WHCF, Box 81.

45. LBJ and Walter Reuther, TC, August 14, 1964, 3:53 p.m., Citation 4926, RTCM.

46. Roy Wilkins to NAACP Branch and Youth Group Presidents, memo, August 12, 1964, Box III A 230, NAACP Papers, Manuscript Division, LOC.

47. LBJ and Roy Wilkins, TC, August 15, 1964, 9:50 a.m., citation 4940, RTCM.

48. H. N. Bassett to Mr. Callahan, memo, January 29, 1975, Folder 8, "1964 DNC Inquiry FBI File," Box 17, Kotz Papers.

49. Cartha D. "Deke" DeLoach Oral History Interview I by Michael L. Gillette, January 11, 1991, transcript, LBJL, at http://www.lbjlib.utexas .edu/johnson/archives.hom/oralhistory.hom/DeLoach/Deloach1-san .PDF.

50. Robert Dallek, *Flawed Giant: Lyndon Johnson and His Times 1961–1973* (New York: Oxford University Press, 1998), 161; Harris Wofford, *Of*

Kennedys and Kings: Making Sense of the Sixties (Pittsburgh: University of Pittsburgh Press, 1992), 419.

51. DeLoach interview, Gillette.

52. LBJ and John Connally, TC, July 23, 1964, 5:31 p.m., Citation 4322, RTCM.

53. DeLoach interview, Gillette.

54. LBJ and James Eastland, TC, August 17, 1964, 12:13 p.m., Citation 4992, RTCM.

55. LBJ and Kenneth O'Donnell, TC, August 14, 1964, 3:29 p.m., Citation 4924, RTCM.

56. Ibid.

57. Ibid.

58. Ibid.

59. Rauh interview, Romaine.

60. "Report of the Subcommittee of the Credentials Committee," August 25, 1964, 2:30 p.m., Box 32, Leventhal Papers, emphasis added.

61. LBJ and James Eastland, TC, August 17, 1964, 12:13 p.m., Citation 4992, RTCM.

62. Ibid.

63. Quoted in David Kraslow, "Presidential Neutrality Urged on Mississippi," *Los Angeles Times,* August 19, 1964.

64. Quoted in Garrow, *Bearing the Cross,* 345–46.

65. Roy Wilkins, with Tom Matthews, *Standing Fast: The Autobiography of Roy Wilkins* (New York: Viking Penguin, 1984), 304.

66. Lee C. White to the President, memo, August 12, 1964, attached to [Lee C. White to the President], note, August 19, 1964, "Ex PL 1/ST 24 Seating Mississippi Delegation at Democratic Convention," WHCF, Box 81.

67. Lee C. White to the President, memo, "re: Conversation with Bayard Rustin," August 13, 1964, attached to [Lee C. White to the President], note, August 19, 1964.

68. Lee C. White to the President, memo, "re: Conversation with Martin Luther King," August 13, 1964, attached to [Lee C. White to the President], note, August 19, 1964.

69. Garrow, *Bearing the Cross,* 344–46; Schedule, the President's Appointments, Wednesday, August 19, 1964, President's Appointment File (Diary Backup), Box 8, LBJL.

70. Parrish, *Citizen Rauh,* 170–71.

71. Press Secretary's News Conference number 383, August 19, 1964, 4:10 p.m., transcript, "August 1964," White House Press Office Files, Box

22, LBJL; Robert E. Baker, "LBJ Gets Negro Warning," *Washington Post,* August 20, 1964.

72. Lee C. White to John Lewis, letter, August 20, 1964, "Ex HU 2/ST 24 7/17/64–11/30/64," WHCF, Box 27.

73. Harold Leventhal to John Bailey and Governor Lawrence, memo, August 17, 1964, "DNC—Credentials 1964—Mississippi," DNC Series II, Box 102.

74. Harold Leventhal to Governor Lawrence, August 19, 1964, "DNC—Credentials 1964—Mississippi," DNC Series II, Box 102; call for the 1964 Democratic National Convention, February 26, 1964, "DNC Credentials 1964—Mississippi," DNC Series II, Box 102.

75. Charles C. Diggs Jr. and others to the President, telegram, August 21, 1964, 12:42 p.m., attached to Lee C. White to Dear Congressman (with list of addressees), letter, August 26, 1964, "Gen PL 1/ST 24 8/26/64–9/13/64," WHCF, Box 81.

76. Rauh interview, Romaine.

12. One Woman in Atlantic City

1. Meeting of the Credentials Committee, Democratic National Convention, August 22, 1964, transcript, 43–44, "DNC—Credentials 1964—Credentials Committee, Atlantic City, N.J., August 22, 1964," DNC Series II, Box 102 (cited hereafter as "Credentials Committee hearing transcript").

2. LBJ and Walter Reuther, TC, August 21, 1964, 8:56 p.m., Citation 5112, RTCM.

3. Chalmers M. Roberts, "Convention Hassle Building Up," *Washington Post,* August 20, 1964.

4. Credentials Committee hearing transcript, 2–4.

5. *MFDP Brief,* 55.

6. "Mississippi Freedom Democratic Party before the Credentials Committee," in Erenrich, ed., *Freedom Is a Constant Struggle,* 309.

7. Credentials Committee hearing transcript, 20.

8. Ibid., 43–44.

9. Ibid., 39–44.

10. Mary McGrory, "Mississippi—Sound of Weeping," *Boston Globe,* August 24, 1964; Tillow interview, Romaine.

11. Quoted in Branch, *Pillar of Fire,* 461, citing *Jet,* September 3, 1964, 22–26.

12. Bob Moses, interviewed for *Eyes on the Prize,* May 19, 1986.

13. Fannie Lou Hamer, oral history interview, April 14, 1972, CRDP.

14. Viorst, *Fire in the Streets,* 263. Others have written that Fannie Lou Hamer's testimony "incensed" Johnson, who broke away from his meeting with the governors "to stage an impromptu press conference" (Nick Kotz, *Judgment Days: Lyndon Baines Johnson, Martin Luther King Jr., and the Laws That Changed America* [New York: Houghton Mifflin, 2005], 205); that Johnson ordered "a hastily called press conference" (Carson, *In Struggle,* 125); and that Johnson "hurriedly called a press conference" (Dittmer, *Local People,* 288). These accounts appear to have originated with Rauh, who said, "It was an awful coincidence that he had to *suddenly* go on the air that Saturday afternoon just in the middle of our presentation" (Rauh interview, Romaine, emphasis added).

15. White House Press Conference number 387, August 21, 1964, 4:25 p.m., White House Press Office, Records of White House Offices, LBJL.

16. President's Daily Diary, August 22, 1964, 3, LBJL, and at http://www.lbjlibrary.net/collections/daily-diary.html.

17. Press Conference number 388, August 22, 1964, 1:12 p.m. MDST, LBJL.

18. Lyndon B. Johnson, "Remarks to a Group of Democratic Governors," August 22, 1964, Item 536 in the *Public Papers of the Presidents* volumes for 1963–1964 at http://www.presidency.ucsb.edu/ws/index.php?pid=26461&st=&st1=.

19. Quoted in Branch, *Pillar of Fire,* 460, citing A/SC27f40, Southern Christian Leadership Conference Records, King Library and Archives, 617, 686.

20. Ibid.; see also King, *The Autobiography of Martin Luther King Jr.,* 253.

21. Morgan Louise Ginther, "From the Closed Society to the Realization of Freedom: The Mississippi Delegation Debate at the 1964 Democratic National Convention," Ph.D. diss., University of Memphis, 2011, 112.

22. *Brief of the Facts and Law (with Supporting Affidavits) Filed with the Committee on Credentials of the Democratic National Committee on Behalf of the Delegates of the Regular Democratic Party in the State of Mississippi,* 1, "Miss. Regular Demo. Party," DNC Series II, Box 102.

23. Ginther, "From the Closed Society," 102.

24. LBJ and Kenneth O'Donnell, TC, August 14, 1964, 3:24 p.m., Citation 4925, RTCM.

25. Credentials Committee hearing transcript, 76.

26. Ibid., 88.

27. Robert Kastenmeier, interviewed by Anne Romaine, August 23, 1967, Folder 72, Romaine Papers, UNC.

28. Theodore White, *The Making of the President 1964* (New York: Atheneum, 1965), 293.

29. Kastenmeier interview, Romaine.

30. Credentials Committee hearing transcript, 113–23; see also Rauh, "Mississippi Freedom Democratic Party, before the Credentials Committee."

31. Credentials Committee hearing transcript, 118, 121.

32. Ibid., 122, 123.

33. Walter F. Mondale, lecture at the symposium "Atlantic City Revisited: The Mississippi Freedom Democratic Party and the 1964 Democratic National Convention," which included a discussion panel, February 11, 2000, Hubert H. Humphrey Institute of Public Affairs, University of Minnesota, Minneapolis, copy in LAT's files courtesy of Walter Mondale, and at http://www.crmvet.org/comm/miller-mondale.htm. Mondale's lecture is cited hereafter as "Mondale lecture" and the discussion panel as "Mondale symposium."

34. Jere Nash and Andy Taggart, *Mississippi Politics* (Jackson: University Press of Mississippi, 2006), 26. These authors state that Johnson asked Humphrey to mediate the dispute when the Credentials Committee decision was postponed, but Humphrey was trying to influence the MFDP to settle as requested by Johnson at least as early as mid-August.

35. David Lawrence to Jeri Joseph, telegram, August 13, 1964, Box 2, Joseph Papers.

36. Rauh, panel, "MFDP and the Atlantic City Convention," 33.

37. Arthur I. Waskow, "Notes on the Democratic National Convention, Atlantic City, August, 1964," 11, "Democratic Party Convention, 1964 Notes," Folder 6, Box 6, Arthur Waskow Papers, MSS 5, WHS; Mendy Samstein, interviewed by Anne Romaine, September 1966, Folder 56, Romaine Papers, UNC, a complete final copy of which is filed as Mendy Samstein Interview, Anne Romaine Papers, SC 1069 M-2, WHS.

38. Waskow, "Notes," 11.

13. Sunday in Atlantic City

1. LBJ and Walter Jenkins, TC, August 23, 1964, 3:58 p.m., Citation 5137, RTCM.

2. LBJ and Walter Reuther, TC, August 17, 1964, 6:14 p.m., Citations 5003, 5004, RTCM.

3. *A Primer for Delegates to the Democratic National Convention Who Haven't Heard about the Mississippi Freedom Democratic Party*, 2, copy in LAT's files and at http://www.thekingcenter.org/archive/document/primer-delegates-democratic-national-convention.

4. Rauh interview, Romaine.

5. "Committee on Credentials," n.d., Box 12, Baker Papers.

6. Chana Kai Lee, *For Freedom's Sake: The Life of Fannie Lou Hamer* (Urbana: University of Illinois Press, 1999), 87.

7. Lester, *Fire in My Soul*, 124.

8. Joyce Ladner, conversations with LAT, Washington, D.C., November 8, 2001, and November 14, 2013.

9. Joyce Ladner, Keynote Speech, SNCC 50th Anniversary Conference, Raleigh, N.C., April 17, 2010.

10. Cobb interview, LAT.

11. Quoted in Branch, *Pillar of Fire*, 457; see also Forman, *The Making of Black Revolutionaries*, 387.

12. Samstein interview, Romaine; see also Lee, *For Freedom's Sake*, 87–88. In turn, Virna Canson thought Mendy Samstein was "suffering from battle fatigue." She saw and talked to Samstein "quite a bit" and described him as "a sensitive, sweet kind of boy, about 20 . . . [he] looks as if he should be a music, art or drama major at some very exclusive school someplace" ("Canson Notes").

13. LBJ and Walter Reuther, TC, August 21, 1964, 3:50 p.m., Citation 5099, RTCM.

14. E. W. Kenworthy, "Rival Delegations from Mississippi Bid for Seats at the Convention," *New York Times*, August 23, 1964.

15. Parrish, *Citizen Rauh*, 171; Tillow telephone interview, LAT.

16. Quotes from this meeting are in notes by Harold Leventhal, Box 32, Leventhal Papers.

17. Half-votes for the delegates and a full vote for each of the two national committee members would make up the total number of votes for the delegation. See Charles M. Hills, "State Demo Convention Opening in Uncertainty," *Jackson Clarion-Ledger*, July 28, 1964.

18. Rauh interview, Romaine.

19. Samstein interview, Romaine.

20. Joe Rauh, interviewed by Finlay Lewis, 1977, Box 1, Finlay Lewis Papers, MHS.

21. Rauh interview, Romaine.

22. Ibid. Rauh interview, Lewis; *Washington Post*, August 26, 1964; Michael Paul Sistrom, "'Authors of the Liberation': The Mississippi Freedom Democrats and the Redefinition of Politics," Ph.D. diss., University of North Carolina at Chapel Hill, 2002, 166; Waskow, "Notes," 14; document stating the "Wyoming compromise," "Ullman substitute," and "Green proposal," n.d., "Convention Credentials Committee: Mississippi Delegation," Box 56, Hubert H. Humphrey Papers, MHS. In Humphrey's papers, the

initial Johnson offer or "formula" became "the Wyoming compromise" or "the unity proposal."

23. Edith Green, Oral History Interview I by Janet Kerr-Tener, August 23, 1985, transcript, LBJL, and at http://web1.millercenter.org/poh/transcripts/green_edith_1985_0823.pdf. Green indicated in this interview that the votes would be divided *equally* among the delegations, but from other references the Green proposal is understood as dividing the votes *proportionately*—that is according to the number of delegates who would take the loyalty oath.

24. Green interview, Kerr-Tener; Tillow telephone interview, LAT; Rauh interview, Romaine.

25. Oregon caucus report signed by Bob Short, "Convention Credentials Committee: Mississippi Delegation," Box 56, Humphrey Papers; see also Tillow telephone interview, LAT.

26. Kastenmeier interview, Romaine.

27. Walter F. Mondale, *The Good Fight: A Life in Liberal Politics* (New York: Scribner, 2010), 25; Steven M. Gillon, *The Democrats' Dilemma: Walter F. Mondale and the Liberal Legacy* (New York: Columbia University Press, 1992), 72; Dittmer, *Local People*, 289.

28. Mondale lecture.

29. William Connell to Walter Mondale, memo, July 22, 1964, "Convention Credentials Committee: Mississippi Delegation," Box 56, Humphrey Papers.

30. Gillon, *The Democrats' Dilemma*, 71.

31. "Freedom Party of Mississippi," Political Policy Resolution, May 16, 1964, Box 14, MSS 3, Americans for Democratic Action Papers, WHS.

32. Rauh interview, Lewis; see also Parrish, *Citizen Rauh*, 166.

33. Mondale, *The Good Fight*, 25. Mondale received his appointment to the U.S. Senate on November 17, 1964.

34. Sherwin J. Markman, Oral History Interview I by Dorothy Pierce McSweeny, May 21, 1969, transcript, LBJL, and at http://web1.millercenter.org/poh/transcripts/markman_sherwin_1969_0521.pdf.

35. "Battle of Credentials," *Newsweek*, September 7, 1964.

36. Rowland Evans and Robert Novak, *Lyndon B. Johnson: The Exercise of Power* (New York: New American Library, 1966), 453; Leslie McLemore, "The Freedom Democratic Party and the Changing Political Status of the Negro in Mississippi," M.A. thesis, Atlantic University, 1965, 64, MFDP Papers, Reel 3, item 10, available in Reel 1556 at MDAH; Bob Moses, interviewed by William H. Chafe, October 7, 1989, Lowenstein Papers.

37. Rauh interview, Lewis.

38. Mondale, *The Good Fight*, 25.

39. Samstein interview, Romaine.

40. Mondale, *The Good Fight*, 25.

41. LBJ and Walter Jenkins, TC, August 23, 1964, 3:58 p.m., Citation 5137, RTCM.

42. Dittmer, *Local People*, 290, quoting Hodgson, *America in Our Time*, 213, 514, who cited as sources his own coverage of the convention as a journalist and his interviews with Rauh. Rauh understood that Connally said, "If those baboons walk on the floor, we walk off" (Rauh interview, Romaine). Again according to Rauh, Connally supposedly said, "You let those bugaboos march in, and the whole South will march out" (Rauh interview, Mulhollan). Rauh later substituted the phrase "those black brothers" for "those bugaboos" in telling this story (Rauh, panel, "MFDP and the Atlantic City Convention," 56). In another story, he said that White House aide Kenneth O'Donnell's "language was so awful" when he told him that he knew that the president wasn't "going to seat those goddam buggers of yours" (Rauh interview, Lewis).

43. LBJ and Walter Jenkins, TC, August 23, 1964, 3:58 p.m., Citation 5137, RTCM.

44. Mondale, *The Good Fight*, 25.

45. Markman interview, McSweeny.

46. Hodding Carter interview, March 30, 2009, LAT.

47. A fair division of the votes that the MFDP found equal was proportionate to the number of delegates, regular and MFDP, willing to take a loyalty oath. See Dittmer, *Local People*, 293.

48. H. N. Bassett to Mr. Callahan, memo, January 29, 1975, "1964 DNC Inquiry FBI File," Folder 8, Box 17, Kotz Papers.

49. Martin Luther King to the President, telegram, August 23, 1964, 7:12 p.m., attached to Paul Popple to the President, memo, August 24, 1964, "Ex PL/ST 24," WHCF, Box 52.

50. Kotz, *Judgment Days*, 210; LBJ and Richard Russell, TC, August 24, 1964, 11:10 a.m., Citation 5143, RTCM.

51. Charles Sherrod, "Mississippi at Atlantic City," *Grain of Salt* (Union Theological Seminary), October 12, 1964, available as an untitled draft, n.d., "MFDP 1964," Folder 3, Box 4, Betty Garman SNCC Files, Schomburg Center.

52. Hogan, *Many Minds One Heart*, 192.

53. Quoted in Sherrod, "Mississippi at Atlantic City."

54. Rauh interview, Lewis; Waskow, "Notes," 12–19; Samstein interview, Romaine. See also Lee, *For Freedom's Sake*, 91–92. Contrary to Lee's

account, however, Rauh and Waskow state that these discussions took place late Sunday evening.

55. Waskow, "Notes," 14.

56. Joe Rauh has said a "good story can't be written without the story of the meeting in King's bedroom that Sunday night," which he called "the most important meeting of the Convention." Allard Lowenstein told him days later that Moses "agreed that the two [votes] was a victory" (Rauh interview, Romaine). Lowenstein also told Ed King that Moses "had indicated . . . [the two-seat compromise] was acceptable under the circumstances of what [the] MFDP might actually get from the Convention" (Ed King to LAT, email, June 6, 2013). Bob Moses has denied the statement (William H. Chafe, *Never Stop Running: Allard Lowenstein and the Struggle to Save American Liberalism* [New York: Basic Books, 1993], 198; Moses interview, Chafe). Ella Baker, who was in the small group in the bedroom meeting, said, "Never, never. I'm sure that never was Bob's position" (Baker interview, Romaine). In a later interview, Rauh acknowledged that he did not know what to believe and was not as clear about what Lowenstein had told him (Richard Cummings, *The Pied Piper Allard K. Lowenstein and the Liberal Dream* [New York: Grove Press, 1985], 266–67).

57. Waskow, "Notes," 15.

58. Rauh interview, Romaine.

59. Charles Sherrod, conversation with LAT, Oxford, Ohio, October 11, 2009.

60. Rauh interview, Lewis.

61. Memorandum for the President, "re: Discussions with Joe Rauh on Mississippi 'Freedom Party,'" August 11, 1964.

62. Rauh interview, Mulhollan.

63. Bob Moses, interviewed by Anne Romaine, September 1966 and November 14, 1987, Folder 52, Romaine Papers, UNC; Moses interview, LAT.

64. Bruce Agnew, "Miss. Rights Group Threatens Floor Fight," *New York Post*, August 24, 1964.

65. Waskow, "Notes," 16.

14. Humphrey's Pleading on Monday

1. Fannie Lou Hamer, interviewed by Anne Romaine and Howard Romaine, November 22, 1966, Folder 58, Romaine Papers, UNC.

2. Quoted in "Humphrey Noncommittal on Vice President Outlook," *Minneapolis Sunday Tribune*, August 23, 1964.

3. Hubert H. Humphrey, *The Education of a Public Man: My Life and Politics* (New York: Doubleday, 1976), 299.

4. Rauh interview, Romaine.

5. LBJ and Hubert H. Humphrey, TC, August 14, 1964, 11:05 a.m., Citations 4917, 4918, RTCM.

6. Dallek, *Flawed Giant,* 157.

7. Doris Kearns Goodwin, *Lyndon Johnson and the American Dream* (New York: St. Martin's Press, 1976), 202.

8. Viorst, *Fire in the Streets,* 264; see also Dittmer, *Local People,* 290–91.

9. Memo to Staff, "re: Convention Activities," August 22, 1964, Box 1, William J. Connell Papers, MHS.

10. Humphrey, *Education of a Public Man,* 299; Tom Wicker, James Reston, Anthony Lewis, Earl Mazo, and E. W. Kenworthy, "The Choice of Humphrey, Step by Step," *New York Times,* August 27, 1964.

11. John Stewart, interviewed by Carl Solberg, Box 2, Carl Solberg Papers, MHS; Humphrey, *Education of a Public Man,* 298, 481 n. 5.

12. LBJ and Hubert Humphrey, TC, August 14, 1964, 8:25 p.m., Citation 4938, RTCM.

13. LBJ and Hubert H. Humphrey, TC, August 14, 1964, 11:05 a.m., Citations 4917, 4918, RTCM. Humphrey wrote that he worked on an initial settlement proposal with Mondale and Reuther that "made certain that overt racial discrimination and intimidation in choosing convention delegates would not be tolerated anywhere in the future" (Humphrey, *Education of a Public Man,* 299).

14. LBJ and Walter Reuther, TC, August 24, 1964, 8:46 a.m., Citation 5140, RTCM.

15. Ibid.

16. Courtland Cox in Joe Davenport, dir., *M.F.D.P.* (Manship Films, 2010).

17. Waskow, "Notes," 16; "MFDP to the Press" from Aaron Henry, August 25, 1964, Box 12, Baker Papers.

18. Vail TC, LAT.

19. Sistrom, "'Authors of the Liberation,'" 169–70.

20. Branch, *Pillar of Fire,* 465; Kay Mills, *This Little Light of Mine: The Life of Fannie Lou Hamer* (New York: Dutton, 1993; reissued, Lexington: University Press of Kentucky, 2007), 125; Ed King interview, Romaine; Sistrom, "'Authors of the Liberation,'" 171–73; Moses interview, LAT.

21. Ed King, Mondale symposium.

22. Ed King, personal papers.

23. Hogan, *Many Minds One Heart,* 189–90.

24. Hamer interview, Romaine. Ed King remembered Hamer arguing with Humphrey and finally saying, "I'm going to pray to Jesus for you" (Ed King, Mondale symposium).

25. Rauh interview, Romaine.

26. "Atlantic City: The Dilemma," *National Guardian,* August 29, 1964; "Canson Notes."

27. Moses interview, Carson.

28. Rauh interview, Romaine, and "Canson Notes"; see also Lee, *For Freedom's Sake,* 93.

29. "Canson Notes."

30. Kotz, *Judgement Days,* 211.

31. Richard Wilson, "Democrats Convene amid Rights Wrangle," *Minneapolis Morning Tribune,* August 25, 1964.

32. "Canson Notes."

33. Rauh interview, Romaine; "Canson Notes"; Mondale lecture.

34. Sistrom, "'Authors of the Liberation,'" 172–73. This meeting does not appear to be reported elsewhere. Sistrom places Ed King's report of Humphrey's statement that Fannie Lou Hamer was an "illiterate woman" at this third Monday meeting, but Ed King has reported it as having been said on Tuesday (Ed King interview, Romaine; Ed King, Mondale symposium). Sistrom says Bayard Rustin was present, but he did not arrive in Atlantic City until Tuesday.

35. LBJ and Walter Jenkins, TC, August 24, 1964, 4:31 p.m., Citation 5156, RTCM.

36. Quoted in Joseph R. Daughen, "It Continues Battle to Be Recognized," *Philadelphia Bulletin,* August 25, 1967; see also "Biographical Sketches of Delegates," Joseph Papers.

37. Quoted in Marguerite Higgins, "Rights Tensions Pose Trouble for Democrats," *Washington Star,* August 25, 1964.

38. Quoted in Daughen, "It Continues Battle to Be Recognized."

39. LBJ and Walter Jenkins, TC, August 24, 1964, 7:08 p.m., Citation 5161, RTCM.

40. *Democratic National Convention 1964 Official Proceedings* (Washington, D.C.: Democratic National Committee, 1968), 4.

41. *Democratic Platform 1964* (Washington, D.C.: Democratic National Committee, 1964), copy in LAT's files courtesy of Mary King.

42. Russ Nixon, "LBJ Buries the Issues," *National Guardian,* September 5, 1964, quoting the *New York Times* and the *New York Herald Tribune.*

43. Beschloss, ed., *Taking Charge,* 526; LBJ and Walter Reuther, TC, August 24, 1964, 8:25 p.m., Citation 5165, RTCM.

44. LBJ and Walter Reuther, TC, August 24, 1964, 8:25 p.m. The conversation calls into question reports based on Rauh's statements that Johnson pressured Reuther to break away from union negotiations for 550,000 auto

workers in Detroit as a strike deadline approached and that Reuther left the negotiations "at Lyndon Johnson's insistence" (Branch, *Pillar of Fire,* 467; Dittmer, *Local People,* 294).

45. Rauh interview in Hampton and Fayer, *Voices of Freedom,* 200. On August 20, Reuther had warned of a strike after the UAW rejected contract offers from the industry's Big Three—General Motors, Ford, and Chrysler—to replace contracts expiring August 31 (Damon Stetson, "Reuther Warns of Auto Strike," *New York Times,* August 21, 1964).

46. Rauh interview, Romaine. Rauh was also concerned that a District of Columbia caucus vote indicated he had lost support from his own delegation for a roll-call vote on a minority report. He feared that Democrats supporting the president had spoken to a union-affiliated delegate from D.C. to influence the delegation against Rauh, but he was later able to obtain a pledge of allegiance from the key D.C. delegate he believed had been targeted.

47. Ibid., emphasis added.

48. Tillow interview, Romaine; see Len Holt, *The Summer That Didn't End* (New York: William Morrow, 1965), 171.

49. "MISSISSIPPI PROBLEM," memo, August 24 and 25, 1964, "Convention Credentials Committee" folders, Box 56, Humphrey Papers. Information and quotations in the subsequent discussion of the findings from Humphrey's staff contacts come from this source.

50. Baker interview, Romaine; see Ransby, *Ella Baker,* 339.

15. Reuther's Manipulation on Tuesday

1. LBJ, Hubert H. Humphrey, and Walter Reuther, TC, August 24, 1964, 2:31 p.m., Citation 5181, RTCM.

2. LBJ and John Bailey, TC, August 25, 1964, 9:22 a.m., Citations 5173, 5174, RTCM.

3. "It's LBJ Week in Atlantic City."

4. Beschloss, ed., *Taking Charge,* 529; LBJ and George Reedy, TC, August 25, 1964, 11:06 a.m., Citation 5176, RTCM. For descriptions of Johnson's deep despair, see also Branch, *Pillar of Fire,* 468 ("depressed . . . distemper"), and Kotz, *Judgment Days,* 212–14 ("depressed and bitter"). (Note that Kotz describes the events as happening on Wednesday, August 25, although they occurred on Tuesday, August 25, 1964.)

5. Lady Bird Johnson, *A White House Diary* (Austin: University of Texas Press, 1970), 192.

6. George E. Reedy, Oral History Interview XXVI by Michael L. Gillette, November 16, 1990, transcript, LBJL, and at http://www.lbjlib.utexas.edu/johnson/archives.hom/oralhistory.hom/Reedy/reedy%20web%2026.pdf.

7. George Reedy, *Lyndon B. Johnson: A Memoir* (Fairway, Kan.: Andrews and McMeel, 1982), 55.

8. Reedy interview, Gillette.

9. Ibid.; see also Kotz, *Judgment Days*, 214.

10. Reedy, *Lyndon B. Johnson*, 58.

11. Goodwin, *Lyndon Johnson and the American Dream*, 203.

12. Bob Moses, interviewed for Connie Field and Mary Mulford, dir., *Freedom on My Mind*, DVD (California Newsreel, 1994); see also Parrish, *Citizen Rauh*, 174.

13. LBJ and Walter Reuther, TC, August 24, 1964, 8:25 p.m., Citation 5165, RTCM.

14. Rauh interview in Hampton and Fayer, *Voices of Freedom*, 200; Rauh interview, Mulhollan.

15. LBJ and Walter Reuther, TC, August 21, 1964, 3:50 p.m., Citation 5099, RTCM.

16. Rauh interview, Romaine. LAT's July 3, 2013, request to Mondale for information about whether he had ever met with MFDP delegates was not answered.

17. Mondale lecture.

18. Markman interview, McSweeny.

19. "Battle of Credentials."

20. David S. Broder, "Dramatic Bid Helped Avert Blowup," *Washington Star*, August 26, 1964.

21. Mondale, *The Good Fight*, 26; Mondale lecture; Broder "Dramatic Bid."

22. Kotz, *Judgment Days*, 214–15. Note that Kotz describes the event as happening on Wednesday, although Reuther's arrival was on Tuesday.

23. Evans and Novak, *Lyndon B. Johnson*, 454, emphasis in original.

24. Hubert H. Humphrey, interviewed by Finlay Lewis, June 29, 1997, Box 1, Lewis Papers.

25. Markman interview, Sweeney.

26. Mondale, *The Good Fight*, 26. Mondale has written that Humphrey showed the offer to Martin Luther King Jr. and Bayard Rustin, who also endorsed it. When King and Rustin received notice of the proposal is unknown.

27. Mondale lecture; in contrast, see Kotz, *Judgment Days*, 214–15, where Kotz refers to Wednesday morning and to the events he describes as taking place on Tuesday.

28. Evans and Novak, *Lyndon B. Johnson*, 455.

29. Ibid.

30. Lee C. White to the President, memo, "re: Discussion with Joe Rauh

on Mississippi 'Freedom Party,'" August 11, 1964, "Ex PL 1/ST 24 Seating Mississippi Delegation at Democratic National Convention," WHCF, Box 81.

31. Waskow, "Notes," 22.

32. Samstein interview, Romaine.

33. Rauh interview, Romaine; see also Ransby, *Ella Baker,* 340, for an account of Baker's public criticism of Rauh, which occurred, however, on Tuesday morning, not after broadcast of a "done deal" late Tuesday afternoon, as Ransby suggests.

34. Rauh interview, Romaine. Twenty-two years later Mondale listed Rauh as well as Humphrey and Reuther as being there during "the long night" that the final offer was hammered out but admits that "it gets a little vague" (Walter Mondale, interviewed for *Eyes on the Prize,* May 5, 1986).

35. LBJ and Walter Jenkins, TC, August 23, 1964, 3:58 p.m., Citations 5136, 5137, RTCM.

36. Rauh interview, Lewis.

37. Sherrod, "Mississippi at Atlantic City." The five points in the compromise Sherrod describes were (1) two at-large delegate seats for named delegates, (2) future state delegations' assurance of pledged electors and nondiscrimination, (3) the seating of the regular delegation, (4) a required loyalty oath, and (5) a committee to assist states in compliance for the 1968 convention. MFDP delegate and political scientist Leslie McLemore relies on Sherrod's paper to describe a "crucial meeting" Tuesday morning "to consider the compromise." However, the final offer had not been received, and the MFDP caucus did not begin until late that afternoon after the Credentials Committee met. McLemore quotes Sherrod as writing that the "hot day dragged on," but in Sherrod's paper the day meant is Wednesday, *after* the convention delegates approved the final resolution of the Convention Challenge. McLemore's omission of the timing of events is relevant to his conclusions that the MFDP refusal of the final offer, which he maintains was decided by Moses, was simply based on a refusal to compromise, when the reasons for the MFDP rejection are in fact more complex (Leslie McLemore, "The Mississippi Freedom Democratic Party: A Case Study of Grass-Roots Politics," Ph.D. diss., University of Massachusetts, 1971, 149, MDAH).

38. Tillow interview, Romaine.

39. Moses interview, Chafe.

40. Rauh interview, Mulhollan.

41. Rauh interview, Romaine. Rauh has described the reporters, while he was on live TV, as observing but unable to hear his conversation in a glass telephone booth. They were anxious for information when he finished the call. Asked who was he was talking to, Rauh said, "It was a pretty girl."

42. Rauh interview in Hampton and Fayer, *Voices of Freedom*, 201.

43. Ibid. Rauh also called Markman "a little shit" (Rauh interview, Lewis). In January 1966, Markman was appointed to the White House counsel staff.

44. LBJ, Hubert H. Humphrey, and Walter Reuther, TC, August 24, 1964, 2:31 p.m., Citation 5181, RTCM. The information in the next two paragraphs also comes from this source.

45. Moses interview, Romaine. "Rustin said he had been called to Atlantic City by Reuther" (Joanne Grant, "Politicos Gag a Cry for Freedom," *National Guardian*, September 4, 1964). The FBI reported that "King had prevailed upon Bayard Rustin to come to Atlantic City" (C. D. DeLoach to Mr. [John P.] Mohr [of the FBI], memo, August 29, 1964, "1964 DNC Inquiry FBI File," Folder 8, Box 17, Kotz Papers).

46. Ed King, personal papers; Ed King, Mondale symposium.

47. "McCarthy Urges LBJ to Choose Humphrey," *Minneapolis Star Tribune*, August 26, 1964.

48. Aaron Henry, with Constance Curry, *The Fire Ever Burning* (Jackson: University Press of Mississippi, 2000), 191.

49. Thelwell interview, LAT.

50. Ed King, Mondale symposium.

51. Moses interview, Chafe. Bob Moses did not seem to Ed King "to have any hint of prior knowledge" (Ed King to LAT, email, June 6, 2013).

52. Ed King, personal papers.

53. LBJ, Hubert H. Humphrey, and Walter Reuther, TC, August 24, 1964, 2:31 p.m.

54. Moses interview, LAT.

55. Ed King interview, Romaine.

56. Hamer interview, Romaine; see also Forman, *The Making of Black Revolutionaries*, 388.

57. Mondale lecture. Based on knowledge of Humphrey's political sense and his decency, there is no reason to credit Humphrey's statement that President Johnson would not allow "that illiterate woman" Fannie Lou Hamer to be an MFDP delegate at-large. The statement was not revealed to the press in Atlantic City or the MFDP caucus but is only the remembrance of Ed King (Ed King interview, Romaine; Ed King, Mondale symposium). I mention it only because it has appeared in practically every account of the MFDP Convention Challenge. Later statements that relied on Ed King's recollection include, among others, Kotz, *Judgment Days*, 216; Carmichael and Thelwell, *Ready for Revolution*, 404; and Marian Wright Edelman, *Lanterns: A Memoir of Mentors* (Boston: Beacon Press, 1999), 88. The reference in Robert P. Moses and Charles E. Cobb Jr., *Radical Equations: Math Literacy and Civil*

Rights (Boston: Beacon Press, 2001), 83, is inaccurate. This account places the statement in the initial meeting with Humphrey on Tuesday, when Mrs. Hamer was actually present. Moses has not recalled hearing the statement (Moses interview, LAT). Charlie Cobb confirmed that Ed King is the only source of the remark (Cobb interview, LAT).

58. Ed King, personal papers.

59. Rauh interview, Romaine; Mondale lecture ("our proposal failed them").

60. Ed King, personal papers.

61. Ibid.

62. Ibid.

63. Ed King, Mondale symposium. The amount that the UAW gave to King and the SCLC has been stated as $176,000 (Tillow interview, Romaine; see also Branch, *Pillar of Fire*, 469).

64. Henry, *The Fire Ever Burning*, 189.

65. Ed King, Mondale symposium; see also Garrow, *Bearing the Cross*, 258.

66. Henry, *The Fire Ever Burning*, 189.

67. Ed King, conversation with LAT, Washington, D.C., May 22, 2008.

68. Rauh interview, Romaine.

69. Ed King, personal papers.

70. Rauh interview, Chafe.

71. Humphrey interview, Lewis.

72. Dallek, *Flawed Giant*, 163; Wofford, *Of Kennedys and Kings*, 419; Cartha D. DeLoach, *Hoover's FBI: The Inside Story by Hoover's Trusted Lieutenant* (Washington, D.C.: Regnery, 1995), 6–8; Kenneth O'Reilly, *"Racial Matters": The FBI's Secret File on Black America 1960–1972* (New York: Free Press, 1989), 186–90; DeLoach interview, Gillette; Ronald Kessler, "FBI Tapped King at 1964 Convention," *Washington Post*, January 26, 1975; FBI report, "Special Squad at Democratic National Convention Atlantic City, New Jersey August 22–28, 1964," January 30, 1975, Folder 8, "1964 DNC Inquiry FBI File," Box 17, Kotz Papers.

73. Kotz found that fifty-two pages was a more accurate page count for the twelve memos sent than is DeLoach's reference to "44 pages" (Nick Kotz to Regina Greenwell, LBJL, memo, June 12, 2002, "DeLoach Personal File," Folder 6, Box 17, Kotz Papers).

74. FBI report, "Special Squad at Democratic National Convention."

75. LBJ to J. Edgar Hoover, letter, August 31, 1964, "July August 1964 White House Documents," Folder 31, Box 10, Kotz Papers.

76. Memo, "re: President Johnson, Politics and the FBI," n.d., "Ervin Committee re 1964 Atlantic City," Folder 5, Box 17, Kotz Papers.

77. Gillon, *The Democrats' Dilemma*, 73, citing Jeri Joseph's notes.

78. Rauh interview in Hampton and Fayer, *Voices of Freedom*, 201.

79. Quoted in Finlay Lewis, *Mondale: Portrait of an American* (New York: Harper & Rowe, 1980), 133–34.

80. Broder, "Dramatic Bid Helped Avert Blowup."

81. Rauh interview, Lewis; see also Rauh interview in Hampton and Fayer, *Voices of Freedom*, 201.

82. Mondale interview, *Eyes on the Prize*.

83. Rauh interview, Romaine. Historians have generally accepted the truth of Rauh's statement that he voted against the final proposal in the Credentials Committee meeting. But see Rothschild, *A Case of Black and White*, 69.

84. Rauh interview in Hampton and Fayer, *Voices of Freedom*, 202.

85. Rauh interview, Lewis.

86. Grant, "Politicos Gag a Cry for Freedom."

87. Rauh interview, Mulhollan.

88. C. D. DeLoach to Mr. [John P.] Mohr [of the FBI], memo, August 25, 1964, Folder 62-109555, Box 103, David Garrow Freedom of Information Collection, Schomburg Center; see Garrow, *Bearing the Cross*, 348, 686 n. 63.

89. Mondale lecture.

90. Samstein interview, Romaine.

91. Courtland Cox interview in Hampton and Fayer, *Voices of Freedom*, 199; Thelwell interview, LAT.

92. Thelwell interview, LAT.

93. Courtland Cox to LAT, email, September 2, 2010.

94. Thelwell interview, LAT.

95. Samstein interview, Romaine; Rauh interview, Romaine; Marshall Ganz interview in Field and Mulford, *Freedom on My Mind;* Marshall Ganz to LAT, email, February 9, 2013; "Handful of Delegates Forced Compromise," *Washington Post*, August 26, 1964; Ed King, personal papers; Ed King to LAT, email, September 17, 2010. SNCC knew about the pressure on Sunday contrary to an FBI reliable source stating that early Tuesday afternoon SNCC learned that Johnson was "reputedly bringing pressure to bear on the delegates of 15 unidentified states" to prevent their support of a floor vote ("Afternoon Summary of Activity, Democratic National Convention, Atlantic City, New Jersey, August 25, 1964," Folder 6, Box 17, Kotz Papers).

96. "Canson Notes."

97. Faythe Canson, telephone interview by Nick Kotz, n.d., Folder 41, Box 24, Kotz Papers.

98. Ed King, personal papers.

99. Kotz, *Judgment Days*, 217; cf. Forman, *Making of Black Revolutionaries*, 388.

100. Rauh interview, Romaine; Rauh interview, Mulhollan.

101. Holt, *The Summer That Didn't End*, 171–72; Lawrence Guyot, Mondale symposium; Grant, "Politicos Gag a Cry for Freedom"; Hogan, *Many Minds One Heart*, 193–94 ("Loans, appointments, and other benefits").

102. News and Information Democratic National Committee, memo, August 29, 1964, Office Files of Bill Moyers, Box 19, LBJL.

103. LBJ and Palmer Hoyt, TC, August 24, 1964, 12:56 p.m., Citation 5146, RTCM.

104. LBJ and Walter Jenkins, TC, August 24, 1964, 1:11 p.m., Citation 5152, RTCM.

105. Kotz, *Judgment Days*, 217.

106. "Credentials Problem—Washington/per Herb Waters via Stinnett," memo, "Convention Credentials Committee: Mississippi Delegation," Box 56, Humphrey Papers.

107. JV [Jack Valenti] [to the President], "For Your Information," memo, August 25, 1964, President's Appointment File (Diary Backup), Box 8, LBJL; see also Dittmer, *Local People*, 296.

108. Rauh interview in Hampton and Fayer, *Voices of Freedom*, 196.

109. Joseph L. Rauh Jr. to Dr. Aaron Henry, letter, September 8, 1964, Box 86, Rauh Papers.

110. Mondale lecture.

111. Rauh interview, Romaine; see also Kotz, *Judgment Days*, 216, and Dittmer, *Local People*, 297 ("a bulletin that the credentials committee had unanimously approved the two-seat compromise").

112. Rauh interview in Hampton and Fayer, *Voices of Freedom*, 202.

113. LBJ and Carl Sanders, TC, August 25, 1964, 4:32 p.m., Citations 5183, 5184, RTCM.

114. Beschloss, ed., *Taking Charge*, 535. Beschloss lists the conversation at 4:32 p.m., with John Connally; Connally got on the phone at the end of the Sanders conversation (LBJ and Carl Sanders, TC, August 25, 1964, 4:32 p.m., Citation 5184, RTCM).

115. LBJ and Walter Jenkins, TC, August 25, 1964, 5:33 p.m., Citation 5186, RTCM.

116. LBJ and Walter Jenkins, TC, August 25, 1964, 7:07 p.m., Citation 5188, RTCM.

117. Thurber, *The Politics of Equality*, 157.

118. Ed King, personal papers.

119. Wallace Roberts, "The Mondale Myth," *New Times* 2, no. 2 (January 25, 1974): 26–31.

120. Ed King interview, Romaine; Dittmer, *Local People,* 297; for "You tricked us!" see Ed King, personal papers, and Gitlin, *The Sixties,* 158.

121. Moses and Cobb, *Radical Equations,* 81–82; see also Ed King, interviewed by LAT, Jackson, Miss., March 22, 2010.

122. Young, *An Easy Burden,* 306, 308–9; Andrew Young telephone interview by LAT.

123. Ed King, Mondale symposium.

124. Cobb interview, LAT.

125. Samstein interview, Romaine.

126. Dittmer, *Local People,* 298.

127. Rauh interview, Romaine.

128. Ibid.

129. Henry, *The Fire Ever Burning,* 193.

130. Joseph L. Rauh Jr. to Arthur I. Waskow, resident fellow, Institute for Policy Studies, letter, September 8, 1964, Box 86, Rauh Papers.

131. Joseph L. Rauh Jr., to Leslie McLemore, letter, June 16, 1965, Box 86, Rauh Papers.

132. Henry, *The Fire Ever Burning,* 197.

133. Rauh interview, Romaine.

134. Rauh interview, Mulhollan.

135. Henry, *The Fire Ever Burning,* 194.

136. Hodding Carter III, "Mississippi Demos Leave Convention," *Delta Democrat-Times,* August 26, 1964; "LBJ Still Silent, Convention Signs Point to Humphrey," *Minneapolis Star,* August 26, 1964.

137. Hodding Carter interview, March 30, 2009, LAT; Hodding Carter III, "Loyalists Were Well Guarded," *Delta Democrat-Times,* August 28, 1964; George Cable Wright, "Negroes Refused Mississippi Seats," *New York Times,* August 27, 1964; see also Mills, *This Little Light of Mine,* 131.

138. Tom Wicker, "Mississippi Delegates Withdraw, Rejecting a Seating Compromise," *New York Times,* August 26, 1964; Mary E. King, "Mississippi Freedom Democrats and the 1964 Democratic National Convention Aug 19–25 daily account," "Other Materials," Folder 75, Romaine Papers, UNC.

139. *Democratic National Convention 1964 Official Proceedings,* 30–31; "Mississippians Walk Out as Delegate Plan Is Voted," *Minneapolis Morning Tribune,* August 26, 1964.

140. Edith Green, oral history interview by Robert Wright, February 21, 1968, Ralph J. Bunche Oral History Collection, Civil Rights Documentation

Project, Moorland–Spingarn Research Center, Howard University; Green interview, Kerr-Tener.

141. Joseph L. Rauh Jr. to Dr. Aaron Henry, letter, September 8, 1964, and Joseph L. Rauh Jr. to Max M. Kampelman, Esq., letter, August 31, 1964, Box 86, Rauh Papers; the "underground railroad" reference meant getting the "maximum number of people on the convention floor" (Henry, *The Fire Ever Burning*, 212).

142. Green interview, Wright.

143. Forman, *The Making of Black Revolutionaries*, 388.

144. Rauh interview, Romaine; John McCormack to Aaron Henry, letter, August 26, 1964, "DNC Credentials 1964," DNC Series II, Box 102.

16. The Mississippi Freedom Democratic Party Turns to Protest

1. Hamer interview, Romaine; Mills, *This Little Light of Mine*, 132.

2. "Atlantic City: The Dilemma."

3. Carmichael and Thelwell, *Ready for Revolution*, 404.

4. Hodding Carter III, interviewed by LAT, Chapel Hill, N.C., April 1, 2010.

5. Courtland Cox, interviewed for *Eyes on the Prize*, May 14, 1979.

6. Kranz interview, LAT.

7. Henry, *The Fire Ever Burning*, 192, 195.

8. George Cable Wright, "Negroes Refused Mississippi Seats," *New York Times*, August 27, 1964. See also Dittmer, *Local People*, 299; Branch, *Pillar of Fire*, 472.

9. Sutherland, *Letters from Mississippi*, 220–21.

10. "Mississippians Walk Out as Delegate Plan Is Voted."

11. State Stallworth Sr., oral history interview, May 25, 2000, CRDP.

12. Anthony Day, "White House Orders Kept Freedom Sit-Ins in Place," *Philadelphia Bulletin*, August 26, 1964; "Biographical Sketches of Delegates," Joseph Papers.

13. Walter Adams to Walter Jenkins, letter, September 1, 1964, "Ex PL1/ST 24 Seating Mississippi Delegation at Democratic Convention," WHCF, Box 81.

14. Branch, *Pillar of Fire*, 472.

15. Day, "White House Orders."

16. Quoted in Sistrom, "'Authors of the Liberation,'" 189.

17. Carter, "Mississippi Demos Leave Convention"; see also Arthur I. Waskow, *From Race Riot to Sit-In, 1919 and the 1960s* (Gloucester, Mass.: Smith, 1979), 275.

18. Mary King, "Mississippi Freedom Democrats," Romaine Papers, UNC.

19. Hamer interview, Romaine; Mills, *This Little Light of Mine*, 132.

20. Branch, *Pillar of Fire*, 475.

21. Richardson interview, LAT. DeLoach reported in his daily FBI reports to Jenkins that fifteen uniforms were available for pickup by someone from the CORE–SNCC storefront office at 6:00 p.m. on Wednesday (memo, August 26, 1964, "DeLoach Personal File," Folder 6, Box 17, Kotz Papers).

22. Adams to Jenkins, letter, September 1, 1964.

23. Holt, *The Summer That Didn't End*, 175.

24. Ed King interview, Romaine.

25. Adams to Jenkins, letter, September 1, 1964.

26. Ed King interview, Romaine; see also Waskow, "Notes," 27–29, and Waskow, *From Race Riot to Sit-In*, 274.

27. Moses interview, Carson.

28. Waskow, *From Race Riot to Sit-In*, 274.

29. "Battle of Credentials."

30. Waskow, *From Race Riot to Sit-In*, 272.

31. Ibid.

17. Wednesday

1. Quoted in Robert Penn Warren, *Who Speaks for the Negro?* (New York: Random House, 1965), 118.

2. Dittmer, *Local People*, 299.

3. Waskow, "Notes," 29.

4. Moses interview, *Eyes on the Prize*.

5. Asking the MFDP delegation to approve possible changes was not feasible, particularly when no changes were presented or likely to be made by the White House (Ed King interview, Romaine).

6. Henry, *The Fire Ever Burning*, 196.

7. Quoted in Unita Blackwell, oral history interview, April 21 and May 12, 1977, CRDP.

8. Hamer interview, CRDP; Moses interview, LAT; Lucille Komisar, "'Don't They Know They've Won?'" *The Village Voice*, September 3, 1964; Ed King to LAT, email, April 22, 2010.

9. Ed King, personal papers.

10. Henry, *The Fire Ever Burning*, 196.

11. Hamer interview, Romaine.

12. King, *The Autobiography of Martin Luther King, Jr.*, 253.

13. Ed King interview, Romaine.

14. Bayard Rustin, "From Protest to Politics: The Future of the Civil Rights Movement," *Commentary*, February 1965.

15. Ed King interview, Romaine.

16. Quoted in Forman, *The Making of Black Revolutionaries*, 392.

17. D'Emilio, *Lost Prophet*, 389.

18. Rustin, "From Protest to Politics."

19. Bayard Rustin to Irving Bluestone, UAW, letter, September 13, 1964, UAW President's Office, Folder 1, "Randolph A. Philip Institute, 1965," Box 518, Reuther Collection.

20. Walter P. Reuther to Bayard Rustin, letter, April 8, 1964, Folder 1, Box 518, Reuther Collection.

21. Quoted in Forman, *The Making of Black Revolutionaries*, 393.

22. Ivanhoe Donaldson, interviewed by Anne Romaine, March 23, 1967, Folder 60, Romaine Papers, UNC.

23. James Farmer, *Lay Bare the Heart: An Autobiography of the Civil Rights Movement* (New York: New American Library, 1985), 299–300.

24. James Farmer to Leslie McLemore, letter, July 15, 1964, quoted in McLemore, "The Mississippi Freedom Democratic Party," 164.

25. Findlay, *Church People in the Struggle*, 115.

26. Forman, *The Making of Black Revolutionaries*, 391.

27. Holt, *The Summer That Didn't End*, 175.

28. Henry, *The Fire Ever Burning*, 31.

29. "Mississippi Problem—Oregon/per Herb Waters," memo, August 25, 1964, Box 56, Humphrey Papers.

30. Edith Green to Leslie McLemore, letter, July 2, 1965, quoted in McLemore, "The Mississippi Freedom Democratic Party," 162.

31. Ed King, personal papers; Rachel B. Reinhard, "Politics of Change: The Mississippi Freedom Democratic Party and the Emergence of a Black Political Voice in Mississippi," Ph.D. diss., University of California, Berkeley, 2005, 113, citing her interview with Leslie Burl McLemore, Jackson, Miss., October 1, 2003. McLemore has written in his dissertation that Moses and others in SNCC actually made the decisions, "handed to the FDP delegation what amounted to a *fait accompli*," "controlled the delegation," and gave the grassroots delegates "little opportunity to participate in the decision-making process" ("The Mississippi Freedom Democratic Party," 153, 156–57).

32. Willie B. (Wazir) Peacock in "The Mississippi Movement and the MFDP," discussion, April, May, June, July 2004, at the CRMV website, http://www.crmvet.org/disc/mfdp.htm#mfdpcontext.

33. Quoted in Wilson, "Democrats Convene amid Rights Wrangle."

34. Mondale interview, *Eyes on the Prize*.

35. Moses and Cobb, *Radical Equations*, 82.

36. Ed King, personal papers.

37. Quoted in Waskow, "Notes," 32.

38. Quoted in Forman, *The Making of Black Revolutionaries*, 393; Bob Moses has been quoted as saying, "We're not here to bring politics into our morality but to bring morality into our politics" (Burner, *And Gently He Shall Lead Them*, 187, citing William Higgs, oral interview by Anne Romaine; see also Branch, *Pillar of Fire*, 474, and Kotz, *Judgment Days*, 220).

39. Visser-Maessen, "A *Lot* of Leaders?" 243.

40. DeLoach to Mohr, memo, August 29, 1964.

41. Hamer interview, Romaine.

42. Donaldson interview, LAT.

43. Henry Sias interview, August 11, 1968, Moorland–Spingarn Research Center; see Lynne Olson, *Freedom's Daughters: The Unsung Heroines of the Civil Rights Movement from 1830 to 1970* (New York: Scribner, 2001), 323.

44. Ed King to LAT, email, April 22, 2010.

45. Ed King, personal papers.

46. Henry, *The Fire Ever Burning*, 197; Waskow, "Notes," 32.

47. Hamer interview, Romaine.

48. Hamer interview, CRDP.

49. McLaurin conversation with LAT.

50. "The Mississippi Movement and the MFDP" discussion.

51. "The Convention Challenge," n.d., Folder 9, "MFDP Challenges," Box 3, Miller Civil Rights Collection; see also Mike Miller, "The Mississippi Freedom Democratic Party," in Erenrich, ed., *Freedom Is a Constant Struggle*, 298.

52. "The Convention Challenge," emphasis added; quotations in the next two paragraphs come from this report.

53. Primer No. 1, *The Convention Challenge and the Freedom Vote*, "Political Primers and Handbooks c. 1964," Folder 13, Box 1, MSS 586, MFDP Records, WHS .

54. *Democratic National Convention 1964 Official Proceedings*, 458–59; Harold Leventhal to John M. Bailey, memo, August 31, 1964, "DNC—Credentials 1964—Mississippi," DNC Series II, Box 102.

55. Leventhal to Bailey, memo, August 31, 1964, emphasis in original.

56. Branch, *Pillar of Fire*, 475.

18. Victory or Defeat

1. Mondale interview, *Eyes on the Prize*.

2. Carmichael and Thelwell, *Ready for Revolution*, 411.

3. MFDP press release, August 29, 1964, "Other Materials," Folder 75, Romaine Papers, UNC.

4. Sutherland, *Letters from Mississippi,* 222.

5. Linda Davis, interviewed by LAT, Washington, D.C., July 27, 2009.

6. Unita Blackwell and JoAnne Prichard Morris, *barefootin'* (New York: Crown, 2006), 117.

7. In "Mississippi: Is This America (1962–1964)," in *Eyes on the Prize,* DVD (Blackside, Inc.), transcript available at http://www.pbs.org/wgbh/amex/eyesontheprize/about/pt_105.html.

8. Bob Moses, in Field and Mulford, *Freedom on My Mind.*

9. Rev. Clifton R. Whitley II to Leslie McLemore, letter, June 15, 1965, quoted in McLemore, "The Mississippi Freedom Democratic Party," 163.

10. Quoted in Grant, "Politicos Gag a Cry for Freedom."

11. Whitley to McLemore, letter quoted in McLemore, "The Mississippi Freedom Democratic Party," 163.

12. Miles interview, Project South.

13. Charles Graves interview, n.d., Project South.

14. "A Commentary on the Civil Rights Movement in Mississippi," Box M379, Folder 1, Peggy Jean Connor Papers, USM.

15. Quoted in Hogan, *Many Minds One Heart,* 198.

16. Lawrence Guyot, interviewed by LAT, Jackson, Miss., March 27, 2008.

17. McLaurin conversation with LAT.

18. Block interview, LAT.

19. M. Susan Orr-Klopfer, *Where Rebels Roost: Mississippi Civil Rights Revisited* (n.p.: Orr-Klopfer, 2005–2006), 522; Block interview, LAT.

20. Michael Thelwell, interviewed by Anne Romaine, November 1987, Folder 67, Romaine Papers, UNC.

21. Ed King interview, Romaine.

22. "Southern Delegations," *New York Times,* August 27, 1964.

23. Murray Kempton, "Conscience of a Convention," *The New Republic,* September 5, 1964.

24. Anthony Lewis, "The Negro and Politics," *New York Times,* August 27, 1964.

25. Komisar, "'Don't They Know They've Won?'"

26. Carson, *In Struggle,* 127 ("embittered"); Dittmer, *Local People,* 320, 324 ("alienated"); Kotz, *Judgment Days,* 221 ("disillusioned"); Lemann, *The Promised Land,* 162 ("bitterly disillusioned"); Henry, *The Fire Ever Burning,* 199 ("disappointment, disillusionment, and disenchantment").

27. Courtland Cox, conversation with LAT, Jackson, Miss., March 23, 2012.

28. Ladner, Keynote Speech, SNCC 50th Anniversary Conference.

29. Ladner, conversation with LAT; see also Dittmer, *Local People*, 302.

30. Lawrence Guyot and Mike Thelwell, "The Politics of Necessity and Survival in Mississippi," *Freedomways* 6, no. 2 (1966): page numbers unavailable, quoted in Stokely Carmichael and Charles V. Hamilton, *Black Power: The Politics of Liberation in America* (New York: Vintage Books, 1967), 95.

31. Dorie Ladner, interviewed for Laura Jane Lipson, dir., *Standing on My Sisters' Shoulders*, DVD (Sadoff Productions, 2002); Rita Bender to LAT, email, March 11, 2013.

32. Sellers, *The River of No Return*, 111.

33. Sherrod, "Mississippi at Atlantic City."

34. Moses interview, LAT.

35. The concentration of religious organizations, including NCC headquarters, in the nineteen-story office building at 475 Riverside Drive in New York City where the meeting was held led to the nickname "the God Box" (Findlay, *Church People in the Struggle*, 36).

36. Dittmer, *Local People*, 315–17; Cummings, *The Pied Piper*, 275–76; Chafe, *Never Stop Running*, 200; Forman, *The Making of Black Revolutionaries*, 399–405; "Rough minutes of a meeting called by the National Council of Churches to discuss the Mississippi Project," September 18, 1964, Forman Papers, and M2007-010, Folder 21, Box 8, Arthur Kinoy Papers, WHS, and at http://content.wisconsinhistory.org/cdm/ref/collection/p15932coll2/id/172.

37. Courtland Cox, interviewed by William H. Chafe, April 26, 1989, Lowenstein Papers.

38. Quoted in Forman, *The Making of Black Revolutionaries*, 401.

39. "Rough minutes."

40. Quoted in Forman, *The Making of Black Revolutionaries*, 400–402, 404.

41. Quoted in ibid., 401, 404; Cox interview, Chafe.

42. Quoted in Forman, *The Making of Black Revolutionaries*, 399.

43. Wilkins, *Standing Fast*, 306.

44. Carmichael and Hamilton, *Black Power*, 96.

45. Lewis and D'Orso, *Walking with the Wind*, 282.

46. Moses interview, Carson.

47. Dittmer, *Local People*, 296–97.

48. Payne, *I've Got the Light of Freedom*, 376.

49. Moses interview, Carson.

50. Moses interview, LAT.

51. Moses interview, Romaine.

52. Quoted in Dittmer, *Local People*, 302.

53. Moses and Cobb, *Radical Equations*, 82.

54. Quoted in "Moses Assails Corruption of Judicial System in South," *National Guardian*, December 5, 1964.

55. Ransby, *Ella Baker*, 342.

56. Vail interview, 2008, LAT.

57. Stephen Bingham, "Mississippi Letter," February 15, 1965, 20, at the CRMV website, http://www.crmvet.org/lets/65_bingham_mslet.pdf. "As things turned out historically," Bingham thinks "the rejection of the Compromise was the right decision. But at the time . . . I [was] not fully attuned to how two seats was viewed as an insulting token solution" (Stephen Bingham to LAT, email, May 27, 2013).

58. In "The Mississippi Movement and the MFDP," discussion.

59. "Rights Rally for Mississippi Raises $2,500," *Summit Herald*, September 10, 1964.

60. White, *The Making of the President 1964*, 294, emphasis added.

61. Quoted in "Mississippi Delegates Withdraw, Rejecting a Seating Compromise."

62. MFDP press release, September 17, 1964, MFDP Papers, Reel 1, item 2, available in Reel 2646 at MDAH.

63. Rauh, in Hampton and Fayer, *Voices of Freedom*, 201; Rauh interview, Mulhollan.

64. "Mississippi: Is This America (1962–1964)," transcript; Joseph L. Rauh Jr. to Professor Louis L. Jaffe, letter, September 4, 1964, Box 86, Rauh Papers.

65. Joseph L. Rauh Jr. to Marcus G. Raskin, letter, September 15, 1964, Box 86, Rauh Papers.

66. Moses interview, Carson.

67. Carmichael and Thelwell, *Ready for Revolution*, 406.

68. Moses interview, LAT.

69. Rauh interview, Chafe.

70. Moses interview, LAT.

71. Mondale interview, *Eyes on the Prize*.

72. Mondale lecture.

73. Dittmer, *Local People*, 337–41, 351–52.

74. McMillen, "Black Enfranchisement in Mississippi," 371.

75. Lyndon B. Johnson, speech to the Congress, March 15, 1965, at http://www.historyplace.com/speeches/johnson.htm.

76. Carson, *In Struggle*, 101.

77. Lyndon Baines Johnson, *The Vantage Point: Perspectives of the Presidency 1963–1969* (New York: Holt, Rinehart and Winston, 1971), quoted in Goodwin, *Lyndon Johnson and the American Dream*, 205–6.

78. The description of Guyot is in Dittmer, "The Transformation of the Mississippi Movement, 1964–68," 22.

79. Moses interview, Carson.

80. Vannessa Lynn Davis, "'Sisters and Brothers All': The Mississippi Freedom Democratic Party and the Struggle for Political Equality," Ph.D. diss., Vanderbilt University, 1966, 209, 225–26.

81. Mondale interview, *Eyes on the Prize*.

82. Amy Goodman, "Alice Walker and Bob Moses Reflect on an Obama Presidency and the Struggle for African Americans to Vote," *Democracy Now!* January 21, 2009, transcript.

83. John Dittmer to LAT, email, November 30, 2010.

84. Roger Wilkins, on the panel "The Transformation of American Presidential Politics," Veterans of the Mississippi Civil Rights Movement conference, March 20, 2009, Jackson, Miss. Wilkins added that others also made it "thinkable" that a black man could become president, mentioning Shirley Chisholm, Jesse Jackson, and Harold Washington.

85. "1964 Presidential General Election Results," at http://uselectionatlas .org/RESULTS/national.php?year=1964.

86. "MFDP and Election Challenges 1964–65," Folder 4, Box 4, Morey Papers; see also Dittmer, *Local People*, 323.

87. "Atlantic City: The Dilemma."

Epilogue

1. Vincent Harding, *Hope and History: Why We Must Share the Story of the Movement* (Maryknoll, N.Y.: Orbis Books, 1990), 189.

2. Mondale interview, *Eyes on the Prize*.

3. John Herbers, "Civil Rights Drive Alters Mississippi," *New York Times*, August 20, 1964.

4. LAT to Joan Karliner, letter, April 30, 1965.

5. Joan Karliner to LAT, letter, July 6, 1965.

6. LAT to Joan Karliner, letter, May 25, 1965.

7. LAT to Joan Karliner, letter, July 6, 1965.

8. Britton interview, Oral History Project: Greenville.

9. Bruce Hilton, *The Delta Ministry* (New York: MacMillan, 1969), 47.

10. Page interview, LAT. Sam Applewhite, Edna Moreton, and Willie Rollins, who were elected delegates or alternates from Washington County

to the state convention, continued to participate in the MFDP in 1965 (Pat Vail, telephone interview by LAT, TC, August 5, 2013). H. C. Anderson, a minister who owned Anderson Photo Service on Nelson Street (1948–1986), understood that "[b]lack people had organized a Freedom Democratic Party in Mississippi, in Jackson," when he decided to run as a Freedom Democrat for the Greenville City Council in the election held December 13, 1965. He also said he "headed" the Freedom Democratic Party (Henry Clay Anderson, *Separate, but Equal: The Mississippi Photographs of Henry Clay Anderson* [New York: Public Affairs, 2002], 14–15, 139; Rev. H. C. Anderson, oral history interview, November 9, 1977, CRDP). LAT saw and heard nothing about this prominent photographer in 1964.

11. Matthew Page, oral history interview, August 7, 1977, CRDP.

12. Hodding Carter interview, March 30, 2009, LAT.

13. Hodding Carter, "The Long Journey Home of Matthew Page," *Saturday Evening Post*, December 17, 1960.

14. Page interview, LAT.

15. Page interview, CRDP.

16. Page interview, LAT.

17. Ibid.

18. Ibid.

19. Mrs. Charles Moore, telephone interview by LAT, March 28, 2010.

20. Bill Johnson, "Former Councilman, Moore, Dies at 79," *Delta Democrat-Times*, March 14, 2006.

21. Franke Keating, telephone interview by LAT, March 25, 2008.

22. Ibid.; Franke Keating, interviewed by LAT, Greenville, Miss., March 17, 2009.

23. See the obituary for Franke Keating in the *Delta Democrat-Times*, November 10, 2011.

24. Johnny Frazier, conversation with LAT, Oxford, Ohio, October 10, 2009.

25. Johnny Frazier, on the panel "Mississippi before and after Freedom Summer," Miami University, Oxford, Ohio, October 11, 2009; Anthony Lewis, *Portrait of a Decade* (New York: Random House, 1964), 288–89.

26. Bob and Betty Jo Boyd, conversation with LAT, Greenville, Miss., March 18, 2009.

27. Page interview, LAT; see also James Carter interview, CRDP, and Cobb interview, LAT.

28. "Remarks by President Obama at the Civil Rights Summit," April 10, 2014, transcript, LBJL, at http://www.lbjlibrary.org/events/remarks-by-president-obama-at-the-civil-rights-summit.

29. Michelle Alexander, *The New Jim Crow: Mass Incarceration in the Age of Colorblindness* (New York: New Press, 2010), 230.

30. Hall interview, CRDP.

31. Vincent Harding, Keynote Address, Veterans of the Mississippi Civil Rights Movement conference, March 20, 2009.

32. Howard Zinn to LAT, letter, January 12, 2005.

Bibliography

I list here only a few of the many works on civil rights; others are cited in the notes. Page references are for parts of the story of the MFDP Convention Challenge told by others. A complete bibliography of civil rights books can be found at the Freedom Movement Bibliography on the Civil Rights Movement Veterans website, www.crmvet.org.

MFDP Convention Challenge in Atlantic City

Branch, Taylor. *Pillar of Fire: America in the King Years 1963–65*. New York: Simon & Schuster, 1998. See pp. 247–56.

Dittmer, John. *Local People: The Struggle for Civil Rights in Mississippi*. Champaign: University of Illinois Press, 1994. See pp. 285–302.

Gitlin, Todd. *The Sixties: Years of Hope, Days of Rage*. New York: Bantam, 1987. See pp. 149–62.

Hogan, Wesley C. *Many Minds One Heart: SNCC's Dream for a New America*. Chapel Hill: University of North Carolina Press, 2007. See pp. 188–96.

Kotz, Nick. *Judgment Days: Lyndon Baines Johnson, Martin Luther King Jr., and the Laws That Changed America*. New York: Houghton Mifflin, 2005. See pp. 198–222.

Mississippi Summer Project, 1964

Belfrage, Sally. *Freedom Summer*. Greenwich, Conn.: Fawcett, 1965; reprint, Charlottesville: University Press of Virginia, 1990.

King, Mary. *Freedom Song: A Personal Story of the 1960s Civil Rights Movement*. New York: William Morrow, 1987.

Marlette, Doug. *Magic Time* (a novel). New York: Picador, 2007.

McAdam, Doug. *Freedom Summer*. New York: Oxford University Press, 1988.

Sutherland, Elizabeth, ed. *Letters from Mississippi*. New York: McGraw-Hill, 1965. Reprinted as Elizabeth Martinez, ed., *Letters from Mississippi: Reports from Civil Rights Volunteers & Poetry of the 1964 Freedom Summer*. Brookline, Mass.: Zephyr Press, 2007.

Mississippi Civil Rights Movement

Dittmer, John. *Local People: The Struggle for Civil Rights in Mississippi.* Champaign: University of Illinois Press, 1994.

Erenrich, Susie, ed. *Freedom Is a Constant Struggle: An Anthology of the Mississippi Civil Rights Movement.* Montgomery, Ala.: Black Belt Press, 1999.

Payne, Charles M. *I've Got the Light of Freedom: The Organizing Tradition and the Mississippi Freedom Struggle.* Berkeley: University of California Press, 1995.

Index

CIVIL RIGHTS AND THE STRUGGLE FOR BLACK EQUALITY
IN THE TWENTIETH CENTURY

SERIES EDITORS
Steven F. Lawson, Rutgers University
Cynthia Griggs Fleming, University of Tennessee

CPSIA information can be obtained at www.ICGtesting.com
Printed in the USA
BVOW07*1336261114

376745BV00001B/1/P